THE QUEEN'S KNIGHT

P9-DNB-076

Queen's Knight Vol. 5
Created by Kim Kang Won

Translation - Lauren Na
English Adaptation - Anina Bennett
Retouch and Lettering - Tram Nguyen
Production Artist - Jose Macasocol, Jr.
Cover Design - Gary Shum

Editor - Troy Lewter
Digital Imaging Manager - Chris Buford
Production Managers - Jennifer Miller and Mutsumi Miyazaki
Managing Editor - Lindsey Johnston
VP of Production - Ron Klamert
Publisher and E.I.C. - Mike Kiley
President and C.O.O. - John Parker
C.E.O. - Stuart Levy

A  Manga

TOKYOPOP Inc.
5900 Wilshire Blvd. Suite 2000
Los Angeles, CA 90036

E-mail: info@TOKYOPOP.com
Come visit us online at www.TOKYOPOP.com

© 2000 KIM KANG WON, HAKSAN PUBLISHING CO., LTD. All rights reserved. No portion of this book may be
All rights reserved. First published in Korea in 2000 by reproduced or transmitted in any form or by any means
HAKSAN PUBLISHING CO., LTD. English translation rights in without written permission from the copyright holders.
North America, UK, NZ, and Australia arranged by This manga is a work of fiction. Any resemblance to
HAKSAN PUBLISHING CO., LTD. actual events or locales or persons, living or dead, is
English text copyright © 2006 TOKYOPOP Inc. entirely coincidental.

ISBN:1-59532-261-2

First TOKYOPOP printing: February 2006
10 9 8 7 6 5 4 3 2 1
Printed in Canada

THE QUEEN'S KNIGHT

VOLUME 5

BY KIM KANG WON

NEW HANOVER COUNTY PUBLIC LIBRARY
201 Chestnut Street
Wilmington, NC 28401

HAMBURG // LONDON // LOS ANGELES // TOKYO

LAST TIME IN...
THE QUEEN'S KNIGHT

YUNA IS A NORMAL GIRL WHO VISITS HER MOTHER IN GERMANY, ONLY TO HAVE A TERRIBLE ACCIDENT. AFTER SHE RETURNS HOME FROM HER ACCIDENT, SHE BEGINS TO HAVE STRANGE DREAMS. IN HER DREAM, A KNIGHT WHO CALLS HIMSELF "RIENO" TELLS YUNA THAT SHE IS HIS QUEEN AND THAT HE IS HER KNIGHT. YUNA'S BROTHERS SEND HER BACK TO GERMANY, WHERE SHE MEETS THE KNIGHT FROM HER DREAMS--WHO THEN PROMPTLY KIDNAPS HER, TAKING HER TO PHANTASMA.

PHANTASMA IS A WORLD COVERED ENTIRELY WITH SNOW, AND YUNA IS FORCED TO LIVE WITH RIENO. BUT JUST WHEN YUNA WAS GETTING USED TO BEING WITH HIM, SPRING ARRIVES, AND YUNA IS TAKEN TO ELYSIAN TO BE PROPERLY INSTALLED AS THE QUEEN OF PHANTASMA. ONCE THERE, YUNA BEFRIENDS THE QUEEN'S GUARDIAN KNIGHTS, EHREN, LEON, SCHILLER, THE HATEFUL CHANCELLOR KENT, AS WELL AS THE QUEEN'S RIVAL, PRINCESS LIBERA.

AFTER YUNA'S CORONATION, A "KNIGHTS TOURNAMENT" IS HELD, WITH THE WINNER TO BE AWARDED A CORONET. LIBERA AND YUNA PLACE A WAGER ON WHICH ONE OF THEM WILL RECEIVE REINO'S CORONET...BUT WHEN YUNA REALIZES SHE HAS BEEN TRICKED BY CHANCELLOR KENT INTO SIGNING AN EXECUTION DECREE, SHE LEAVES THE TOURNAMENT. RIENO HAS NO CHOICE BUT TO GIVE HIS CORONET TO LIBERA. THAT NIGHT, A WOUNDED EHREN ARRIVES AT THE CASTLE, AND YUNA TAKES HIM TO HER ROOM TO DRESS HIS WOUNDS. RIENO ARRIVES AND IMMEDIATELY GETS JEALOUS, AND YUNA ANGRILY TELLS HIM THAT HE CAN GO BE LIBERA'S KNIGHT. LATER, YUNA SECRETLY LEAVES THE CASTLE WITH SCHILLER AND LEON, ONLY TO BE ROBBED AND BRANDED AS FUGITIVES.

THE QUEEN'S KNIGHT

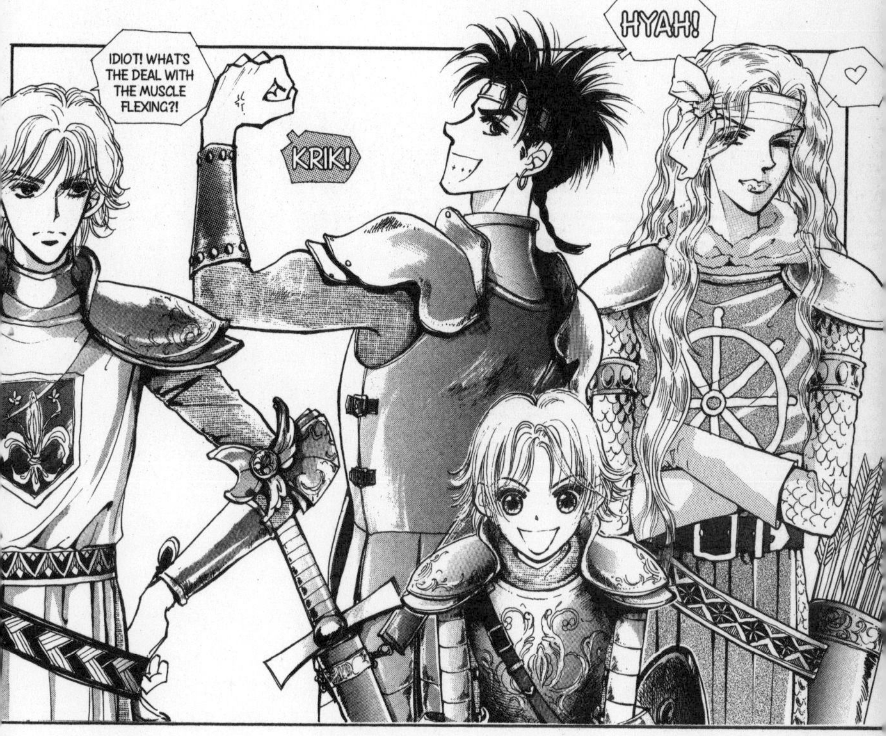
IDIOT! WHAT'S THE DEAL WITH THE MUSCLE FLEXING?!
KRIK!
HYAH!
♡

VOLUME 5

Kim Kang Won

TEUER--The Hamlet of Ehren Furst

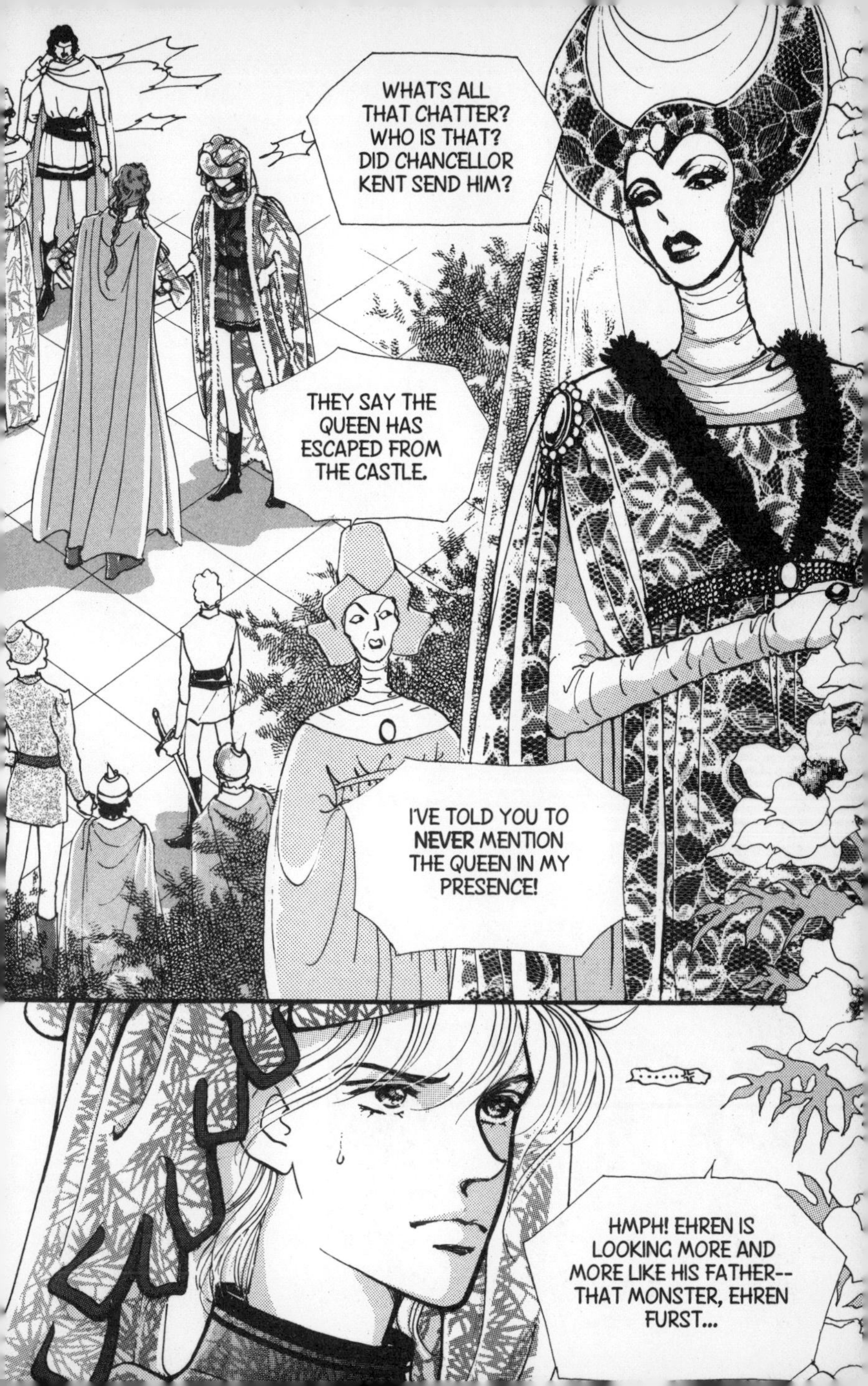
WHAT'S ALL THAT CHATTER? WHO IS THAT? DID CHANCELLOR KENT SEND HIM?
THEY SAY THE QUEEN HAS ESCAPED FROM THE CASTLE.
I'VE TOLD YOU TO NEVER MENTION THE QUEEN IN MY PRESENCE!
HMPH! EHREN IS LOOKING MORE AND MORE LIKE HIS FATHER-- THAT MONSTER, EHREN FURST...

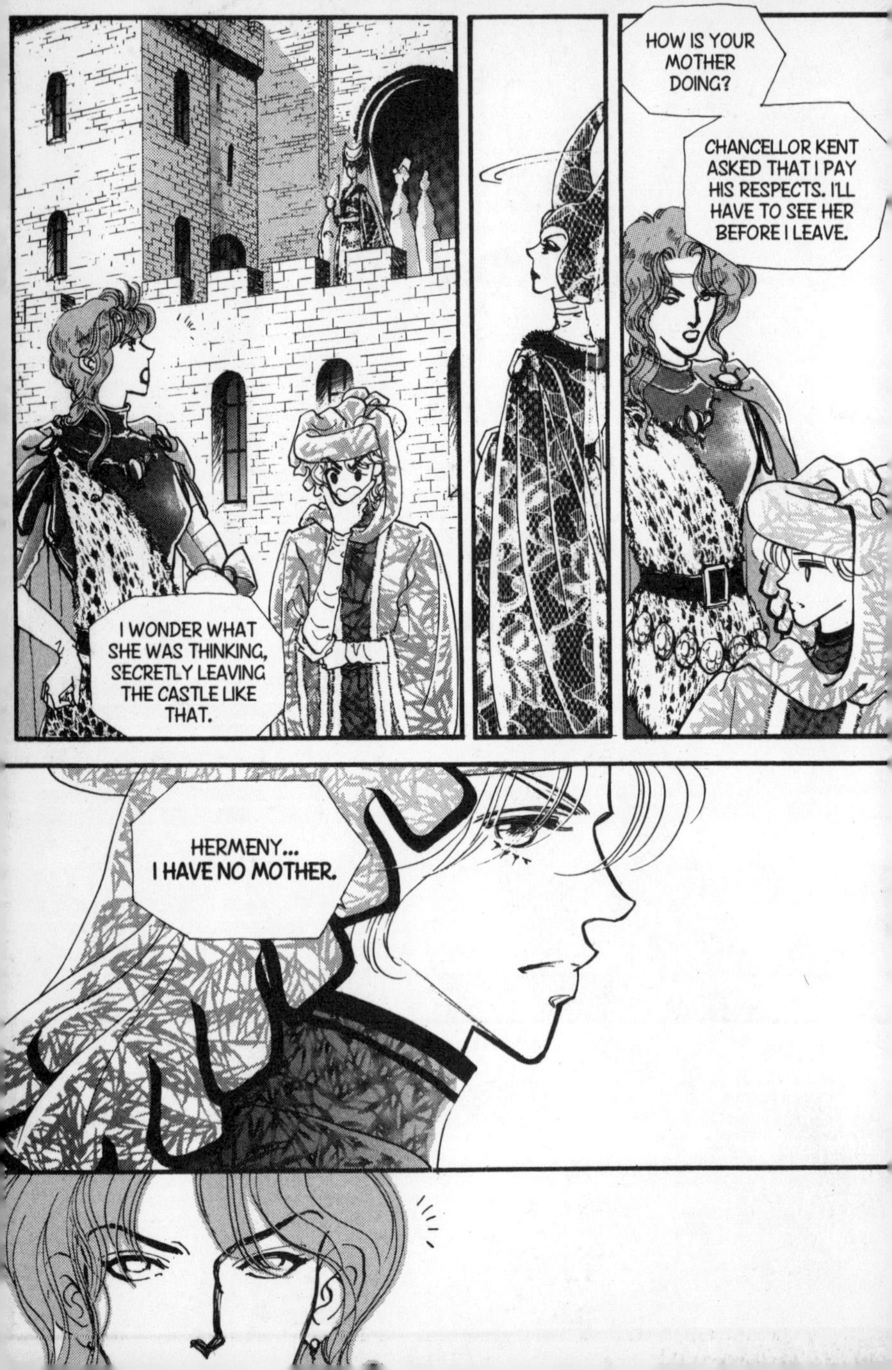
I WONDER WHAT SHE WAS THINKING, SECRETLY LEAVING THE CASTLE LIKE THAT.
HOW IS YOUR MOTHER DOING?
CHANCELLOR KENT ASKED THAT I PAY HIS RESPECTS. I'LL HAVE TO SEE HER BEFORE I LEAVE.
HERMENY... I HAVE NO MOTHER.

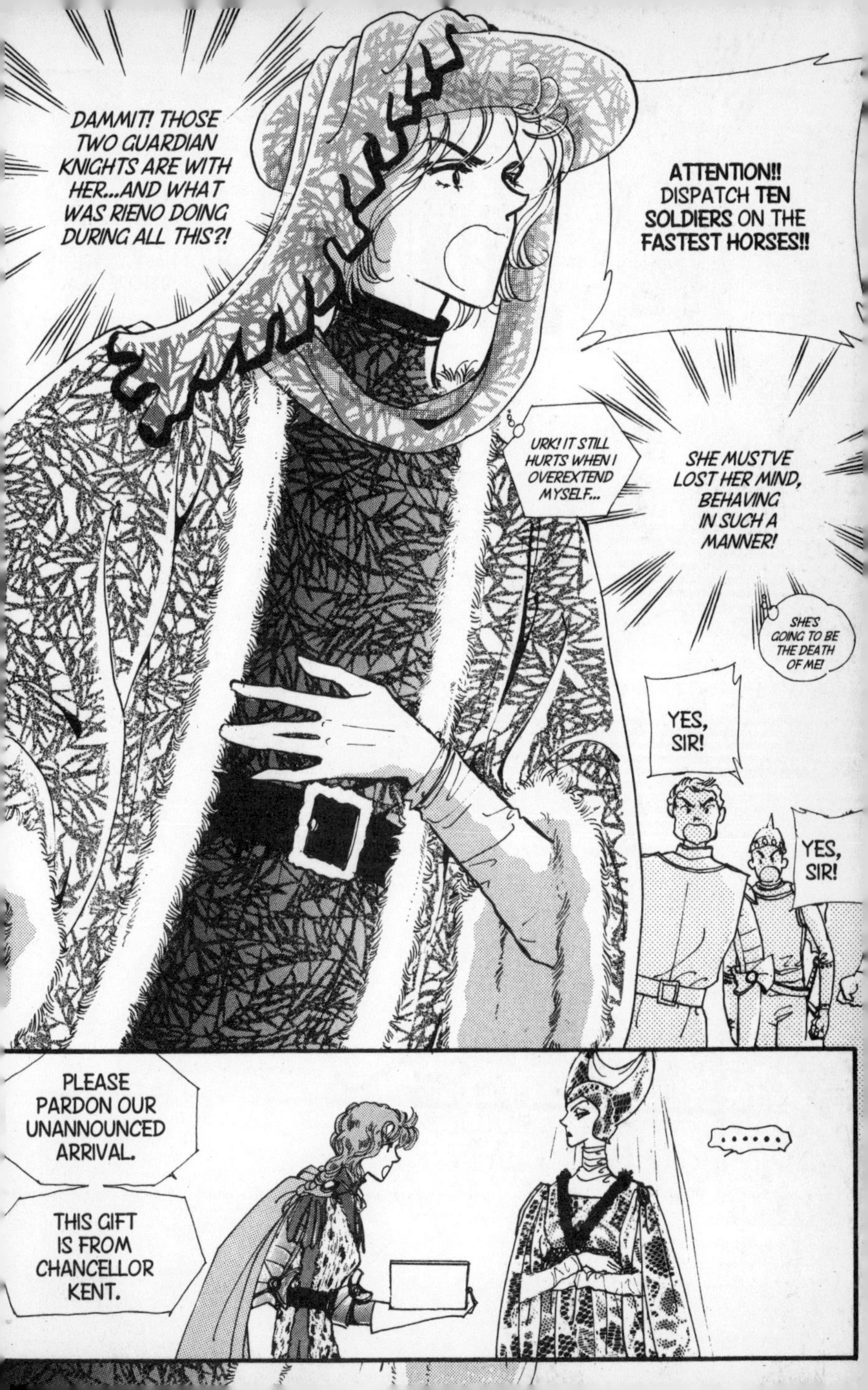
DAMMIT! THOSE TWO GUARDIAN KNIGHTS ARE WITH HER...AND WHAT WAS RIENO DOING DURING ALL THIS?!
ATTENTION!! DISPATCH TEN SOLDIERS ON THE FASTEST HORSES!!
URK! IT STILL HURTS WHEN I OVEREXTEND MYSELF...
SHE MUSTVE LOST HER MIND, BEHAVING IN SUCH A MANNER!
SHE'S GOING TO BE THE DEATH OF ME!
YES, SIR!
YES, SIR!
PLEASE PARDON OUR UNANNOUNCED ARRIVAL.
THIS GIFT IS FROM CHANCELLOR KENT.
.....

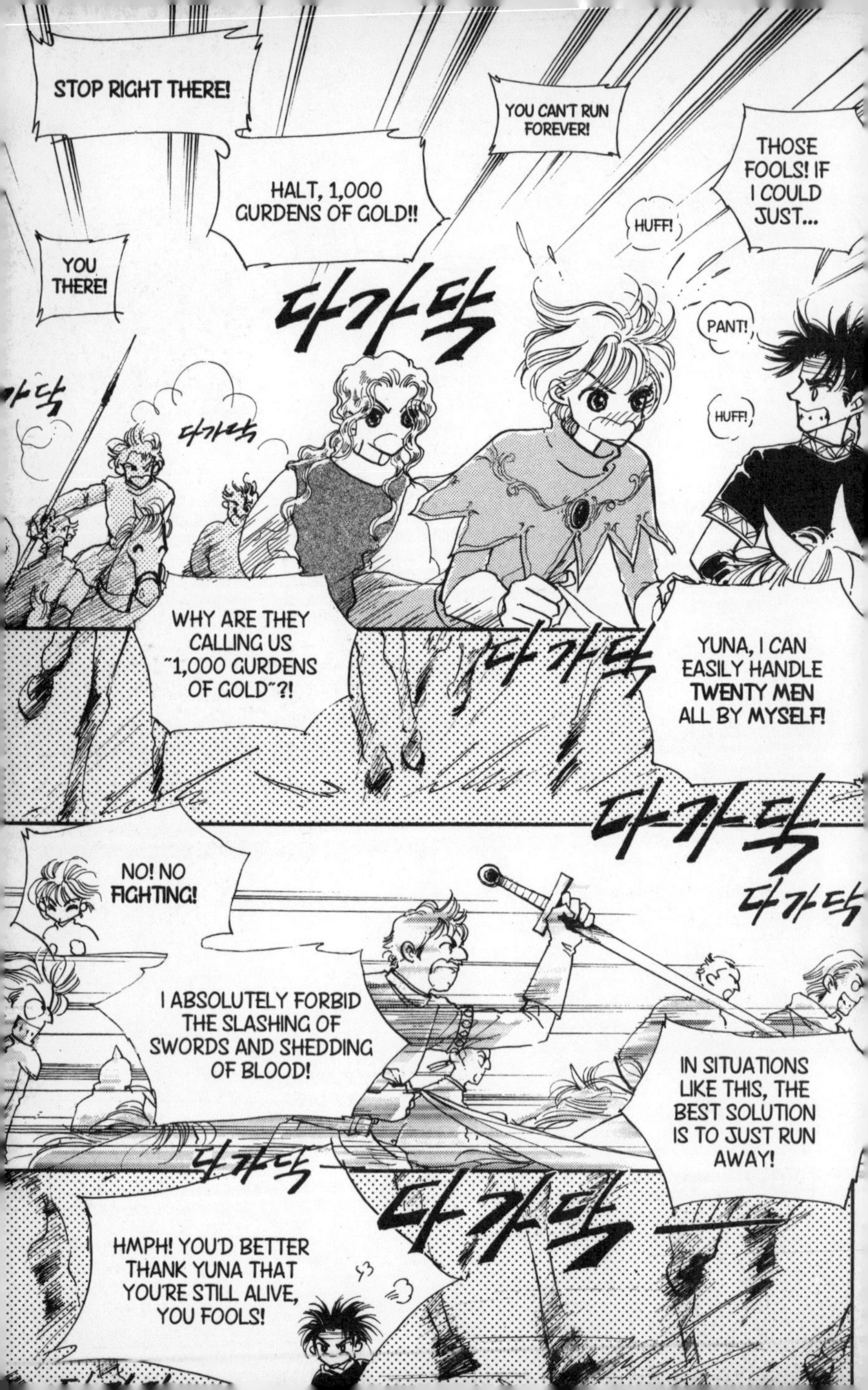
STOP RIGHT THERE!
YOU THERE!
HALT, 1,000 GURDENS OF GOLD!!
다가닥
YOU CAN'T RUN FOREVER!
HUFF!
THOSE FOOLS! IF I COULD JUST...
PANT!
HUFF!
가닥
다가닥
WHY ARE THEY CALLING US "1,000 GURDENS OF GOLD"?!
다가닥
YUNA, I CAN EASILY HANDLE TWENTY MEN ALL BY MYSELF!
다가닥
다가닥
NO! NO FIGHTING!
I ABSOLUTELY FORBID THE SLASHING OF SWORDS AND SHEDDING OF BLOOD!
IN SITUATIONS LIKE THIS, THE BEST SOLUTION IS TO JUST RUN AWAY!
다가닥
다가닥
HMPH! YOU'D BETTER THANK YUNA THAT YOU'RE STILL ALIVE, YOU FOOLS!

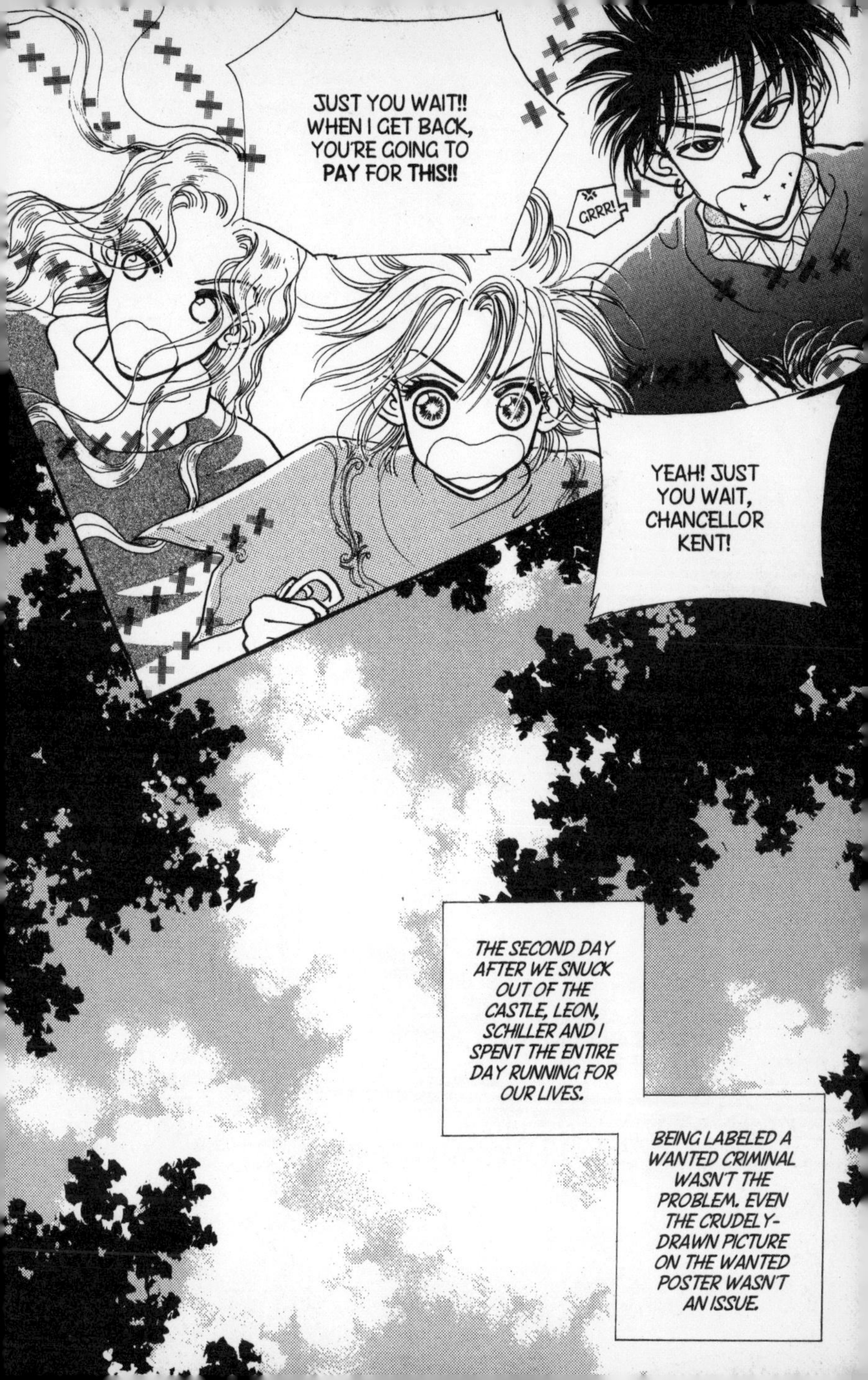
JUST YOU WAIT!! WHEN I GET BACK, YOU'RE GOING TO PAY FOR THIS!!
GRRR!
YEAH! JUST YOU WAIT, CHANCELLOR KENT!
THE SECOND DAY AFTER WE SNUCK OUT OF THE CASTLE, LEON, SCHILLER AND I SPENT THE ENTIRE DAY RUNNING FOR OUR LIVES.
BEING LABELED A WANTED CRIMINAL WASN'T THE PROBLEM. EVEN THE CRUDELY-DRAWN PICTURE ON THE WANTED POSTER WASN'T AN ISSUE.

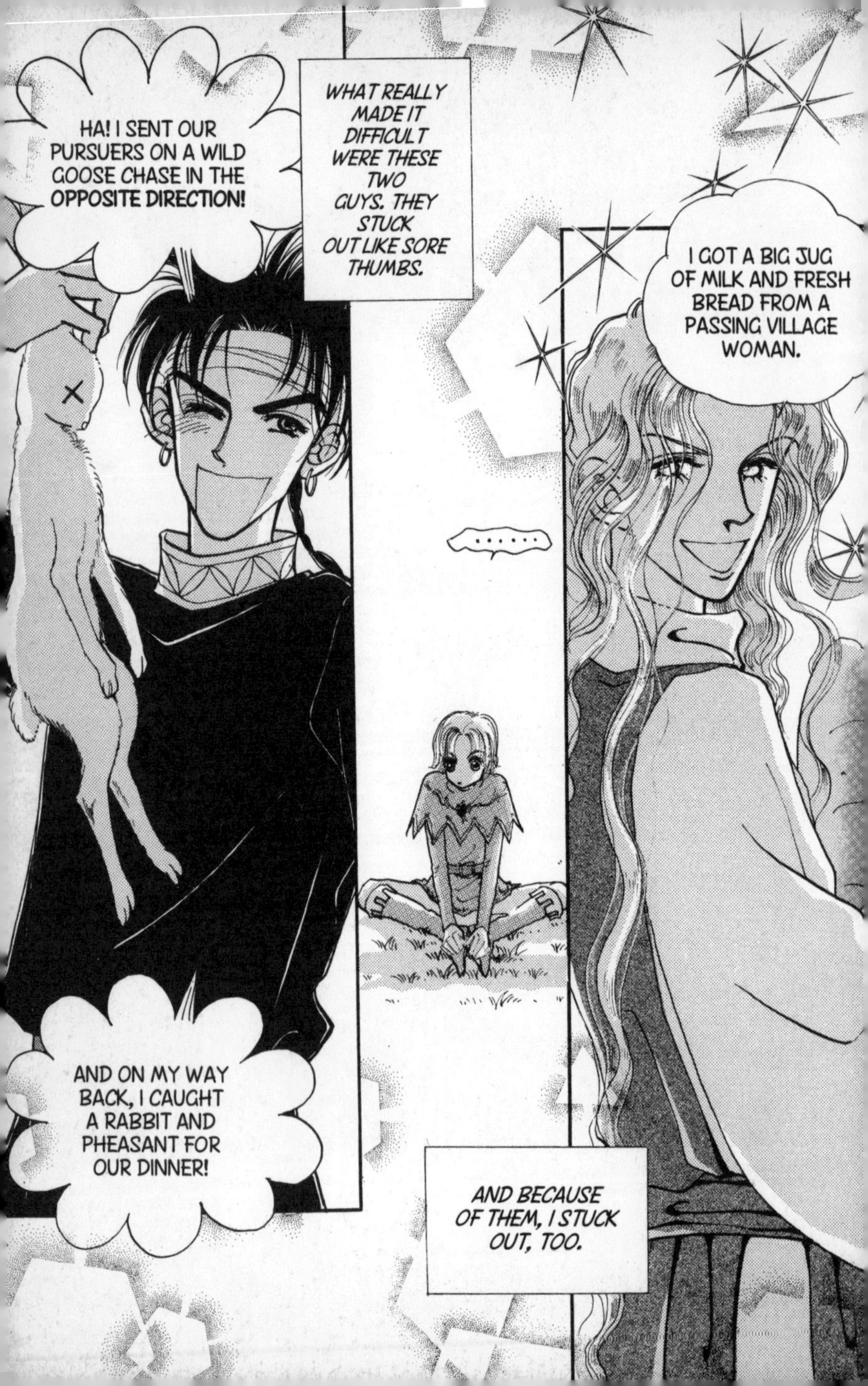
HA! I SENT OUR PURSUERS ON A WILD GOOSE CHASE IN THE OPPOSITE DIRECTION!
AND ON MY WAY BACK, I CAUGHT A RABBIT AND PHEASANT FOR OUR DINNER!
WHAT REALLY MADE IT DIFFICULT WERE THESE TWO GUYS. THEY STUCK OUT LIKE SORE THUMBS.
......
AND BECAUSE OF THEM, I STUCK OUT, TOO.
I GOT A BIG JUG OF MILK AND FRESH BREAD FROM A PASSING VILLAGE WOMAN.

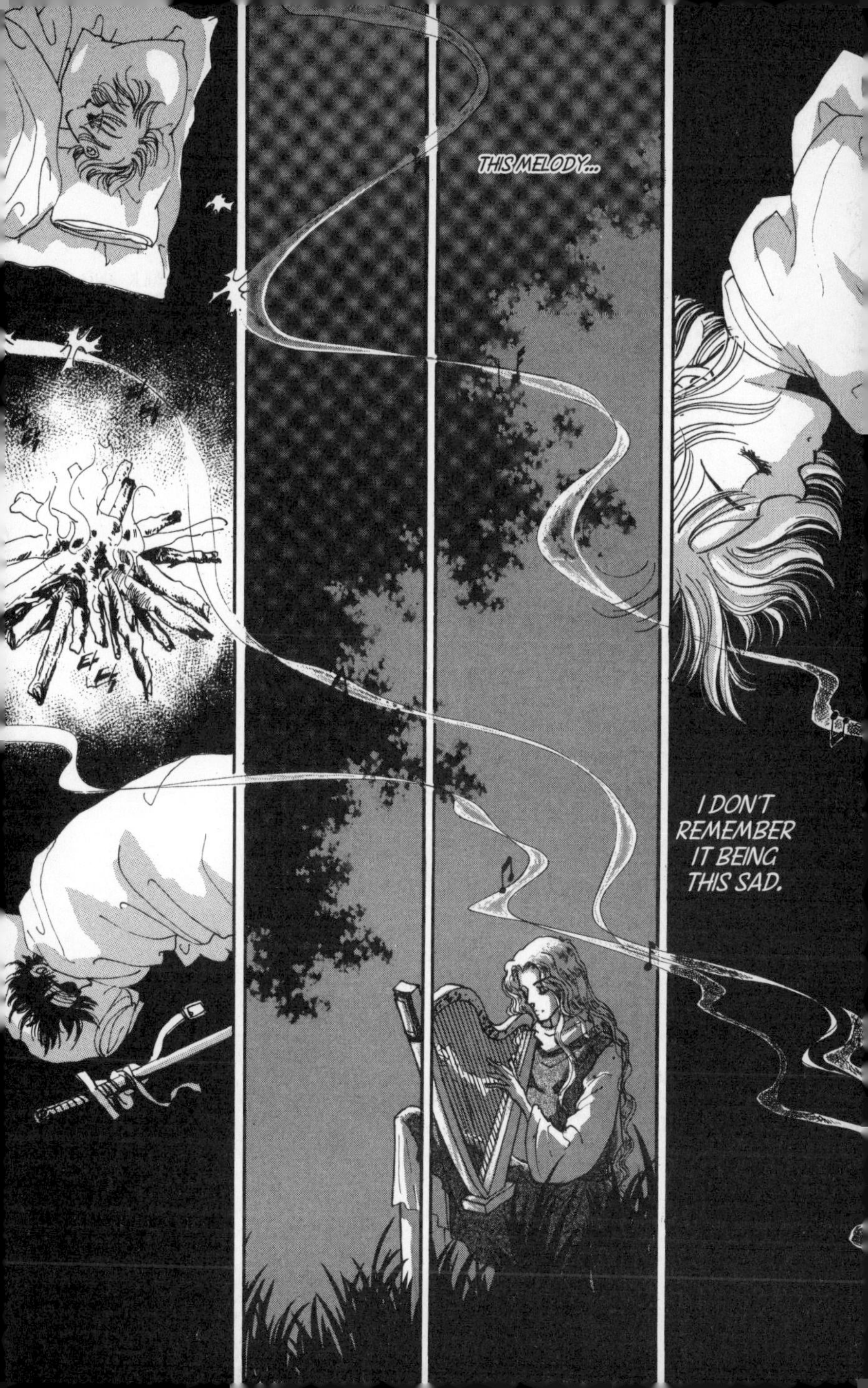
THIS MELODY...
I DON'T REMEMBER IT BEING THIS SAD.

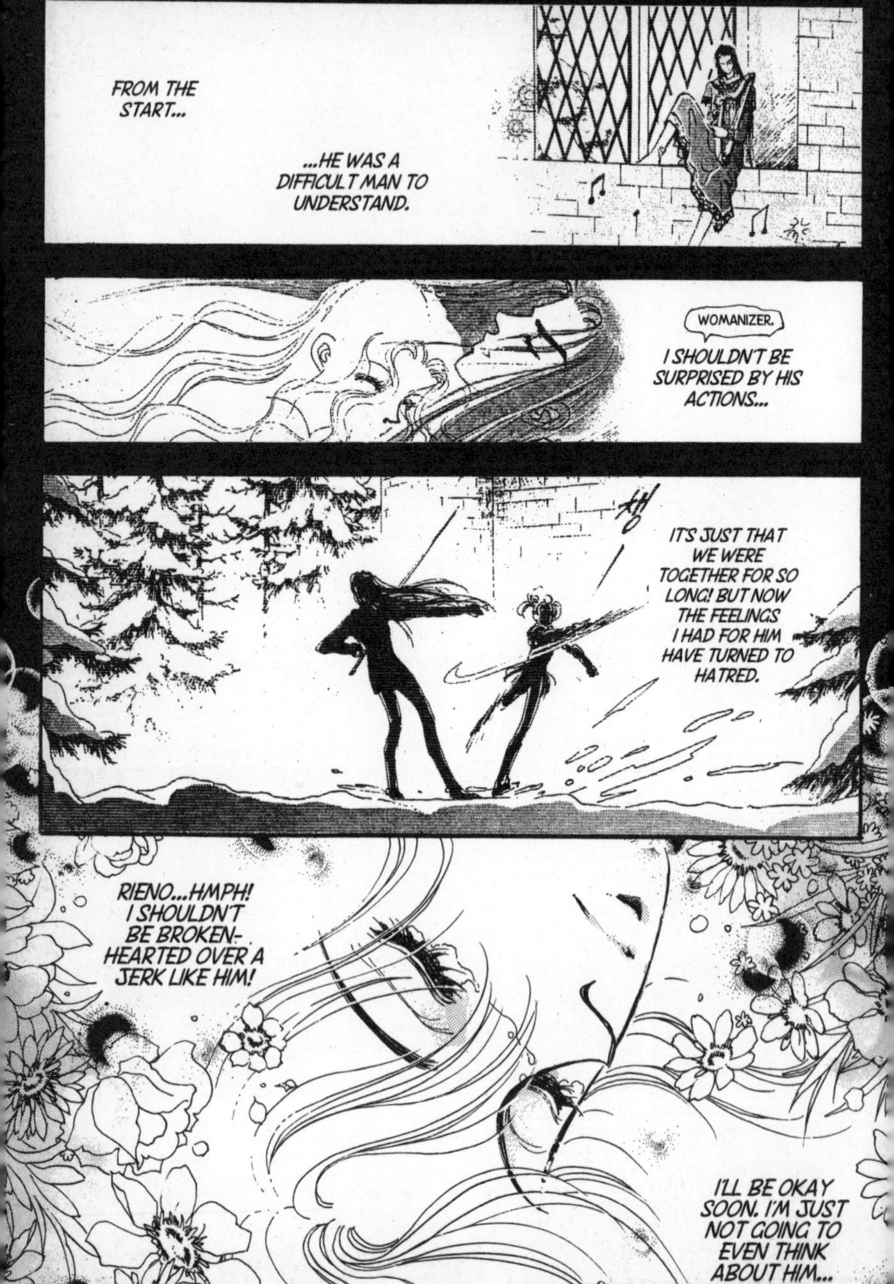
FROM THE START...
...HE WAS A DIFFICULT MAN TO UNDERSTAND.
WOMANIZER.
I SHOULDN'T BE SURPRISED BY HIS ACTIONS...
IT'S JUST THAT WE WERE TOGETHER FOR SO LONG! BUT NOW THE FEELINGS I HAD FOR HIM HAVE TURNED TO HATRED.
RIENO...HMPH! I SHOULDN'T BE BROKEN-HEARTED OVER A JERK LIKE HIM!
I'LL BE OKAY SOON. I'M JUST NOT GOING TO EVEN THINK ABOUT HIM...

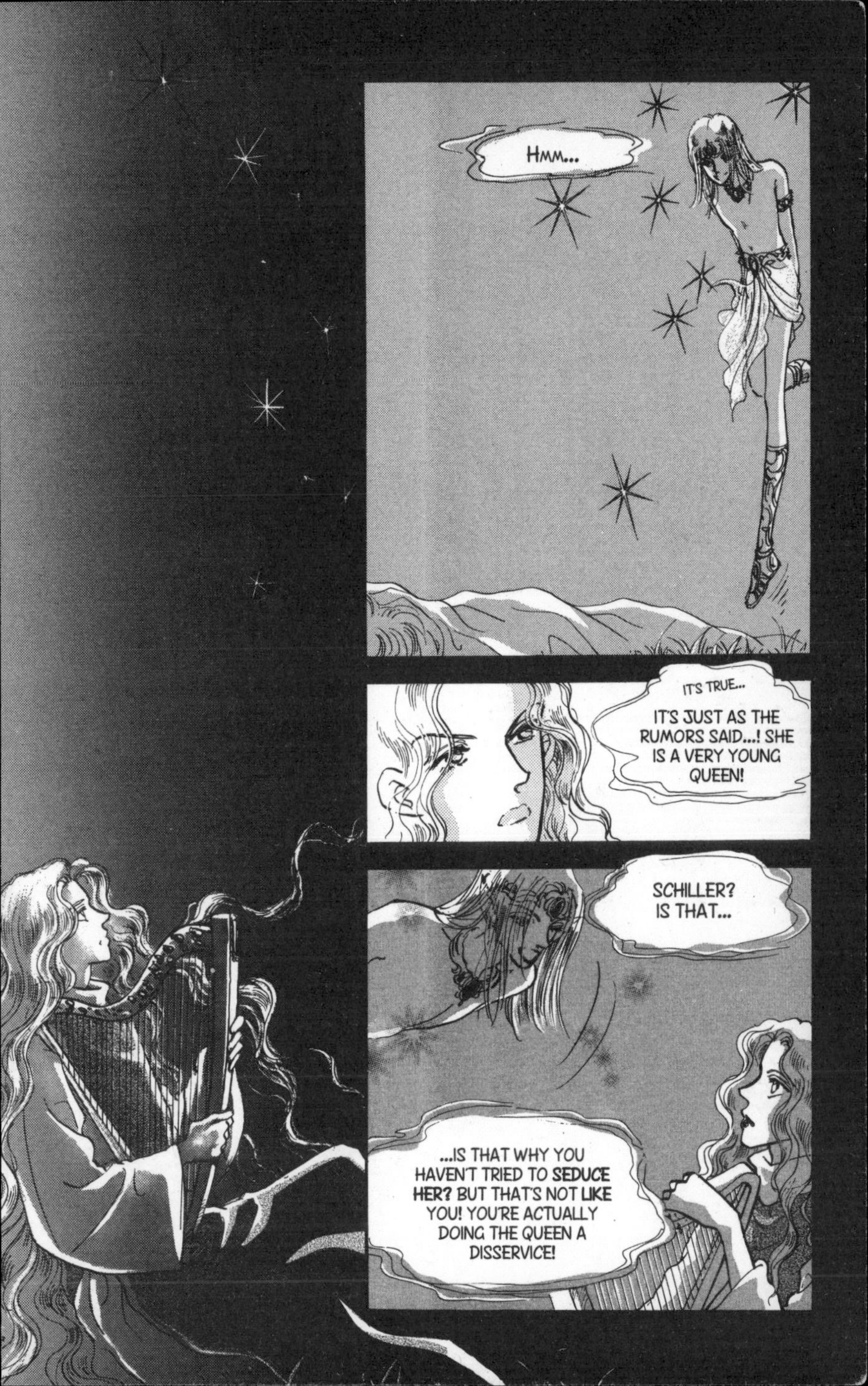
HMM...
IT'S TRUE...
IT'S JUST AS THE RUMORS SAID...! SHE IS A VERY YOUNG QUEEN!
SCHILLER? IS THAT...
...IS THAT WHY YOU HAVEN'T TRIED TO SEDUCE HER? BUT THAT'S NOT LIKE YOU! YOU'RE ACTUALLY DOING THE QUEEN A DISSERVICE!

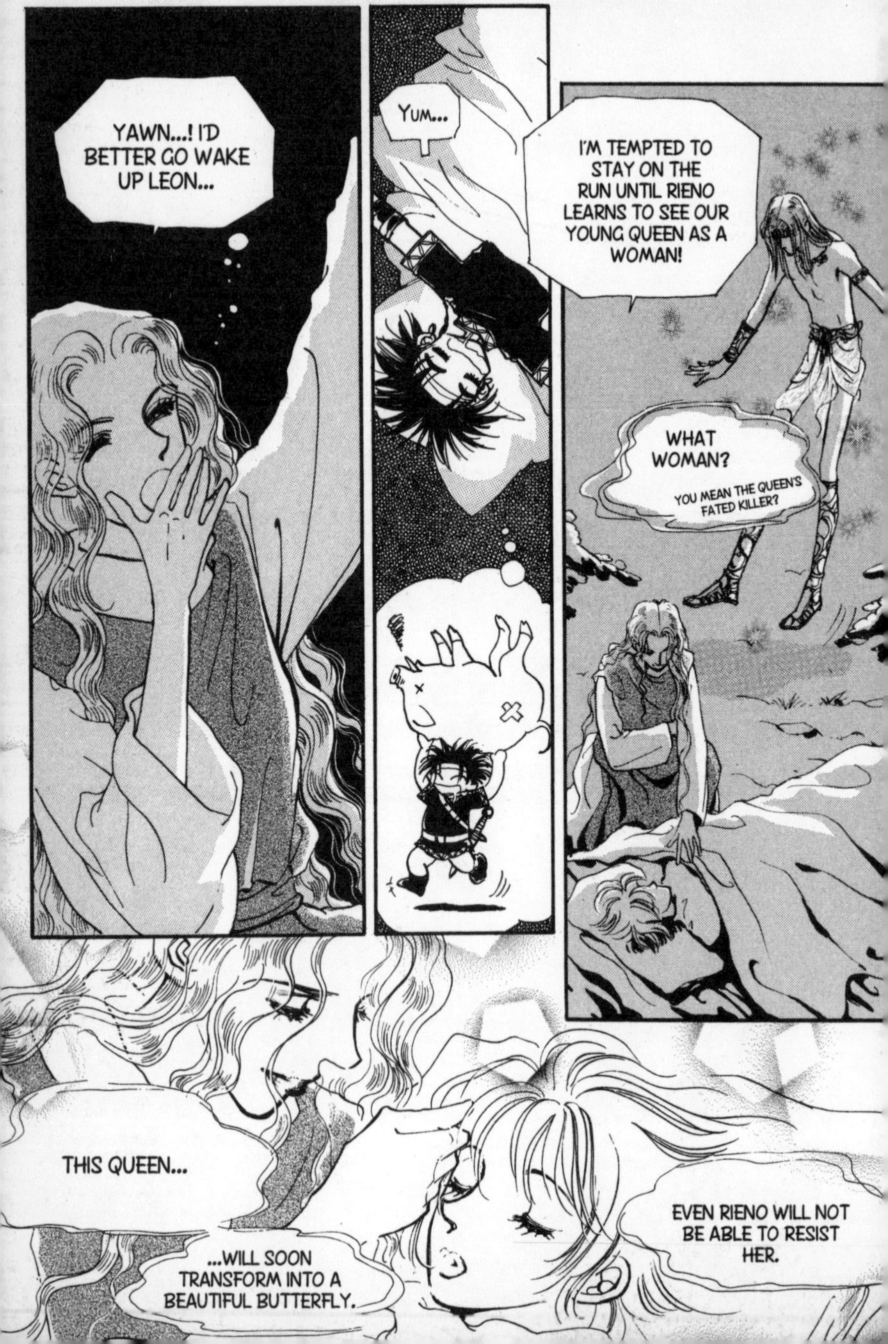
YAWN...! I'D BETTER GO WAKE UP LEON...
YUM...
I'M TEMPTED TO STAY ON THE RUN UNTIL RIENO LEARNS TO SEE OUR YOUNG QUEEN AS A WOMAN!
WHAT WOMAN?
YOU MEAN THE QUEEN'S FATED KILLER?
THIS QUEEN...
...WILL SOON TRANSFORM INTO A BEAUTIFUL BUTTERFLY.
EVEN RIENO WILL NOT BE ABLE TO RESIST HER.

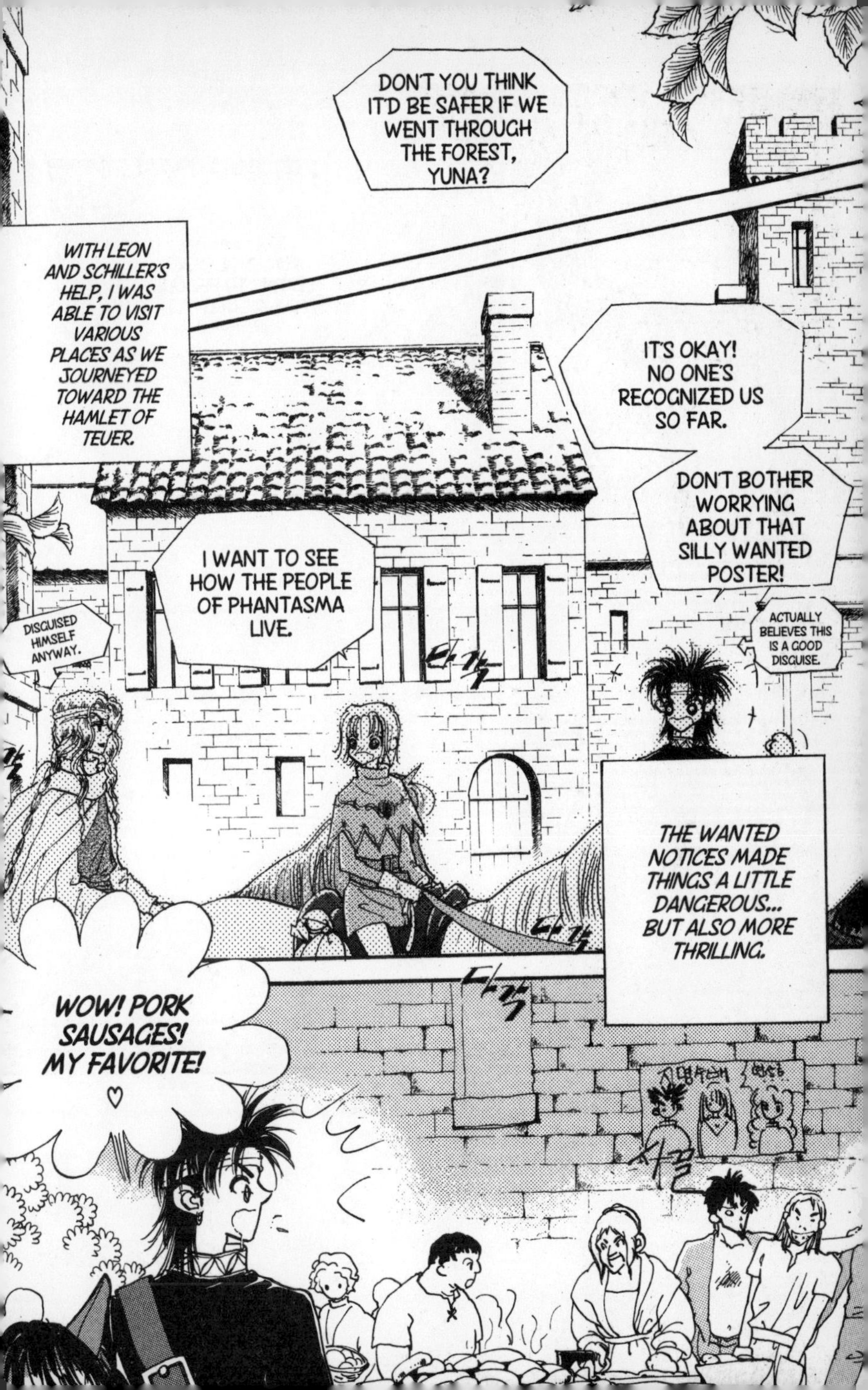
DON'T YOU THINK IT'D BE SAFER IF WE WENT THROUGH THE FOREST, YUNA?
WITH LEON AND SCHILLER'S HELP, I WAS ABLE TO VISIT VARIOUS PLACES AS WE JOURNEYED TOWARD THE HAMLET OF TEUER.
IT'S OKAY! NO ONE'S RECOGNIZED US SO FAR.
DON'T BOTHER WORRYING ABOUT THAT SILLY WANTED POSTER!
I WANT TO SEE HOW THE PEOPLE OF PHANTASMA LIVE.
DISGUISED HIMSELF ANYWAY.
ACTUALLY BELIEVES THIS IS A GOOD DISGUISE.
THE WANTED NOTICES MADE THINGS A LITTLE DANGEROUS... BUT ALSO MORE THRILLING.
WOW! PORK SAUSAGES! MY FAVORITE! ♡

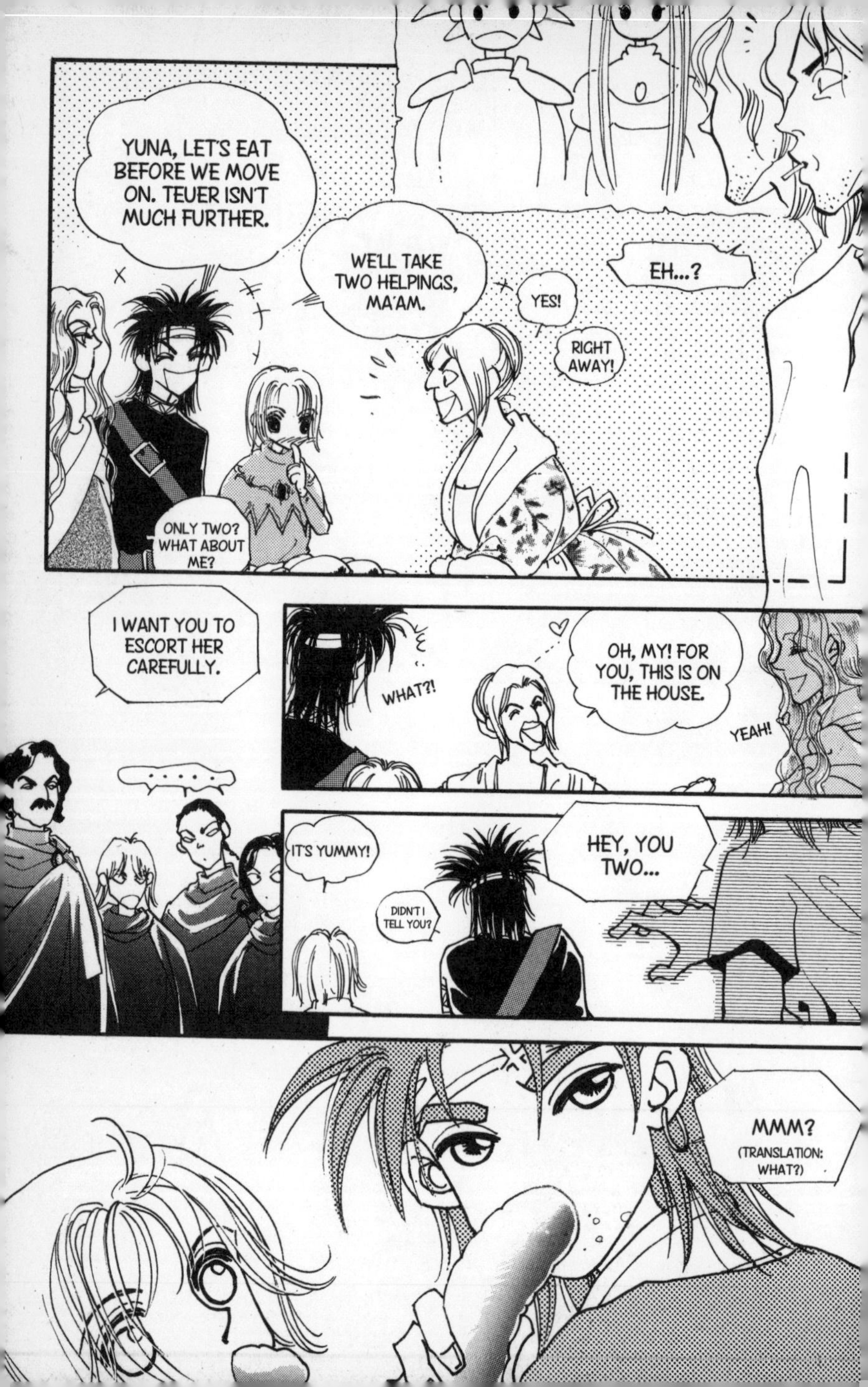

YUNA, LET'S EAT BEFORE WE MOVE ON. TEUER ISN'T MUCH FURTHER.
WE'LL TAKE TWO HELPINGS, MA'AM.
YES!
RIGHT AWAY!
EH...?
ONLY TWO? WHAT ABOUT ME?
I WANT YOU TO ESCORT HER CAREFULLY.
WHAT?!
OH, MY! FOR YOU, THIS IS ON THE HOUSE.
YEAH!
.....
IT'S YUMMY!
DIDN'T I TELL YOU?
HEY, YOU TWO...
MMM? (TRANSLATION: WHAT?)

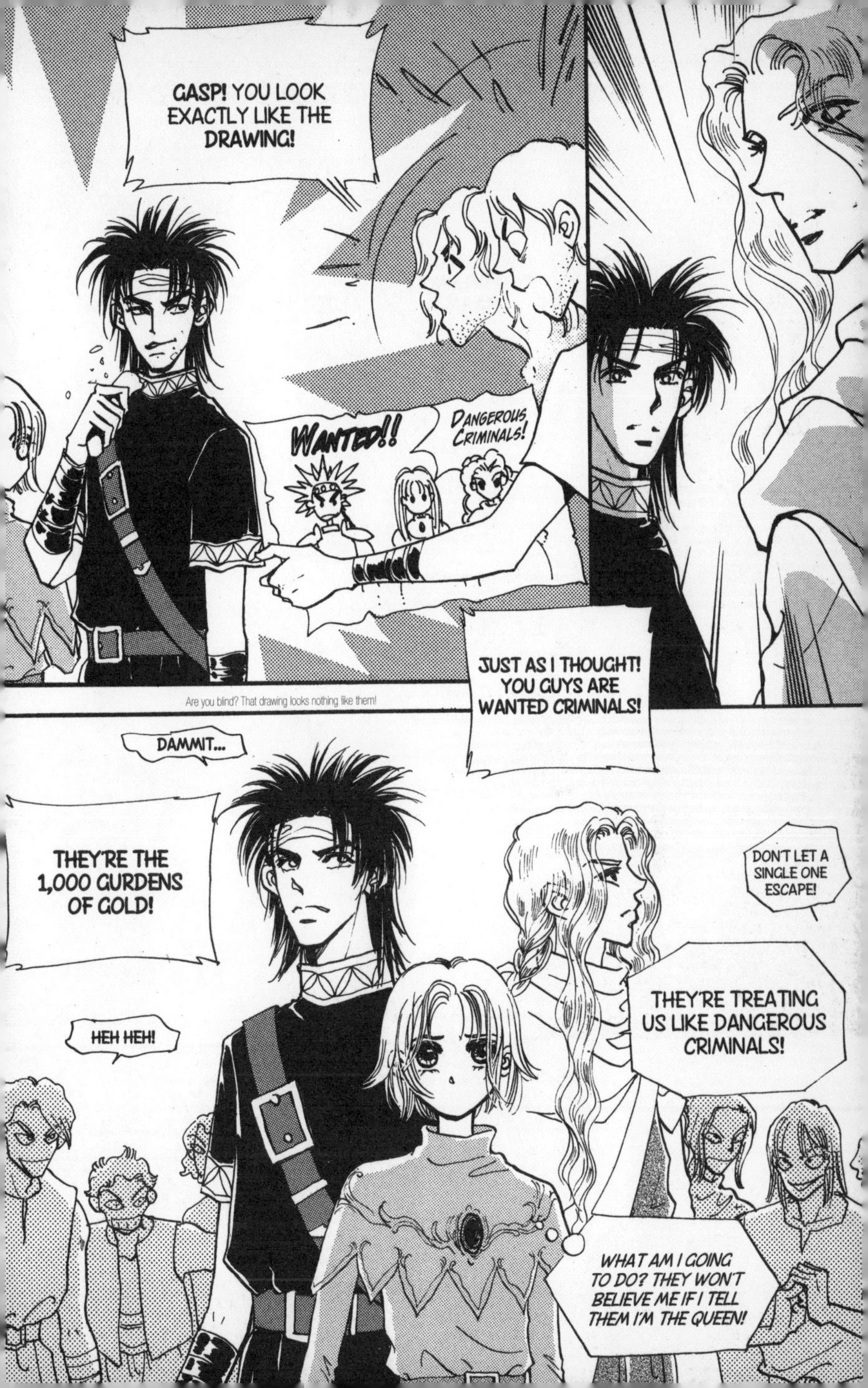

GASP! YOU LOOK EXACTLY LIKE THE DRAWING!
WANTED!!
DANGEROUS CRIMINALS!
Are you blind? That drawing looks nothing like them!
JUST AS I THOUGHT! YOU GUYS ARE WANTED CRIMINALS!
DAMMIT...
THEY'RE THE 1,000 GURDENS OF GOLD!
HEH HEH!
DON'T LET A SINGLE ONE ESCAPE!
THEY'RE TREATING US LIKE DANGEROUS CRIMINALS!
WHAT AM I GOING TO DO? THEY WON'T BELIEVE ME IF I TELL THEM I'M THE QUEEN!

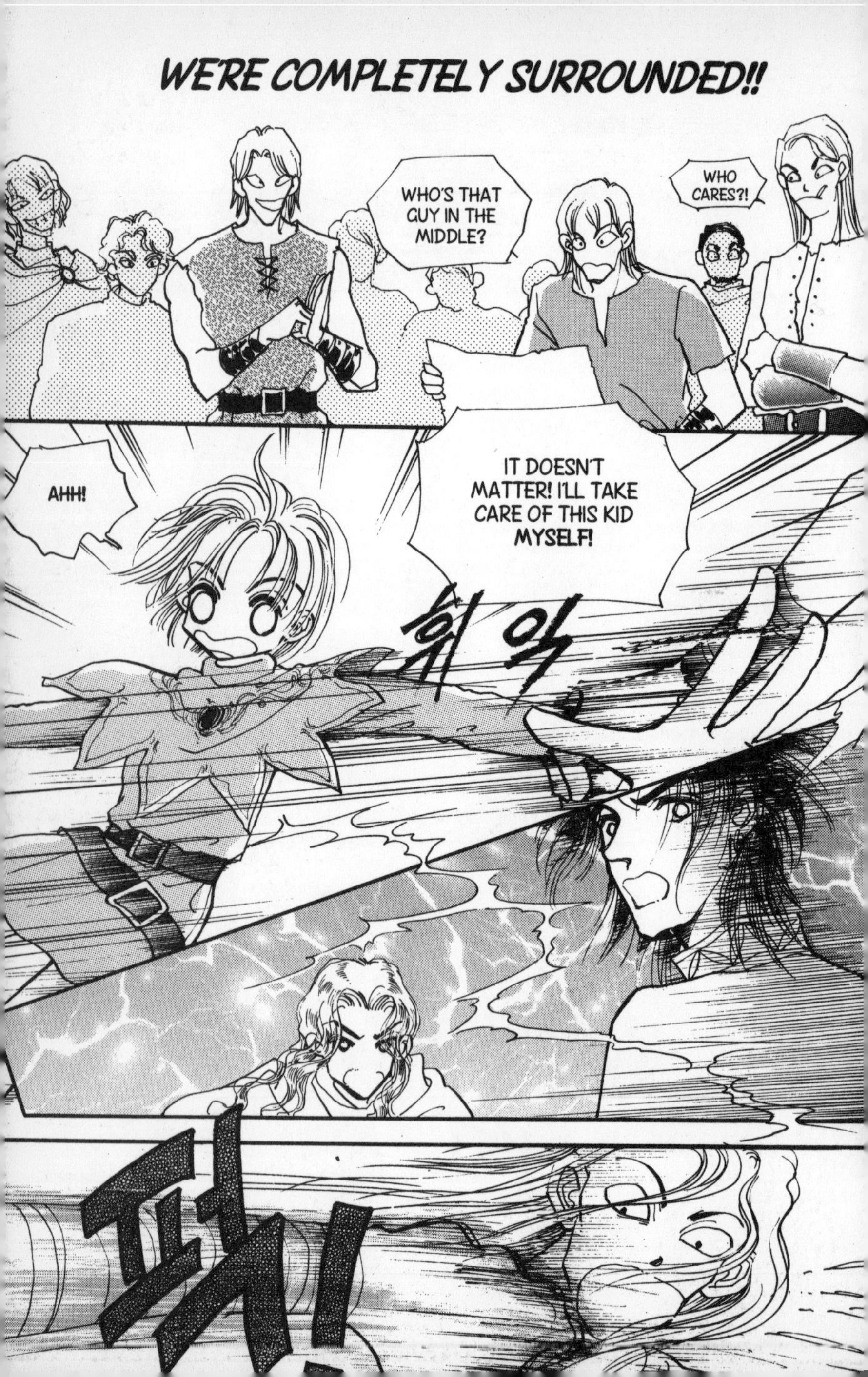
WE'RE COMPLETELY SURROUNDED!!
WHO'S THAT GUY IN THE MIDDLE?
WHO CARES?!
AHH!
IT DOESN'T MATTER! I'LL TAKE CARE OF THIS KID MYSELF!
휘 익

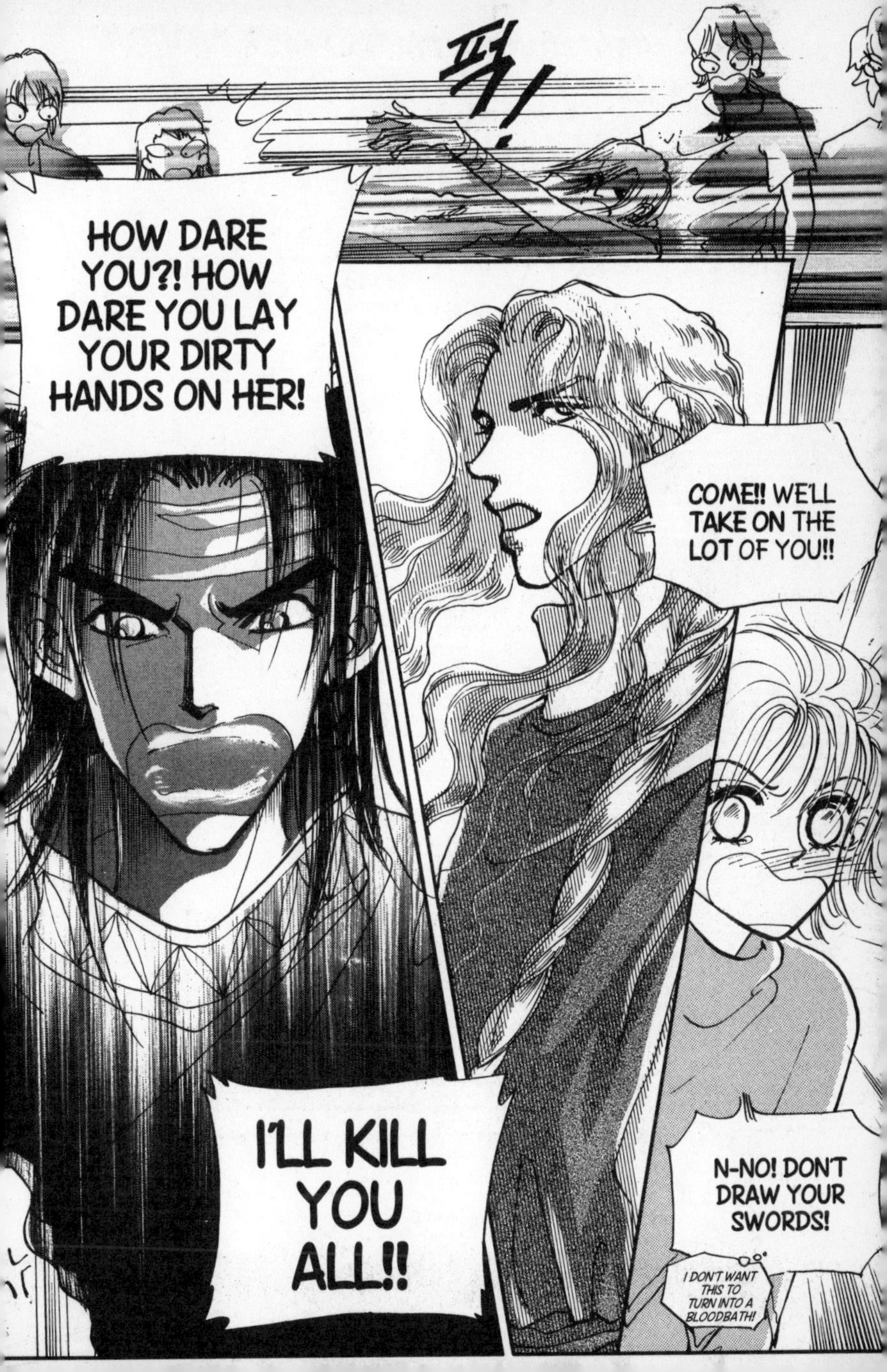
퍽!
HOW DARE YOU?! HOW DARE YOU LAY YOUR DIRTY HANDS ON HER!
I'LL KILL YOU ALL!!
COME!! WE'LL TAKE ON THE LOT OF YOU!!
N-NO! DON'T DRAW YOUR SWORDS!
I DON'T WANT THIS TO TURN INTO A BLOODBATH!

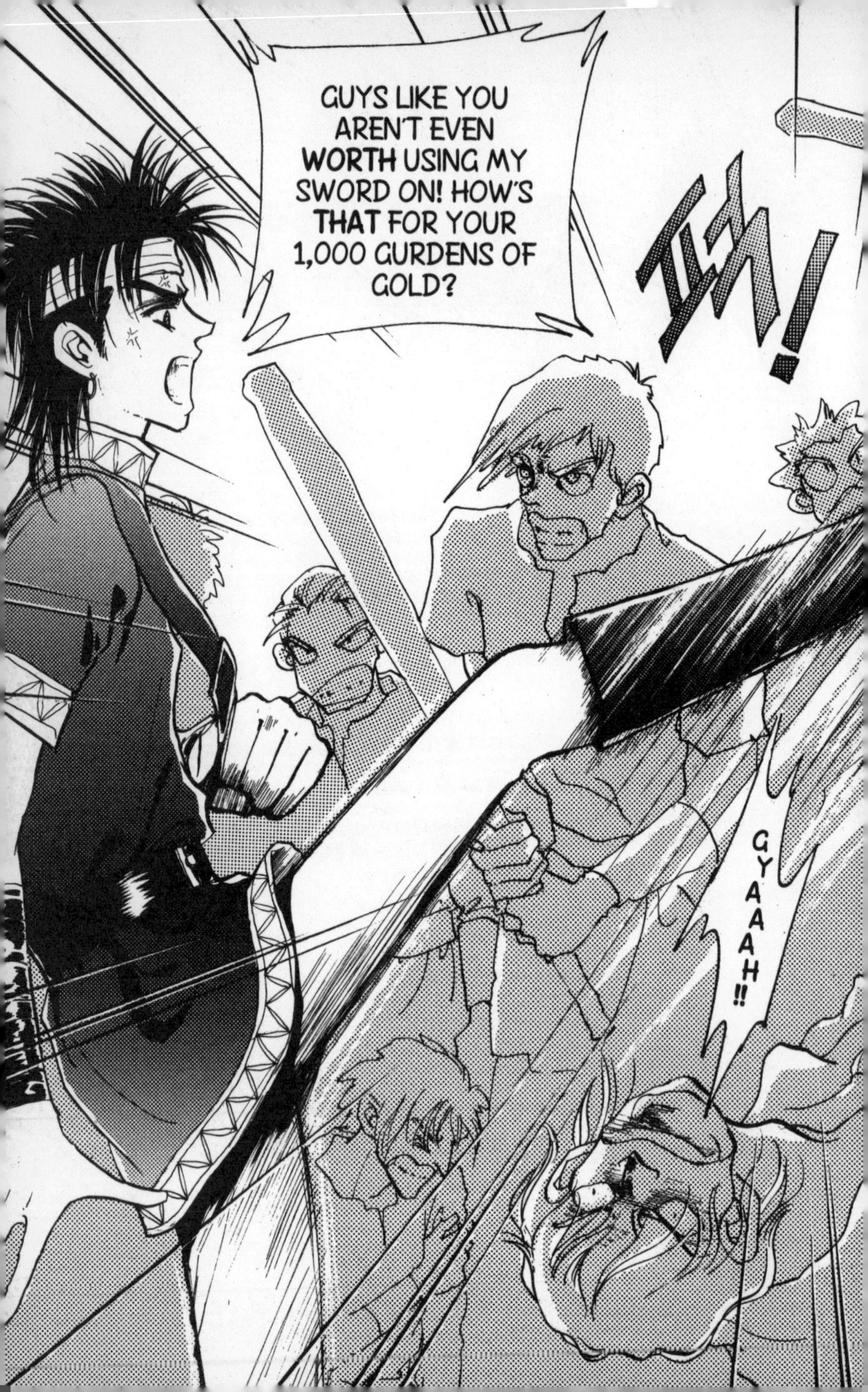
GUYS LIKE YOU AREN'T EVEN WORTH USING MY SWORD ON! HOW'S THAT FOR YOUR 1,000 GURDENS OF GOLD?
GYAAAH!!

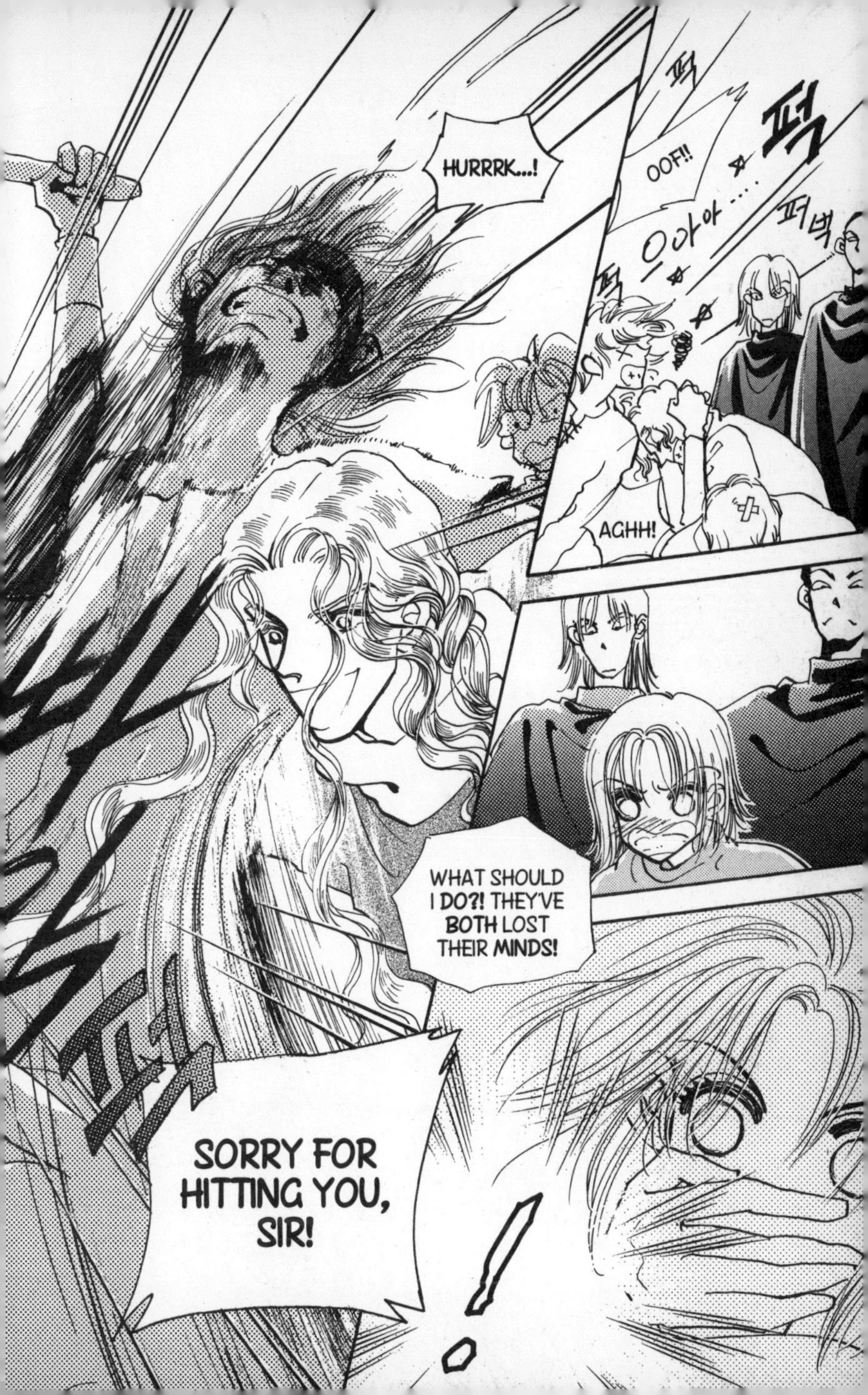
HURRRK...!
퍽
OOF!!
퍽
으아아....
퍼벅
퍽
AGHH!
WHAT SHOULD I DO?! THEY'VE BOTH LOST THEIR MINDS!
SORRY FOR HITTING YOU, SIR!

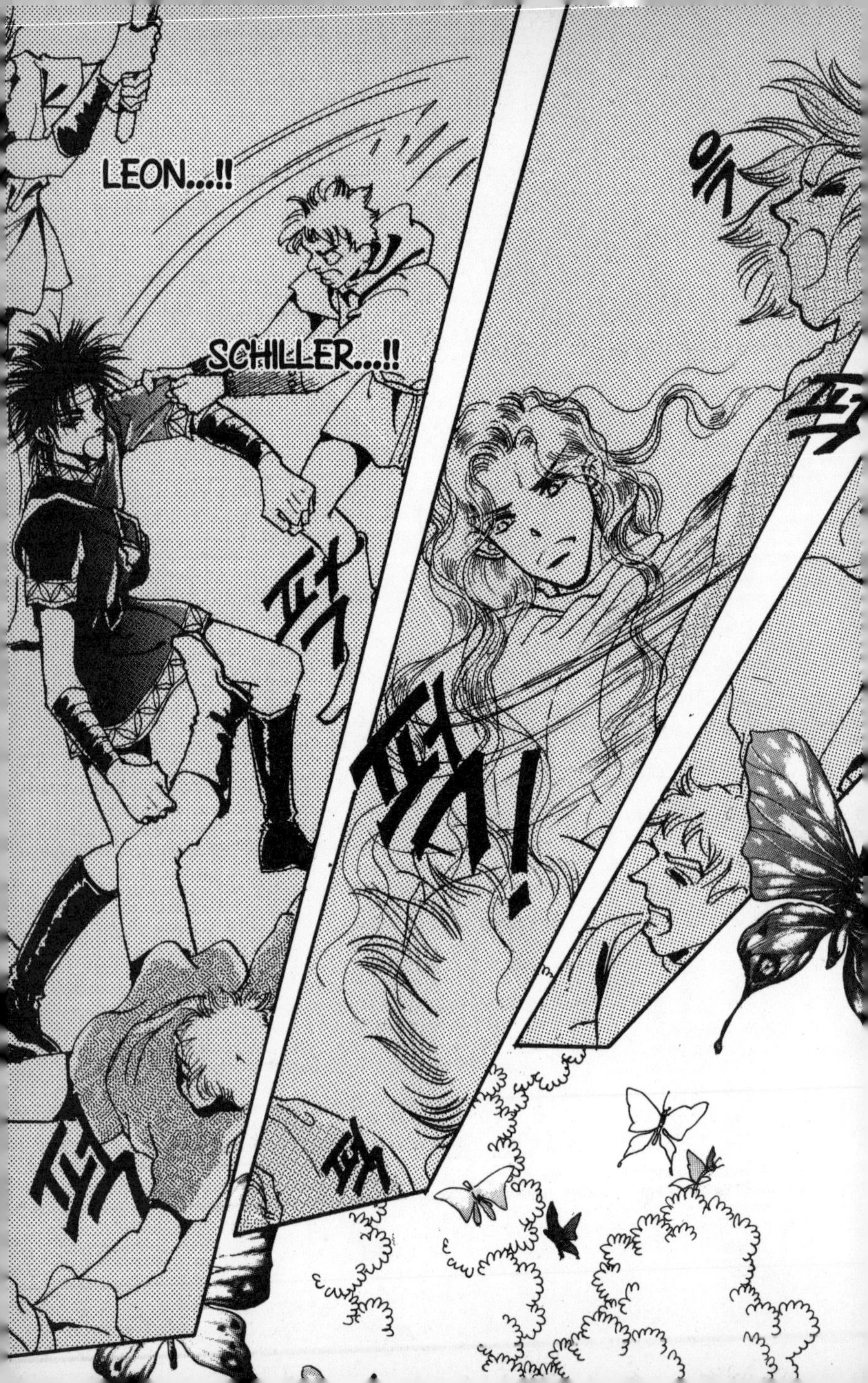
LEON...!!
SCHILLER...!!

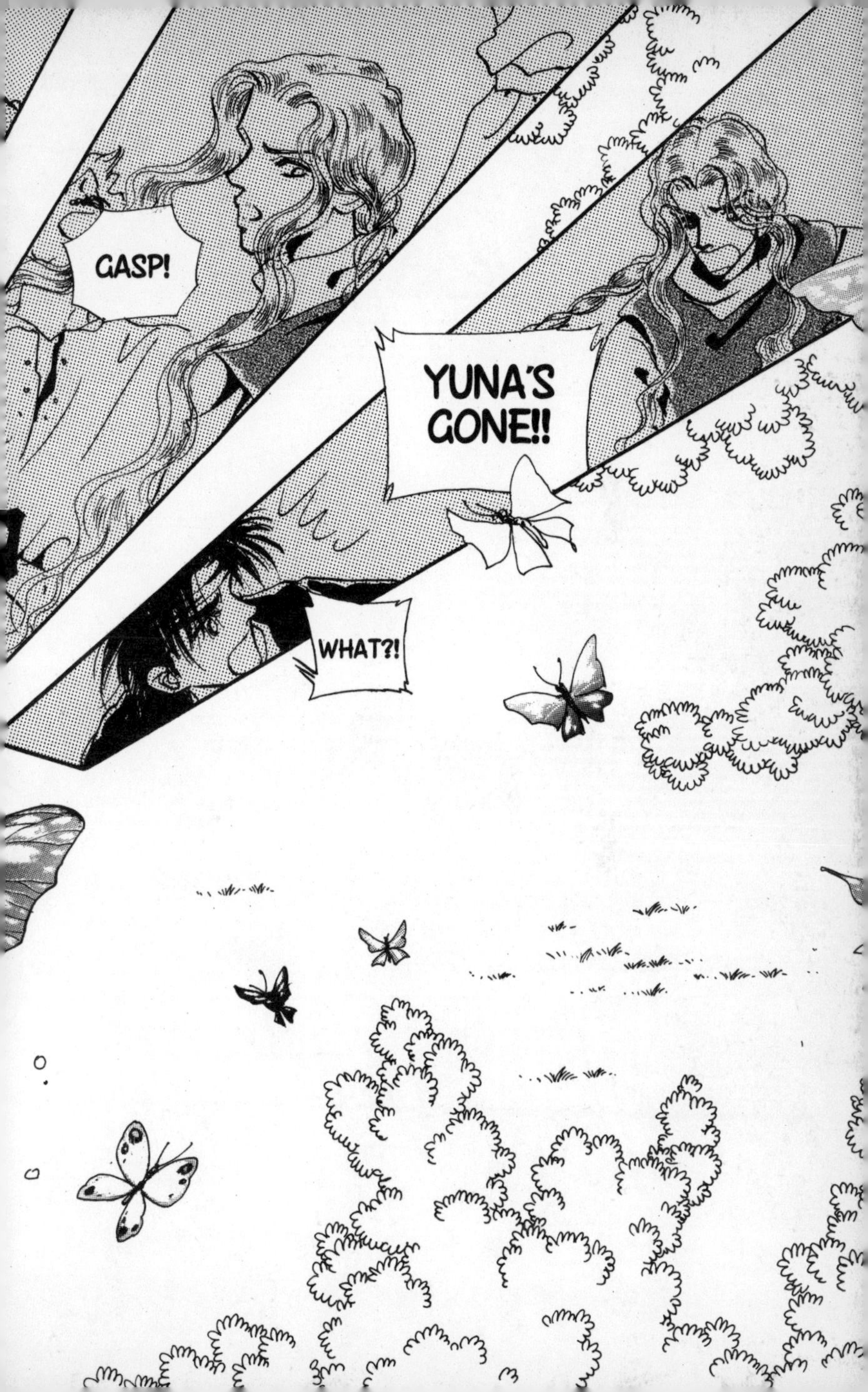
GASP!
YUNA'S GONE!!
WHAT?!

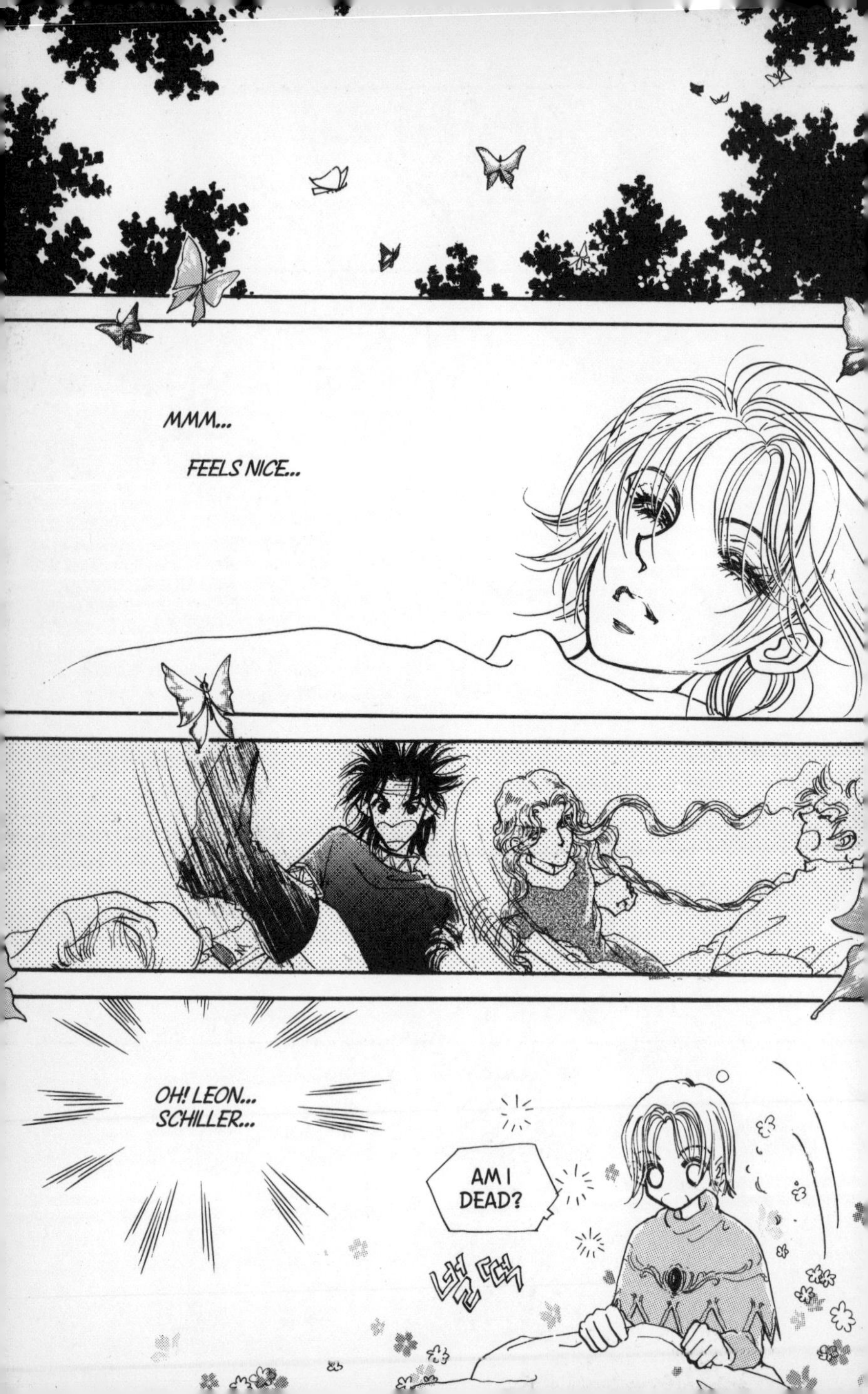
MMM...
FEELS NICE...
OH! LEON... SCHILLER...
AM I DEAD?

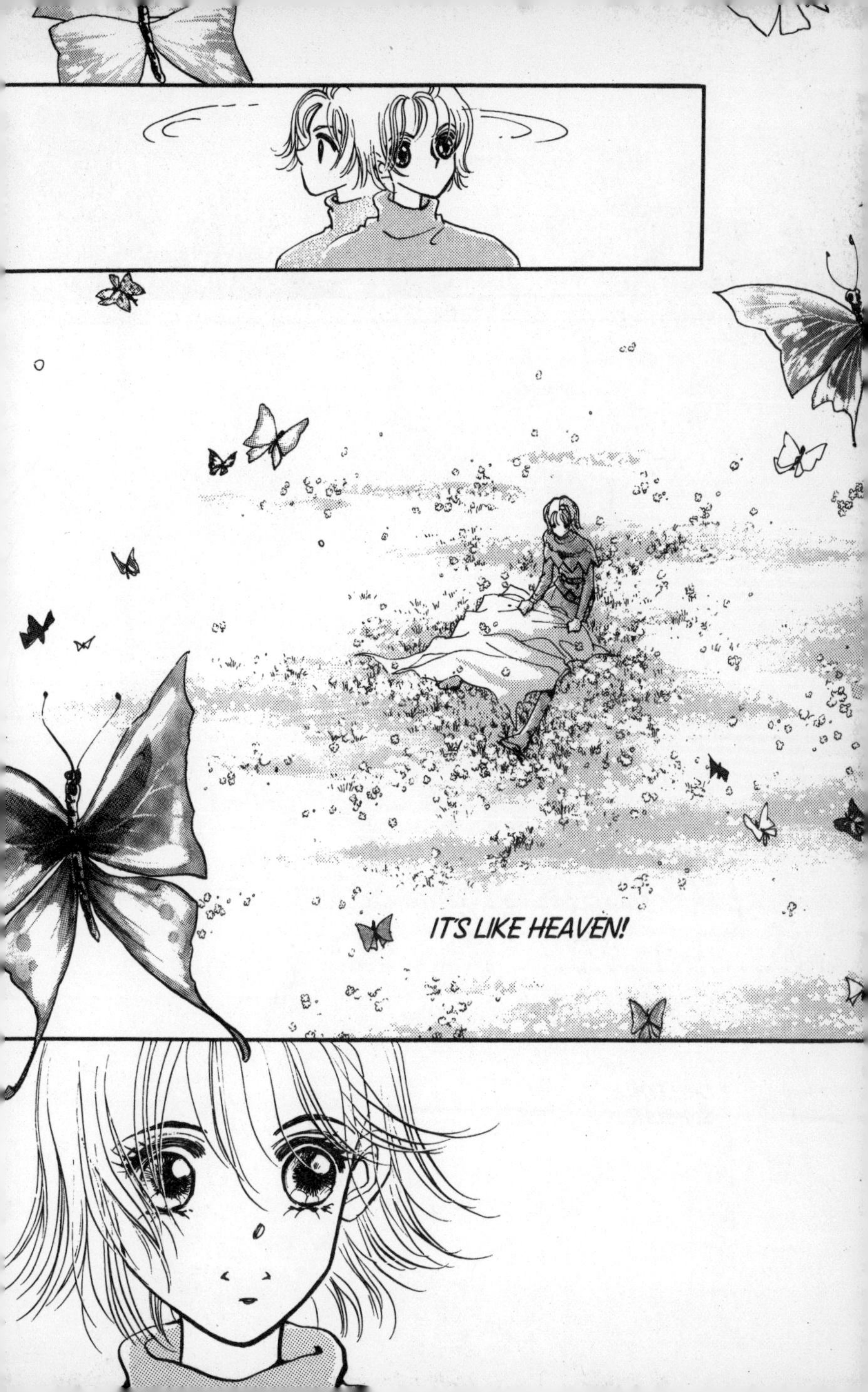
IT'S LIKE HEAVEN!

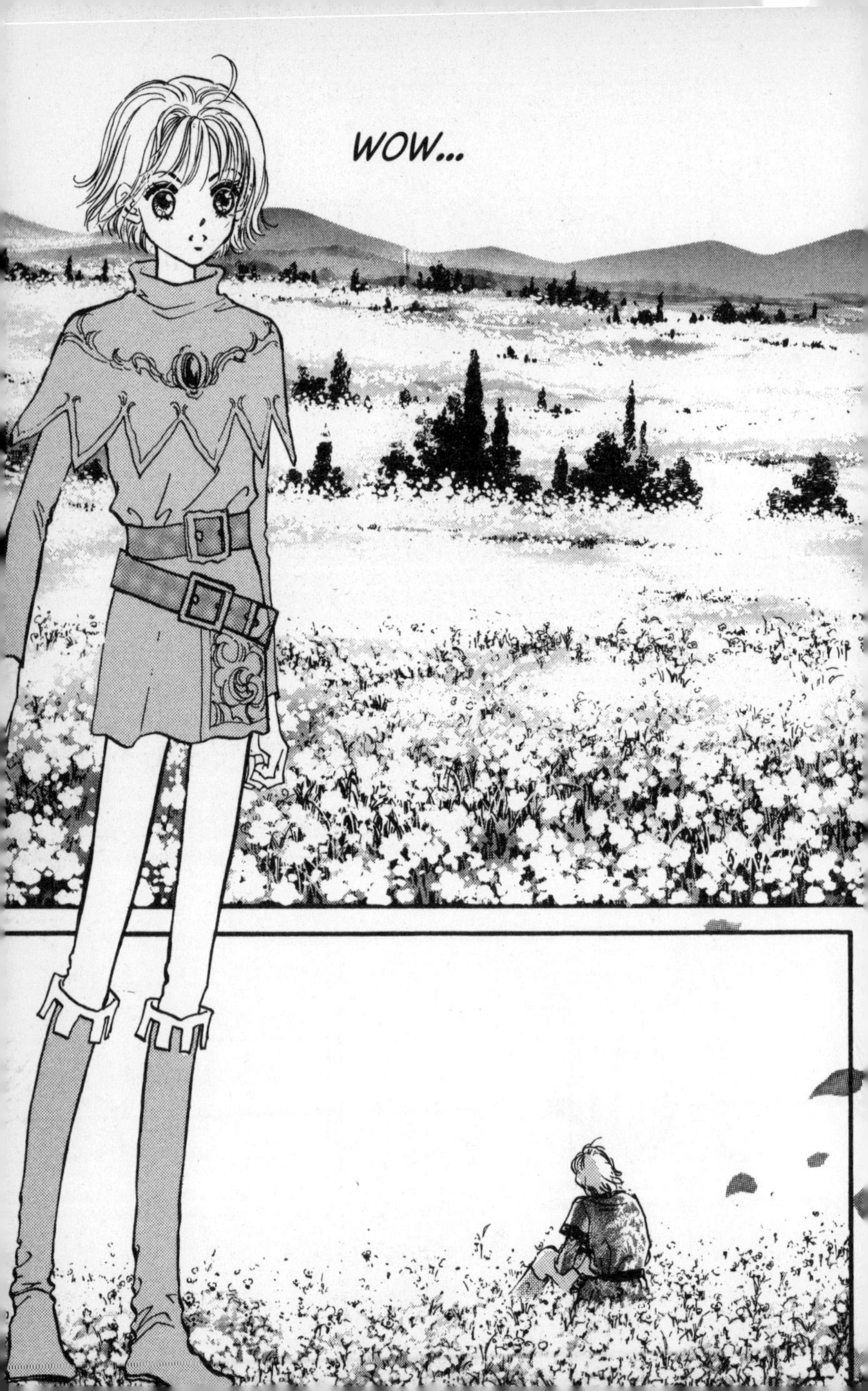
WOW...

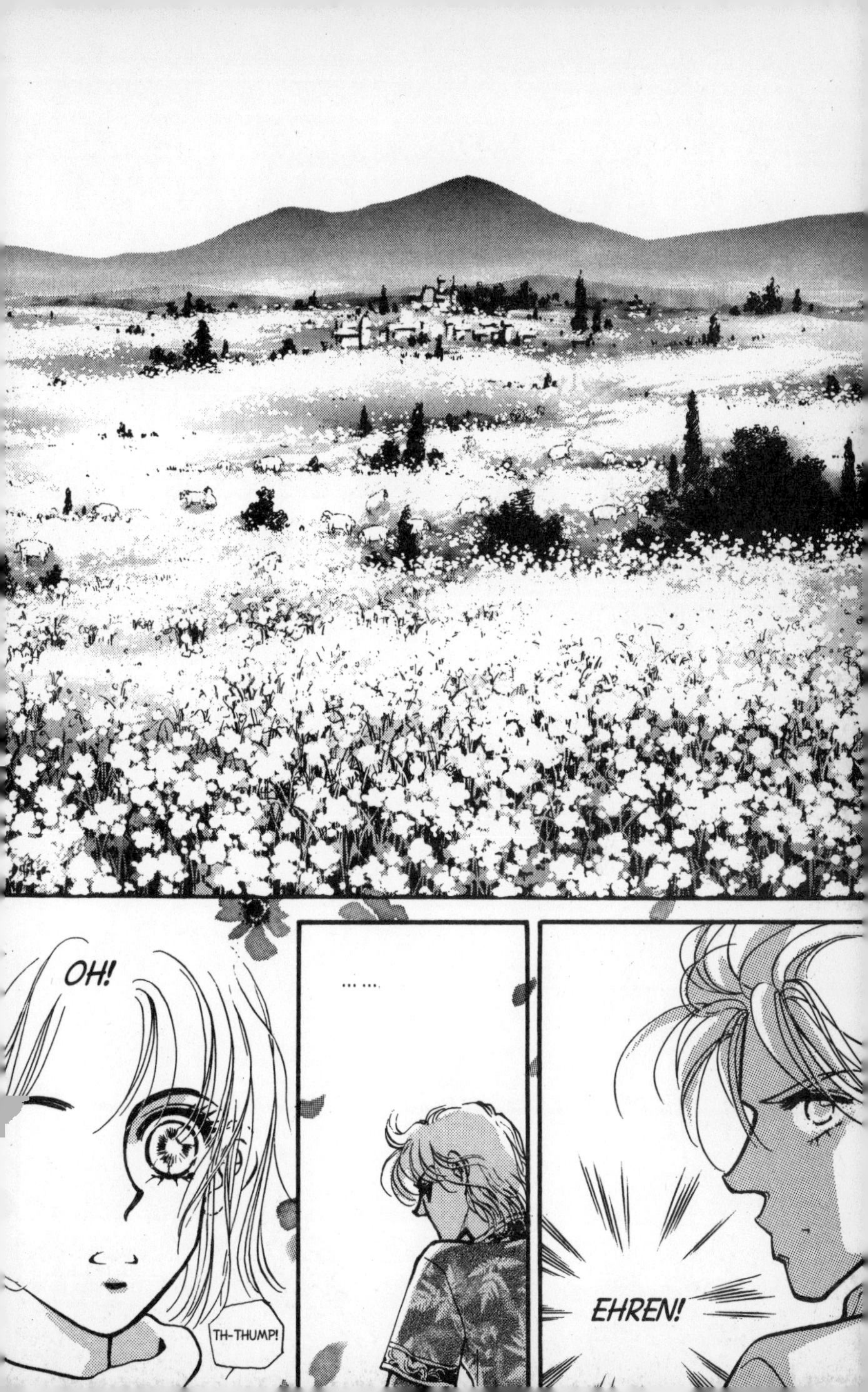
OH!
TH-THUMP!
... ...
EHREN!

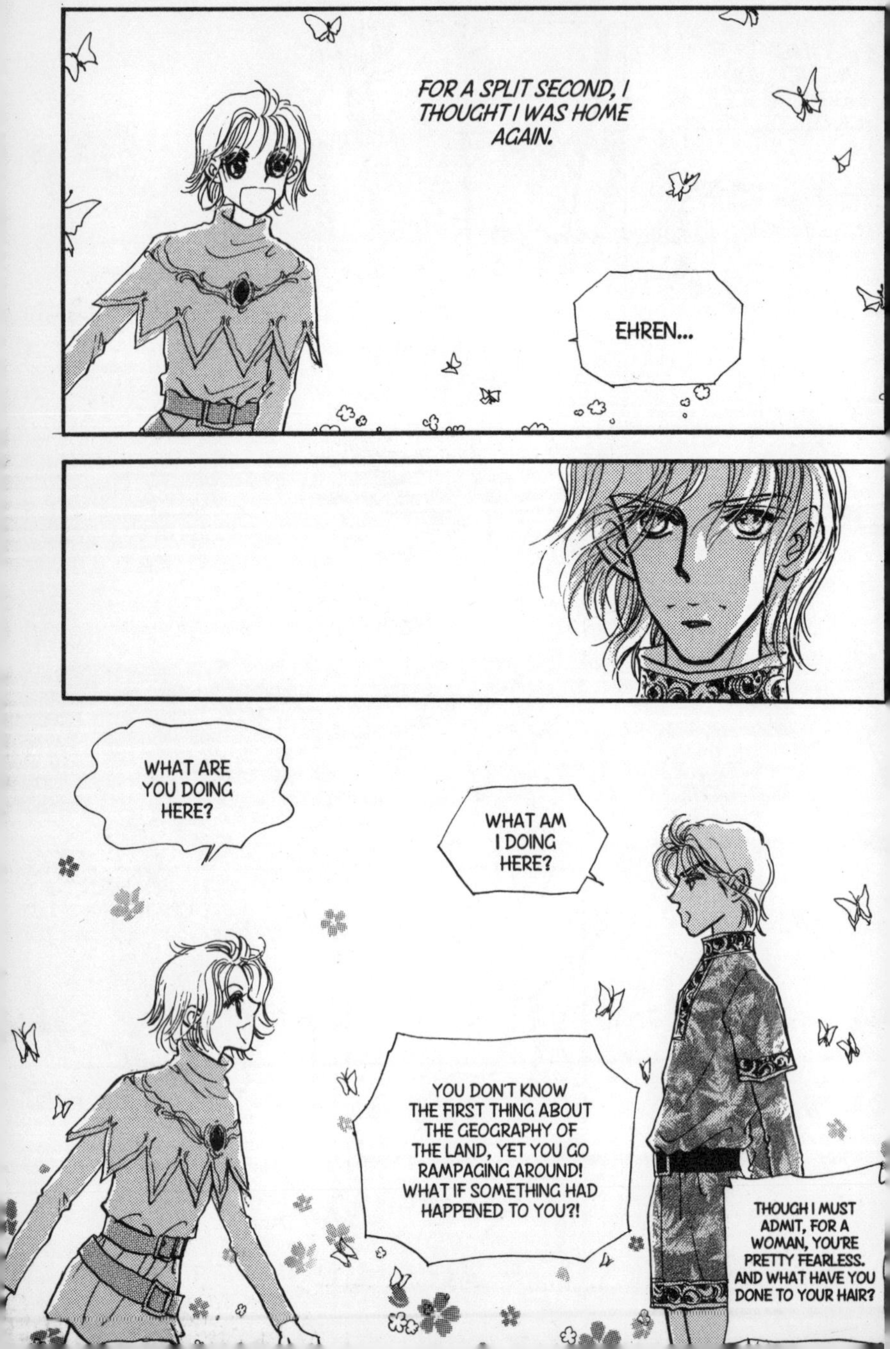
FOR A SPLIT SECOND, I THOUGHT I WAS HOME AGAIN.
EHREN...
WHAT ARE YOU DOING HERE?
WHAT AM I DOING HERE?
YOU DON'T KNOW THE FIRST THING ABOUT THE GEOGRAPHY OF THE LAND, YET YOU GO RAMPAGING AROUND! WHAT IF SOMETHING HAD HAPPENED TO YOU?!
THOUGH I MUST ADMIT, FOR A WOMAN, YOU'RE PRETTY FEARLESS. AND WHAT HAVE YOU DONE TO YOUR HAIR?

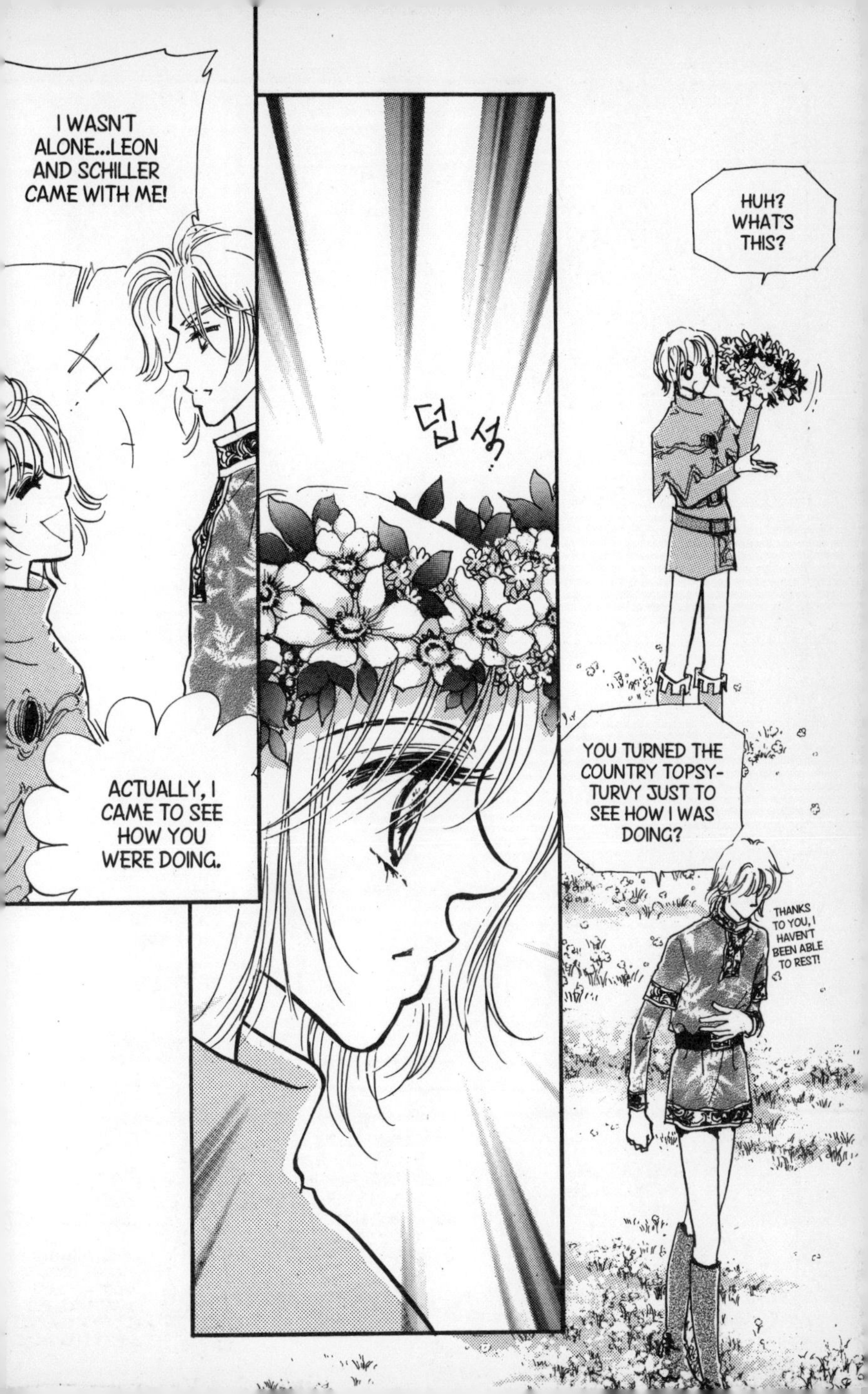
I WASN'T ALONE...LEON AND SCHILLER CAME WITH ME!
ACTUALLY, I CAME TO SEE HOW YOU WERE DOING.
덥석
HUH? WHAT'S THIS?
YOU TURNED THE COUNTRY TOPSY-TURVY JUST TO SEE HOW I WAS DOING?
THANKS TO YOU, I HAVEN'T BEEN ABLE TO REST!

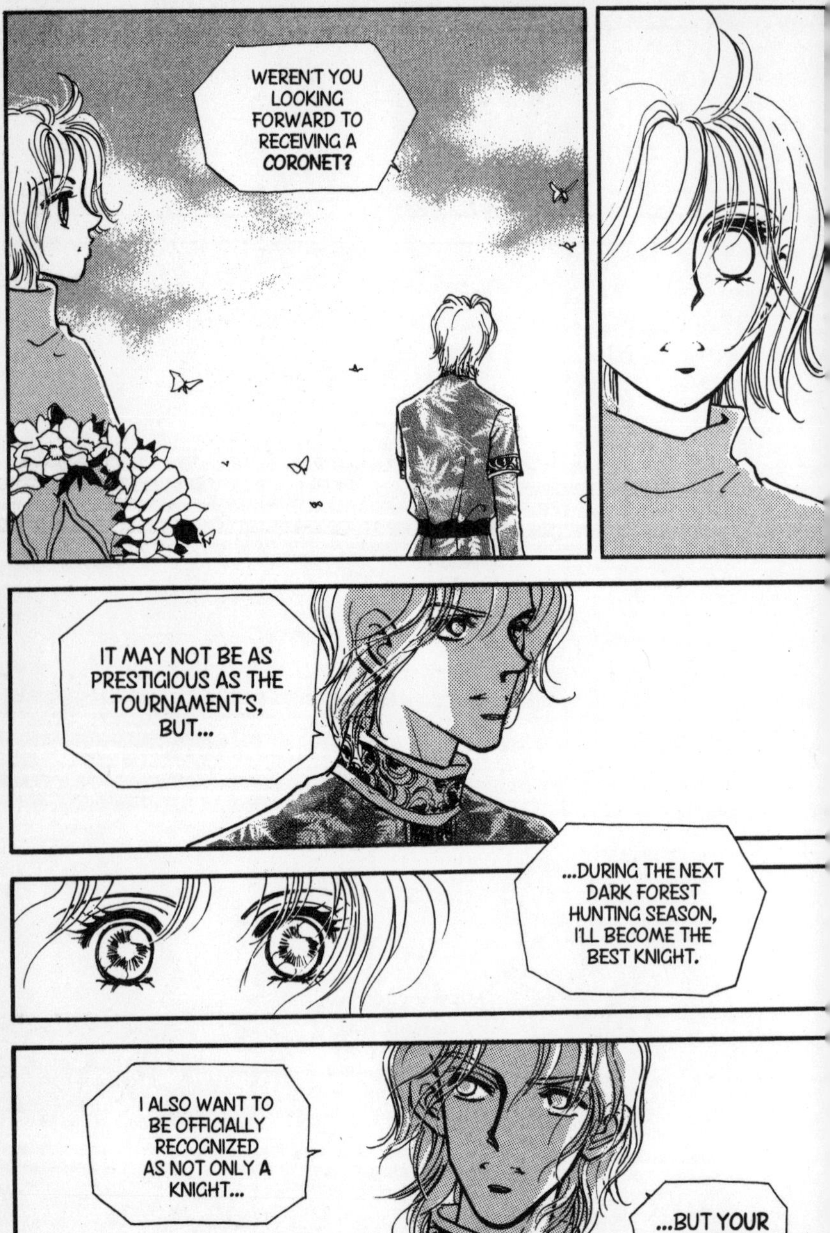
WEREN'T YOU LOOKING FORWARD TO RECEIVING A CORONET?
IT MAY NOT BE AS PRESTIGIOUS AS THE TOURNAMENT'S, BUT...
...DURING THE NEXT DARK FOREST HUNTING SEASON, I'LL BECOME THE BEST KNIGHT.
I ALSO WANT TO BE OFFICIALLY RECOGNIZED AS NOT ONLY A KNIGHT...
...BUT YOUR KNIGHT.

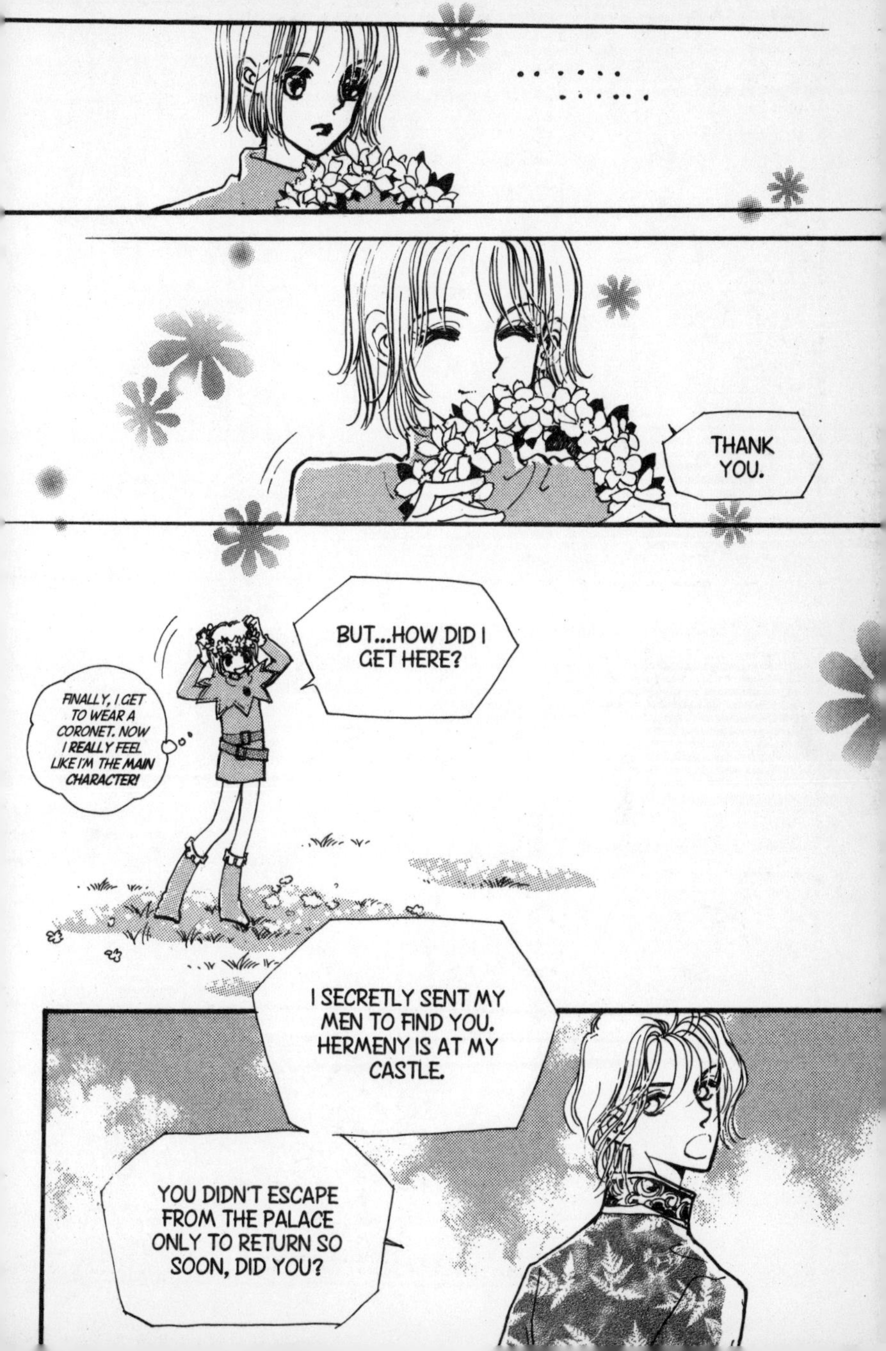
......
......
THANK YOU.
FINALLY, I GET TO WEAR A CORONET. NOW I REALLY FEEL LIKE I'M THE MAIN CHARACTER!
BUT...HOW DID I GET HERE?
I SECRETLY SENT MY MEN TO FIND YOU. HERMENY IS AT MY CASTLE.
YOU DIDN'T ESCAPE FROM THE PALACE ONLY TO RETURN SO SOON, DID YOU?

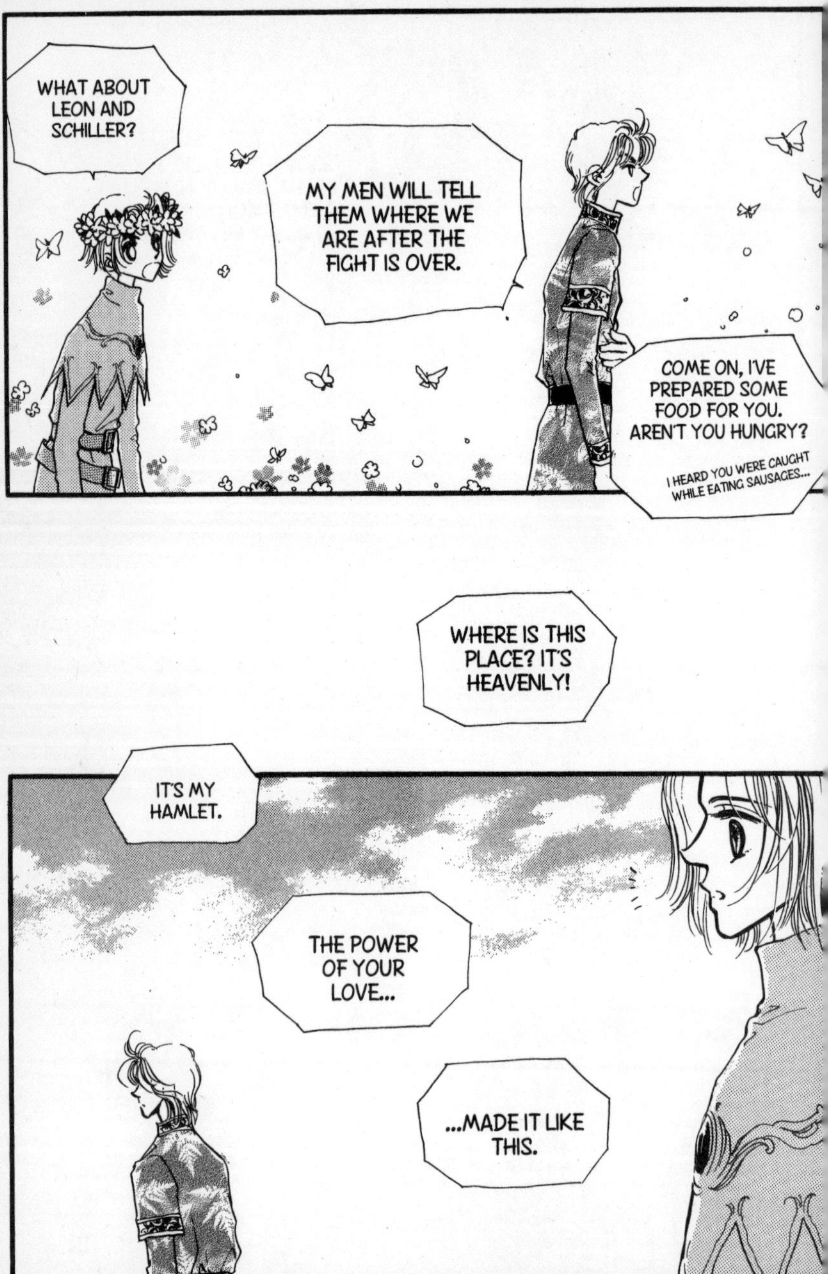
WHAT ABOUT LEON AND SCHILLER?
MY MEN WILL TELL THEM WHERE WE ARE AFTER THE FIGHT IS OVER.
COME ON, I'VE PREPARED SOME FOOD FOR YOU. AREN'T YOU HUNGRY?
I HEARD YOU WERE CAUGHT WHILE EATING SAUSAGES...
WHERE IS THIS PLACE? IT'S HEAVENLY!
IT'S MY HAMLET.
THE POWER OF YOUR LOVE...
...MADE IT LIKE THIS.

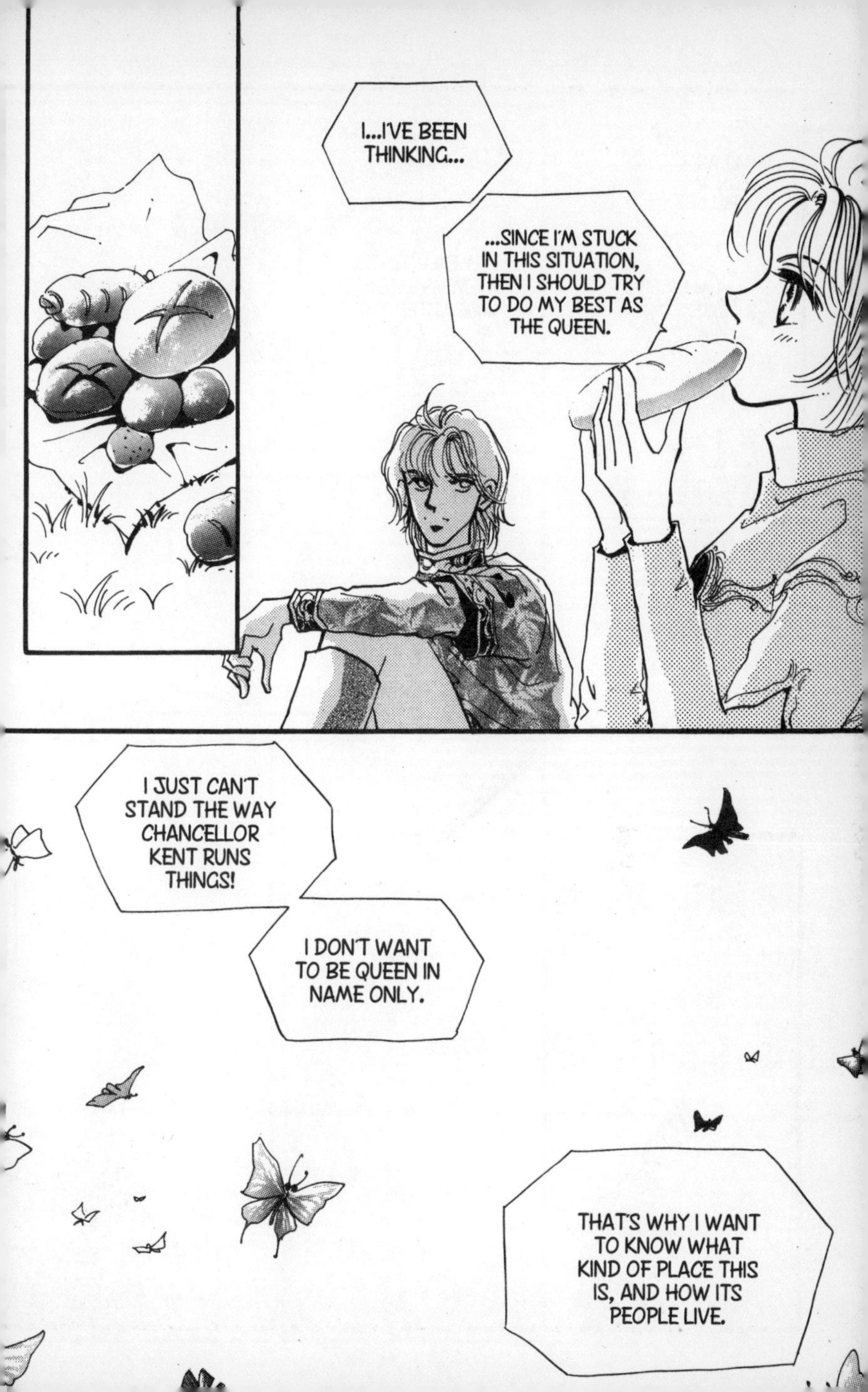
I...I'VE BEEN THINKING...
...SINCE I'M STUCK IN THIS SITUATION, THEN I SHOULD TRY TO DO MY BEST AS THE QUEEN.
I JUST CAN'T STAND THE WAY CHANCELLOR KENT RUNS THINGS!
I DON'T WANT TO BE QUEEN IN NAME ONLY.
THAT'S WHY I WANT TO KNOW WHAT KIND OF PLACE THIS IS, AND HOW ITS PEOPLE LIVE.

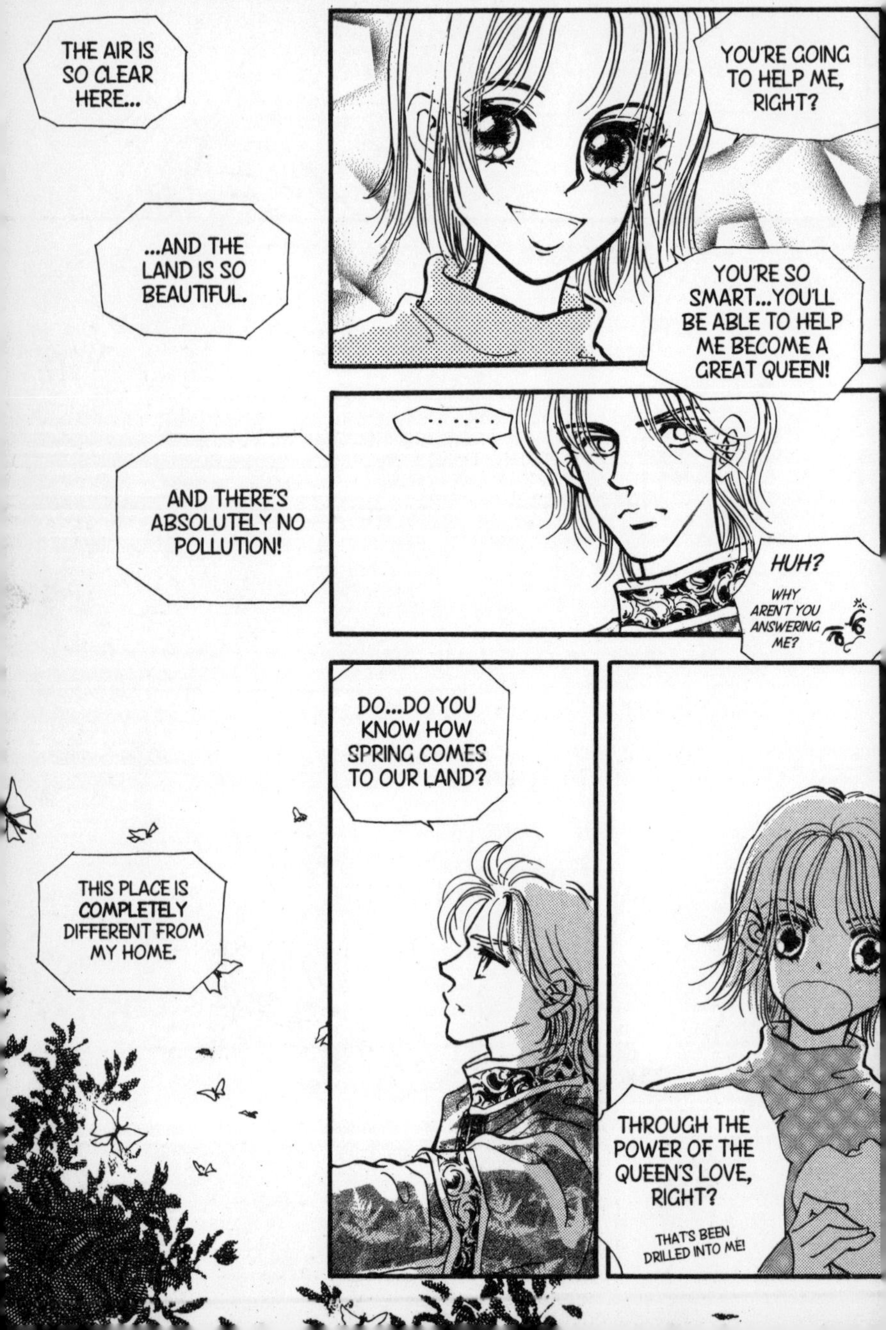
THE AIR IS SO CLEAR HERE...
YOU'RE GOING TO HELP ME, RIGHT?
...AND THE LAND IS SO BEAUTIFUL.
YOU'RE SO SMART...YOU'LL BE ABLE TO HELP ME BECOME A GREAT QUEEN!
AND THERE'S ABSOLUTELY NO POLLUTION!
.. ... .
HUH?
WHY AREN'T YOU ANSWERING ME?
DO...DO YOU KNOW HOW SPRING COMES TO OUR LAND?
THIS PLACE IS COMPLETELY DIFFERENT FROM MY HOME.
THROUGH THE POWER OF THE QUEEN'S LOVE, RIGHT?
THAT'S BEEN DRILLED INTO ME!

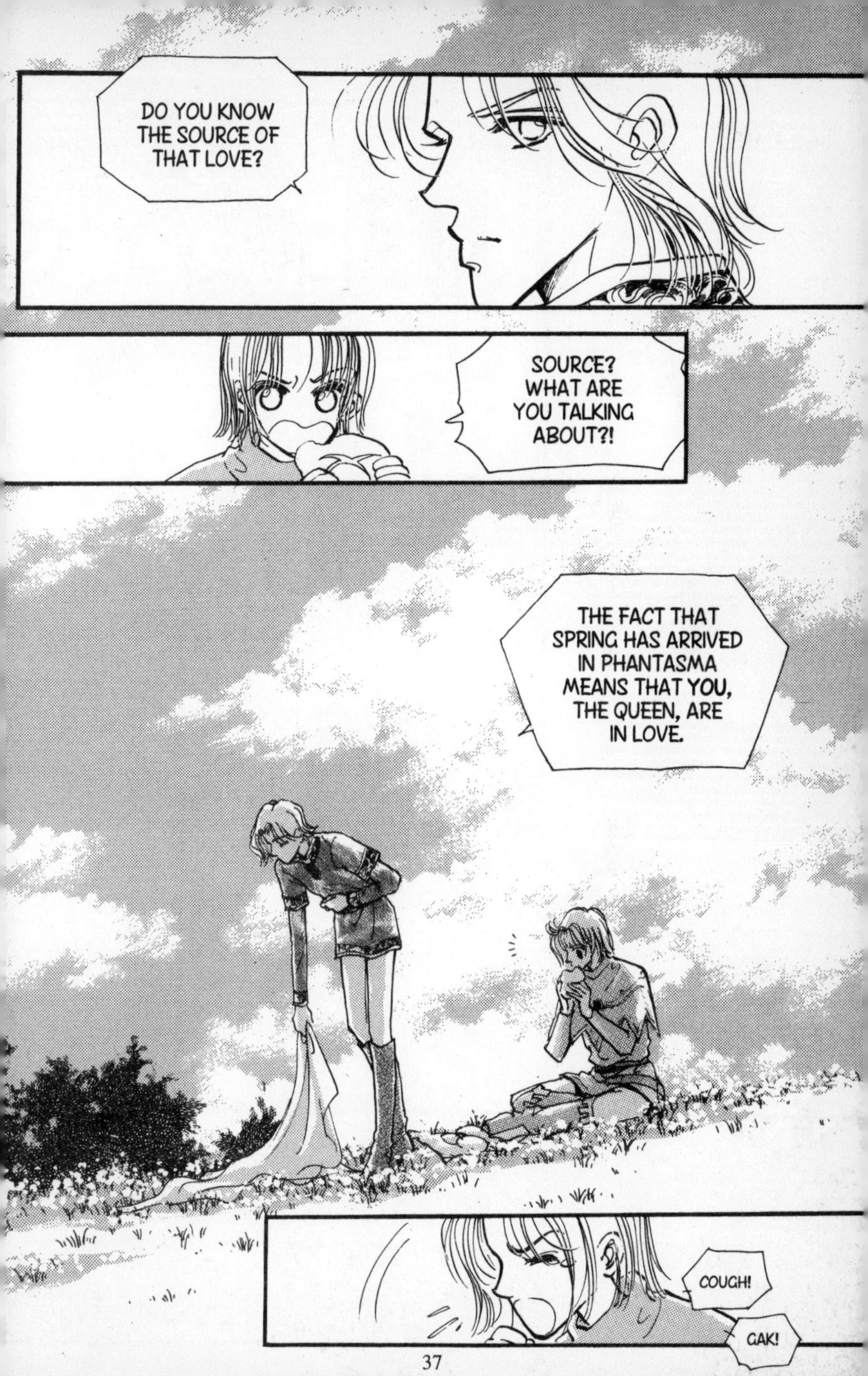
DO YOU KNOW THE SOURCE OF THAT LOVE?
SOURCE? WHAT ARE YOU TALKING ABOUT?!
THE FACT THAT SPRING HAS ARRIVED IN PHANTASMA MEANS THAT YOU, THE QUEEN, ARE IN LOVE.
COUGH!
GAK!

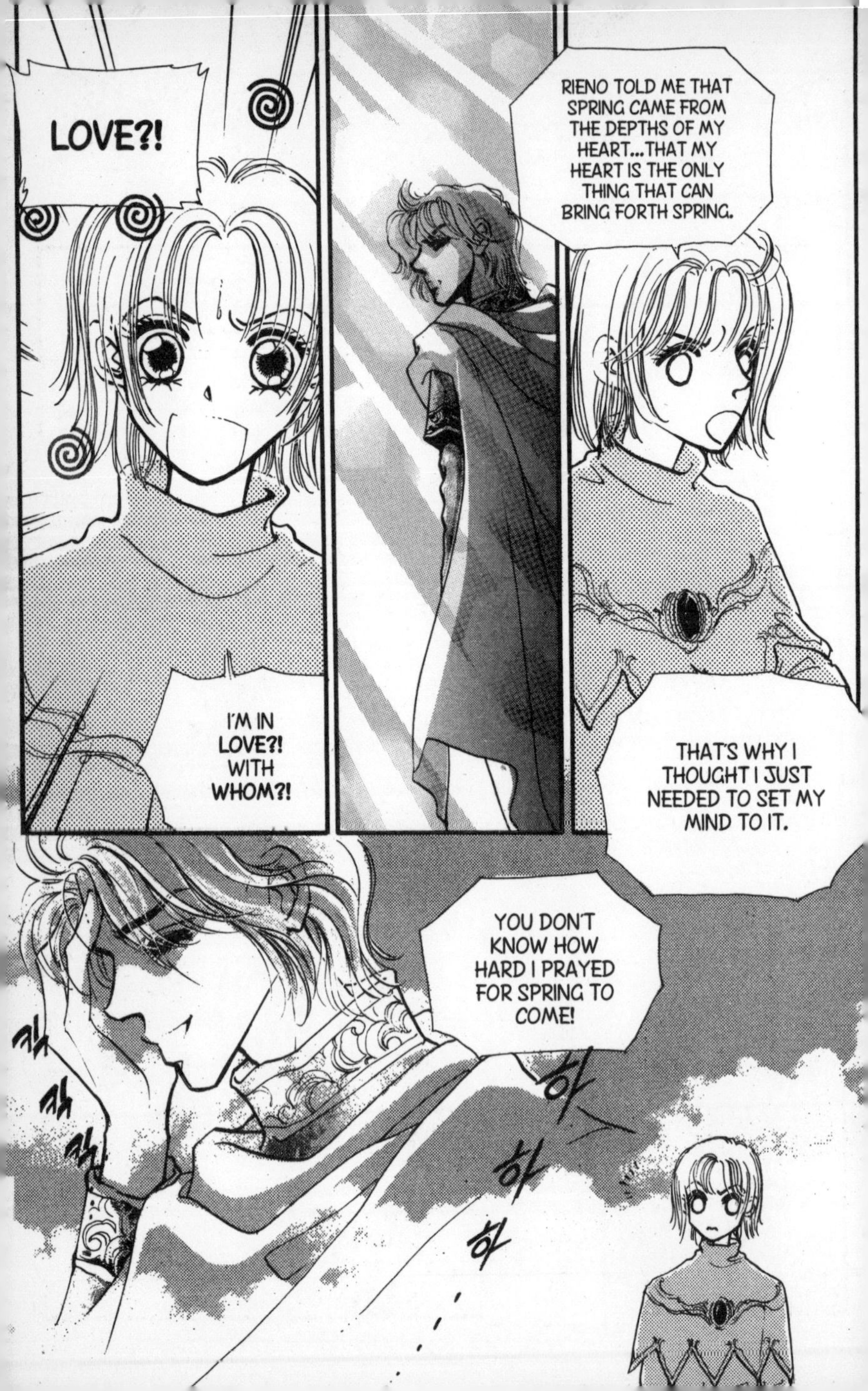

LOVE?!
I'M IN LOVE?! WITH WHOM?!
RIENO TOLD ME THAT SPRING CAME FROM THE DEPTHS OF MY HEART...THAT MY HEART IS THE ONLY THING THAT CAN BRING FORTH SPRING.
THAT'S WHY I THOUGHT I JUST NEEDED TO SET MY MIND TO IT.
YOU DON'T KNOW HOW HARD I PRAYED FOR SPRING TO COME!
칵
칵
칵
하
하
하

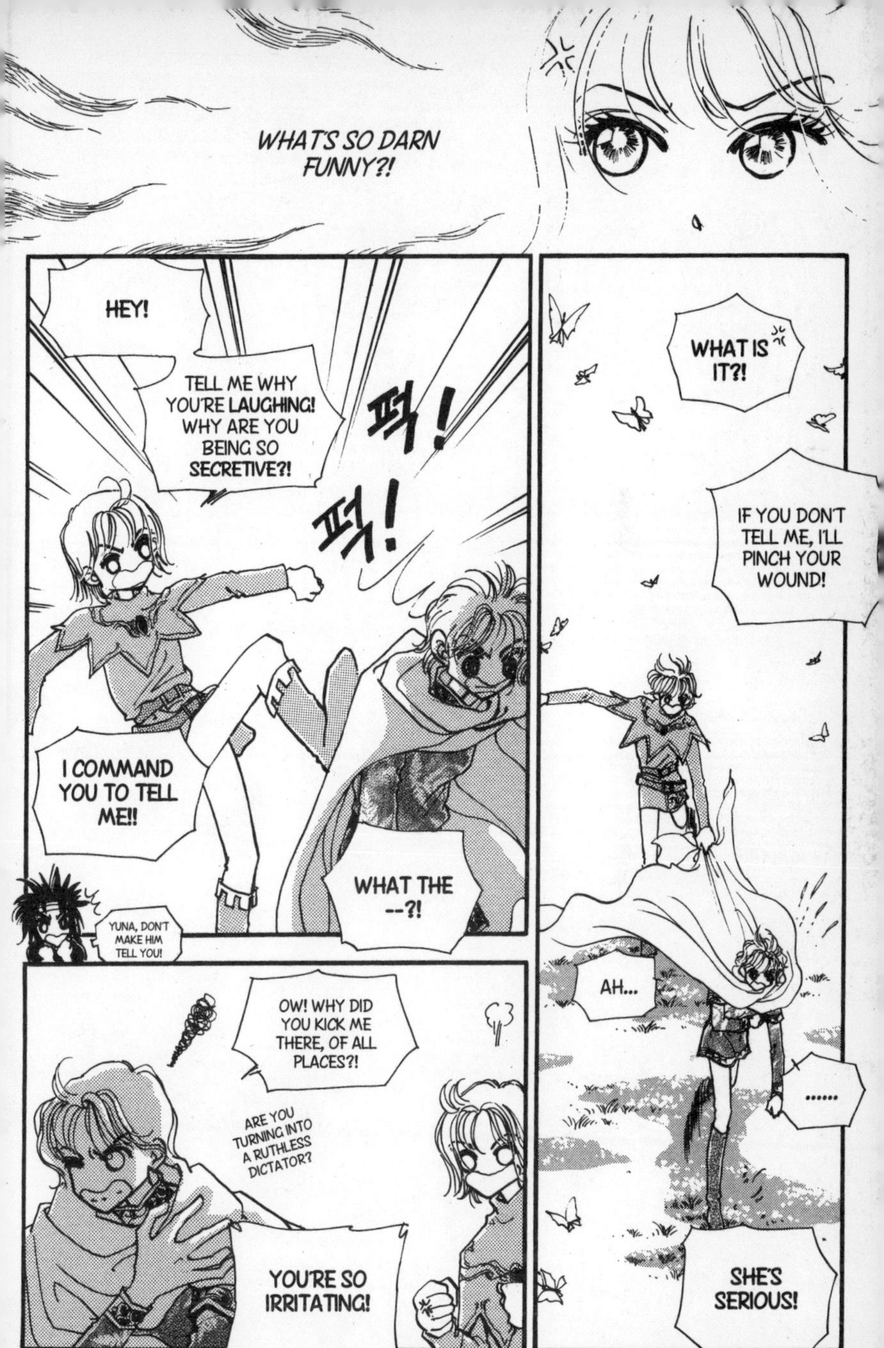
WHAT'S SO DARN FUNNY?!
HEY!
TELL ME WHY YOU'RE LAUGHING! WHY ARE YOU BEING SO SECRETIVE?!
퍽!
퍽!
I COMMAND YOU TO TELL ME!!
WHAT THE --?!
YUNA, DON'T MAKE HIM TELL YOU!
OW! WHY DID YOU KICK ME THERE, OF ALL PLACES?!
ARE YOU TURNING INTO A RUTHLESS DICTATOR?
YOU'RE SO IRRITATING!
WHAT IS IT?!
IF YOU DON'T TELL ME, I'LL PINCH YOUR WOUND!
AH...
......
SHE'S SERIOUS!

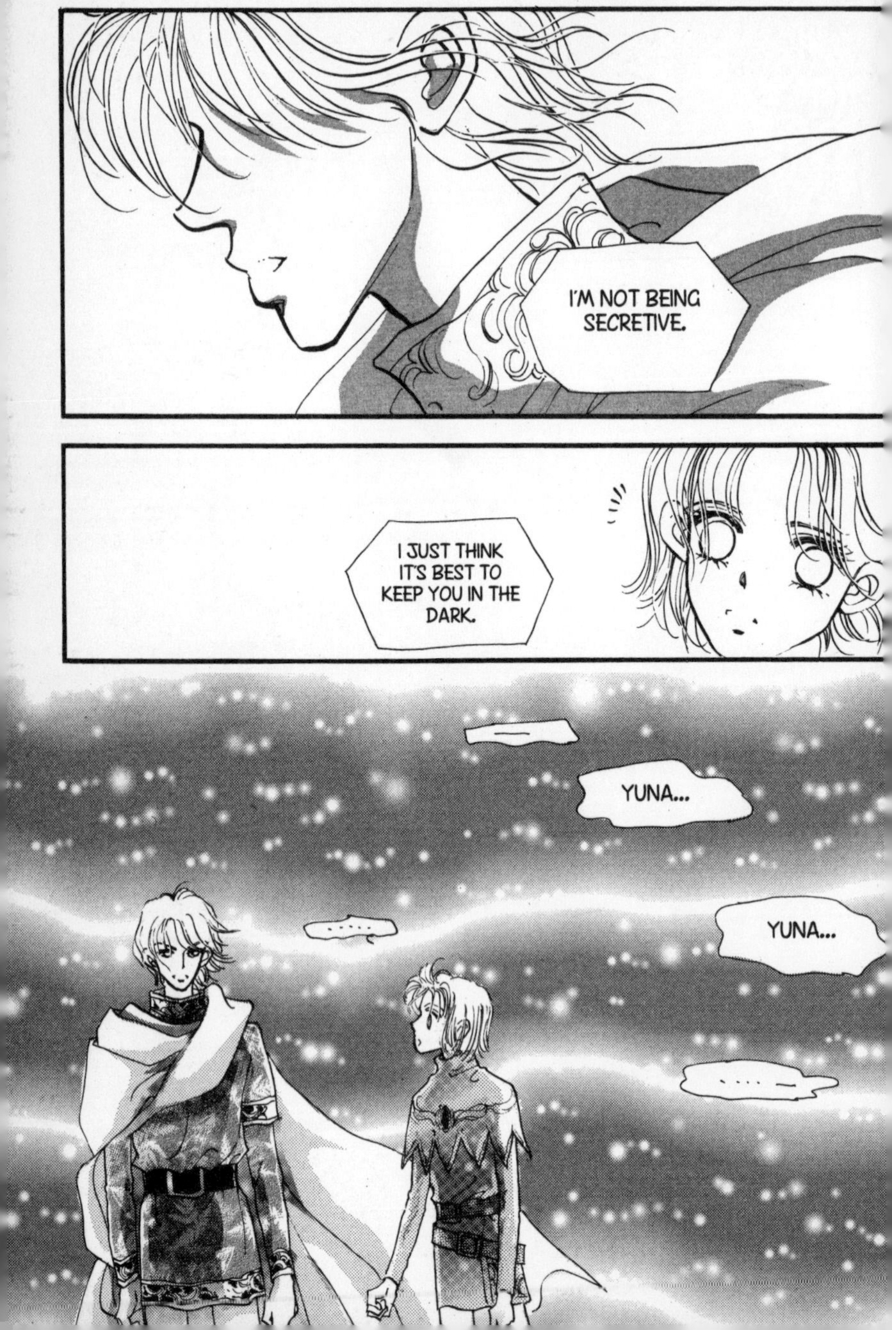
I'M NOT BEING SECRETIVE.
I JUST THINK IT'S BEST TO KEEP YOU IN THE DARK.
—
YUNA...
......
YUNA...
....—

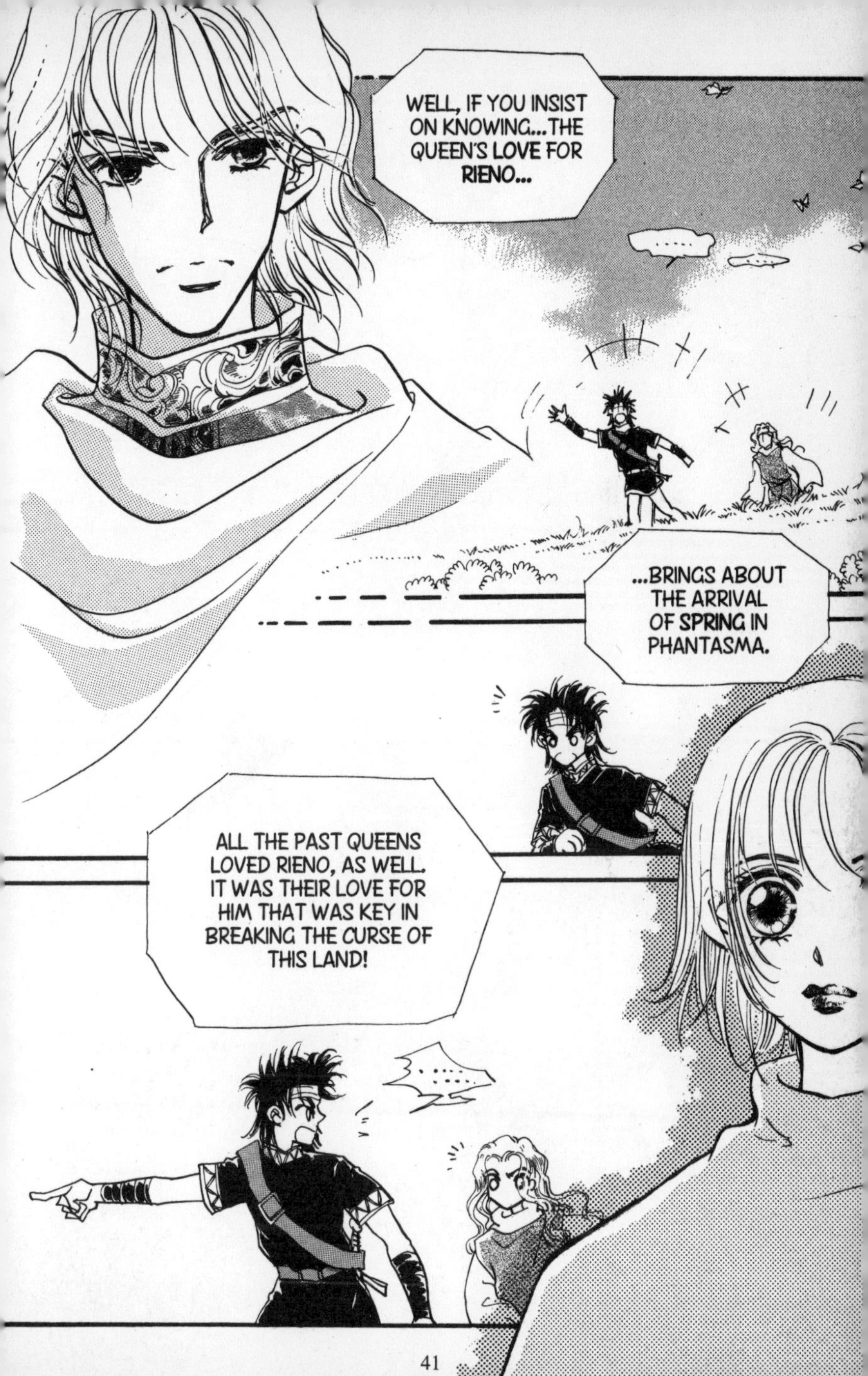
WELL, IF YOU INSIST ON KNOWING...THE QUEEN'S LOVE FOR RIENO...
...BRINGS ABOUT THE ARRIVAL OF SPRING IN PHANTASMA.
ALL THE PAST QUEENS LOVED RIENO, AS WELL. IT WAS THEIR LOVE FOR HIM THAT WAS KEY IN BREAKING THE CURSE OF THIS LAND!

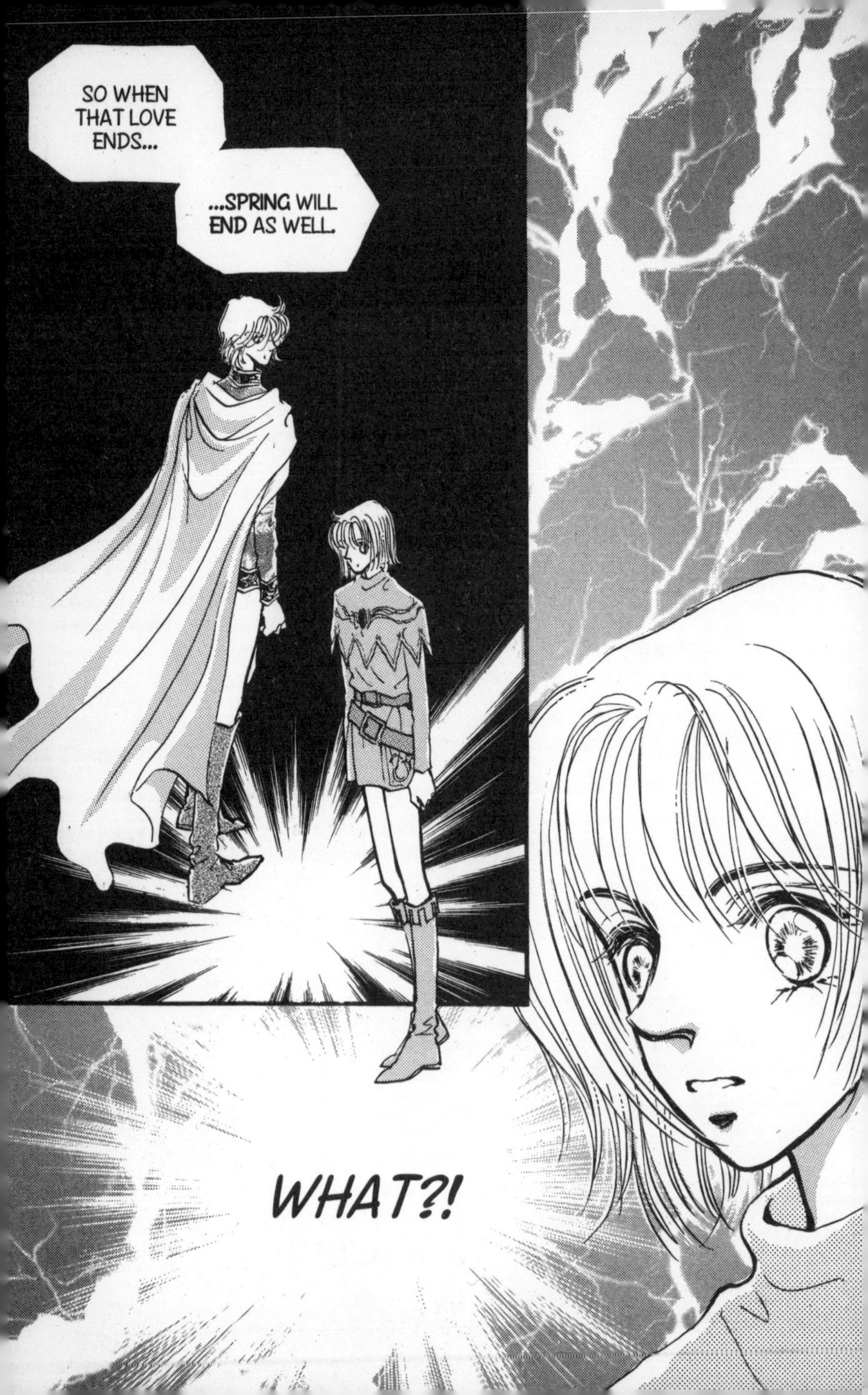
SO WHEN THAT LOVE ENDS...
...SPRING WILL END AS WELL.
WHAT?!

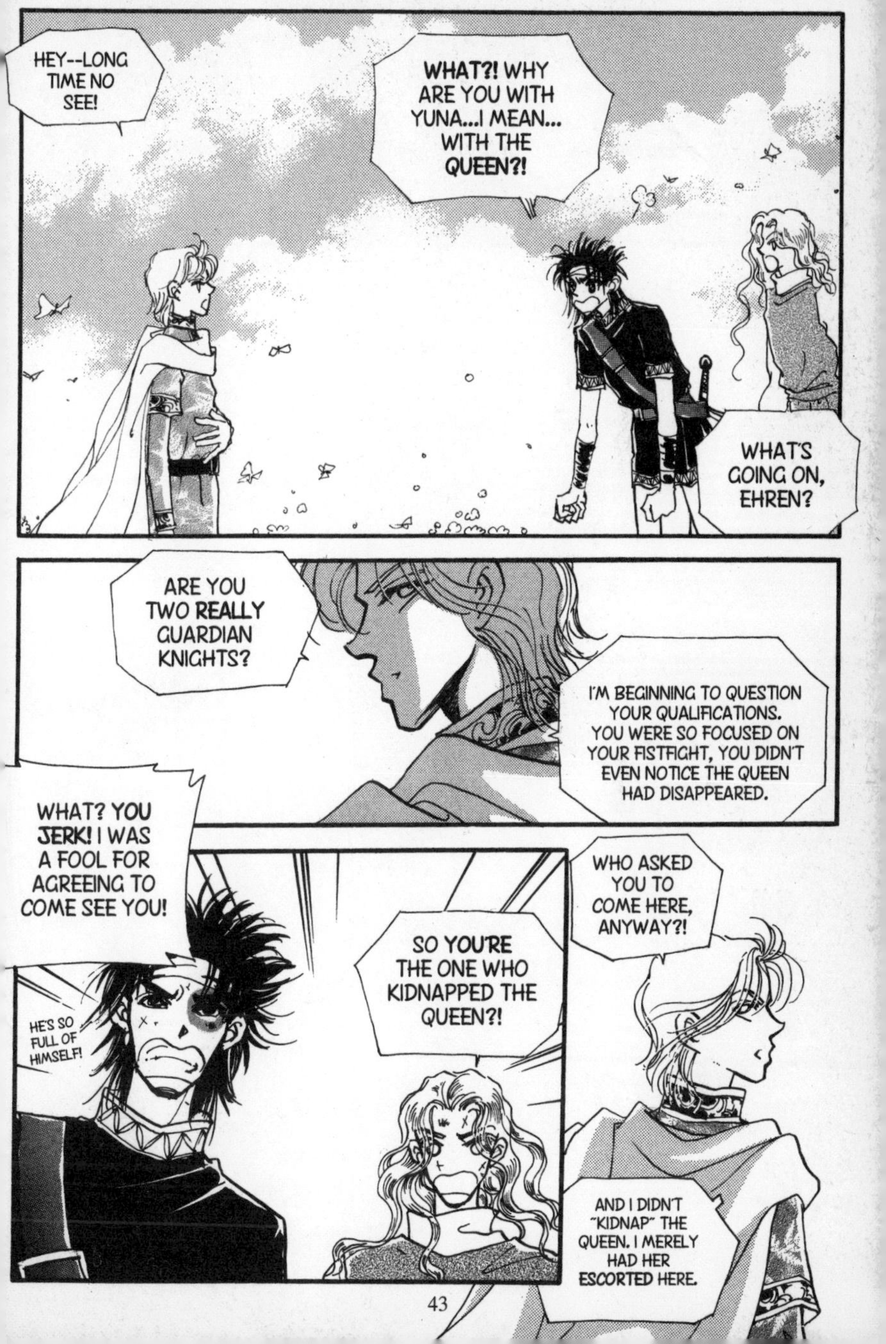

HEY--LONG TIME NO SEE!
WHAT?! WHY ARE YOU WITH YUNA...I MEAN... WITH THE QUEEN?!
WHAT'S GOING ON, EHREN?
ARE YOU TWO REALLY GUARDIAN KNIGHTS?
I'M BEGINNING TO QUESTION YOUR QUALIFICATIONS. YOU WERE SO FOCUSED ON YOUR FISTFIGHT, YOU DIDN'T EVEN NOTICE THE QUEEN HAD DISAPPEARED.
WHAT? YOU JERK! I WAS A FOOL FOR AGREEING TO COME SEE YOU!
HE'S SO FULL OF HIMSELF!
SO YOU'RE THE ONE WHO KIDNAPPED THE QUEEN?!
WHO ASKED YOU TO COME HERE, ANYWAY?!
AND I DIDN'T "KIDNAP" THE QUEEN. I MERELY HAD HER ESCORTED HERE.

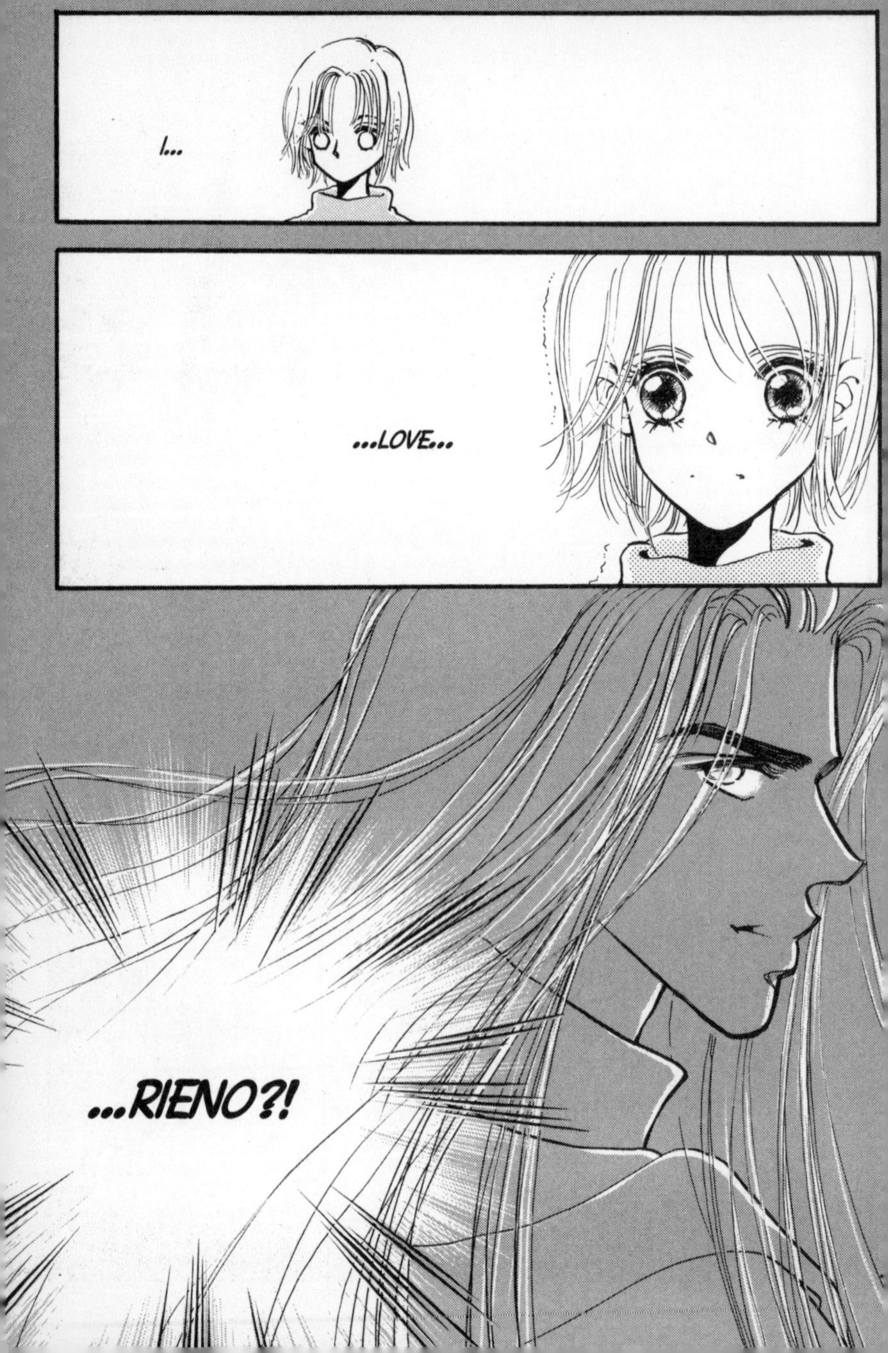
I...
...LOVE...
...RIENO?!

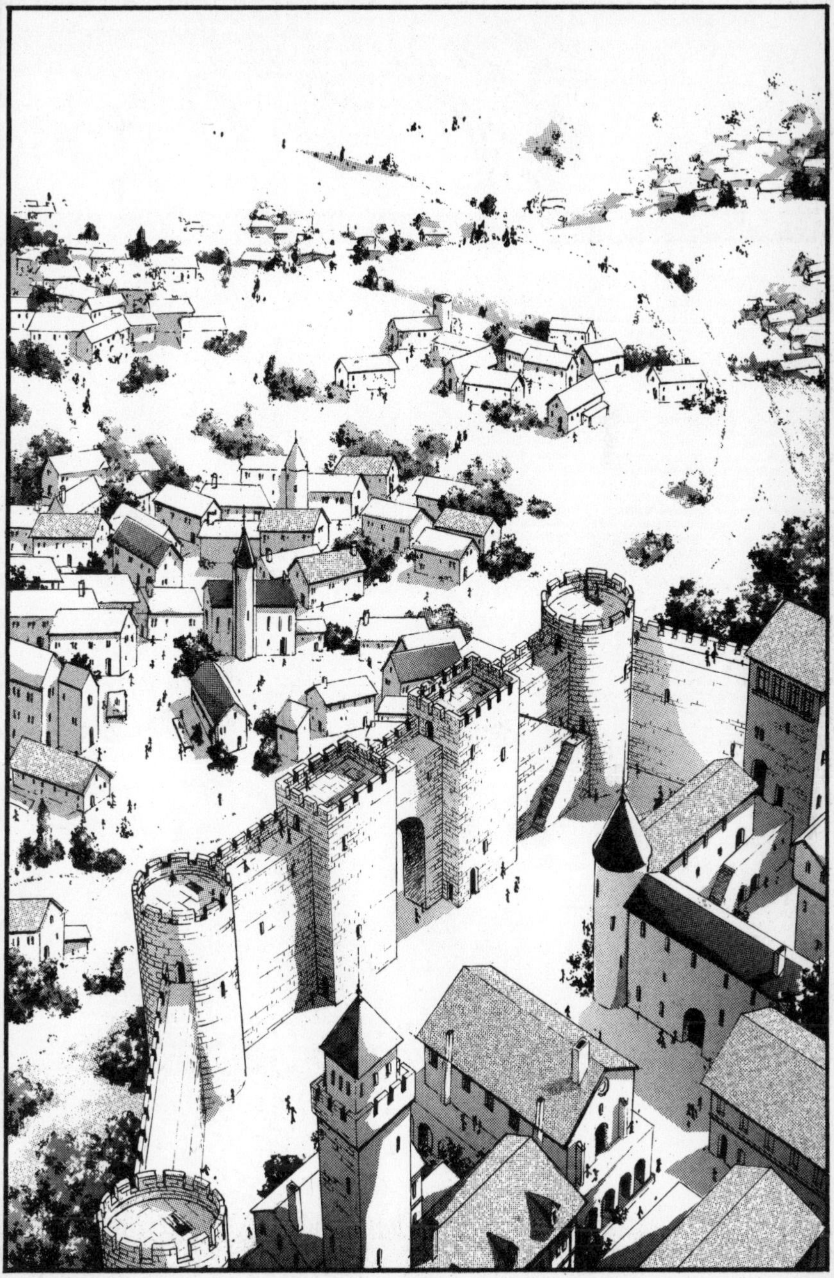

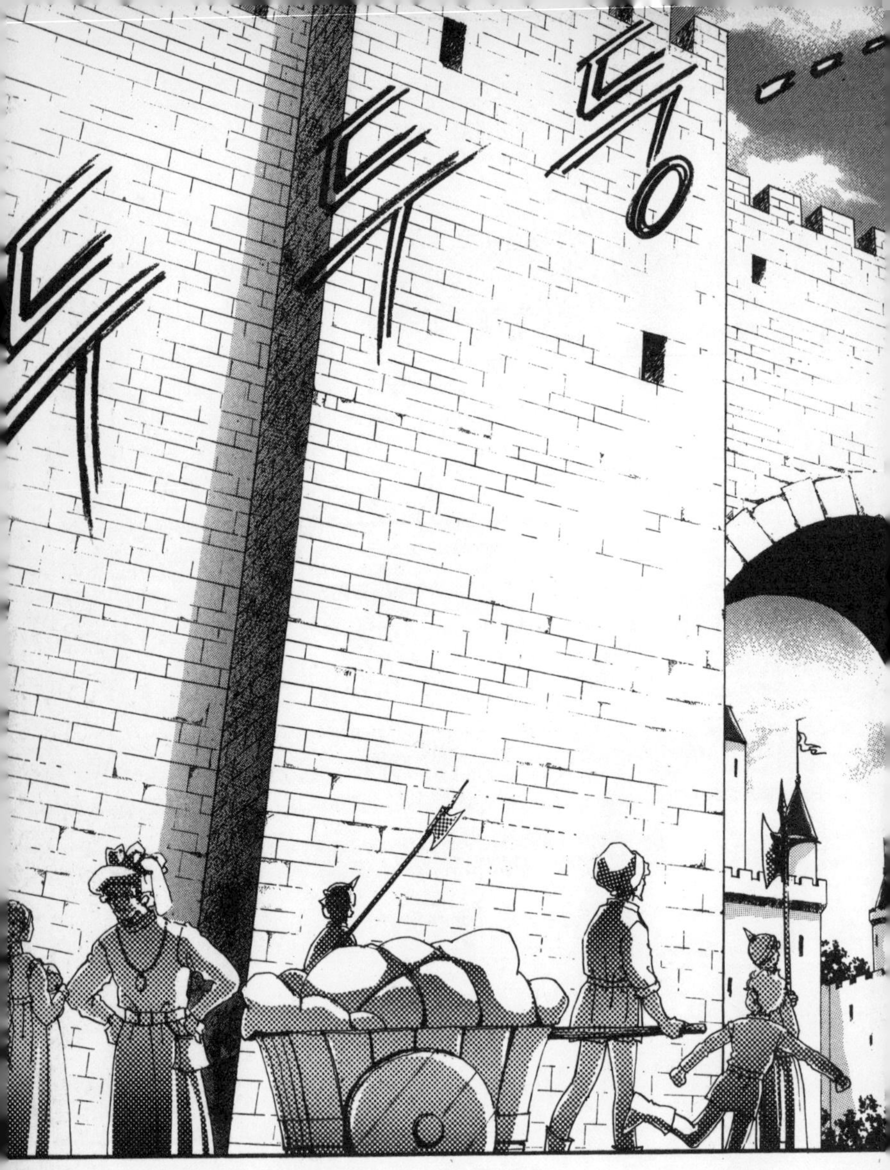

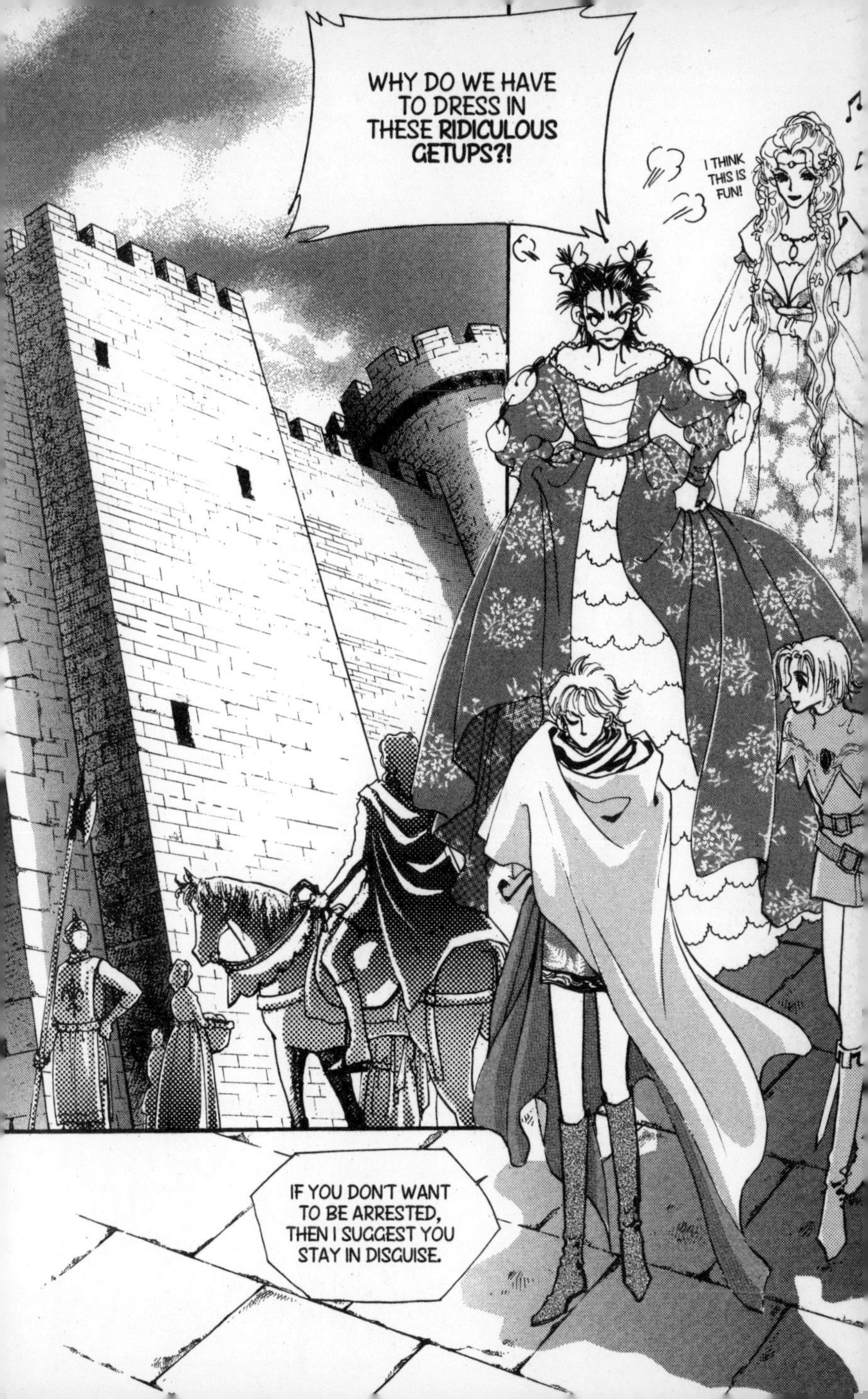
WHY DO WE HAVE TO DRESS IN THESE RIDICULOUS GETUPS?!
I THINK THIS IS FUN!
IF YOU DON'T WANT TO BE ARRESTED, THEN I SUGGEST YOU STAY IN DISGUISE.

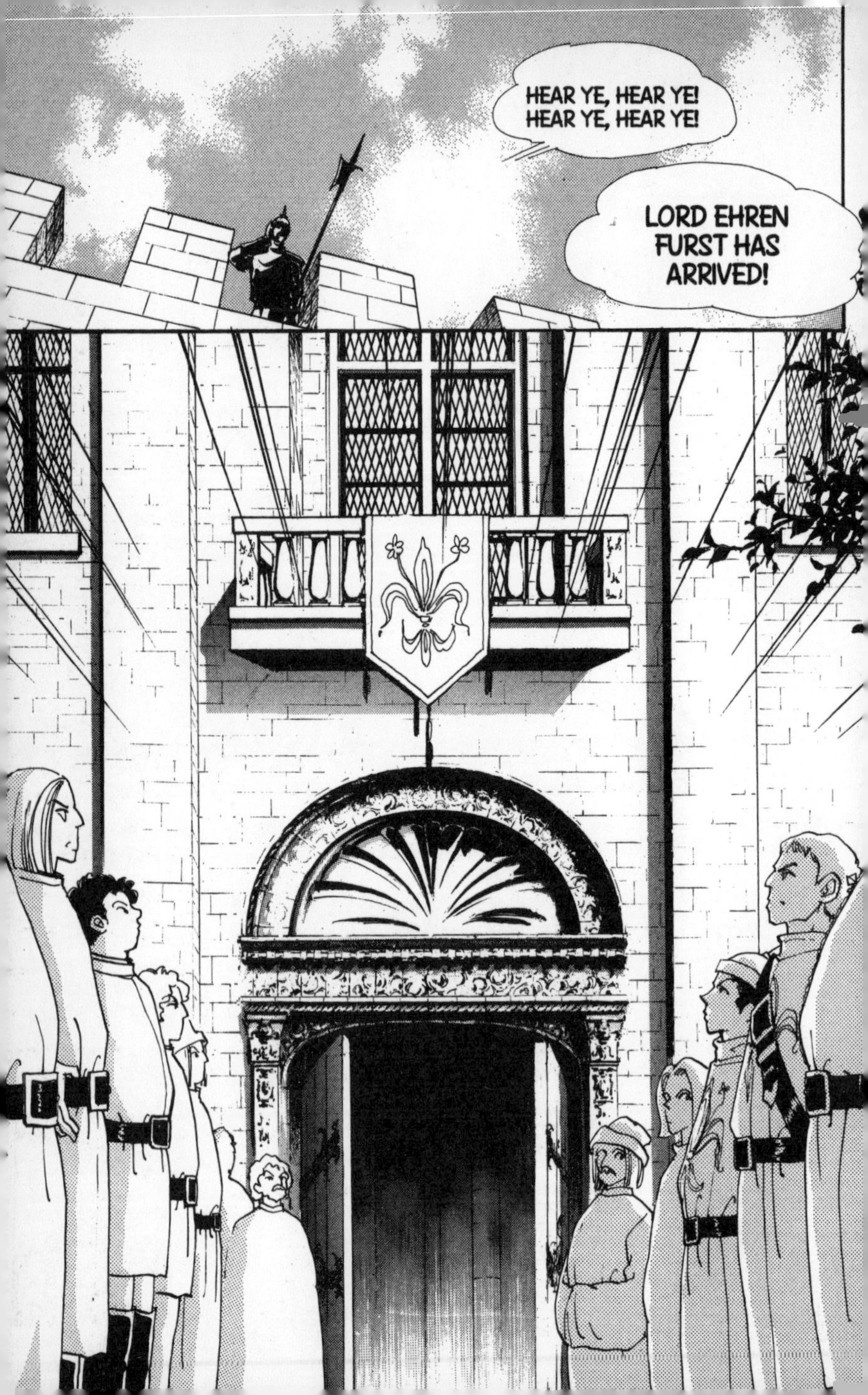
HEAR YE, HEAR YE! HEAR YE, HEAR YE!
LORD EHREN FURST HAS ARRIVED!

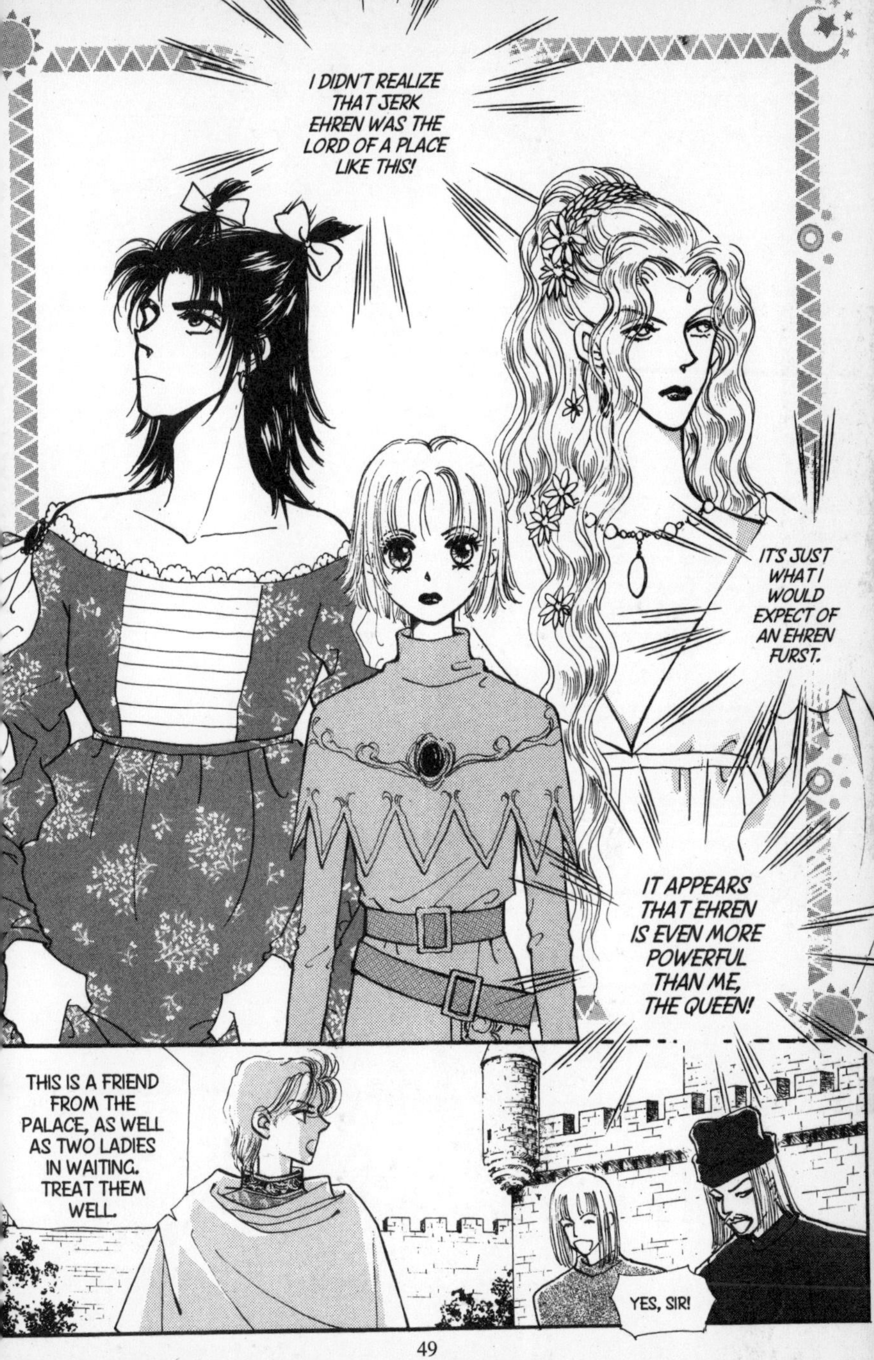
I DIDN'T REALIZE THAT JERK EHREN WAS THE LORD OF A PLACE LIKE THIS!
IT'S JUST WHAT I WOULD EXPECT OF AN EHREN FURST.
IT APPEARS THAT EHREN IS EVEN MORE POWERFUL THAN ME, THE QUEEN!
THIS IS A FRIEND FROM THE PALACE, AS WELL AS TWO LADIES IN WAITING. TREAT THEM WELL.
YES, SIR!

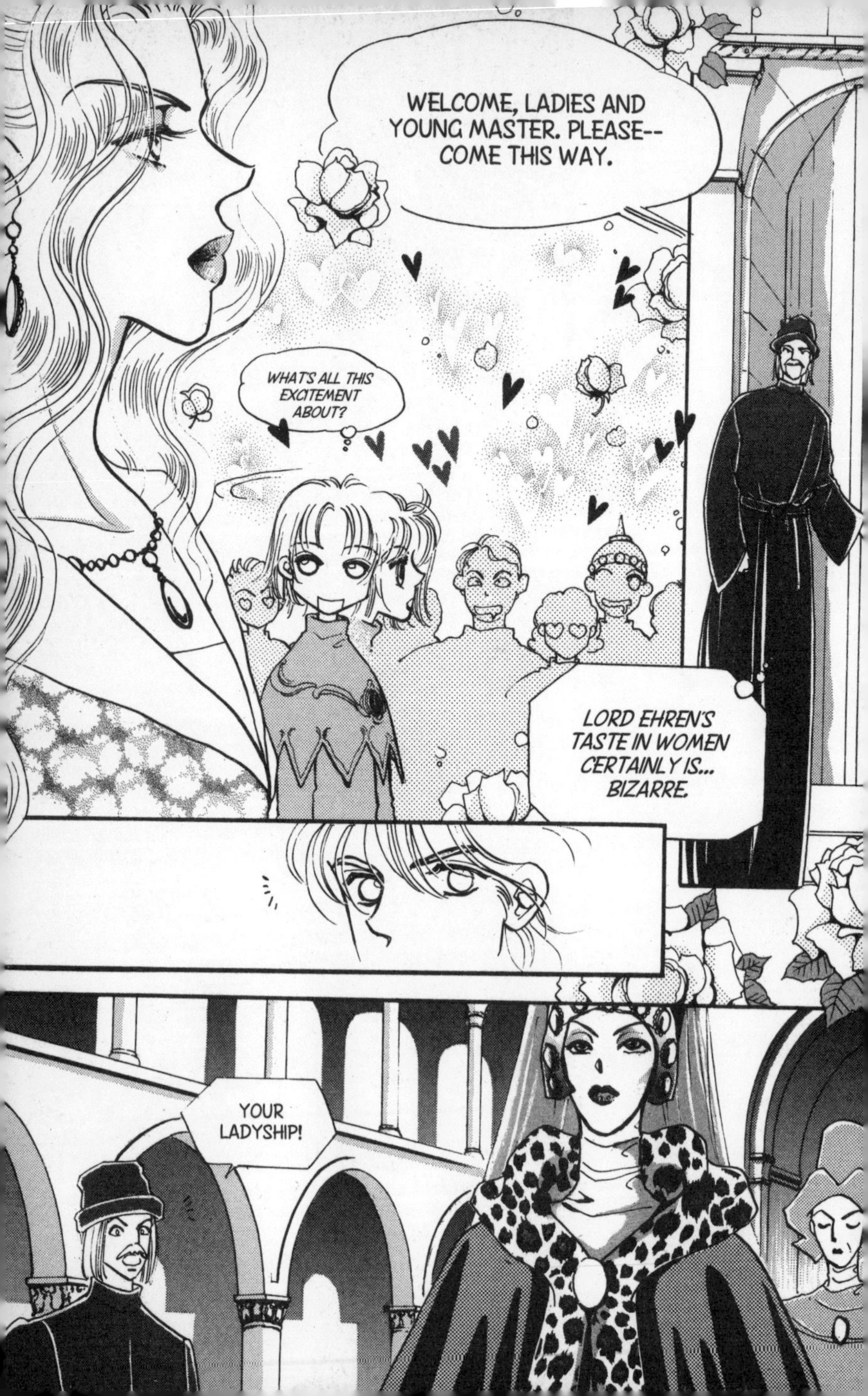
WELCOME, LADIES AND YOUNG MASTER. PLEASE-- COME THIS WAY.
WHAT'S ALL THIS EXCITEMENT ABOUT?
LORD EHREN'S TASTE IN WOMEN CERTAINLY IS... BIZARRE.
YOUR LADYSHIP!

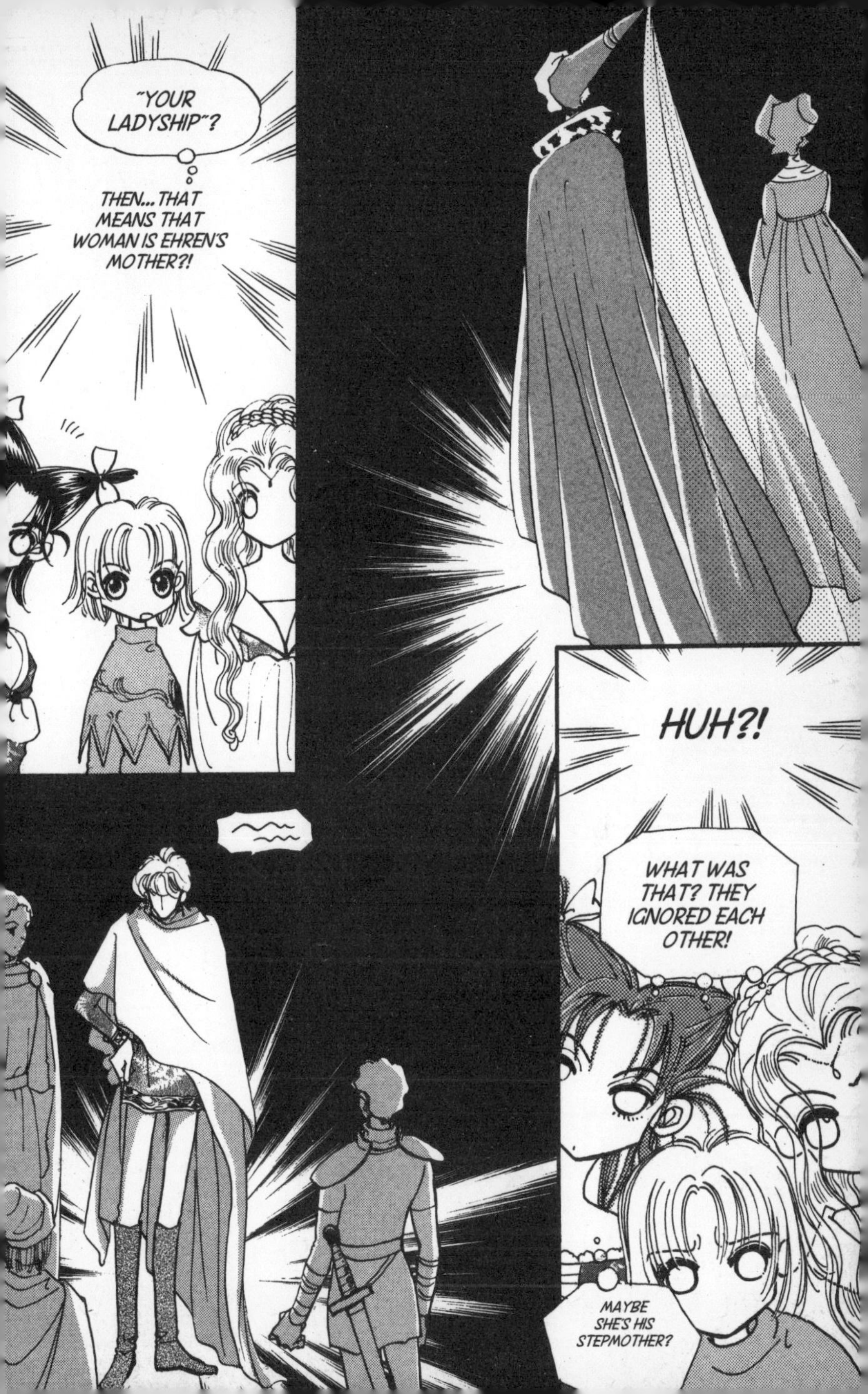
"YOUR LADYSHIP"?
THEN... THAT MEANS THAT WOMAN IS EHREN'S MOTHER?!
HUH?!
WHAT WAS THAT? THEY IGNORED EACH OTHER!
MAYBE SHE'S HIS STEPMOTHER?

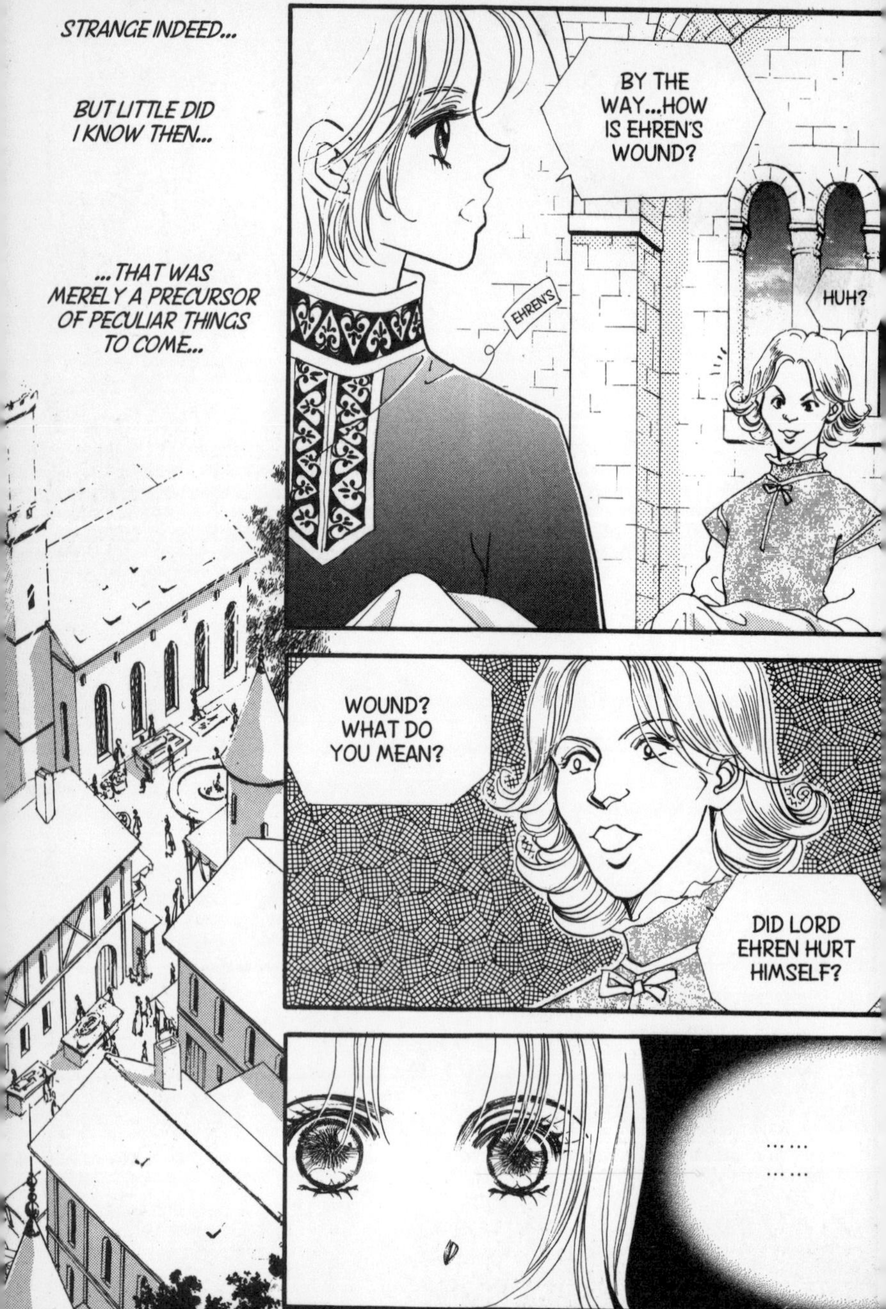
STRANGE INDEED...
BUT LITTLE DID I KNOW THEN...
...THAT WAS MERELY A PRECURSOR OF PECULIAR THINGS TO COME...
BY THE WAY...HOW IS EHREN'S WOUND?
EHREN'S
HUH?
WOUND? WHAT DO YOU MEAN?
DID LORD EHREN HURT HIMSELF?
.....
.....

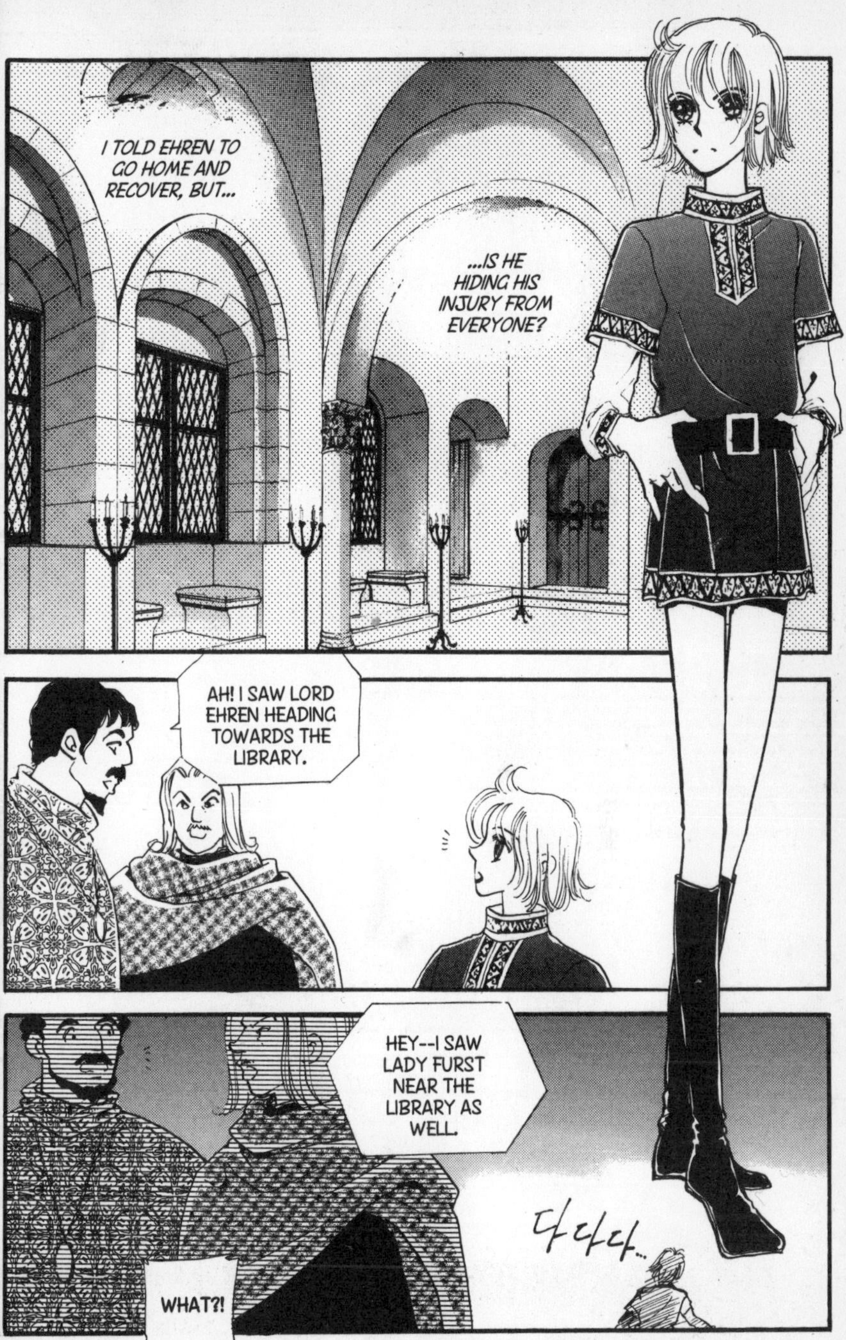
I TOLD EHREN TO GO HOME AND RECOVER, BUT...
...IS HE HIDING HIS INJURY FROM EVERYONE?
AH! I SAW LORD EHREN HEADING TOWARDS THE LIBRARY.
HEY--I SAW LADY FURST NEAR THE LIBRARY AS WELL.
WHAT?!
다다다...

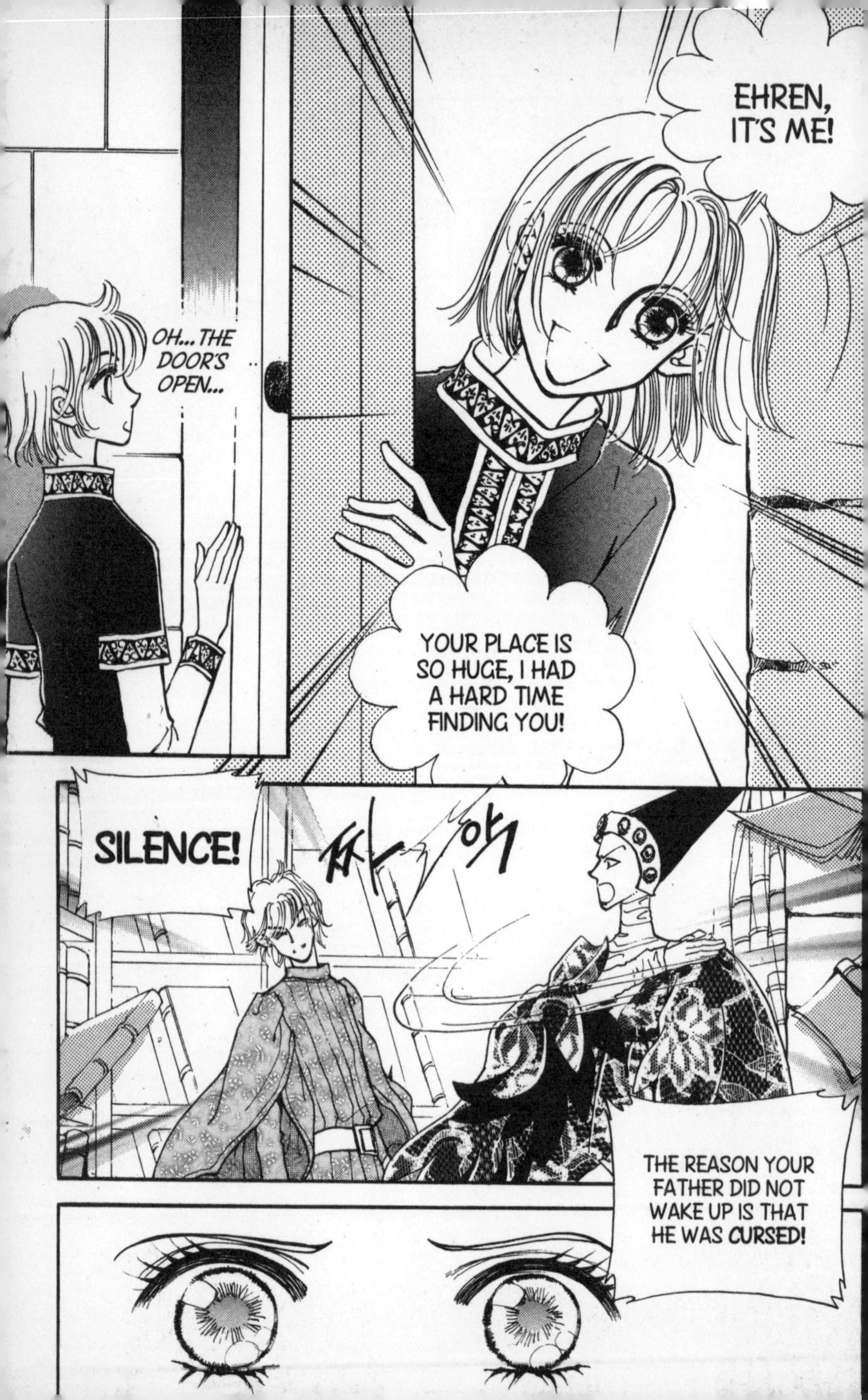
OH...THE DOOR'S OPEN...
EHREN, IT'S ME!
YOUR PLACE IS SO HUGE, I HAD A HARD TIME FINDING YOU!
SILENCE!
쫘-악
THE REASON YOUR FATHER DID NOT WAKE UP IS THAT HE WAS **CURSED**!

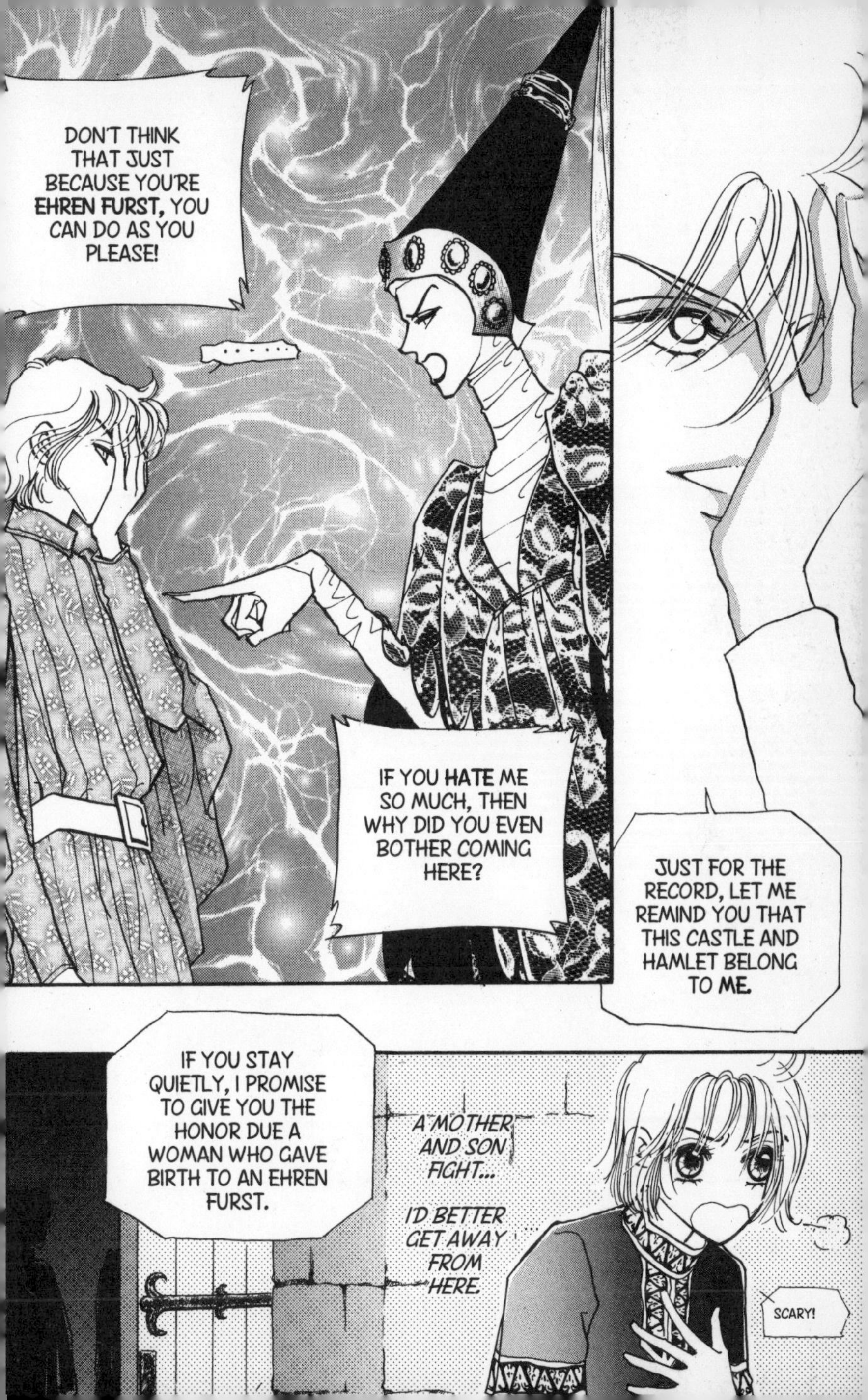
DON'T THINK THAT JUST BECAUSE YOU'RE EHREN FURST, YOU CAN DO AS YOU PLEASE!
......
IF YOU HATE ME SO MUCH, THEN WHY DID YOU EVEN BOTHER COMING HERE?
JUST FOR THE RECORD, LET ME REMIND YOU THAT THIS CASTLE AND HAMLET BELONG TO ME.
IF YOU STAY QUIETLY, I PROMISE TO GIVE YOU THE HONOR DUE A WOMAN WHO GAVE BIRTH TO AN EHREN FURST.
A MOTHER AND SON FIGHT...
I'D BETTER GET AWAY FROM HERE.
SCARY!

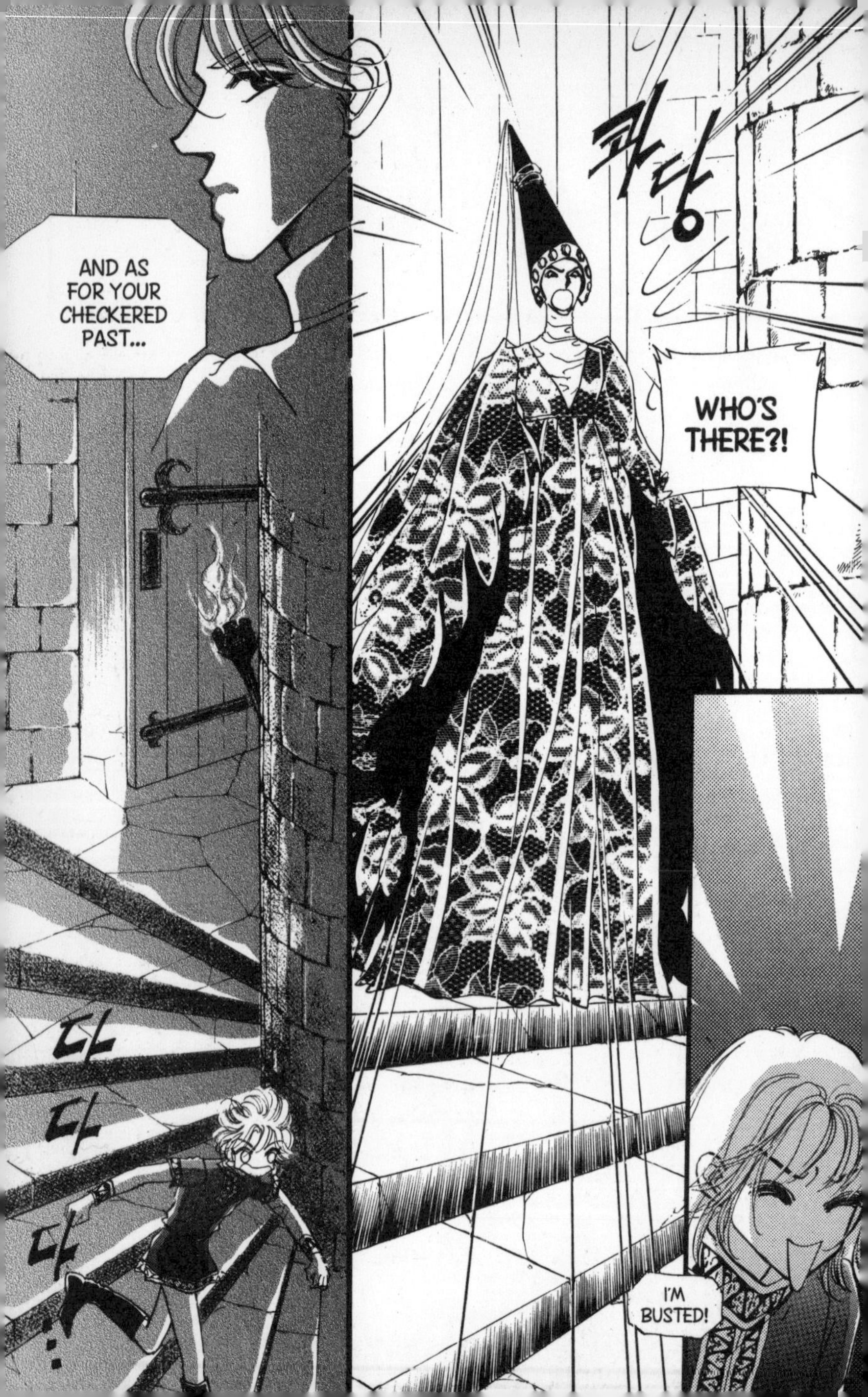
AND AS FOR YOUR CHECKERED PAST...
다 다 다
콰당
WHO'S THERE?!
I'M BUSTED!

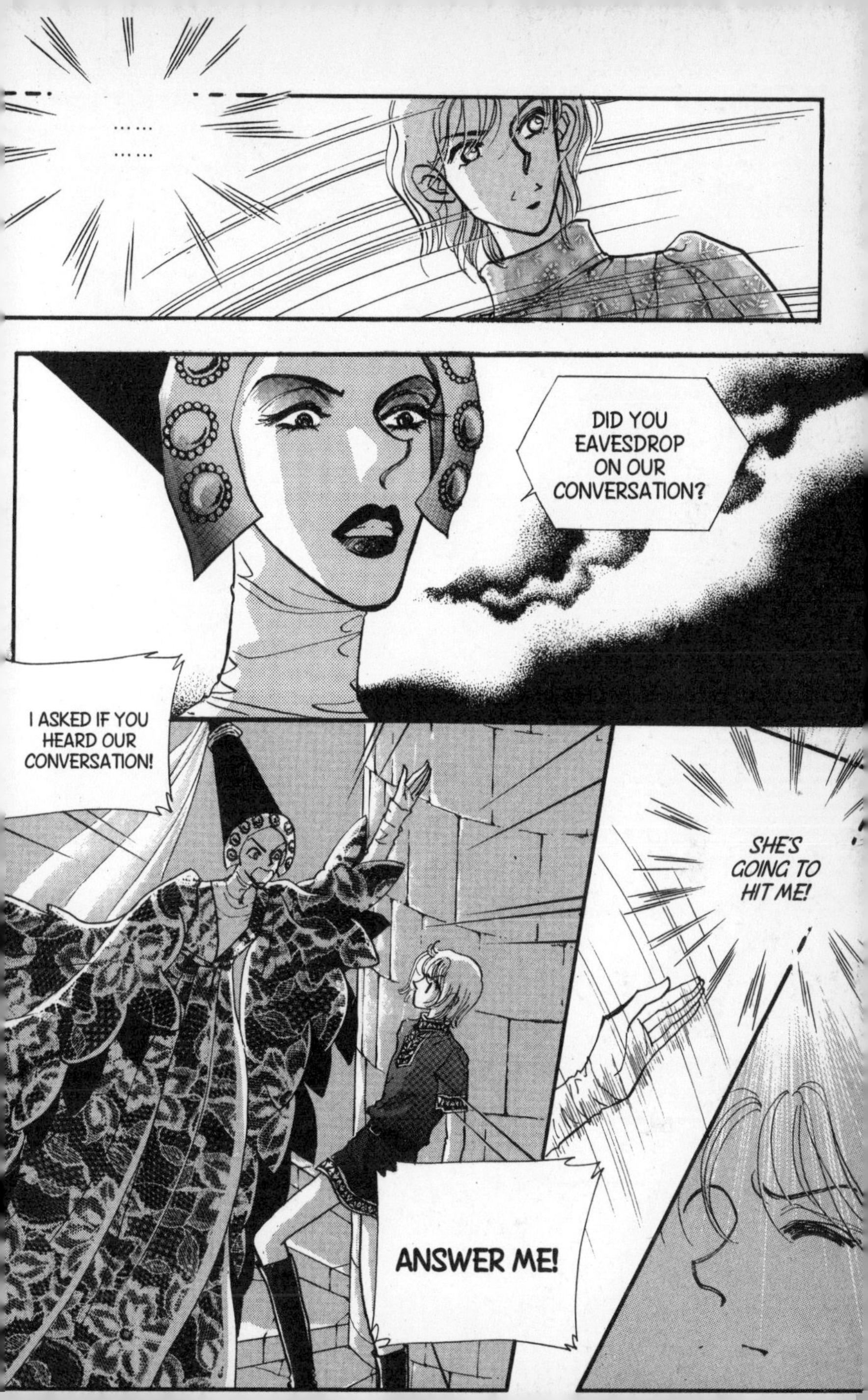

......
......
DID YOU EAVESDROP ON OUR CONVERSATION?
I ASKED IF YOU HEARD OUR CONVERSATION!
SHE'S GOING TO HIT ME!
ANSWER ME!

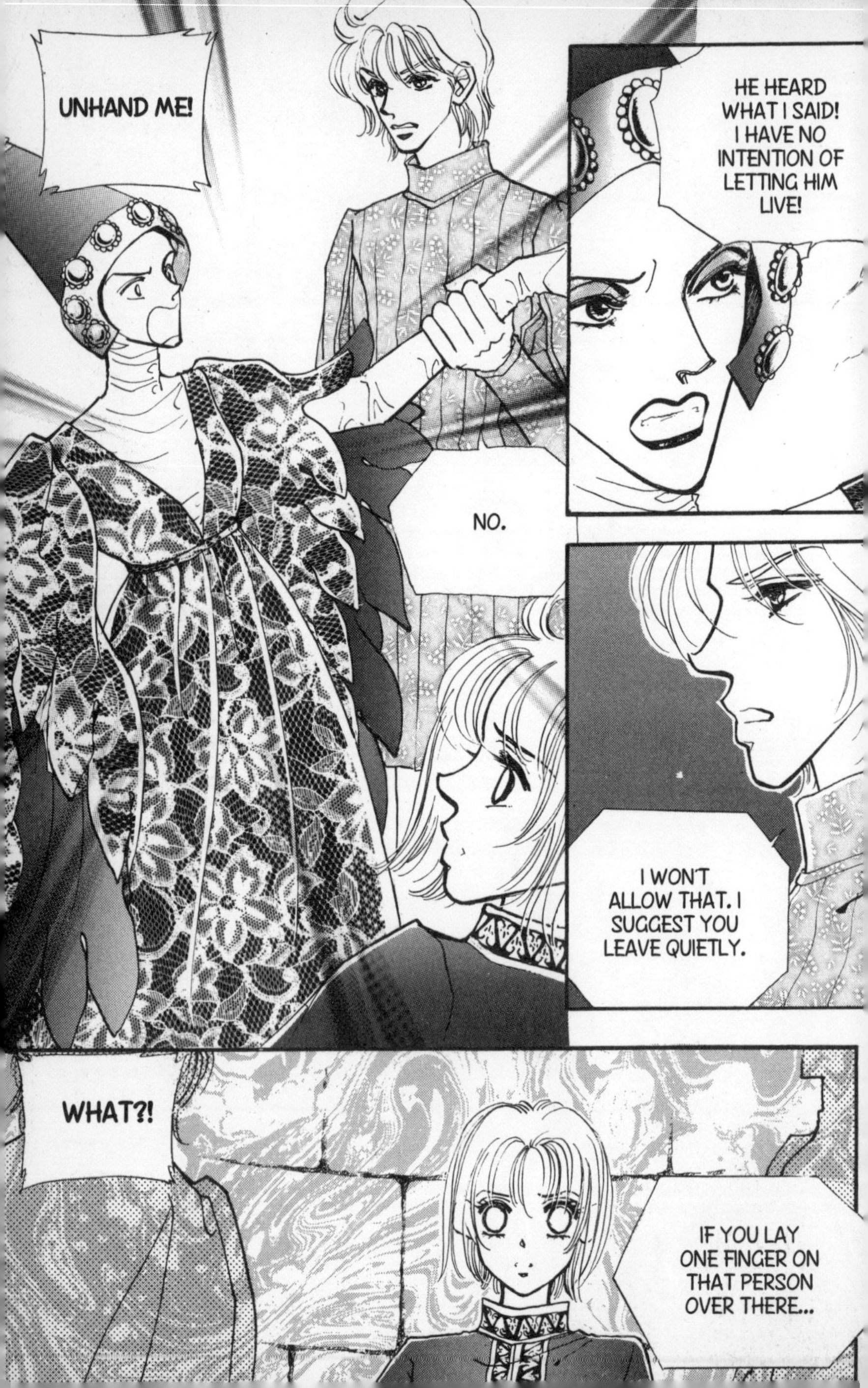
UNHAND ME!
NO.
HE HEARD WHAT I SAID! I HAVE NO INTENTION OF LETTING HIM LIVE!
I WON'T ALLOW THAT. I SUGGEST YOU LEAVE QUIETLY.
WHAT?!
IF YOU LAY ONE FINGER ON THAT PERSON OVER THERE...

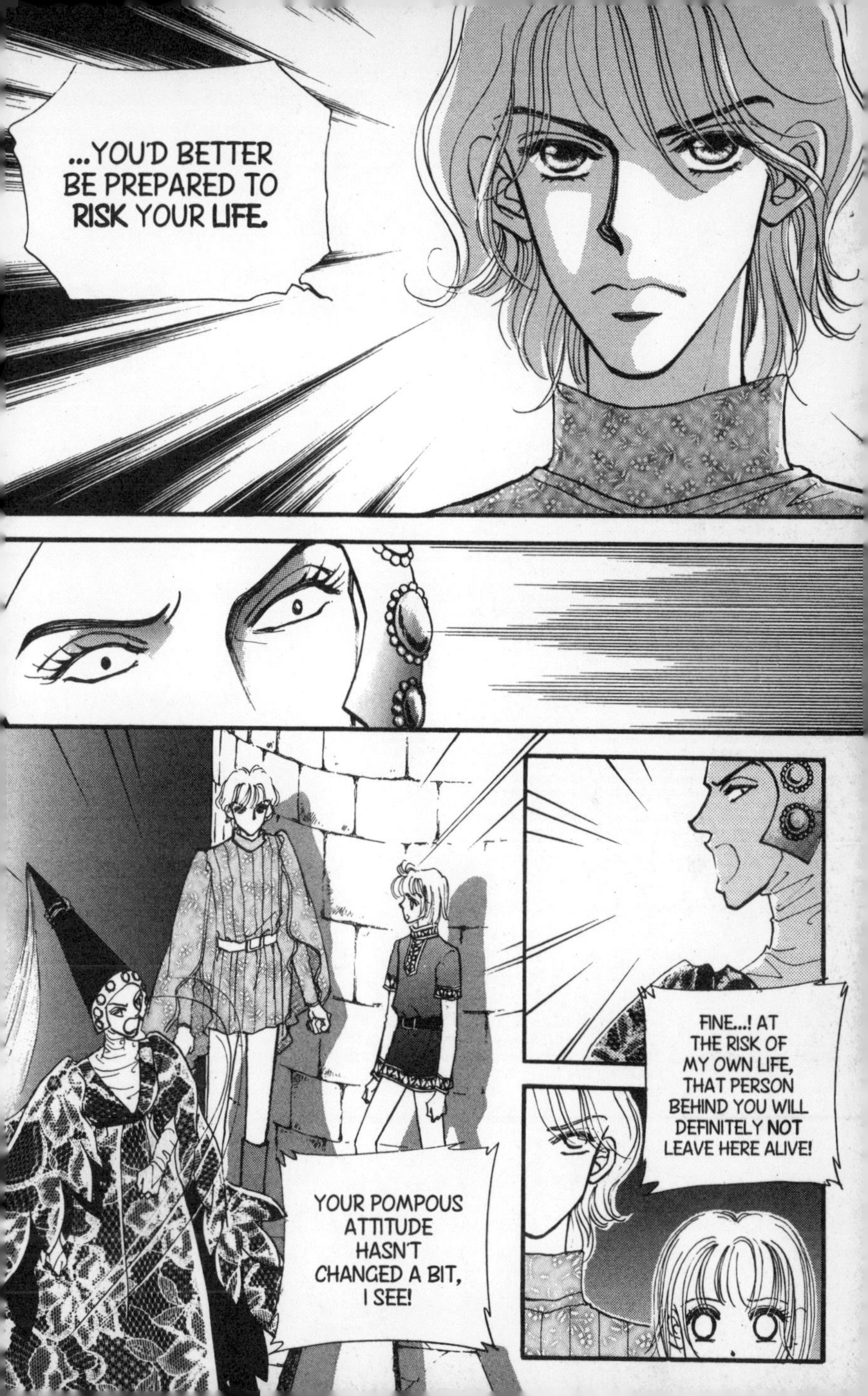
...YOU'D BETTER BE PREPARED TO RISK YOUR LIFE.
YOUR POMPOUS ATTITUDE HASN'T CHANGED A BIT, I SEE!
FINE...! AT THE RISK OF MY OWN LIFE, THAT PERSON BEHIND YOU WILL DEFINITELY NOT LEAVE HERE ALIVE!

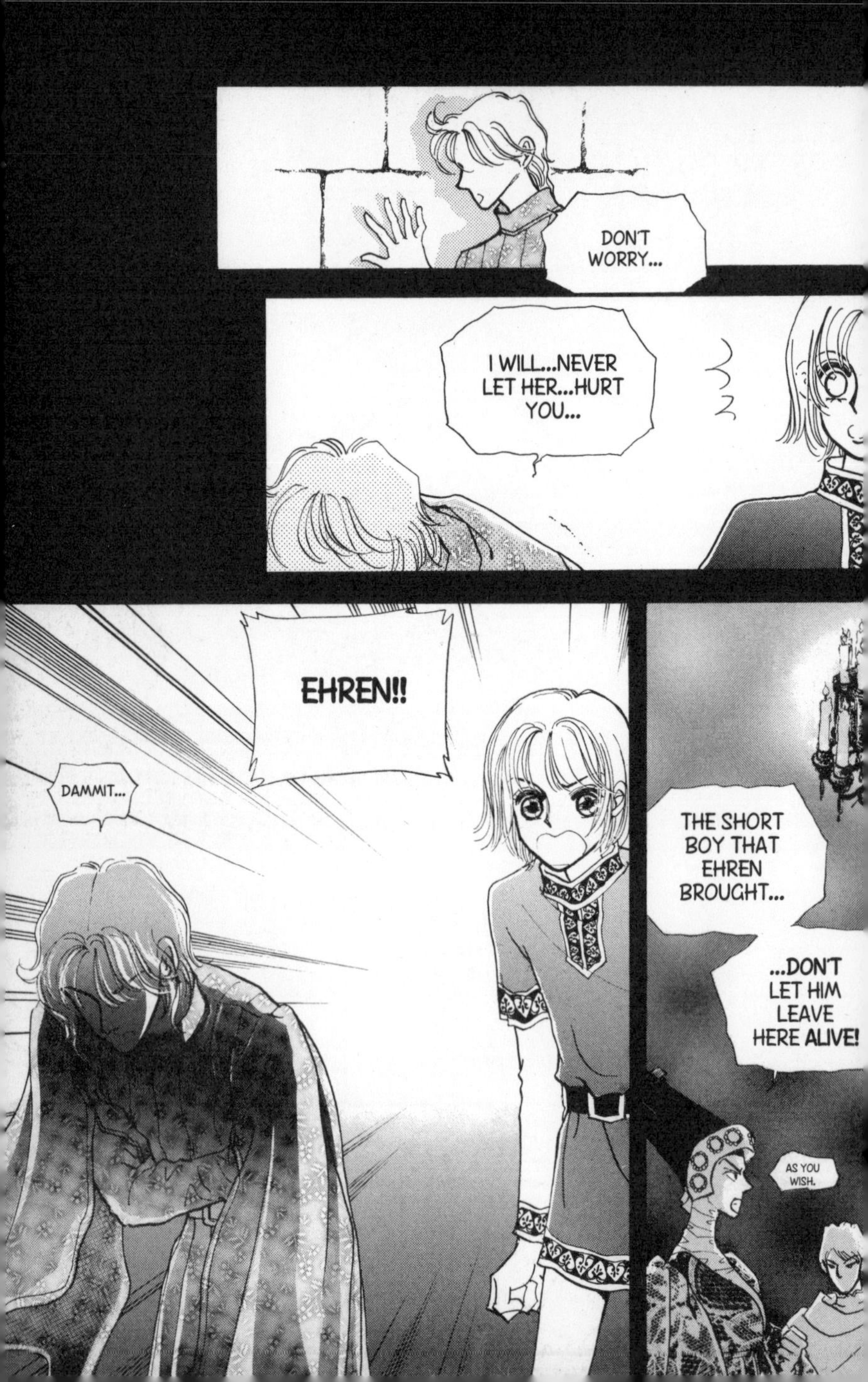
DON'T WORRY...
I WILL...NEVER LET HER...HURT YOU...
EHREN!!
DAMMIT...
THE SHORT BOY THAT EHREN BROUGHT...
...DON'T LET HIM LEAVE HERE ALIVE!
AS YOU WISH.

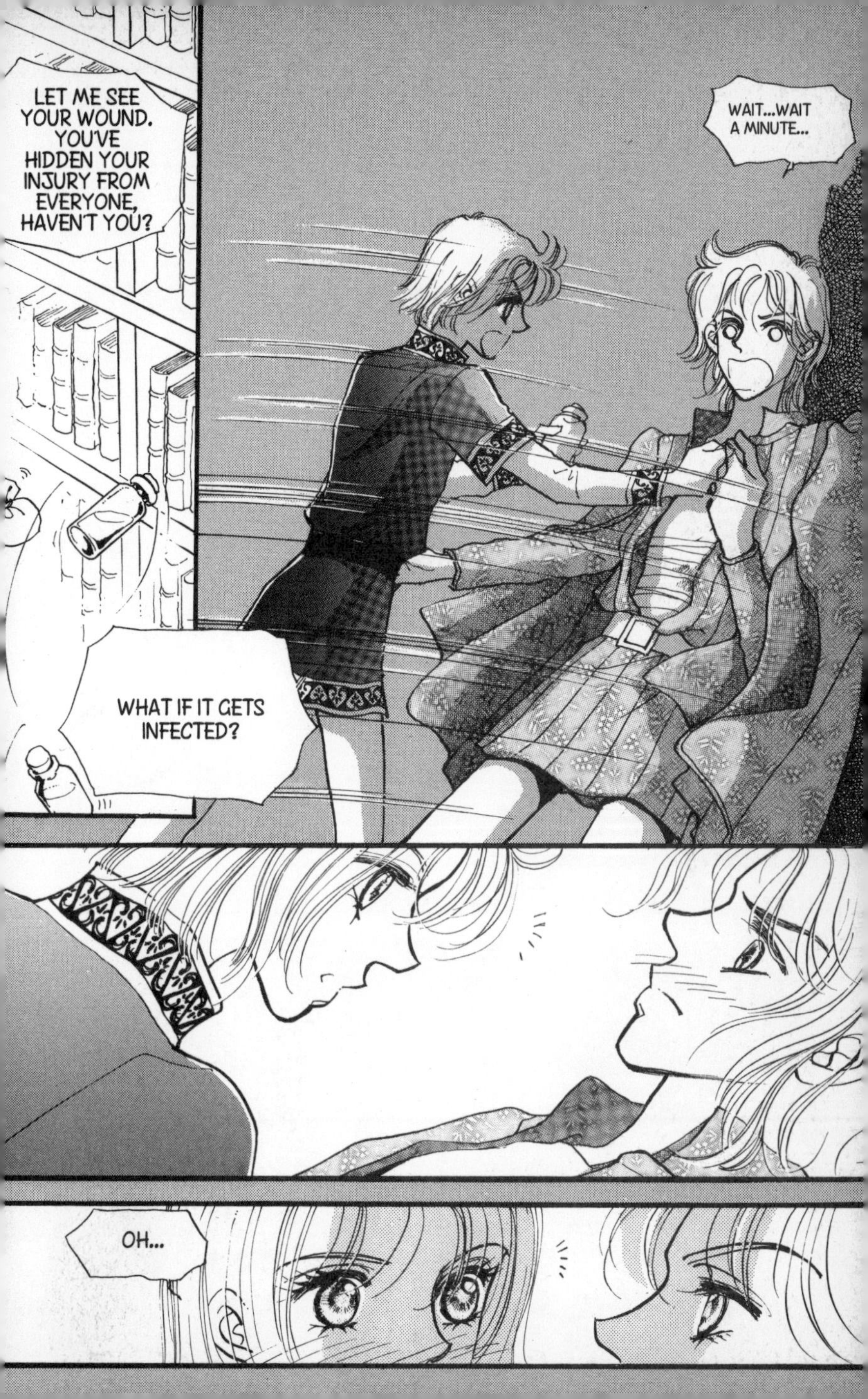
LET ME SEE YOUR WOUND. YOU'VE HIDDEN YOUR INJURY FROM EVERYONE, HAVEN'T YOU?
WAIT...WAIT A MINUTE...
WHAT IF IT GETS INFECTED?
OH...

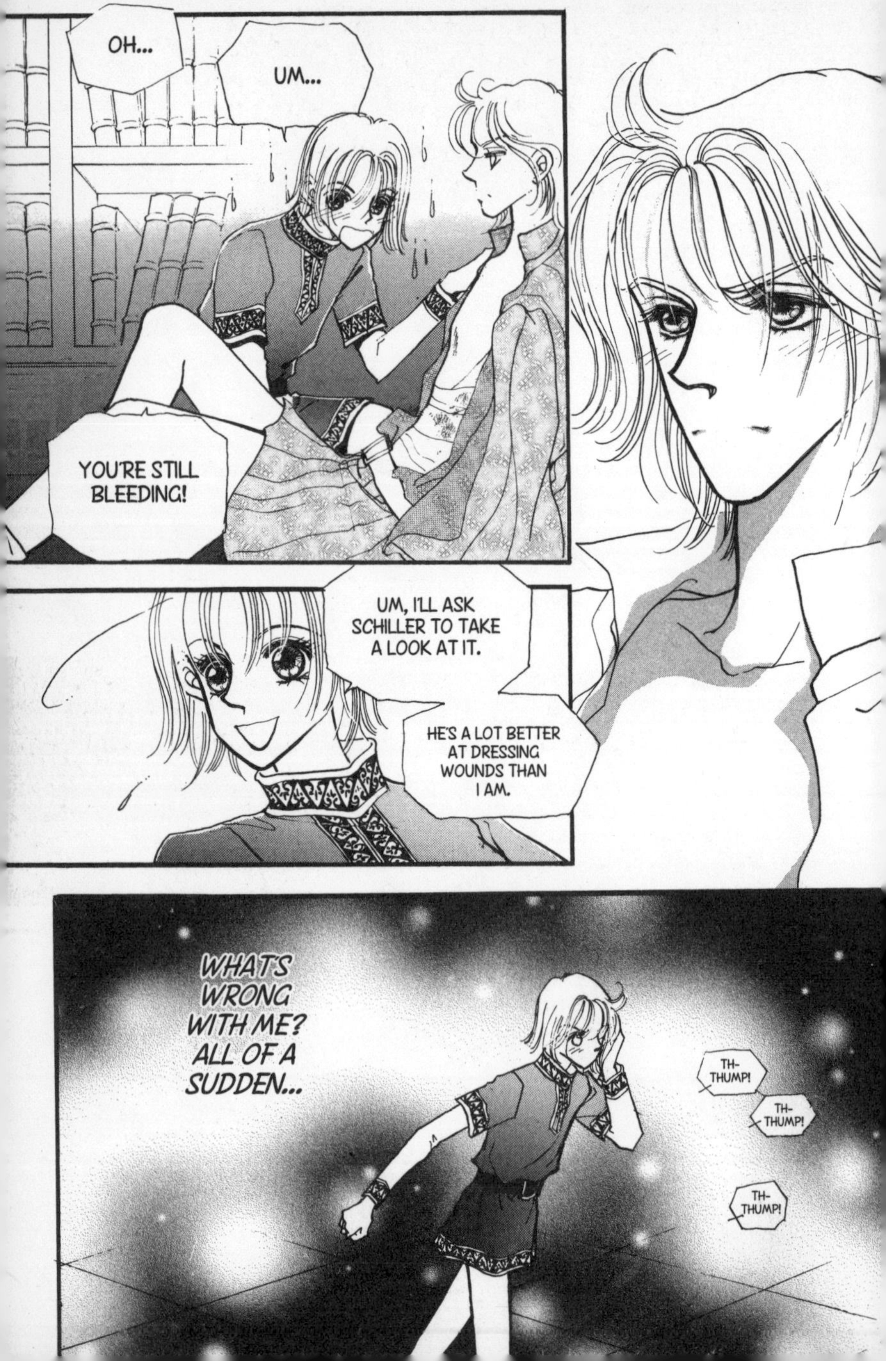
OH...
UM...
YOU'RE STILL BLEEDING!
UM, I'LL ASK SCHILLER TO TAKE A LOOK AT IT.
HE'S A LOT BETTER AT DRESSING WOUNDS THAN I AM.
WHAT'S WRONG WITH ME? ALL OF A SUDDEN...
TH-THUMP!
TH-THUMP!
TH-THUMP!

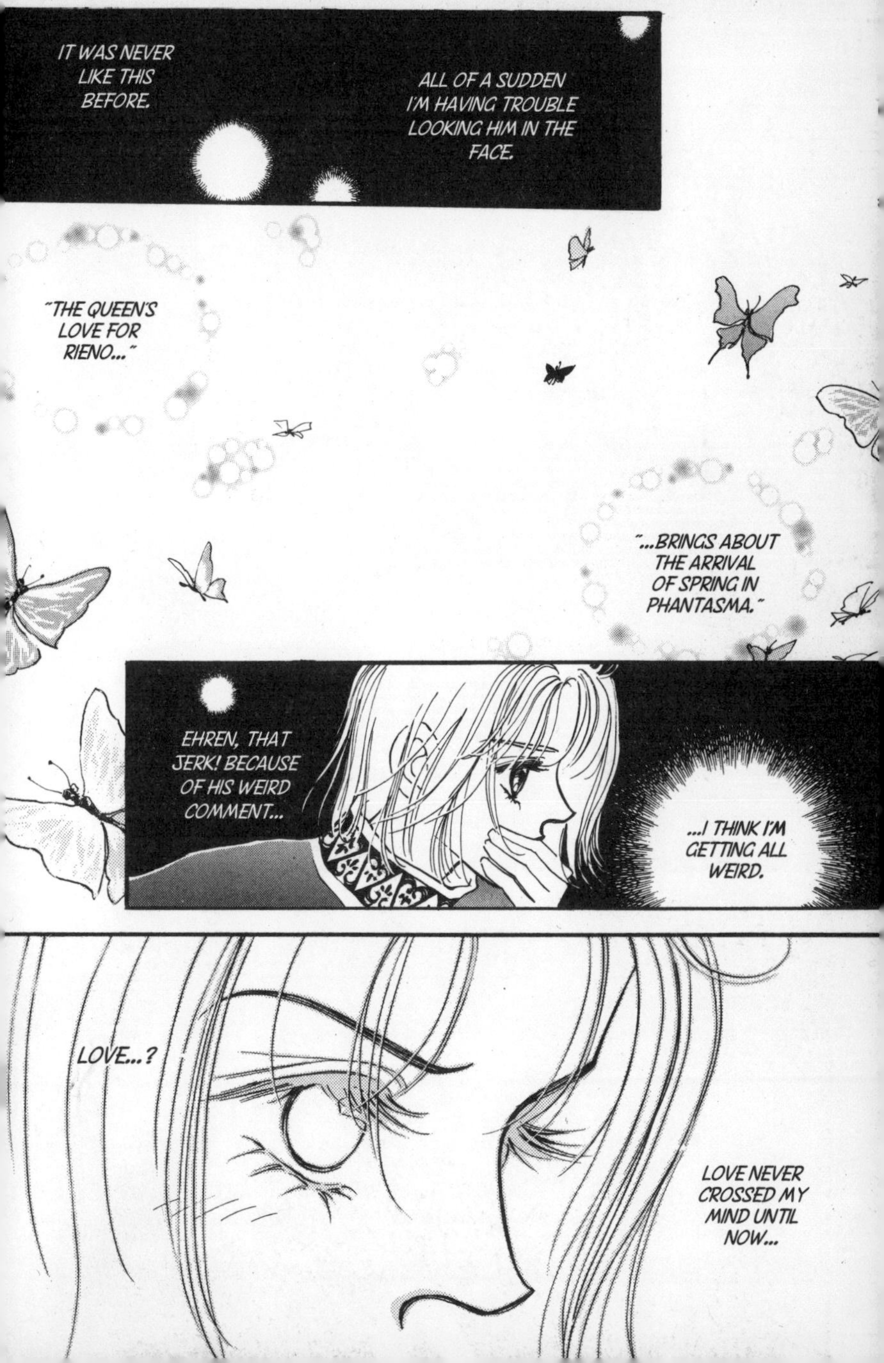
IT WAS NEVER LIKE THIS BEFORE.
ALL OF A SUDDEN I'M HAVING TROUBLE LOOKING HIM IN THE FACE.
"THE QUEEN'S LOVE FOR RIENO..."
"...BRINGS ABOUT THE ARRIVAL OF SPRING IN PHANTASMA."
EHREN, THAT JERK! BECAUSE OF HIS WEIRD COMMENT...
...I THINK I'M GETTING ALL WEIRD.
LOVE...?
LOVE NEVER CROSSED MY MIND UNTIL NOW...

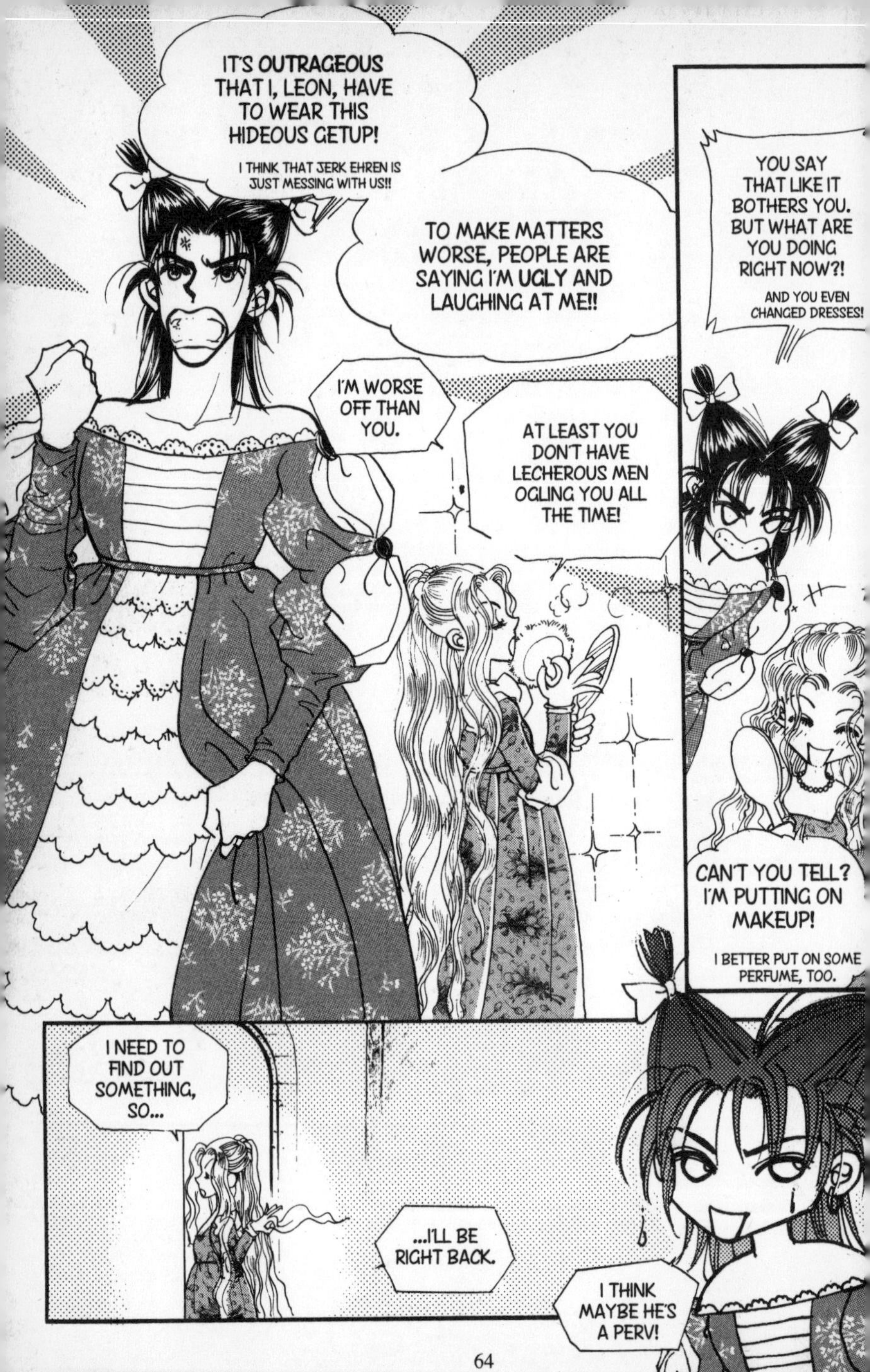
IT'S OUTRAGEOUS THAT I, LEON, HAVE TO WEAR THIS HIDEOUS GETUP!
I THINK THAT JERK EHREN IS JUST MESSING WITH US!!
TO MAKE MATTERS WORSE, PEOPLE ARE SAYING I'M UGLY AND LAUGHING AT ME!!
I'M WORSE OFF THAN YOU.
AT LEAST YOU DON'T HAVE LECHEROUS MEN OGLING YOU ALL THE TIME!
YOU SAY THAT LIKE IT BOTHERS YOU. BUT WHAT ARE YOU DOING RIGHT NOW?!
AND YOU EVEN CHANGED DRESSES!
CAN'T YOU TELL? I'M PUTTING ON MAKEUP!
I BETTER PUT ON SOME PERFUME, TOO.
I NEED TO FIND OUT SOMETHING, SO...
...I'LL BE RIGHT BACK.
I THINK MAYBE HE'S A PERV!

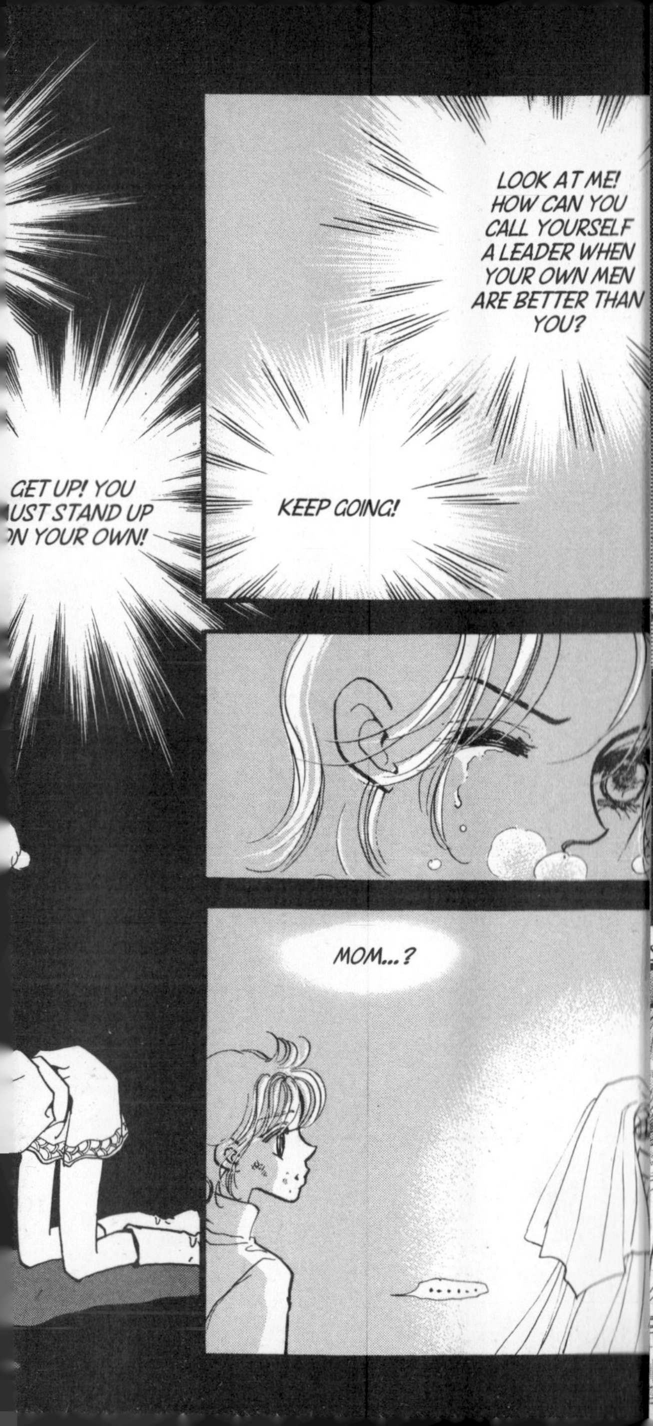
GET UP! YOU
UST STAND UP
N YOUR OWN!
LOOK AT ME! HOW CAN YOU CALL YOURSELF A LEADER WHEN YOUR OWN MEN ARE BETTER THAN YOU?
KEEP GOING!
MOM...?
......
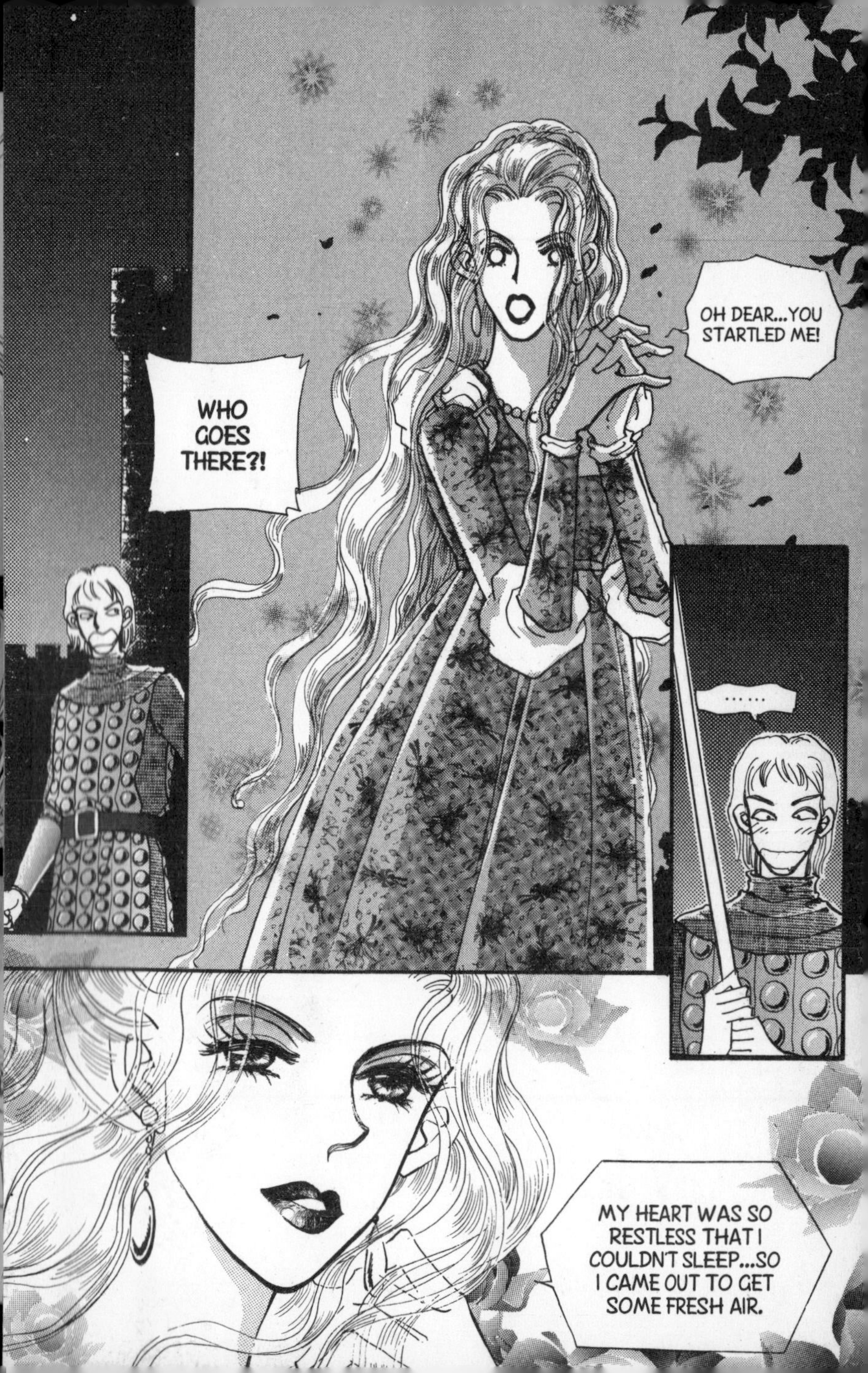
WHO GOES THERE?!
OH DEAR...YOU STARTLED ME!
......
MY HEART WAS SO RESTLESS THAT I COULDN'T SLEEP...SO I CAME OUT TO GET SOME FRESH AIR.

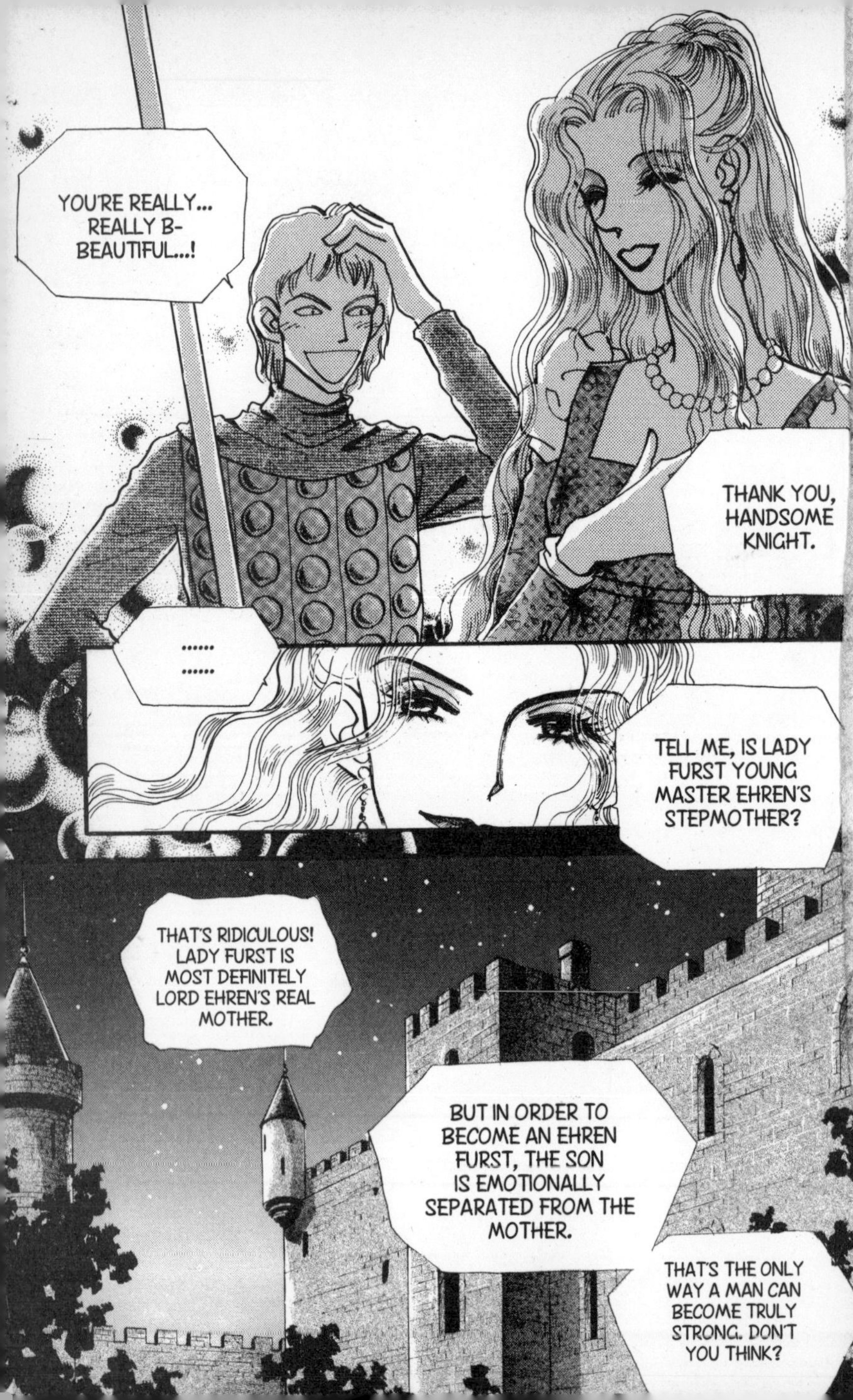
YOU'RE REALLY... REALLY B-BEAUTIFUL...!
THANK YOU, HANDSOME KNIGHT.
....
TELL ME, IS LADY FURST YOUNG MASTER EHREN'S STEPMOTHER?
THAT'S RIDICULOUS! LADY FURST IS MOST DEFINITELY LORD EHREN'S REAL MOTHER.
BUT IN ORDER TO BECOME AN EHREN FURST, THE SON IS EMOTIONALLY SEPARATED FROM THE MOTHER.
THAT'S THE ONLY WAY A MAN CAN BECOME TRULY STRONG. DON'T YOU THINK?

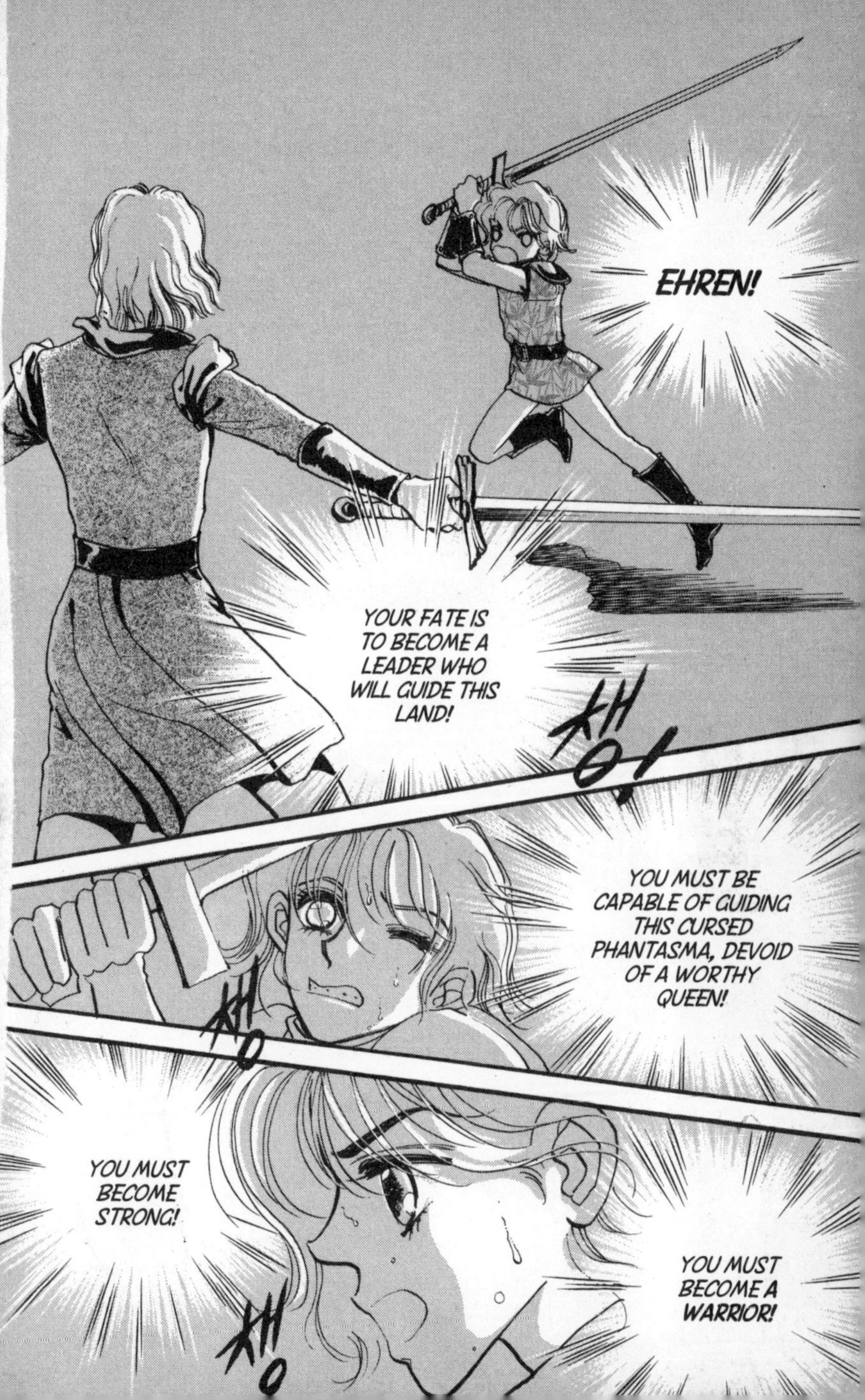
EHREN!
YOUR FATE IS TO BECOME A LEADER WHO WILL GUIDE THIS LAND!
KHO!
YOU MUST BE CAPABLE OF GUIDING THIS CURSED PHANTASMA, DEVOID OF A WORTHY QUEEN!
KHO
YOU MUST BECOME STRONG!
YOU MUST BECOME A WARRIOR!
KHO

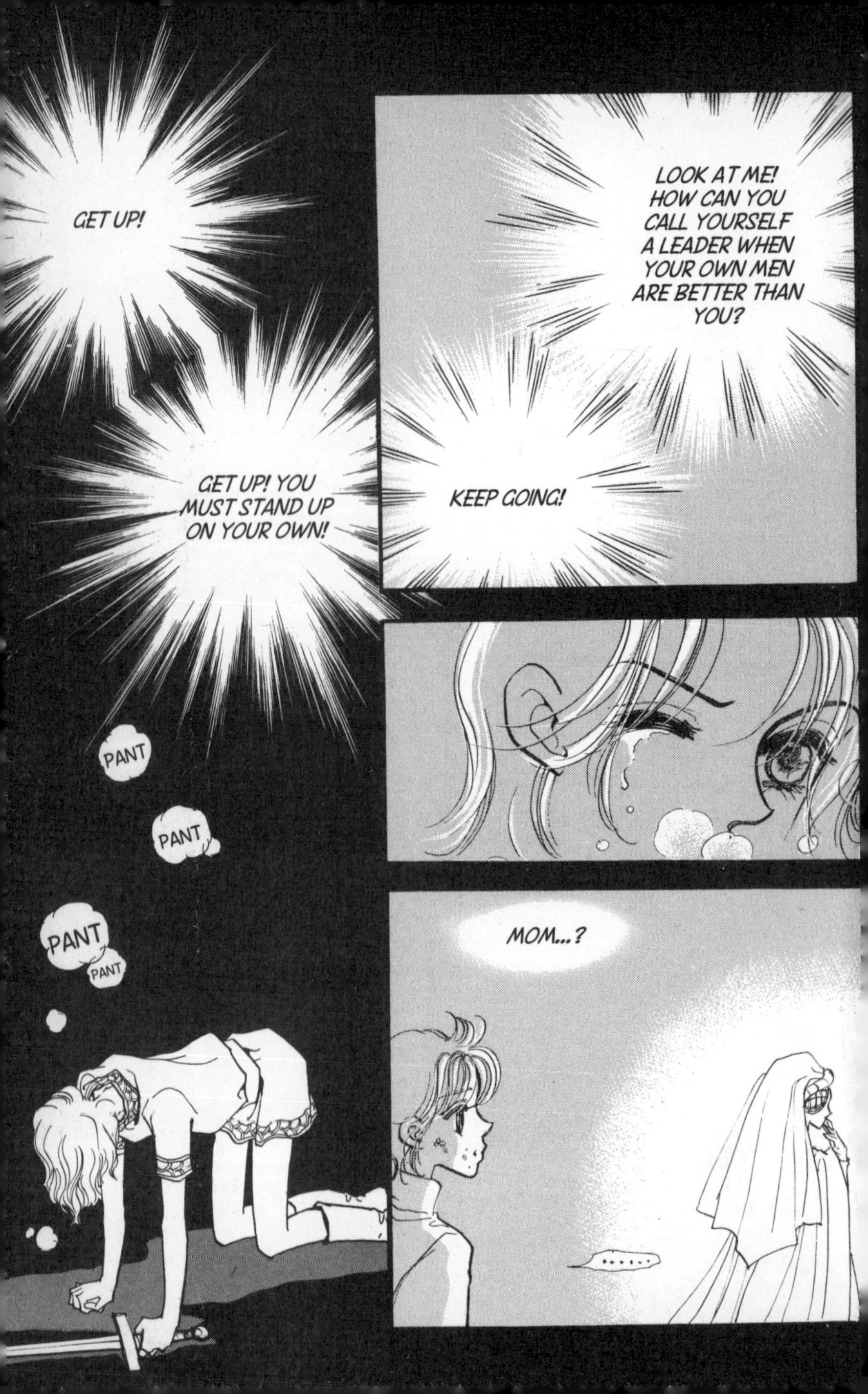
GET UP!
GET UP! YOU MUST STAND UP ON YOUR OWN!
PANT
PANT
PANT
PANT
LOOK AT ME! HOW CAN YOU CALL YOURSELF A LEADER WHEN YOUR OWN MEN ARE BETTER THAN YOU?
KEEP GOING!
MOM...?
......

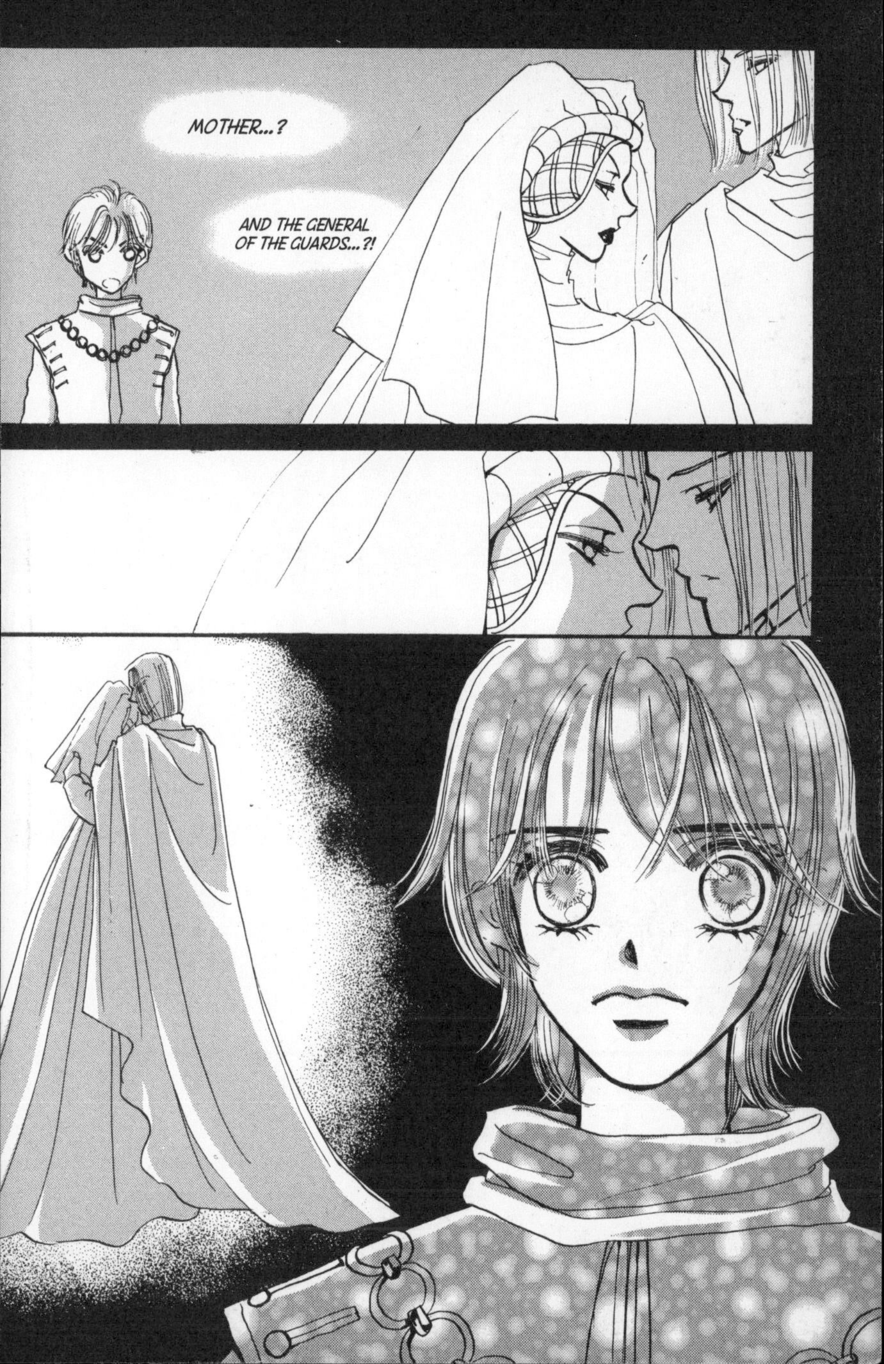
MOTHER...?
AND THE GENERAL OF THE GUARDS...?!

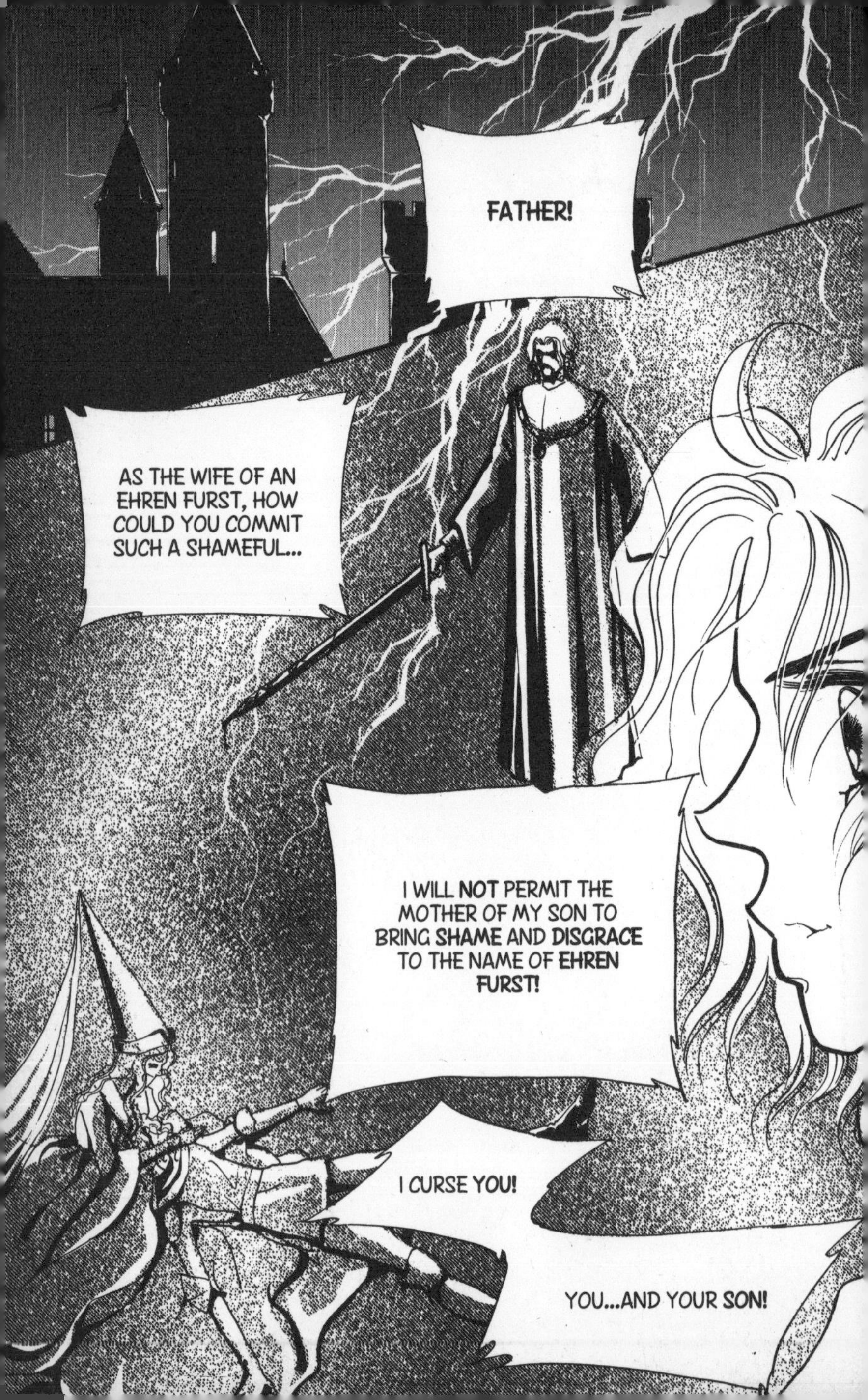
FATHER!
AS THE WIFE OF AN EHREN FURST, HOW COULD YOU COMMIT SUCH A SHAMEFUL...
I WILL NOT PERMIT THE MOTHER OF MY SON TO BRING SHAME AND DISGRACE TO THE NAME OF EHREN FURST!
I CURSE YOU!
YOU...AND YOUR SON!

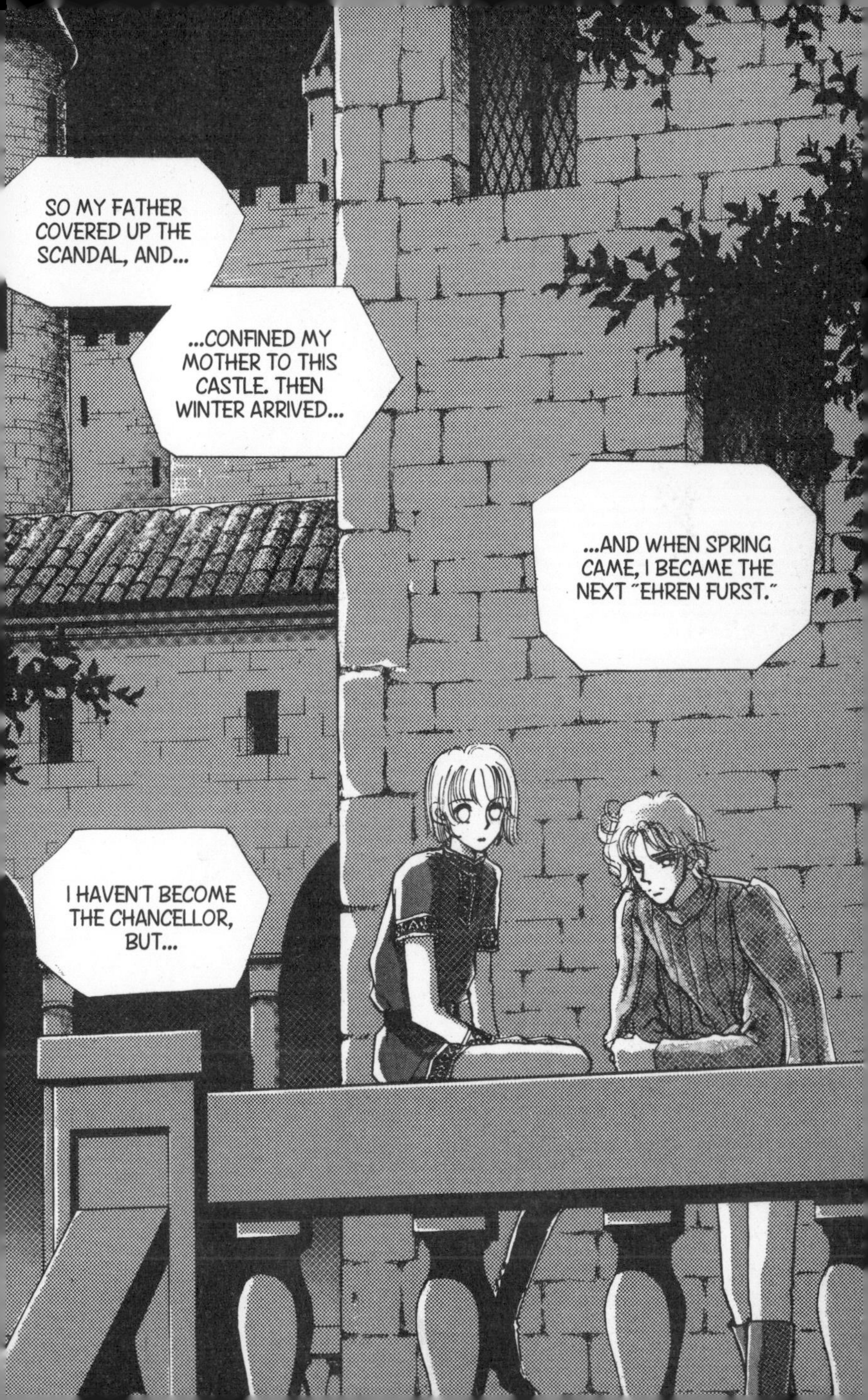
SO MY FATHER COVERED UP THE SCANDAL, AND...
...CONFINED MY MOTHER TO THIS CASTLE. THEN WINTER ARRIVED...
...AND WHEN SPRING CAME, I BECAME THE NEXT "EHREN FURST."
I HAVEN'T BECOME THE CHANCELLOR, BUT...

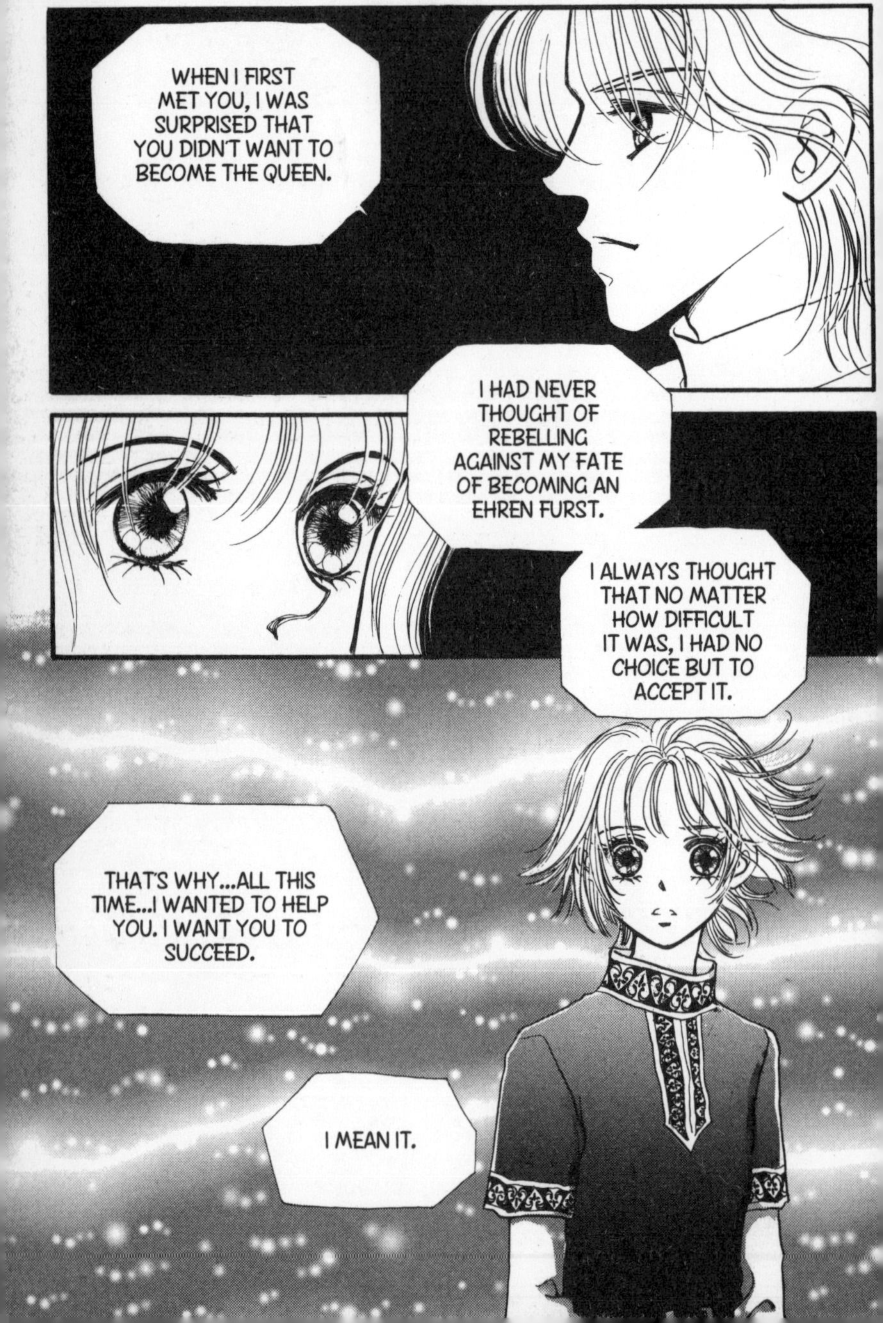
WHEN I FIRST MET YOU, I WAS SURPRISED THAT YOU DIDN'T WANT TO BECOME THE QUEEN.
I HAD NEVER THOUGHT OF REBELLING AGAINST MY FATE OF BECOMING AN EHREN FURST.
I ALWAYS THOUGHT THAT NO MATTER HOW DIFFICULT IT WAS, I HAD NO CHOICE BUT TO ACCEPT IT.
THAT'S WHY...ALL THIS TIME...I WANTED TO HELP YOU. I WANT YOU TO SUCCEED.
I MEAN IT.

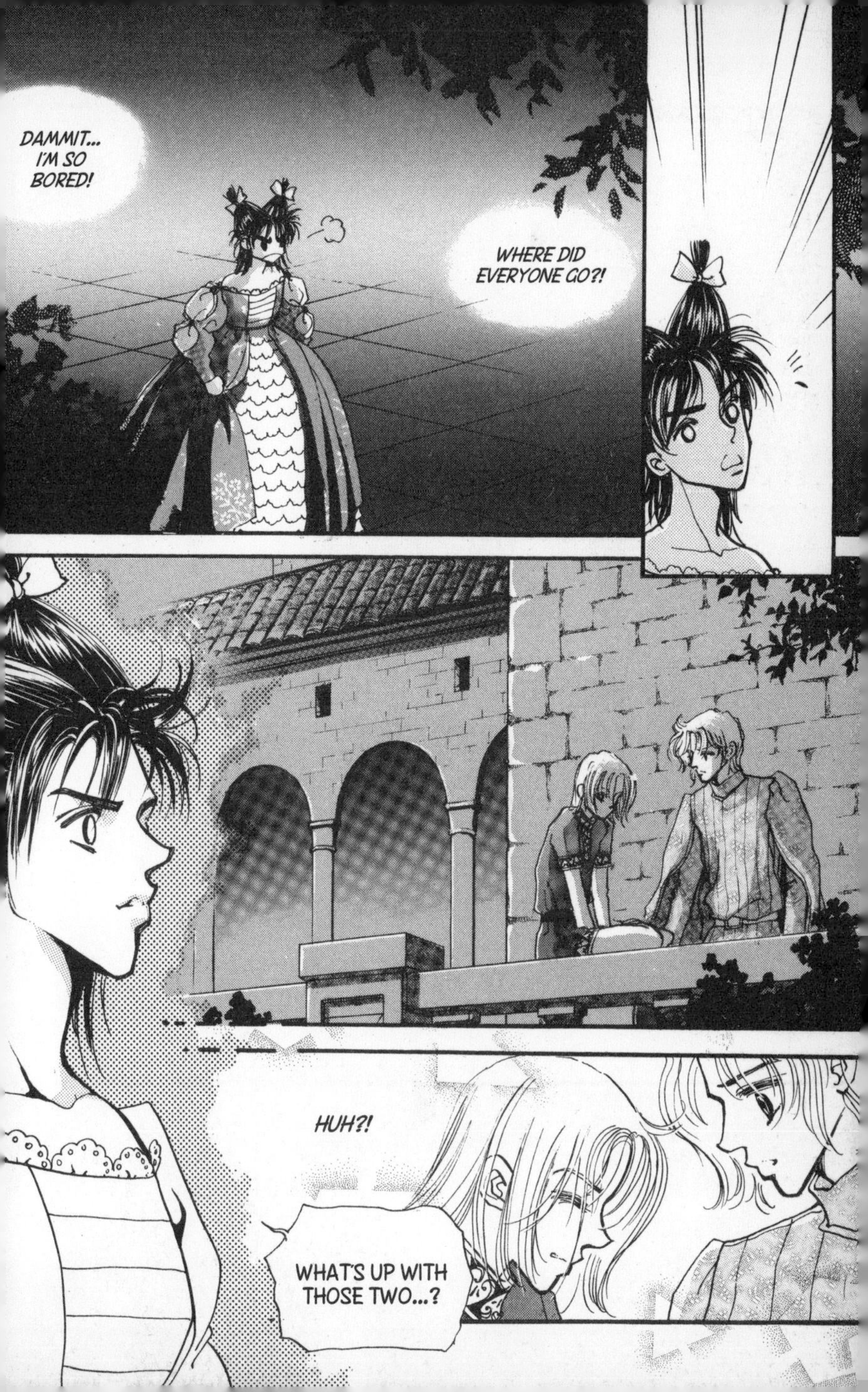
DAMMIT... I'M SO BORED!
WHERE DID EVERYONE GO?!
HUH?!
WHAT'S UP WITH THOSE TWO...?

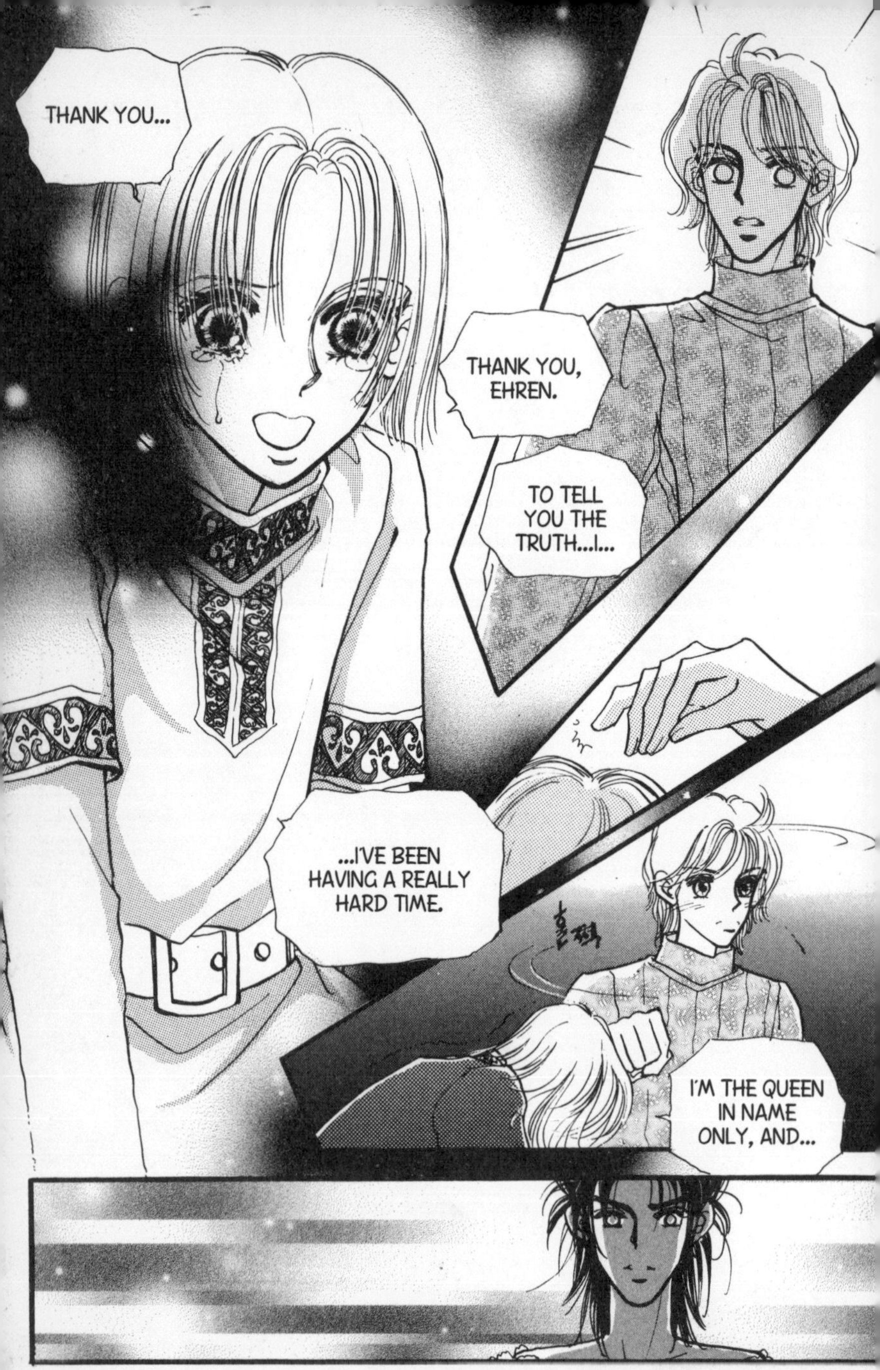
THANK YOU...
THANK YOU, EHREN.
TO TELL YOU THE TRUTH...I...
...I'VE BEEN HAVING A REALLY HARD TIME.
I'M THE QUEEN IN NAME ONLY, AND...

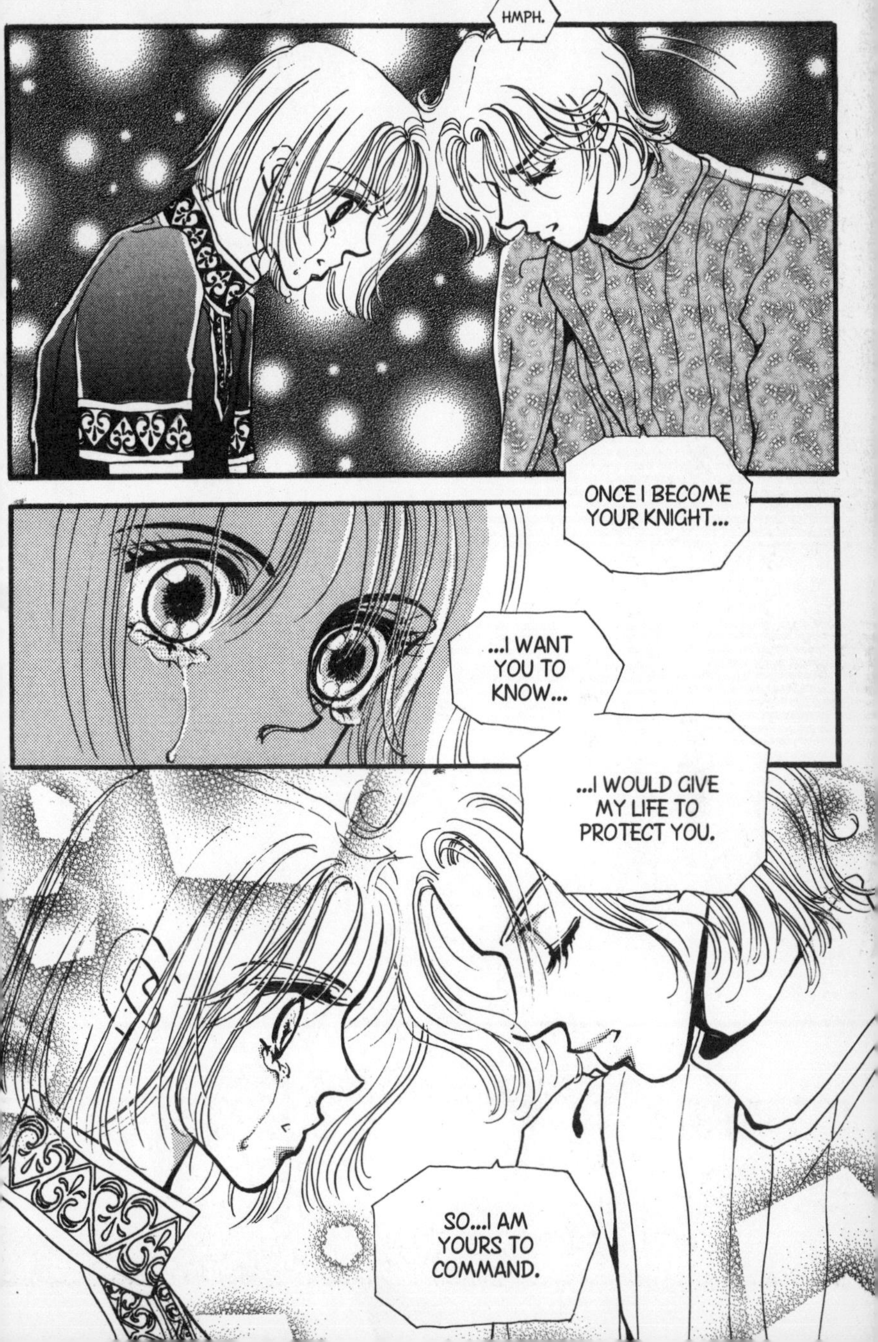
HMPH.
ONCE I BECOME YOUR KNIGHT...
...I WANT YOU TO KNOW...
...I WOULD GIVE MY LIFE TO PROTECT YOU.
SO...I AM YOURS TO COMMAND.

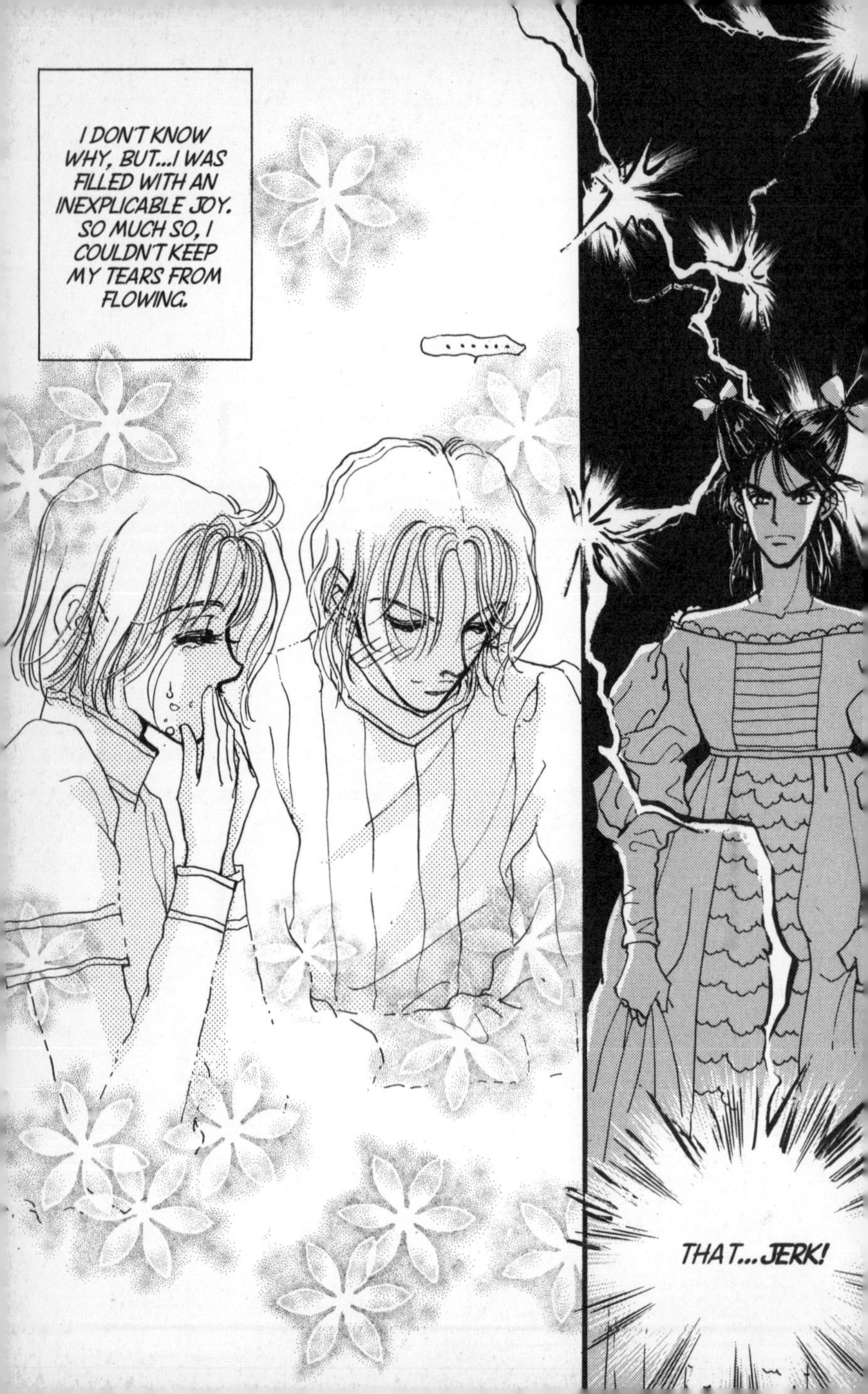
I DON'T KNOW WHY, BUT...I WAS FILLED WITH AN INEXPLICABLE JOY. SO MUCH SO, I COULDN'T KEEP MY TEARS FROM FLOWING.
......
THAT...JERK!

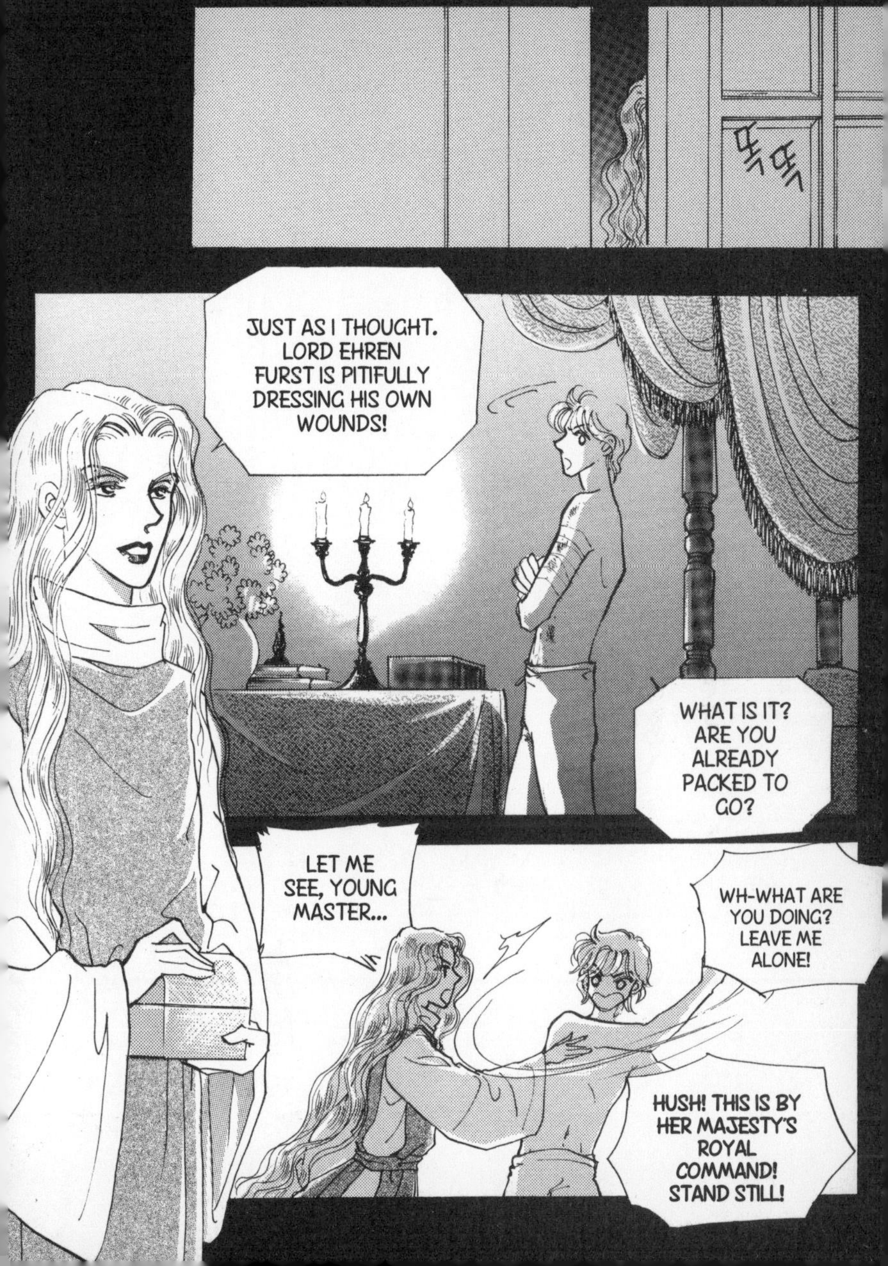
똑똑
JUST AS I THOUGHT. LORD EHREN FURST IS PITIFULLY DRESSING HIS OWN WOUNDS!
WHAT IS IT? ARE YOU ALREADY PACKED TO GO?
LET ME SEE, YOUNG MASTER...
WH-WHAT ARE YOU DOING? LEAVE ME ALONE!
HUSH! THIS IS BY HER MAJESTY'S ROYAL COMMAND! STAND STILL!

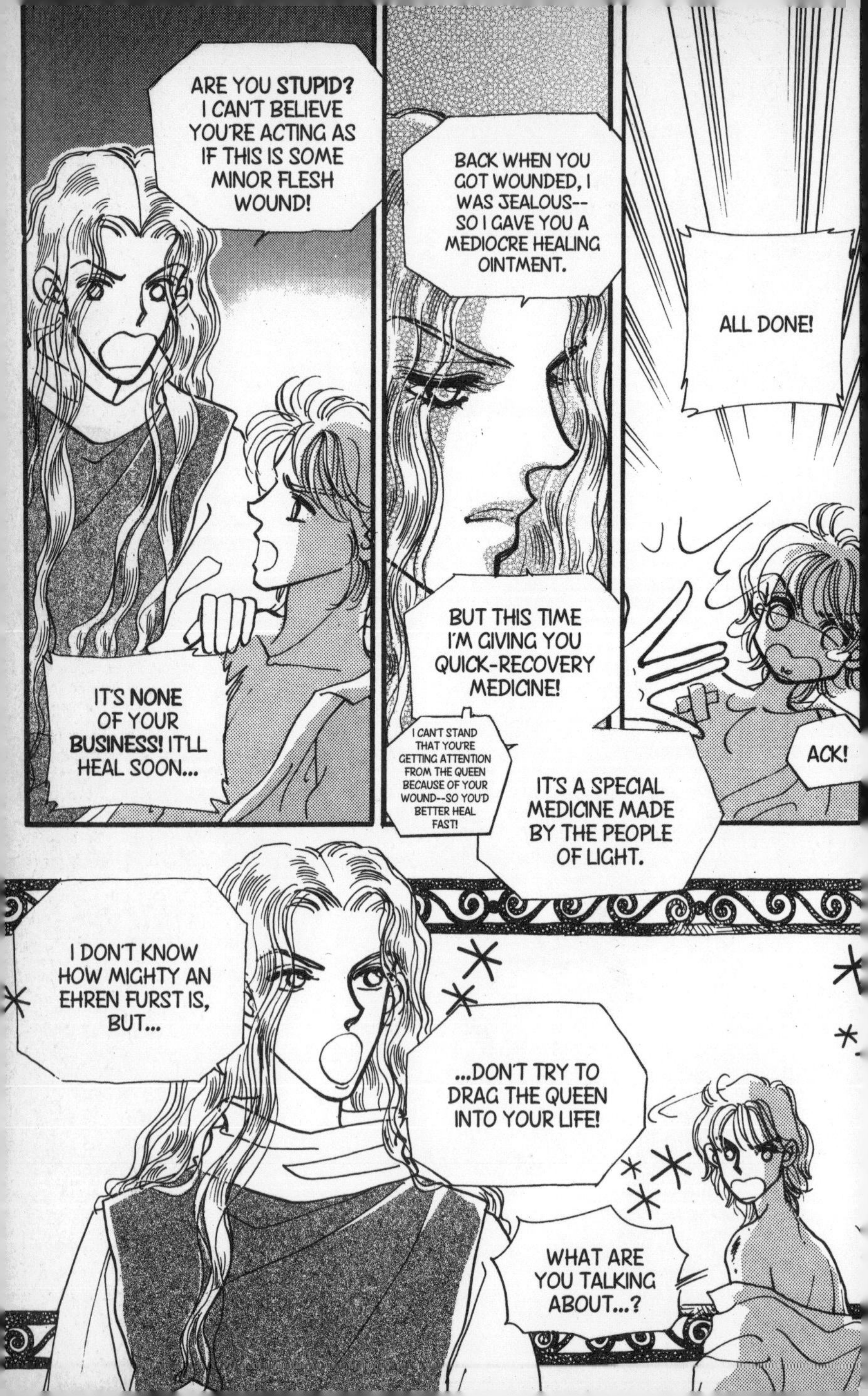
ARE YOU STUPID? I CAN'T BELIEVE YOU'RE ACTING AS IF THIS IS SOME MINOR FLESH WOUND!
IT'S NONE OF YOUR BUSINESS! IT'LL HEAL SOON...
BACK WHEN YOU GOT WOUNDED, I WAS JEALOUS-- SO I GAVE YOU A MEDIOCRE HEALING OINTMENT.
BUT THIS TIME I'M GIVING YOU QUICK-RECOVERY MEDICINE!
I CAN'T STAND THAT YOU'RE GETTING ATTENTION FROM THE QUEEN BECAUSE OF YOUR WOUND--SO YOU'D BETTER HEAL FAST!
IT'S A SPECIAL MEDICINE MADE BY THE PEOPLE OF LIGHT.
ALL DONE!
ACK!
I DON'T KNOW HOW MIGHTY AN EHREN FURST IS, BUT...
...DON'T TRY TO DRAG THE QUEEN INTO YOUR LIFE!
WHAT ARE YOU TALKING ABOUT...?

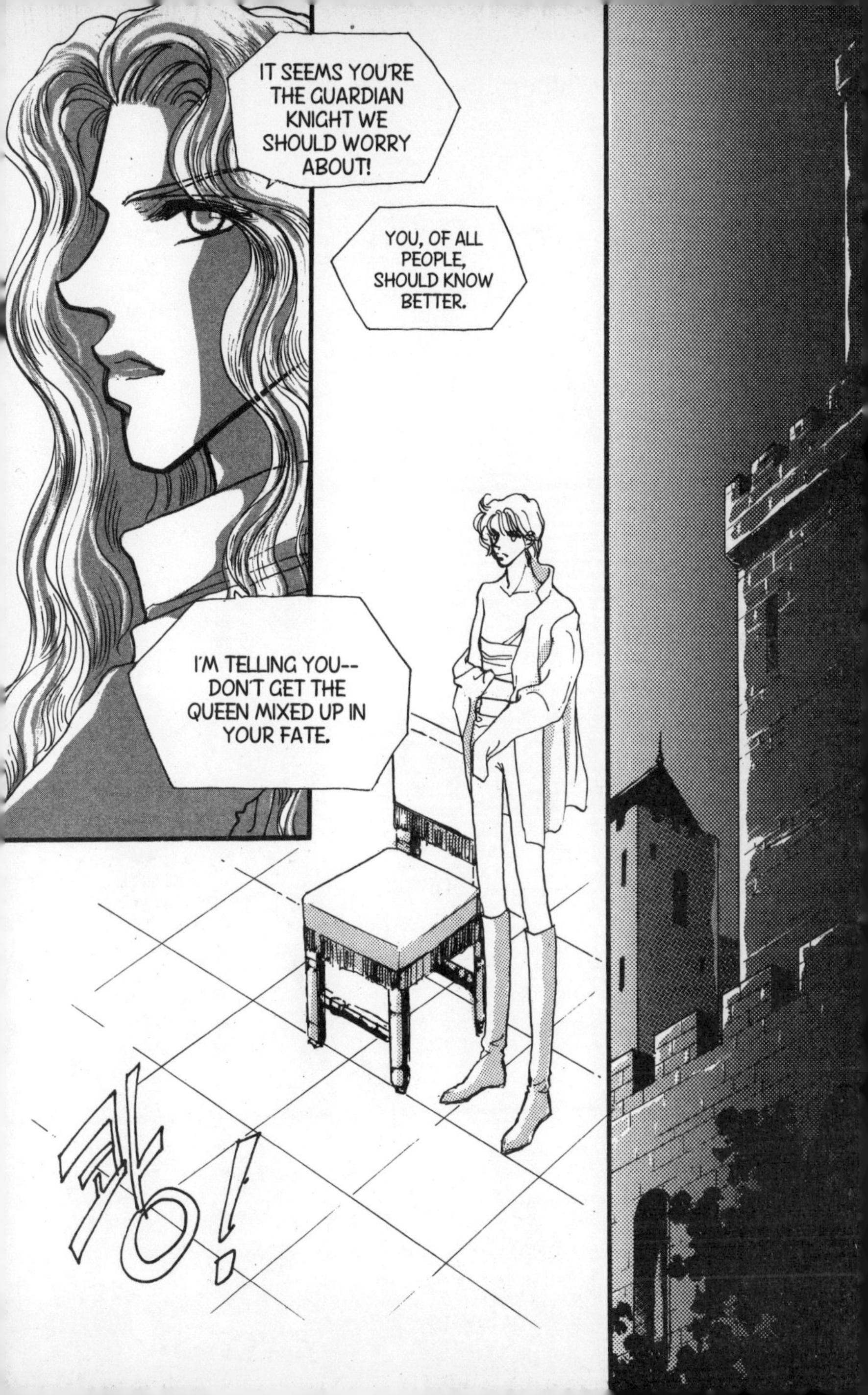
IT SEEMS YOU'RE THE GUARDIAN KNIGHT WE SHOULD WORRY ABOUT!
YOU, OF ALL PEOPLE, SHOULD KNOW BETTER.
I'M TELLING YOU-- DON'T GET THE QUEEN MIXED UP IN YOUR FATE.

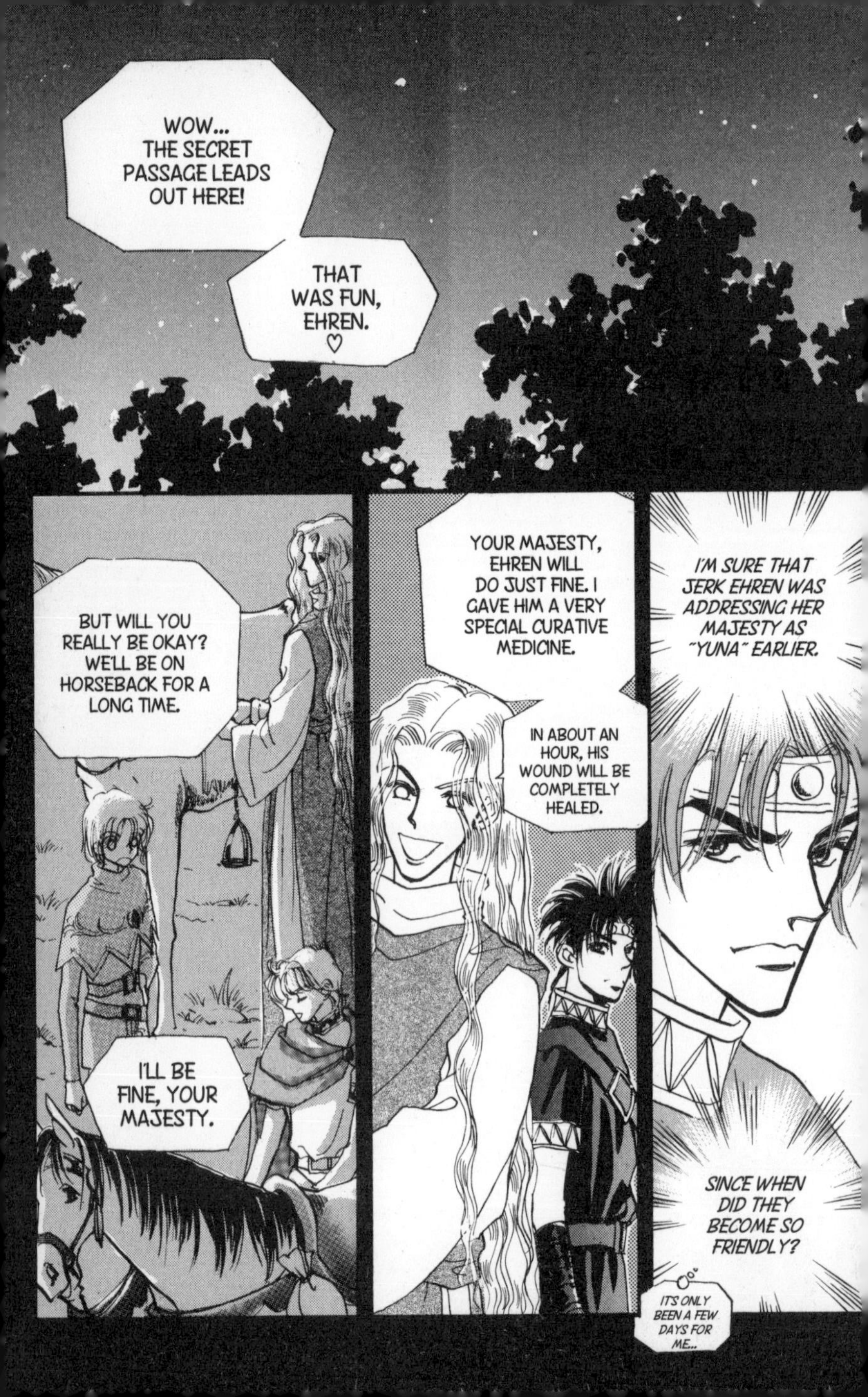
WOW... THE SECRET PASSAGE LEADS OUT HERE!
THAT WAS FUN, EHREN. ♡
BUT WILL YOU REALLY BE OKAY? WE'LL BE ON HORSEBACK FOR A LONG TIME.
I'LL BE FINE, YOUR MAJESTY.
YOUR MAJESTY, EHREN WILL DO JUST FINE. I GAVE HIM A VERY SPECIAL CURATIVE MEDICINE.
IN ABOUT AN HOUR, HIS WOUND WILL BE COMPLETELY HEALED.
I'M SURE THAT JERK EHREN WAS ADDRESSING HER MAJESTY AS "YUNA" EARLIER.
SINCE WHEN DID THEY BECOME SO FRIENDLY?
IT'S ONLY BEEN A FEW DAYS FOR ME...

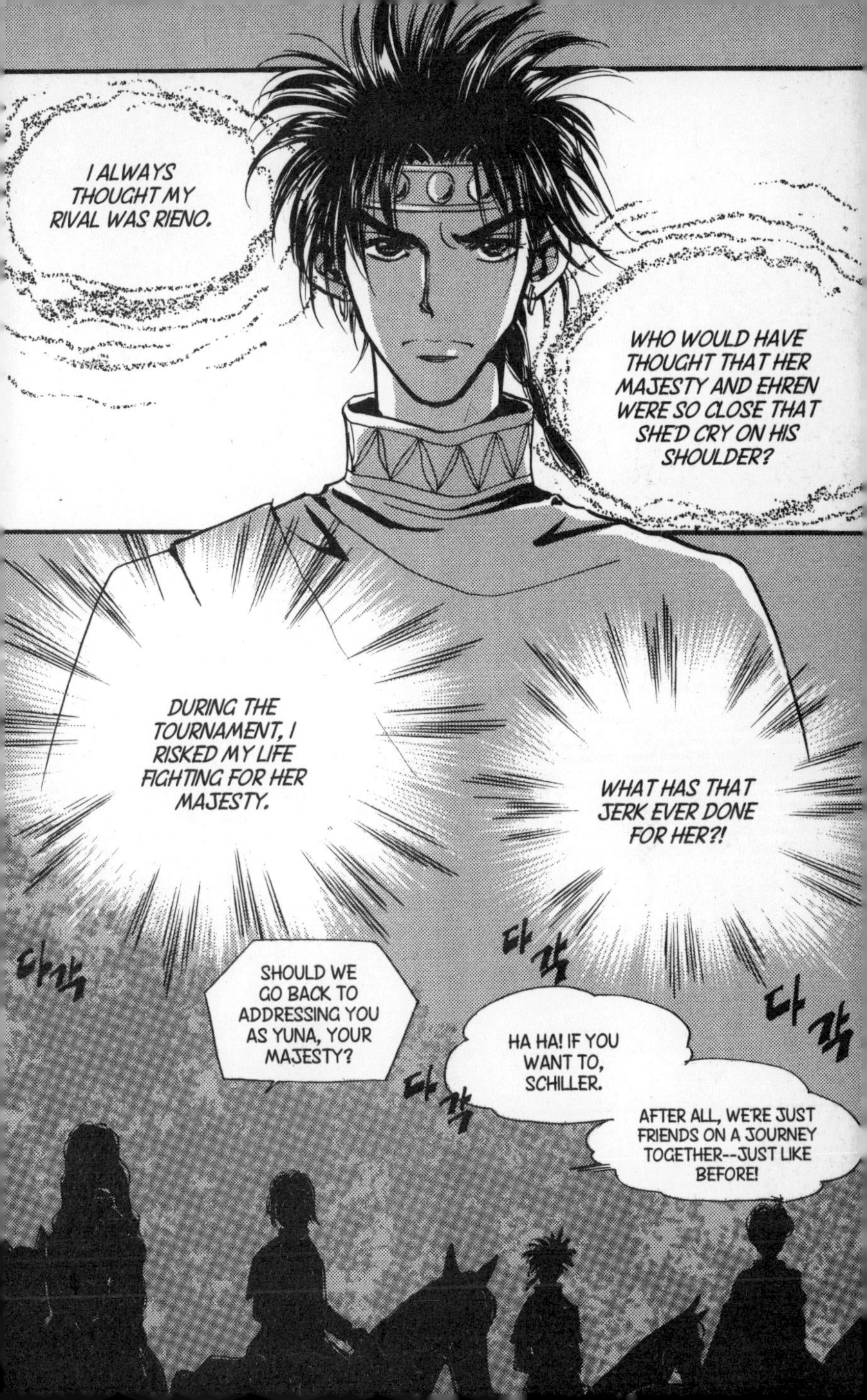
I ALWAYS THOUGHT MY RIVAL WAS RIENO.
WHO WOULD HAVE THOUGHT THAT HER MAJESTY AND EHREN WERE SO CLOSE THAT SHE'D CRY ON HIS SHOULDER?
DURING THE TOURNAMENT, I RISKED MY LIFE FIGHTING FOR HER MAJESTY.
WHAT HAS THAT JERK EVER DONE FOR HER?!
다각
다각
다각
다각
SHOULD WE GO BACK TO ADDRESSING YOU AS YUNA, YOUR MAJESTY?
HA HA! IF YOU WANT TO, SCHILLER.
AFTER ALL, WE'RE JUST FRIENDS ON A JOURNEY TOGETHER--JUST LIKE BEFORE!

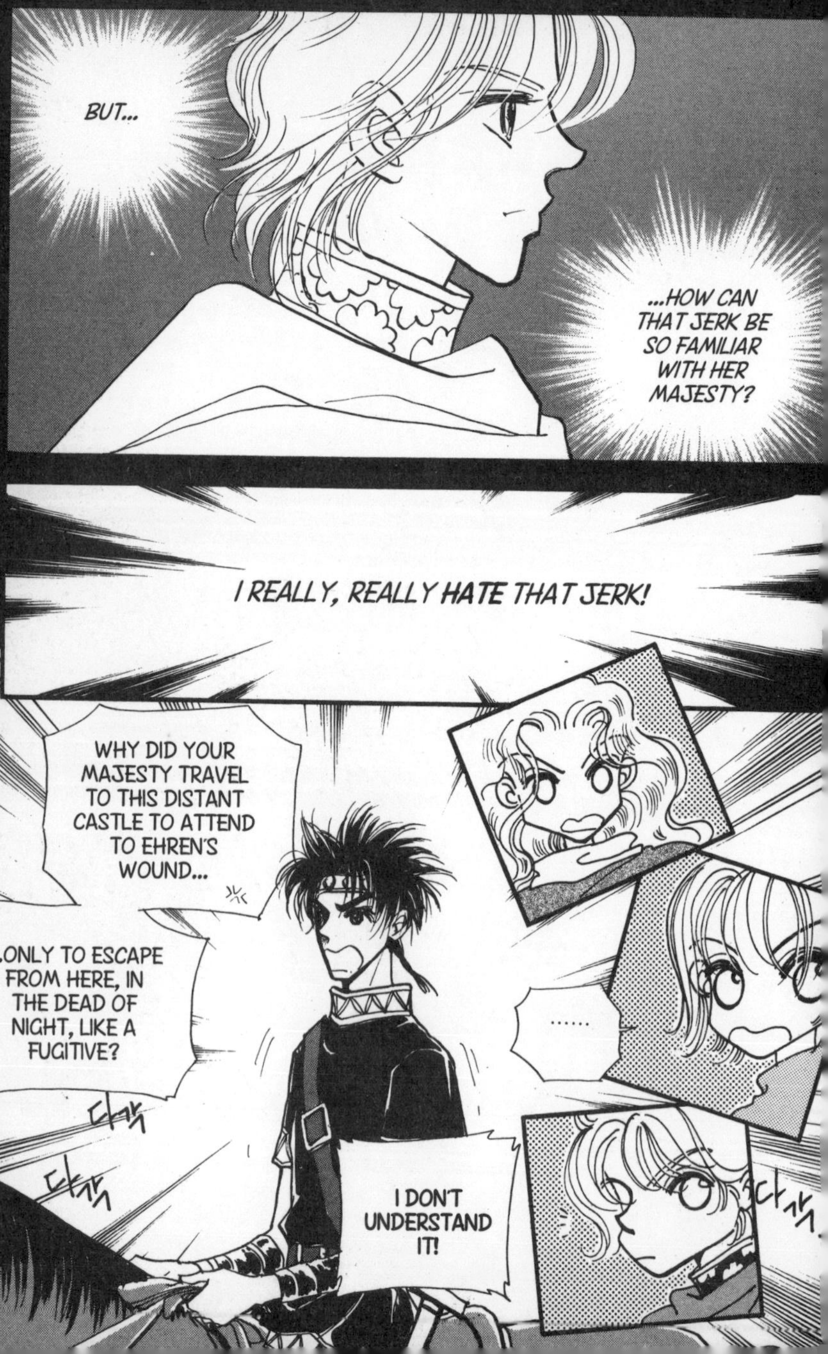
BUT...
...HOW CAN THAT JERK BE SO FAMILIAR WITH HER MAJESTY?
I REALLY, REALLY HATE THAT JERK!
WHY DID YOUR MAJESTY TRAVEL TO THIS DISTANT CASTLE TO ATTEND TO EHREN'S WOUND...
...ONLY TO ESCAPE FROM HERE, IN THE DEAD OF NIGHT, LIKE A FUGITIVE?
......
I DON'T UNDERSTAND IT!

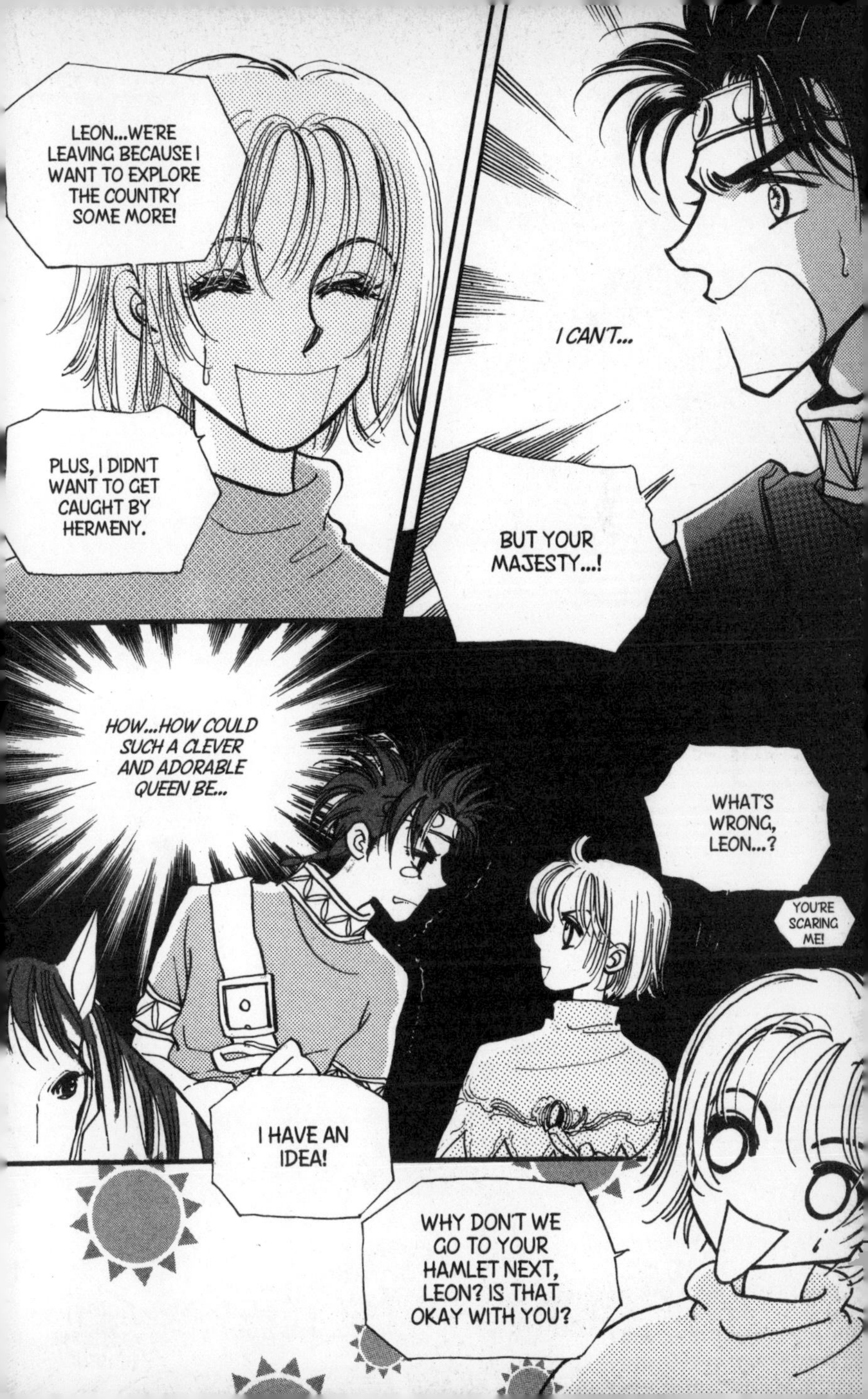
LEON...WE'RE LEAVING BECAUSE I WANT TO EXPLORE THE COUNTRY SOME MORE!
PLUS, I DIDN'T WANT TO GET CAUGHT BY HERMENY.
I CAN'T...
BUT YOUR MAJESTY...!
HOW...HOW COULD SUCH A CLEVER AND ADORABLE QUEEN BE...
WHAT'S WRONG, LEON...?
YOU'RE SCARING ME!
I HAVE AN IDEA!
WHY DON'T WE GO TO YOUR HAMLET NEXT, LEON? IS THAT OKAY WITH YOU?

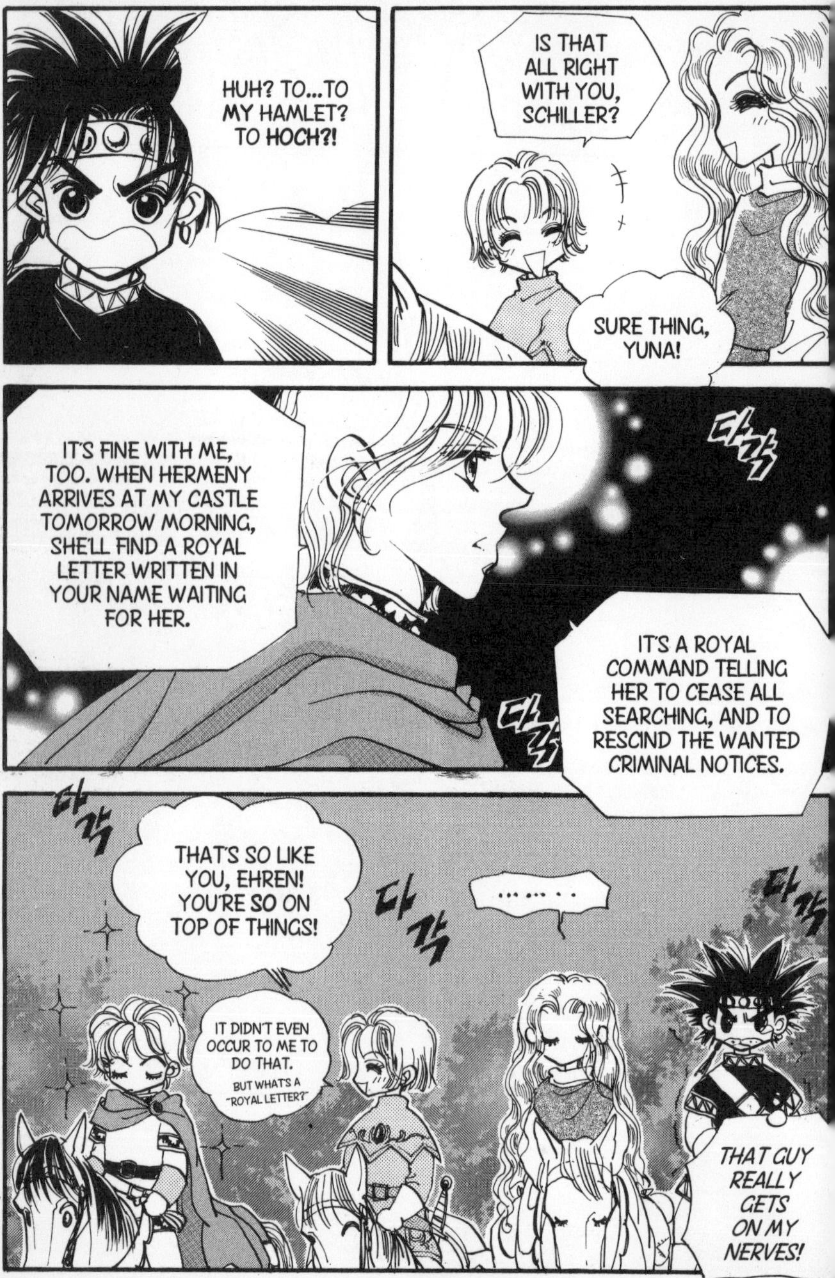
HUH? TO...TO MY HAMLET? TO HOCH?!
IS THAT ALL RIGHT WITH YOU, SCHILLER?
SURE THING, YUNA!
IT'S FINE WITH ME, TOO. WHEN HERMENY ARRIVES AT MY CASTLE TOMORROW MORNING, SHE'LL FIND A ROYAL LETTER WRITTEN IN YOUR NAME WAITING FOR HER.
다각
다각
IT'S A ROYAL COMMAND TELLING HER TO CEASE ALL SEARCHING, AND TO RESCIND THE WANTED CRIMINAL NOTICES.
다각
THAT'S SO LIKE YOU, EHREN! YOU'RE SO ON TOP OF THINGS!
다각
......
다각
IT DIDN'T EVEN OCCUR TO ME TO DO THAT.
BUT WHAT'S A "ROYAL LETTER?"
THAT GUY REALLY GETS ON MY NERVES!

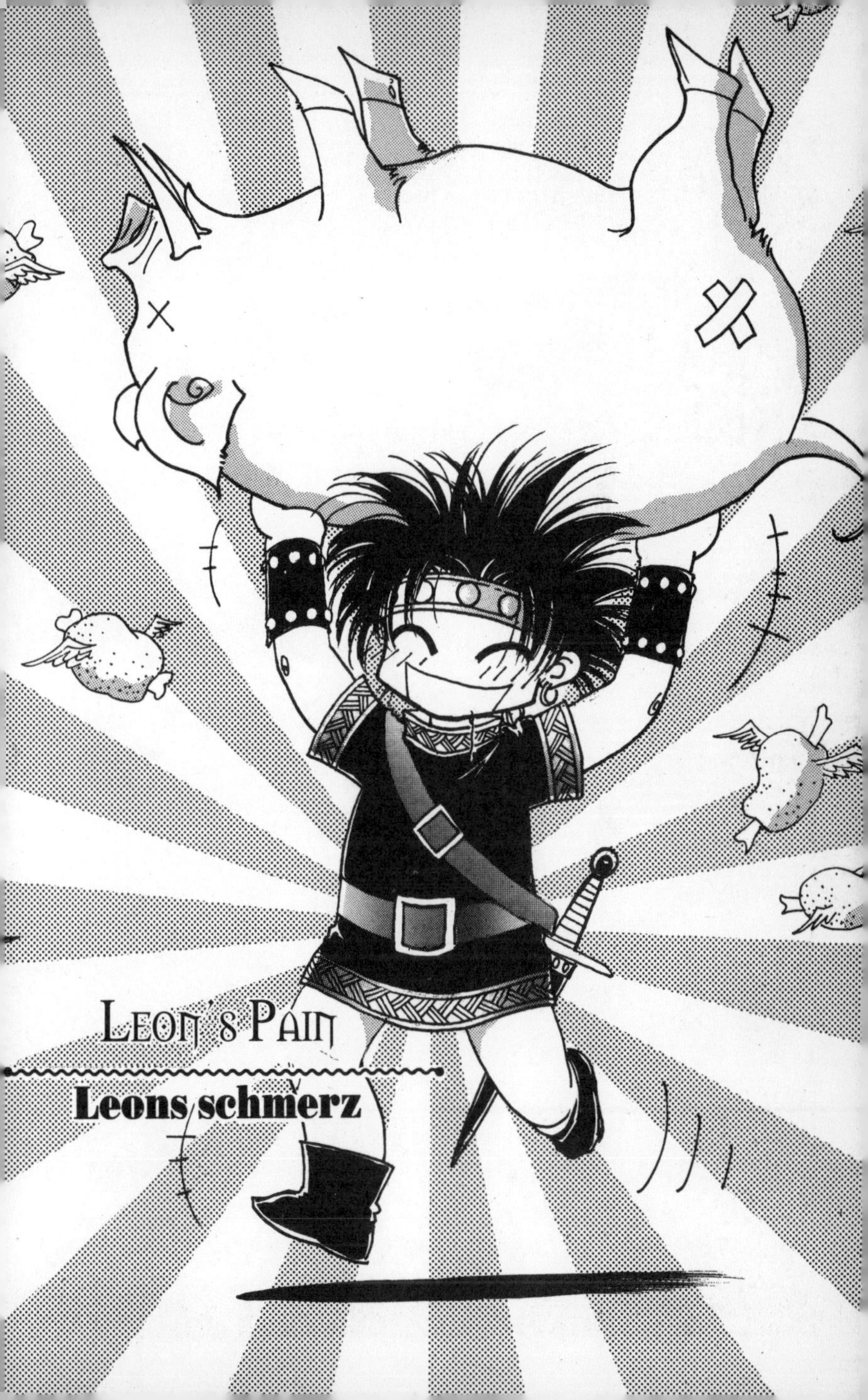

Leon's Pain

Leons schmerz

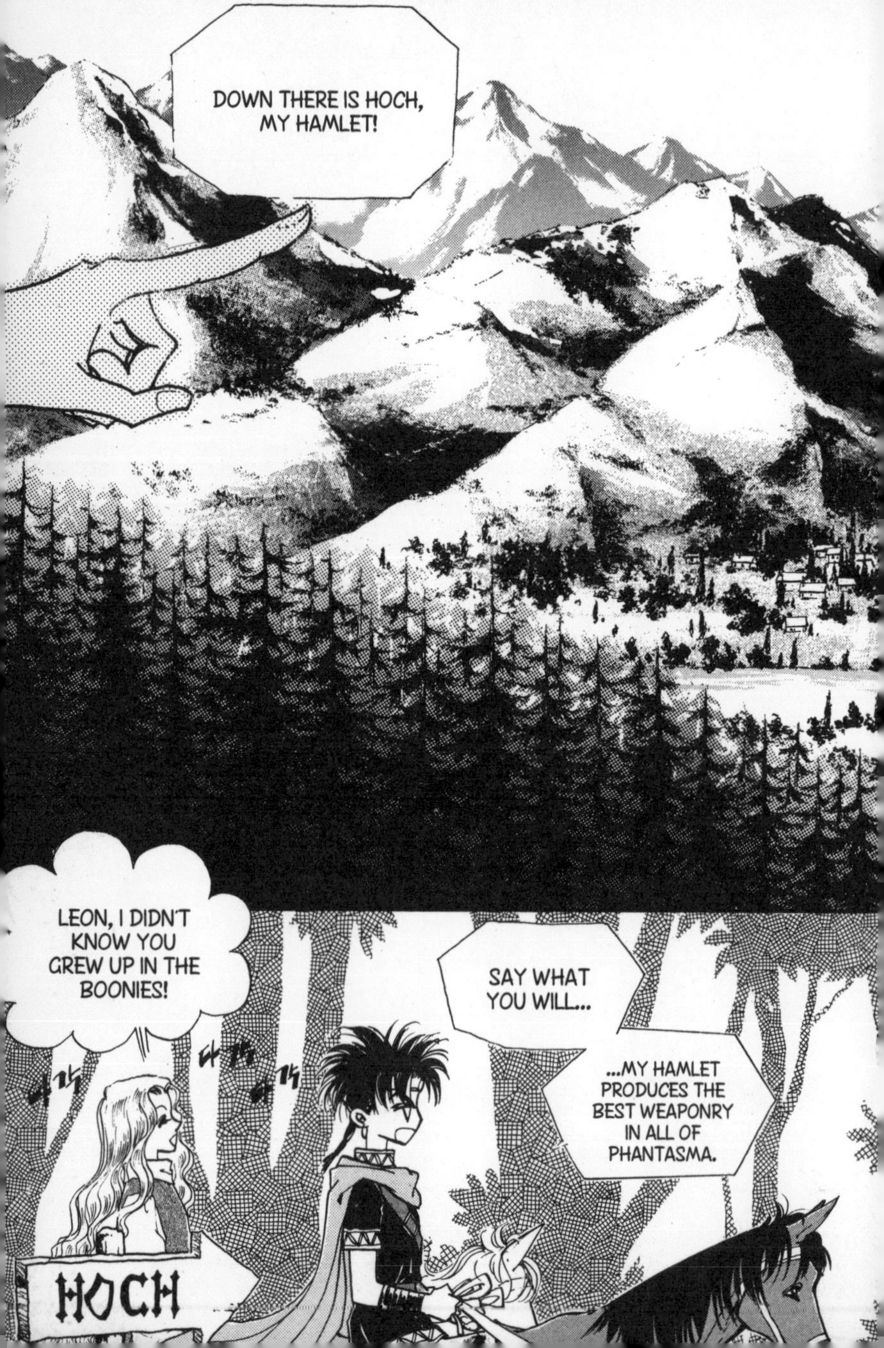
DOWN THERE IS HOCH, MY HAMLET!
LEON, I DIDN'T KNOW YOU GREW UP IN THE BOONIES!
SAY WHAT YOU WILL...
...MY HAMLET PRODUCES THE BEST WEAPONRY IN ALL OF PHANTASMA.
HOCH

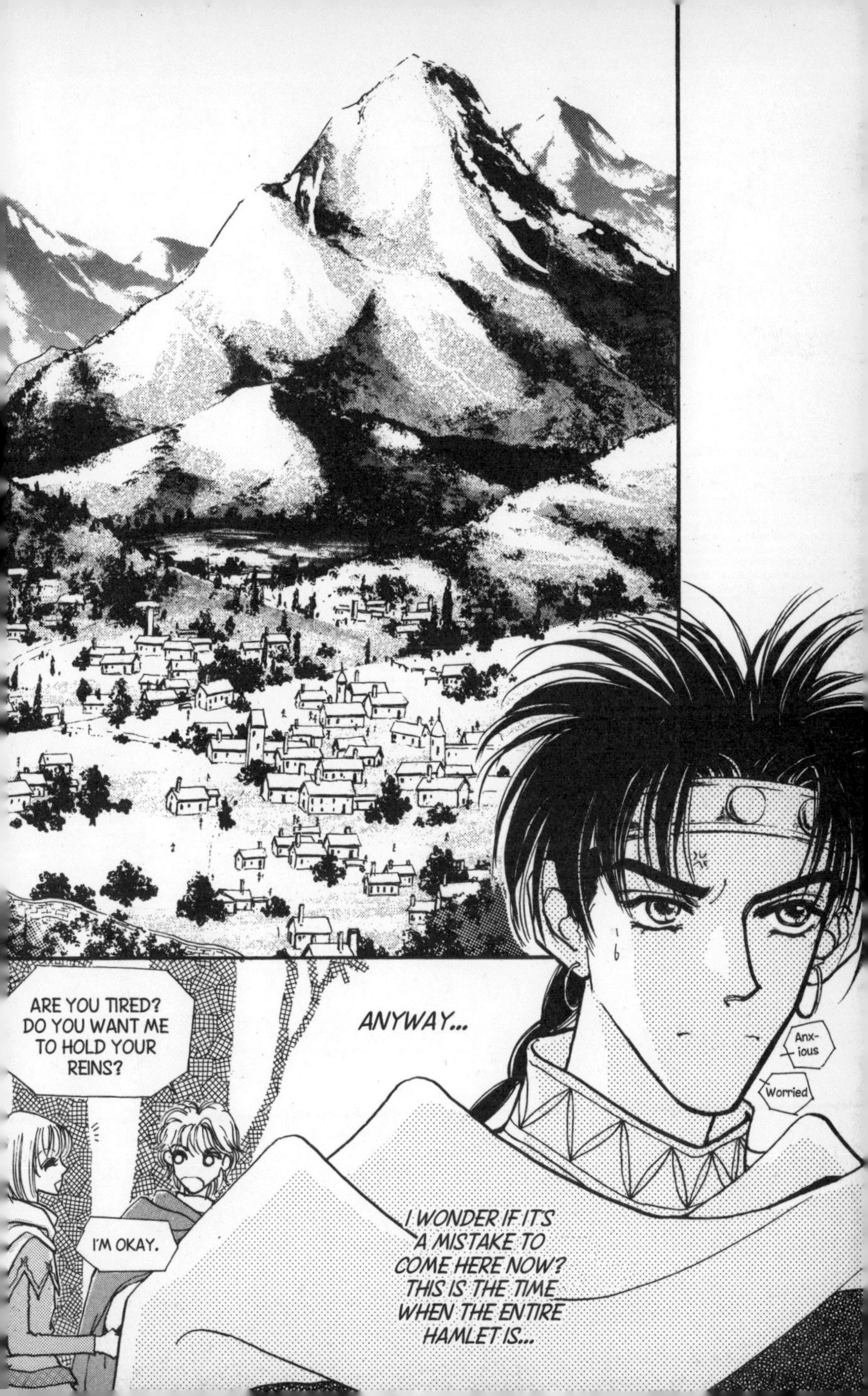
ARE YOU TIRED? DO YOU WANT ME TO HOLD YOUR REINS?
I'M OKAY.
ANYWAY...
Anx-ious
Worried
I WONDER IF IT'S A MISTAKE TO COME HERE NOW? THIS IS THE TIME WHEN THE ENTIRE HAMLET IS...

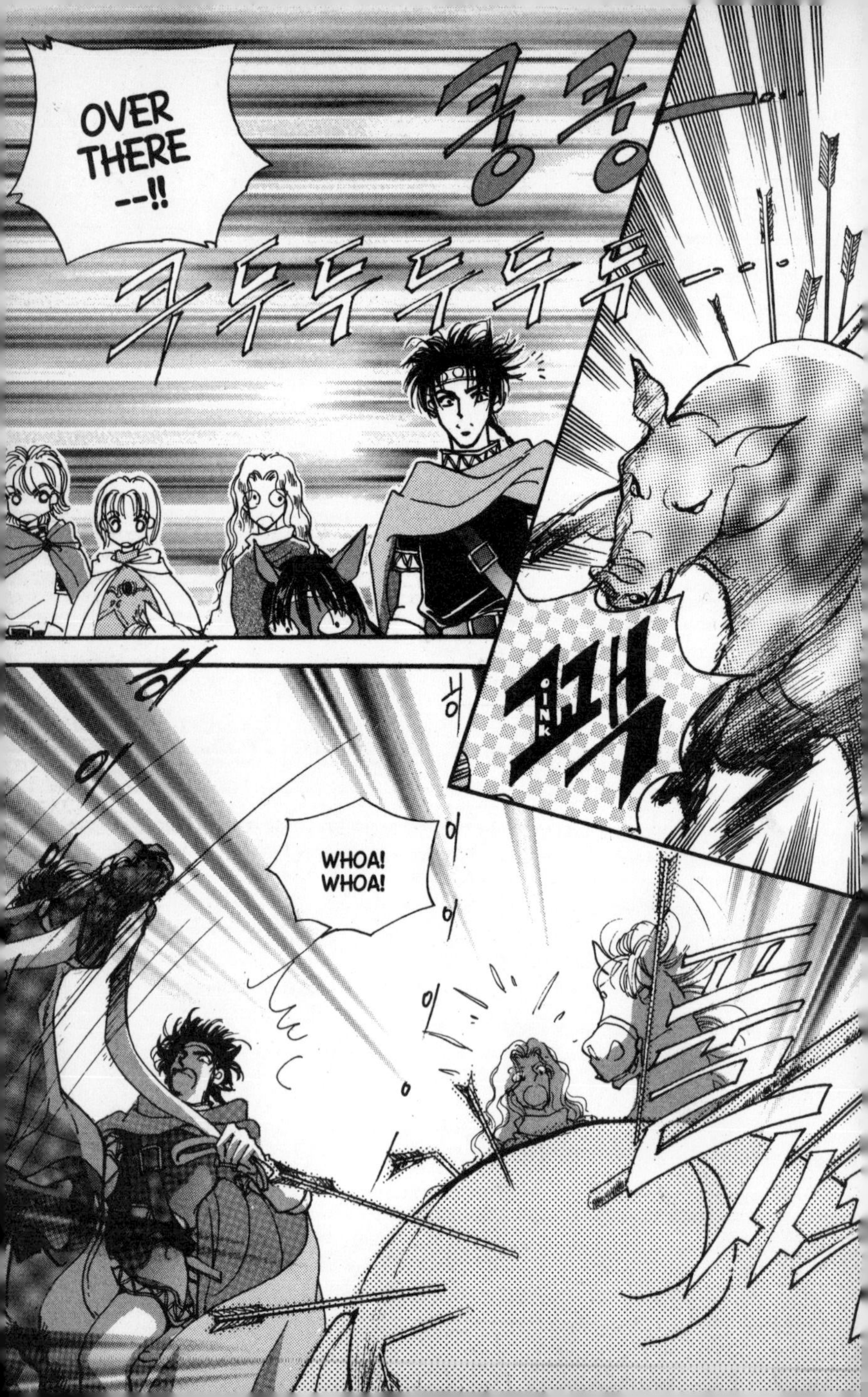
OVER THERE --!!
쿵쿵---
쿠두두두두두---
꾸액
OINK
히이이이이잉
WHOA! WHOA!

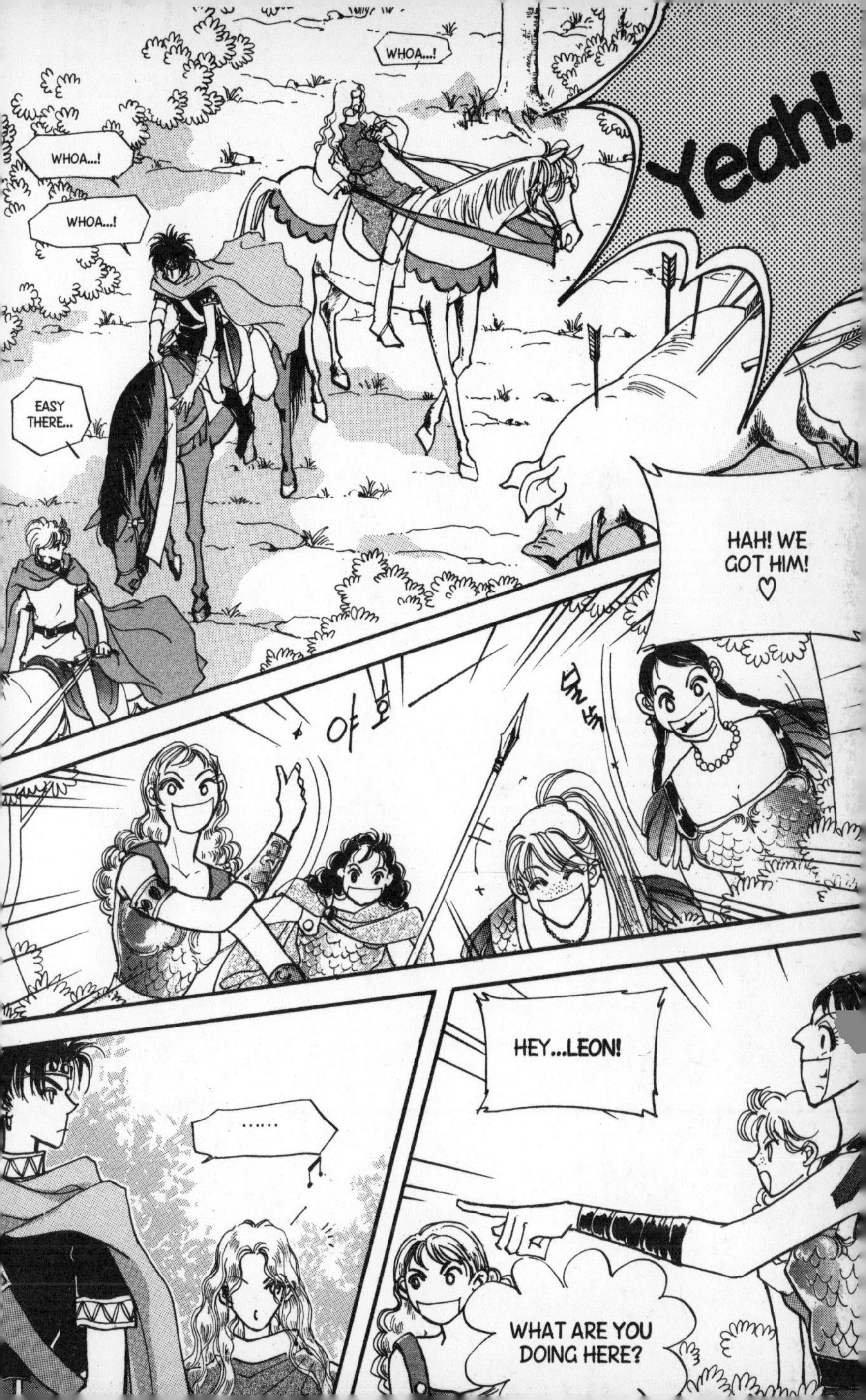
WHOA...!
WHOA...!
WHOA...!
EASY THERE...
Yeah!
HAH! WE GOT HIM! ♡
야호
......
HEY...LEON!
WHAT ARE YOU DOING HERE?

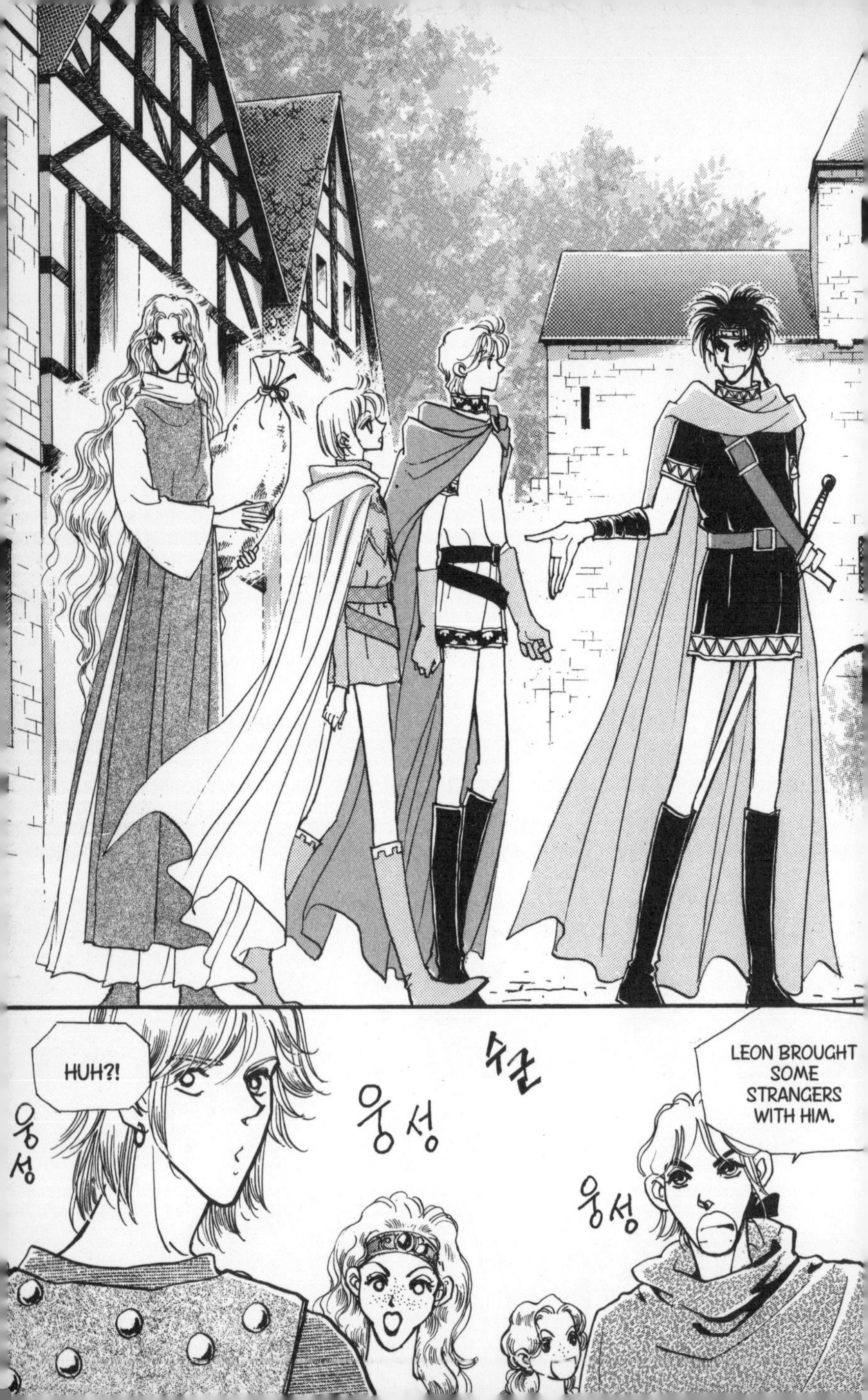
HUH?!
웅성
수군
웅성
LEON BROUGHT SOME STRANGERS WITH HIM.
웅성

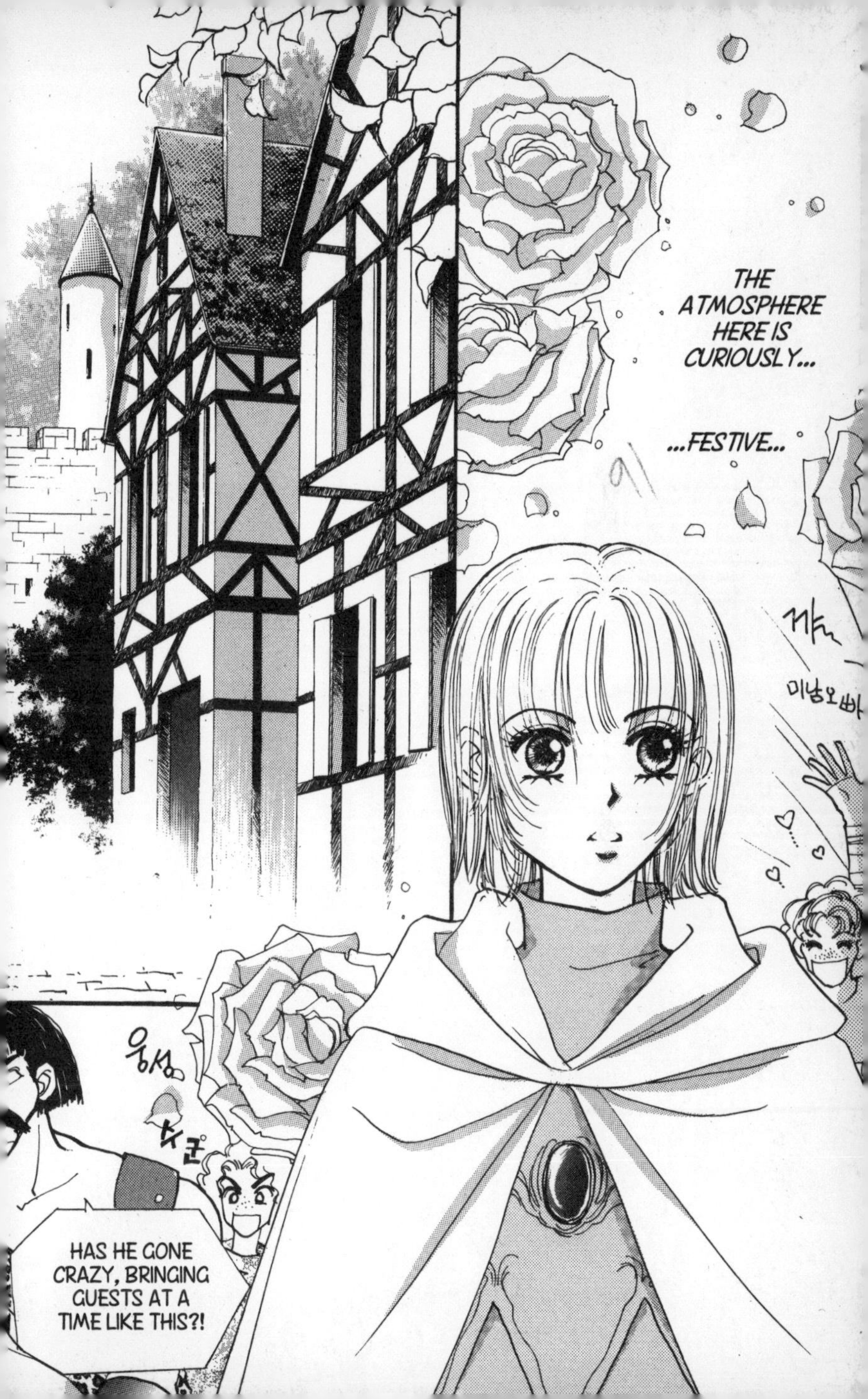
THE ATMOSPHERE HERE IS CURIOUSLY...
...FESTIVE...
꺄~
미남오빠
웅성
수군
HAS HE GONE CRAZY, BRINGING GUESTS AT A TIME LIKE THIS?!

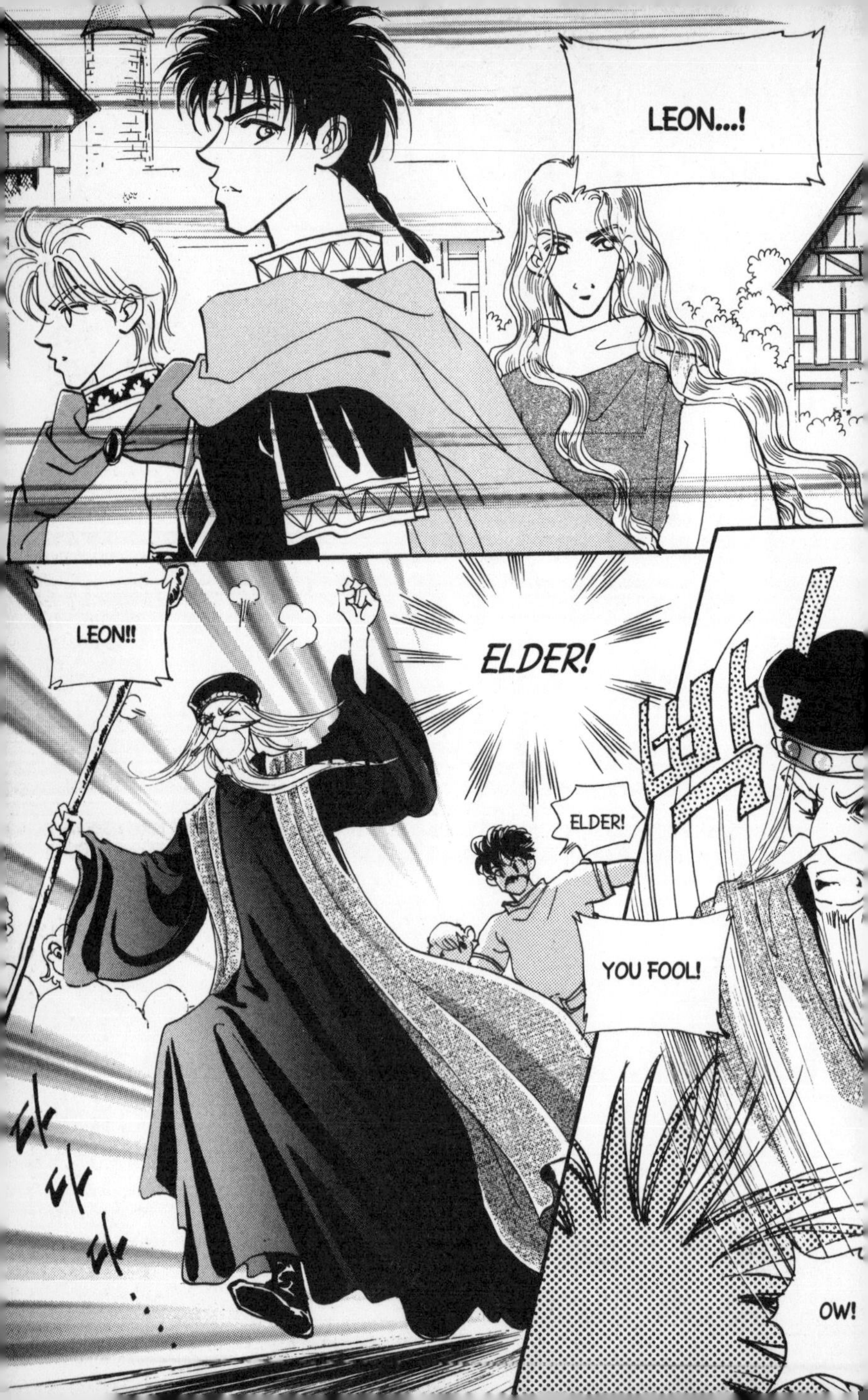
LEON...!
LEON!!
ELDER!
ELDER!
YOU FOOL!
OW!

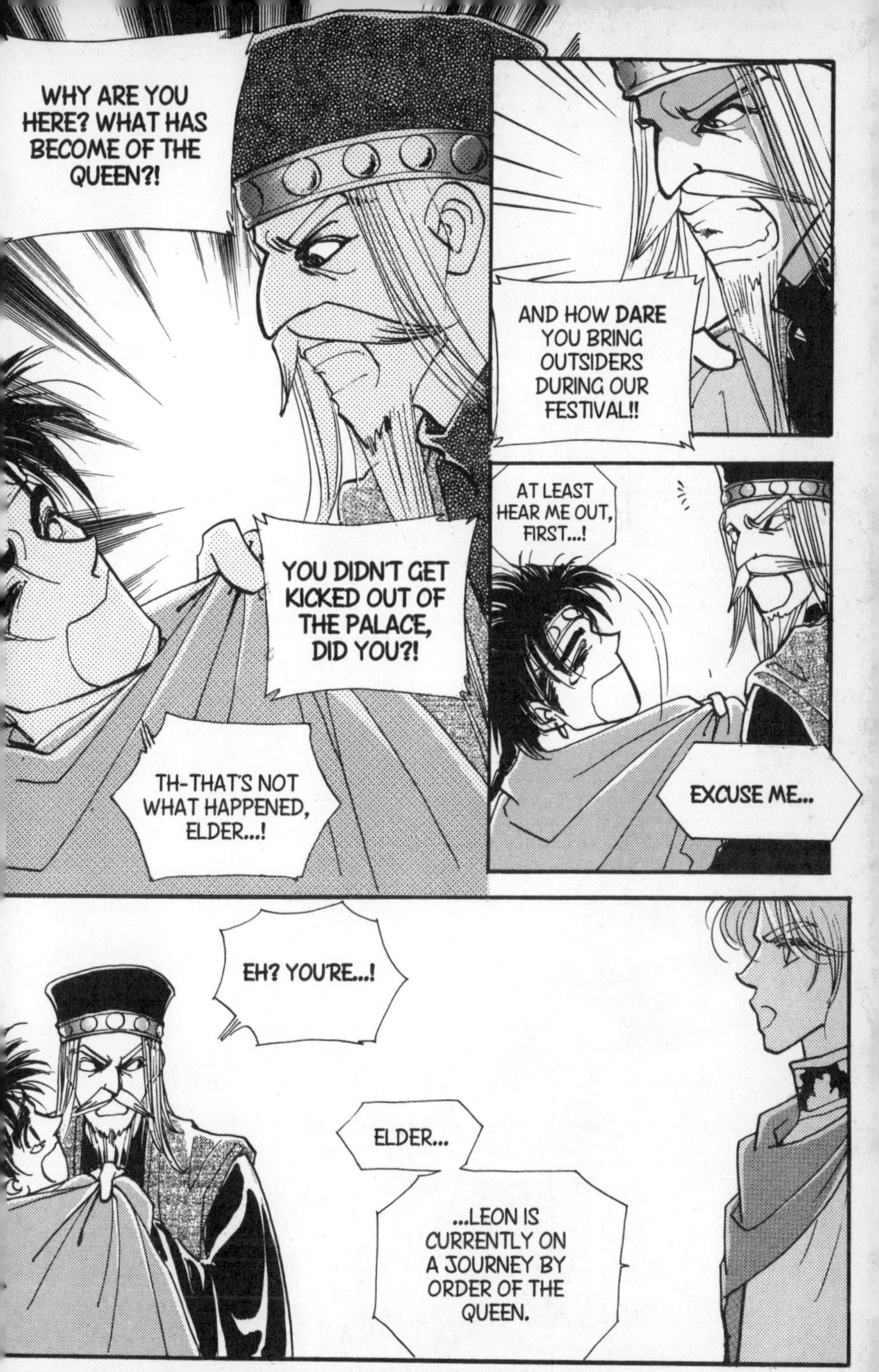
WHY ARE YOU HERE? WHAT HAS BECOME OF THE QUEEN?!
YOU DIDN'T GET KICKED OUT OF THE PALACE, DID YOU?!
TH-THAT'S NOT WHAT HAPPENED, ELDER...!
AND HOW DARE YOU BRING OUTSIDERS DURING OUR FESTIVAL!!
AT LEAST HEAR ME OUT, FIRST...!
EXCUSE ME...
EH? YOU'RE...!
ELDER...
...LEON IS CURRENTLY ON A JOURNEY BY ORDER OF THE QUEEN.

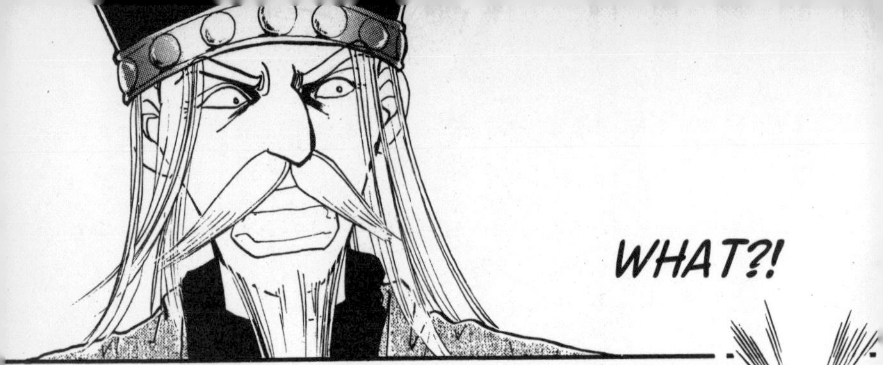
WHAT?!
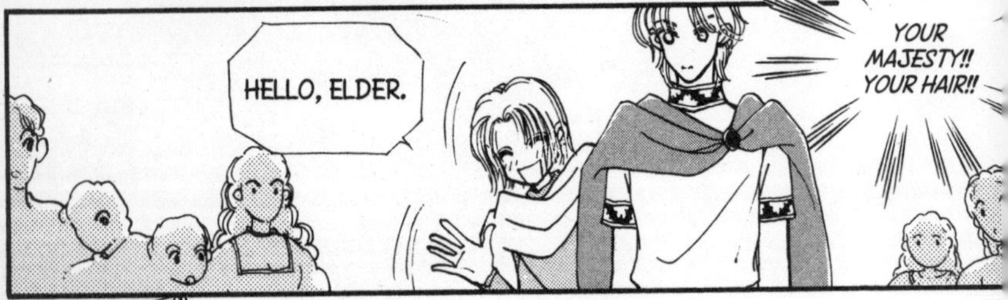
HELLO, ELDER.
YOUR MAJESTY!! YOUR HAIR!!
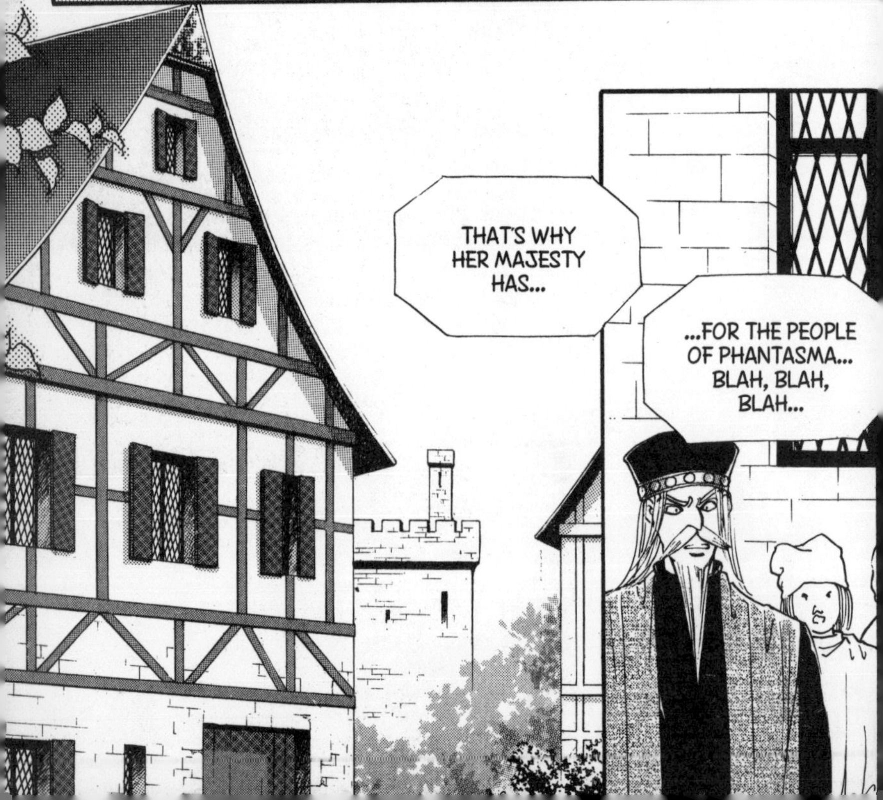
THAT'S WHY HER MAJESTY HAS...
...FOR THE PEOPLE OF PHANTASMA... BLAH, BLAH, BLAH...

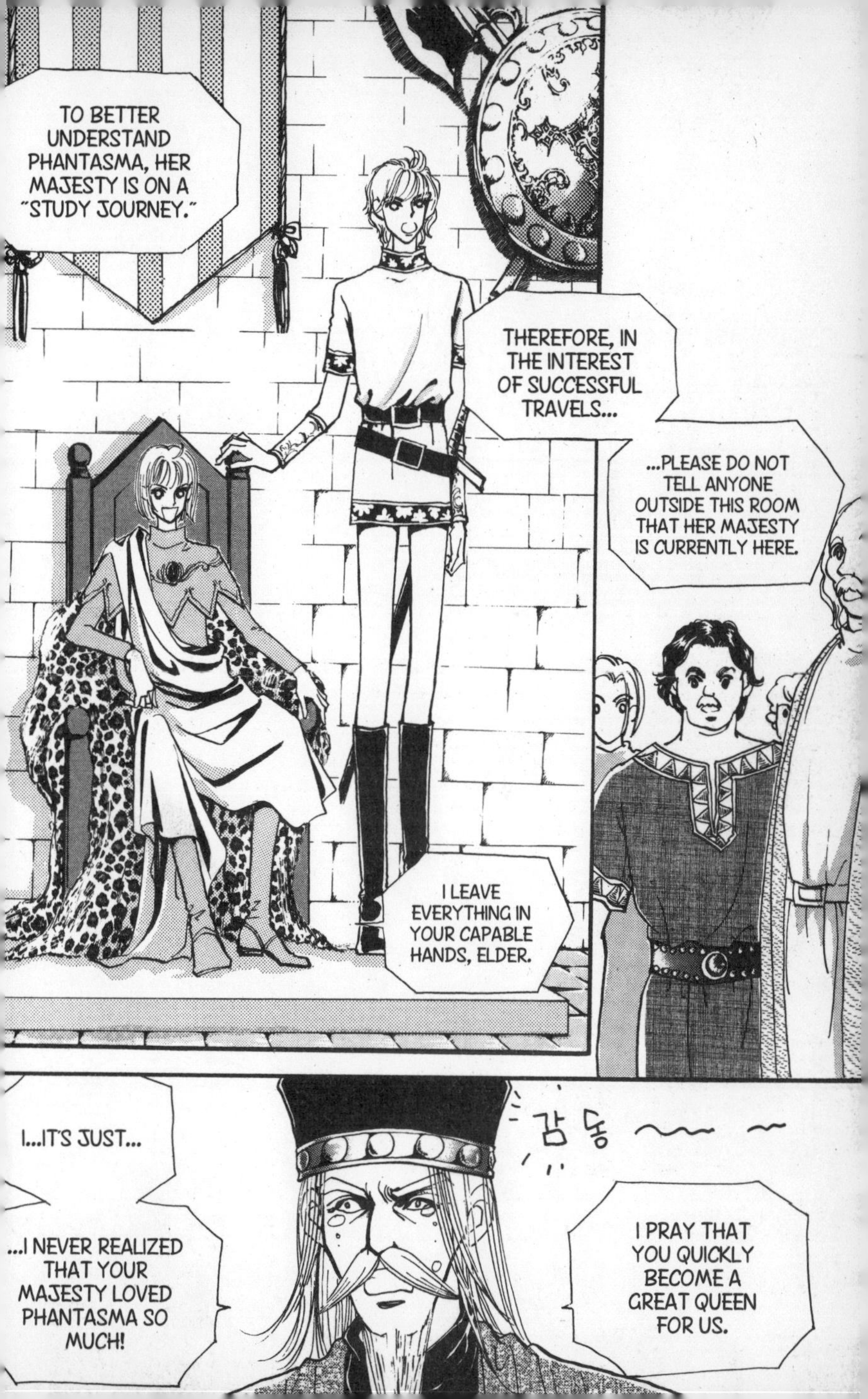
TO BETTER UNDERSTAND PHANTASMA, HER MAJESTY IS ON A "STUDY JOURNEY."
THEREFORE, IN THE INTEREST OF SUCCESSFUL TRAVELS...
...PLEASE DO NOT TELL ANYONE OUTSIDE THIS ROOM THAT HER MAJESTY IS CURRENTLY HERE.
I LEAVE EVERYTHING IN YOUR CAPABLE HANDS, ELDER.
I...IT'S JUST...
...I NEVER REALIZED THAT YOUR MAJESTY LOVED PHANTASMA SO MUCH!
감동
I PRAY THAT YOU QUICKLY BECOME A GREAT QUEEN FOR US.

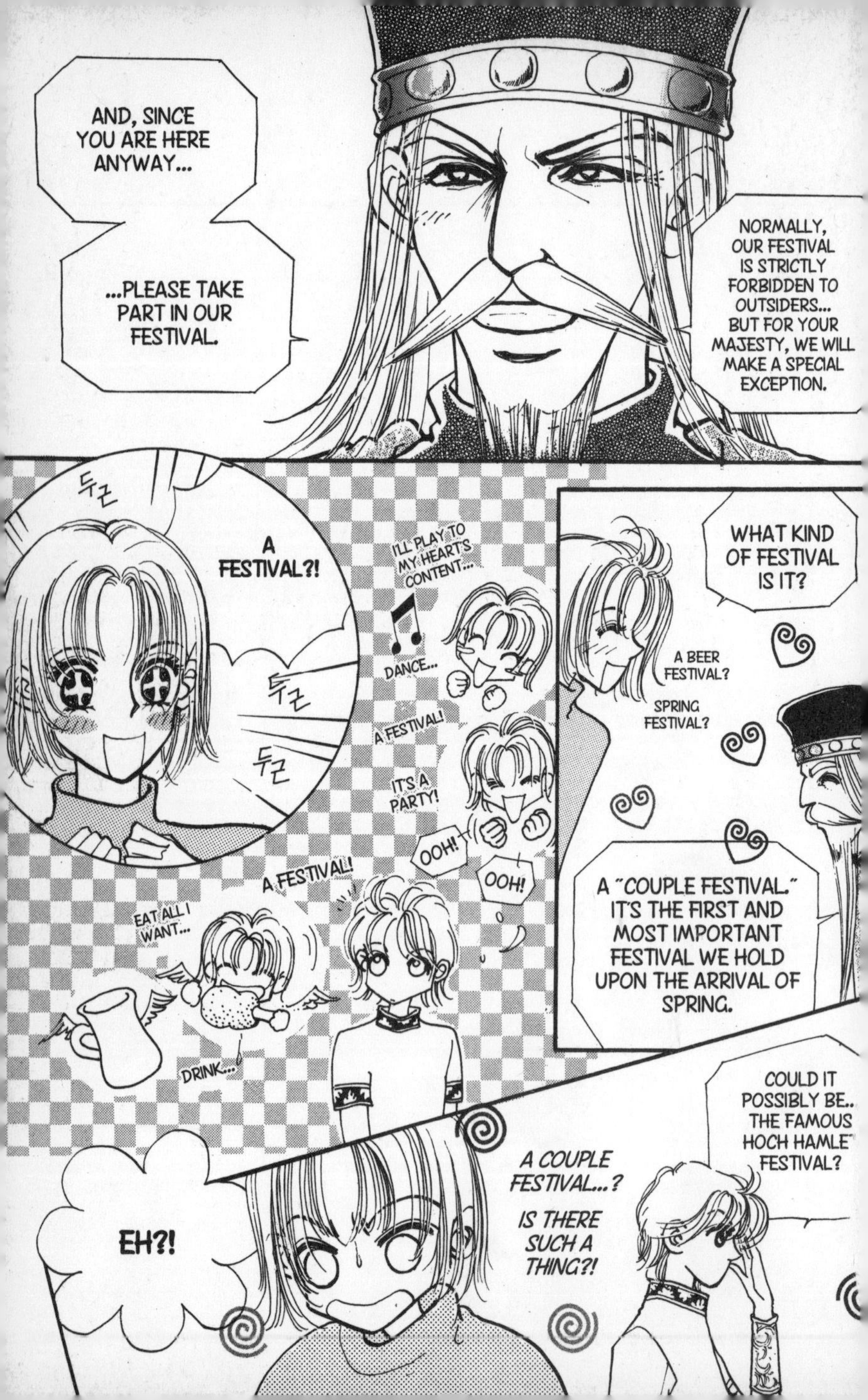
AND, SINCE YOU ARE HERE ANYWAY...
...PLEASE TAKE PART IN OUR FESTIVAL.
NORMALLY, OUR FESTIVAL IS STRICTLY FORBIDDEN TO OUTSIDERS... BUT FOR YOUR MAJESTY, WE WILL MAKE A SPECIAL EXCEPTION.
두근
A FESTIVAL?!
두근
두근
I'LL PLAY TO MY HEART'S CONTENT...
DANCE...
A FESTIVAL!
IT'S A PARTY!
OOH!
OOH!
A FESTIVAL!
EAT ALL I WANT...
DRINK...
WHAT KIND OF FESTIVAL IS IT?
A BEER FESTIVAL?
SPRING FESTIVAL?
A "COUPLE FESTIVAL." IT'S THE FIRST AND MOST IMPORTANT FESTIVAL WE HOLD UPON THE ARRIVAL OF SPRING.
EH?!
A COUPLE FESTIVAL...?
IS THERE SUCH A THING?!
COULD IT POSSIBLY BE.. THE FAMOUS HOCH HAMLE FESTIVAL?

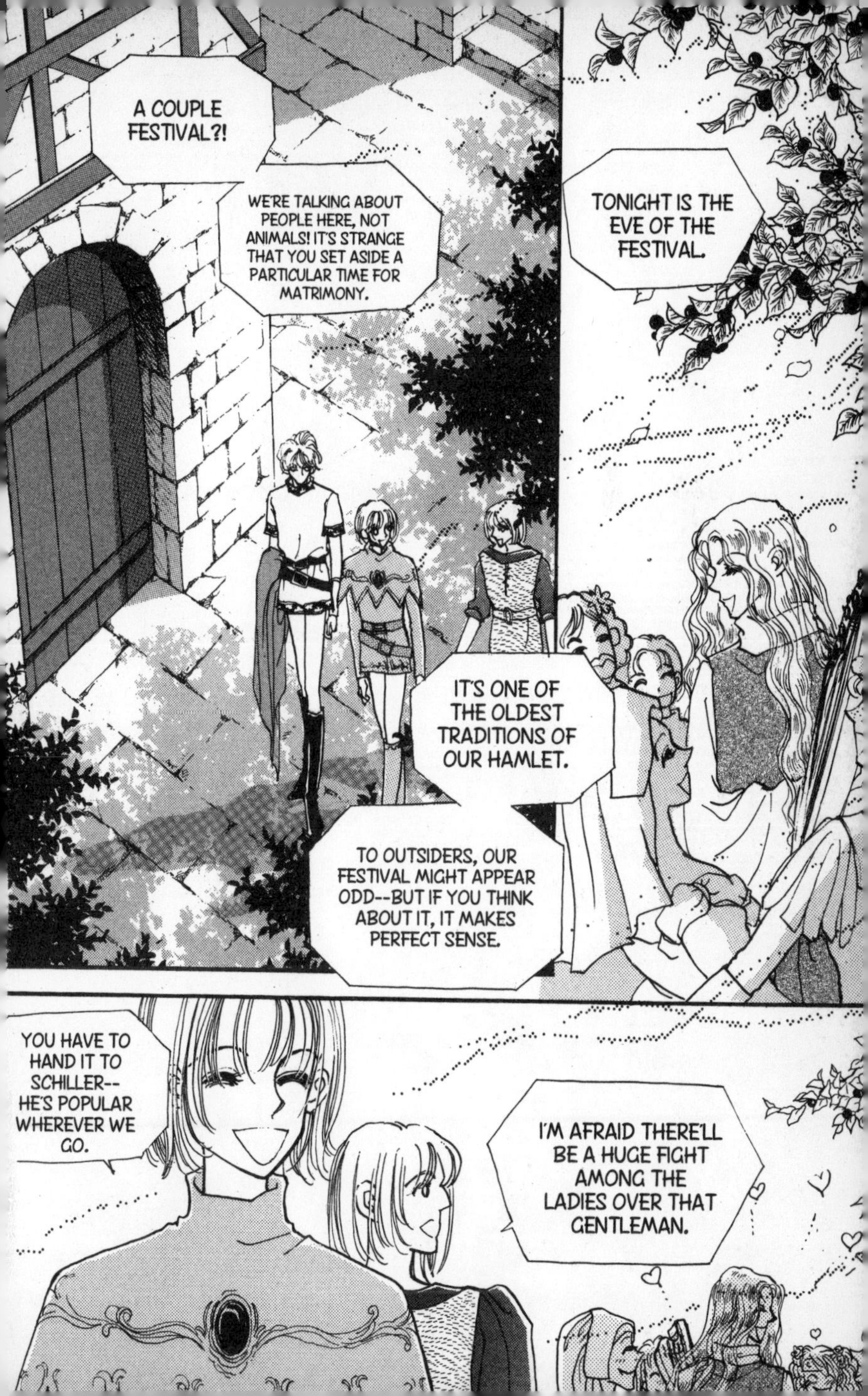
A COUPLE FESTIVAL?!
WE'RE TALKING ABOUT PEOPLE HERE, NOT ANIMALS! IT'S STRANGE THAT YOU SET ASIDE A PARTICULAR TIME FOR MATRIMONY.
TONIGHT IS THE EVE OF THE FESTIVAL.
IT'S ONE OF THE OLDEST TRADITIONS OF OUR HAMLET.
TO OUTSIDERS, OUR FESTIVAL MIGHT APPEAR ODD--BUT IF YOU THINK ABOUT IT, IT MAKES PERFECT SENSE.
YOU HAVE TO HAND IT TO SCHILLER-- HE'S POPULAR WHEREVER WE GO.
I'M AFRAID THERE'LL BE A HUGE FIGHT AMONG THE LADIES OVER THAT GENTLEMAN.

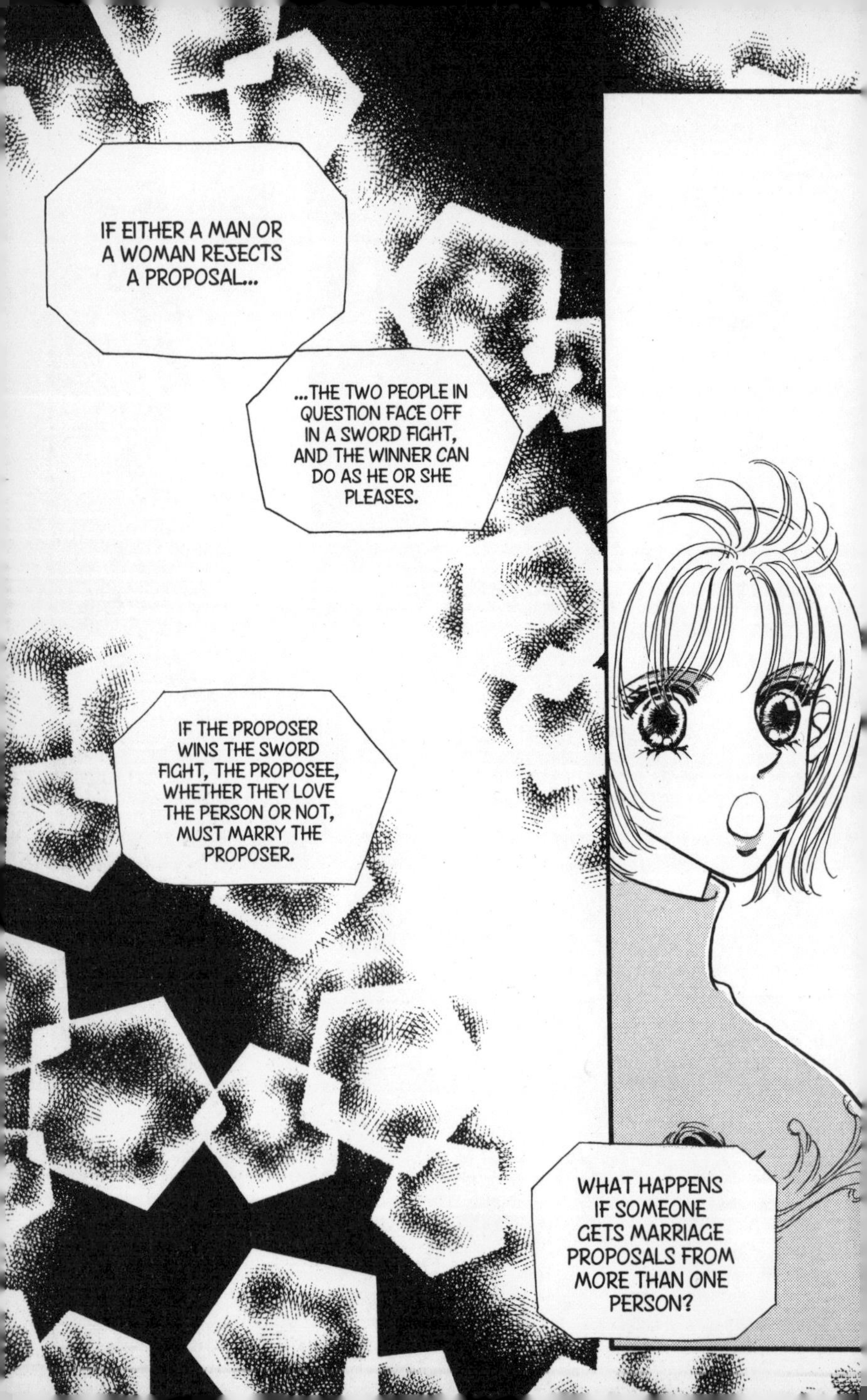
IF EITHER A MAN OR A WOMAN REJECTS A PROPOSAL...
...THE TWO PEOPLE IN QUESTION FACE OFF IN A SWORD FIGHT, AND THE WINNER CAN DO AS HE OR SHE PLEASES.
IF THE PROPOSER WINS THE SWORD FIGHT, THE PROPOSEE, WHETHER THEY LOVE THE PERSON OR NOT, MUST MARRY THE PROPOSER.
WHAT HAPPENS IF SOMEONE GETS MARRIAGE PROPOSALS FROM MORE THAN ONE PERSON?

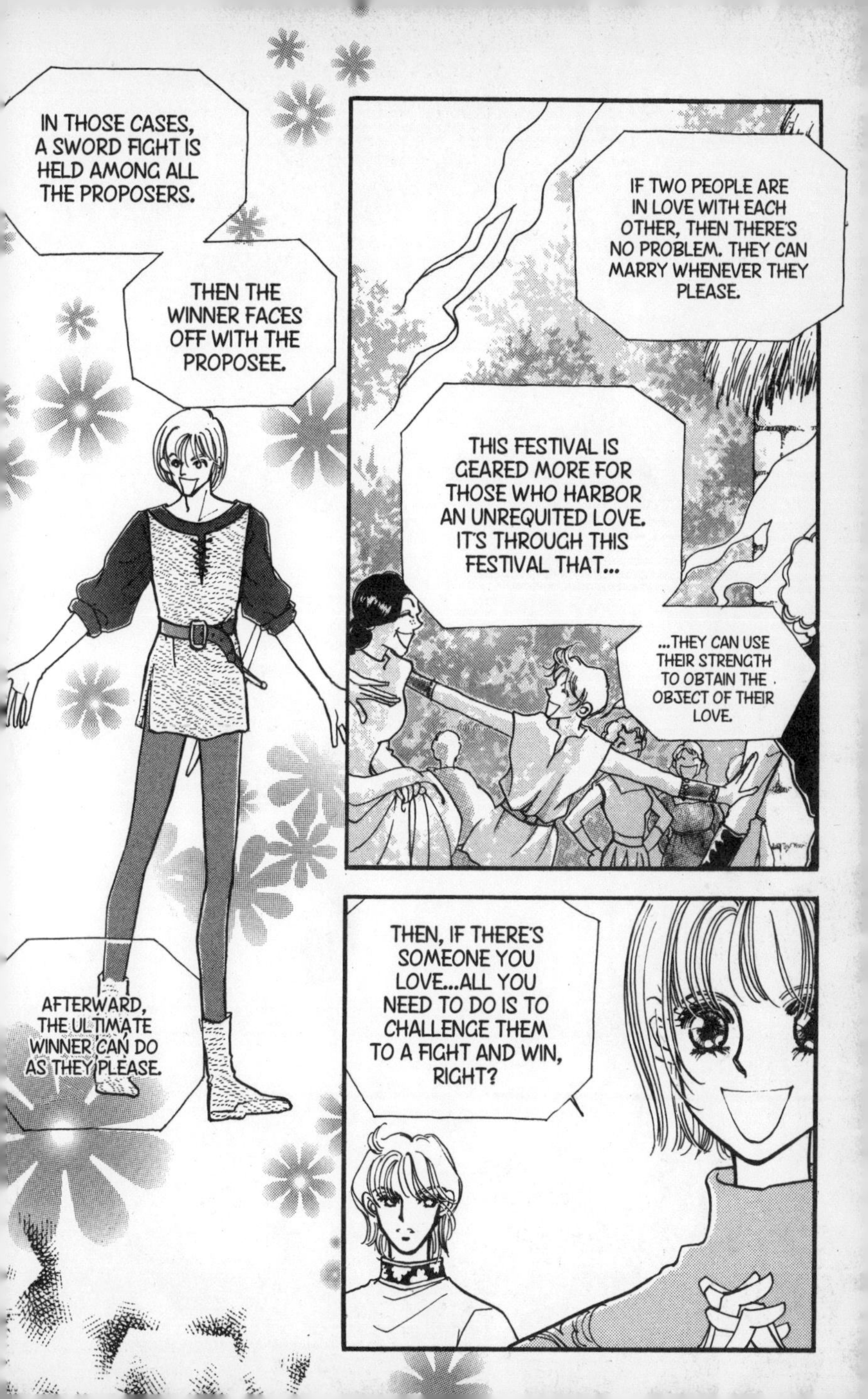

IN THOSE CASES, A SWORD FIGHT IS HELD AMONG ALL THE PROPOSERS.
THEN THE WINNER FACES OFF WITH THE PROPOSEE.
AFTERWARD, THE ULTIMATE WINNER CAN DO AS THEY PLEASE.
IF TWO PEOPLE ARE IN LOVE WITH EACH OTHER, THEN THERE'S NO PROBLEM. THEY CAN MARRY WHENEVER THEY PLEASE.
THIS FESTIVAL IS GEARED MORE FOR THOSE WHO HARBOR AN UNREQUITED LOVE. IT'S THROUGH THIS FESTIVAL THAT...
...THEY CAN USE THEIR STRENGTH TO OBTAIN THE OBJECT OF THEIR LOVE.
THEN, IF THERE'S SOMEONE YOU LOVE...ALL YOU NEED TO DO IS TO CHALLENGE THEM TO A FIGHT AND WIN, RIGHT?

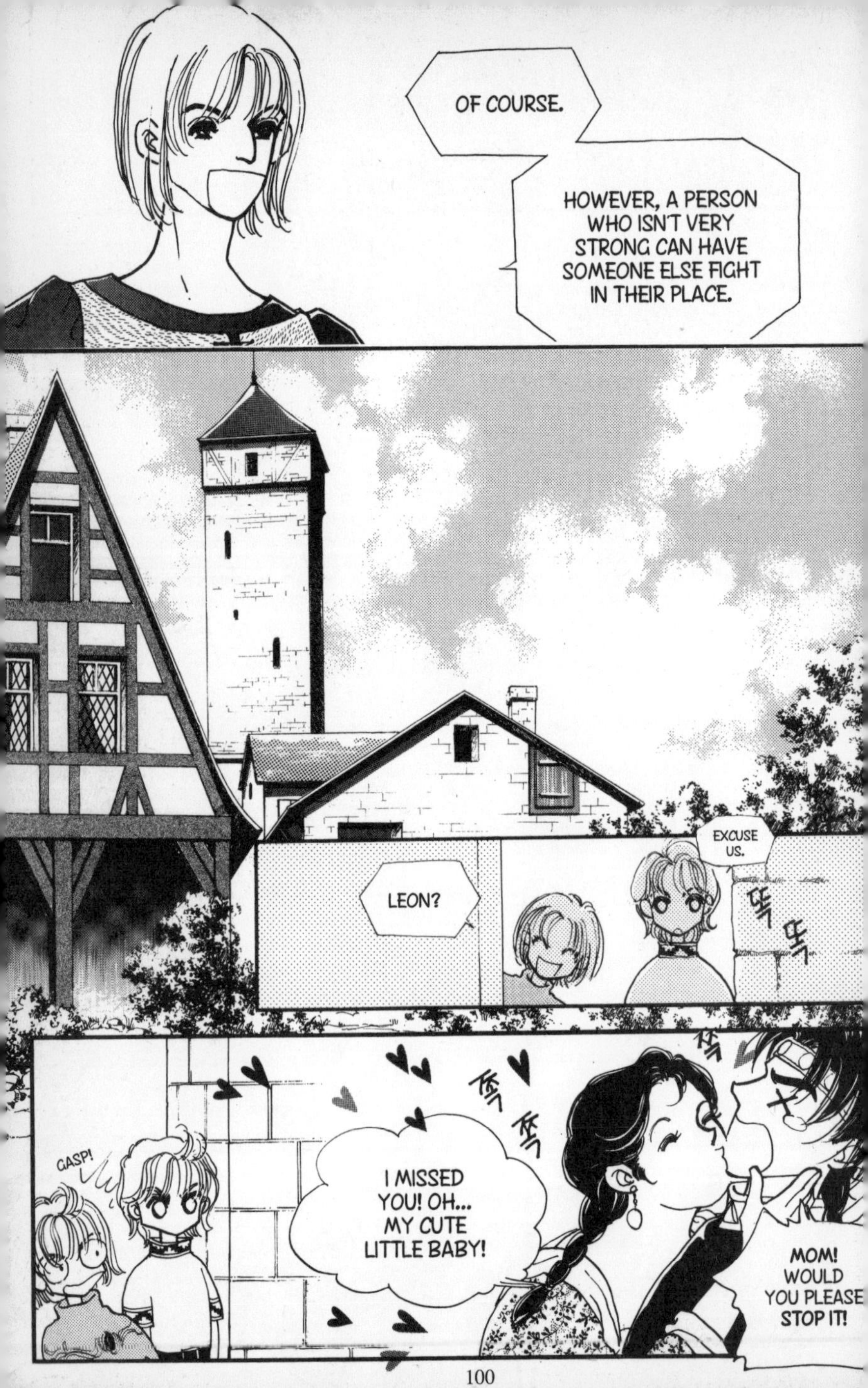
OF COURSE.
HOWEVER, A PERSON WHO ISN'T VERY STRONG CAN HAVE SOMEONE ELSE FIGHT IN THEIR PLACE.
LEON?
EXCUSE US.
똑 똑
GASP!
I MISSED YOU! OH... MY CUTE LITTLE BABY!
쪽 쪽
쪽
MOM! WOULD YOU PLEASE STOP IT!

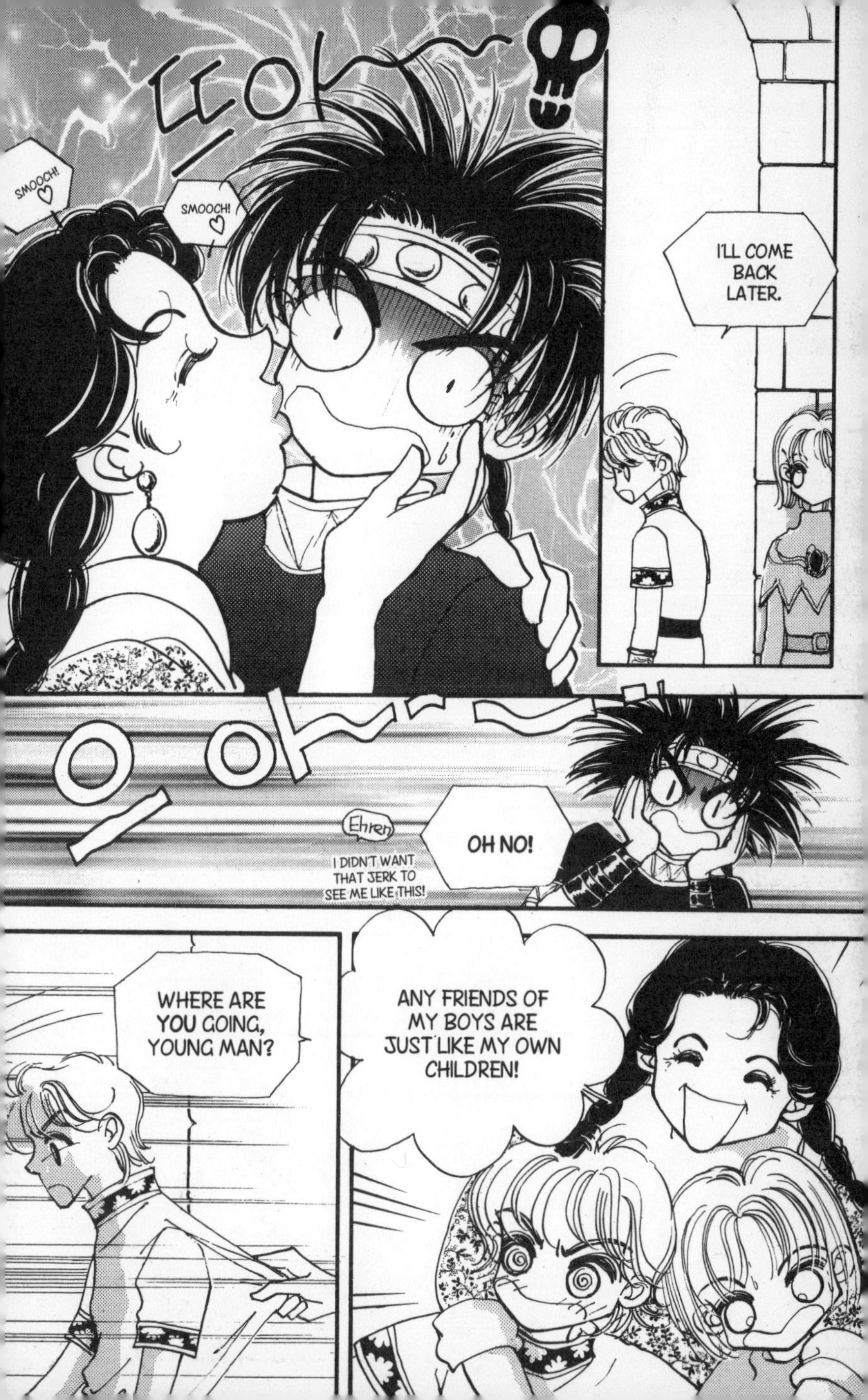
SMOOCH! ♡
SMOOCH! ♡
EEOK~
I'LL COME BACK LATER.
OOK~~!
Ehren
I DIDN'T WANT THAT JERK TO SEE ME LIKE THIS!
OH NO!
WHERE ARE YOU GOING, YOUNG MAN?
ANY FRIENDS OF MY BOYS ARE JUST LIKE MY OWN CHILDREN!

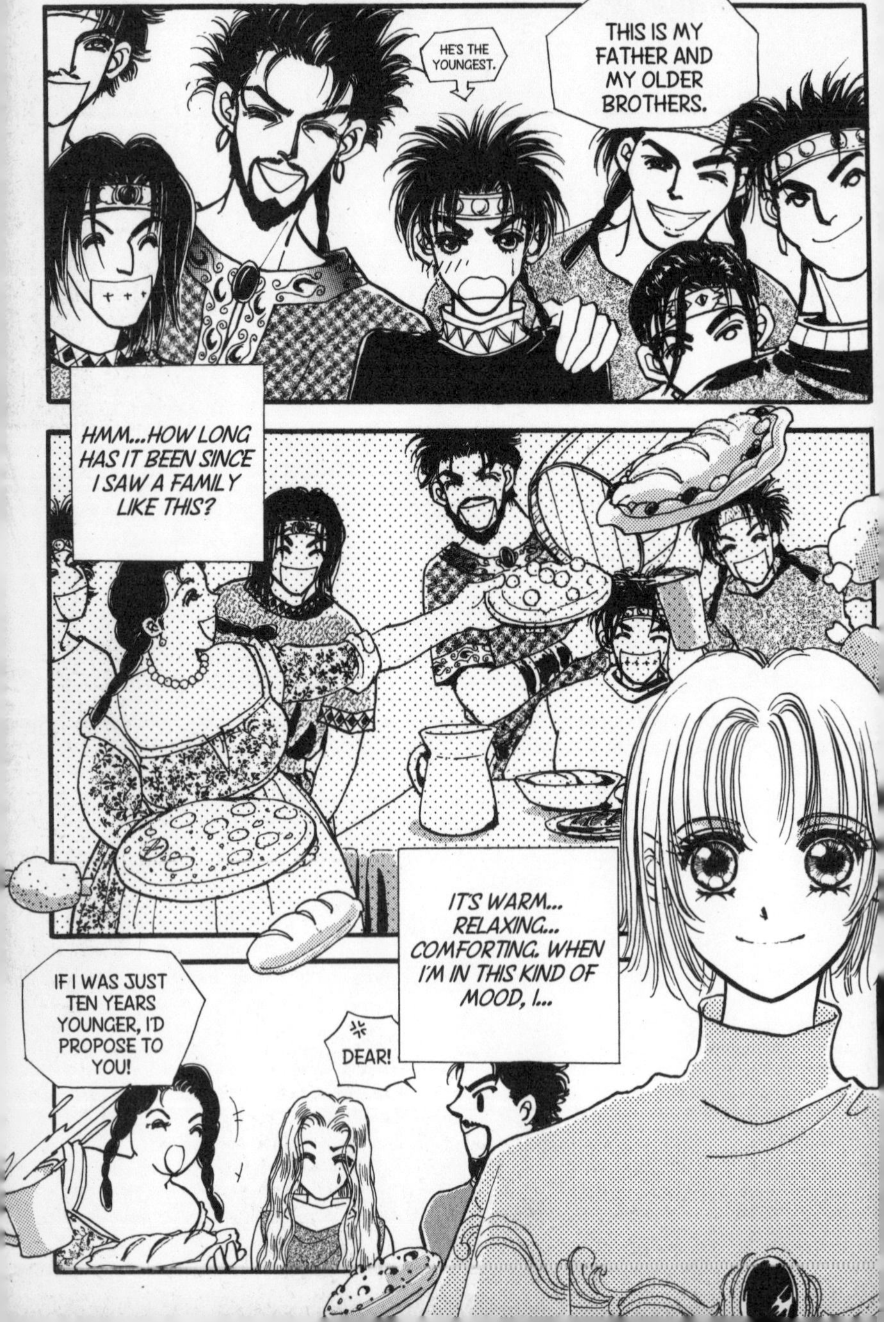
HE'S THE YOUNGEST.
THIS IS MY FATHER AND MY OLDER BROTHERS.
HMM...HOW LONG HAS IT BEEN SINCE I SAW A FAMILY LIKE THIS?
IT'S WARM... RELAXING... COMFORTING. WHEN I'M IN THIS KIND OF MOOD, I...
IF I WAS JUST TEN YEARS YOUNGER, I'D PROPOSE TO YOU!
DEAR!

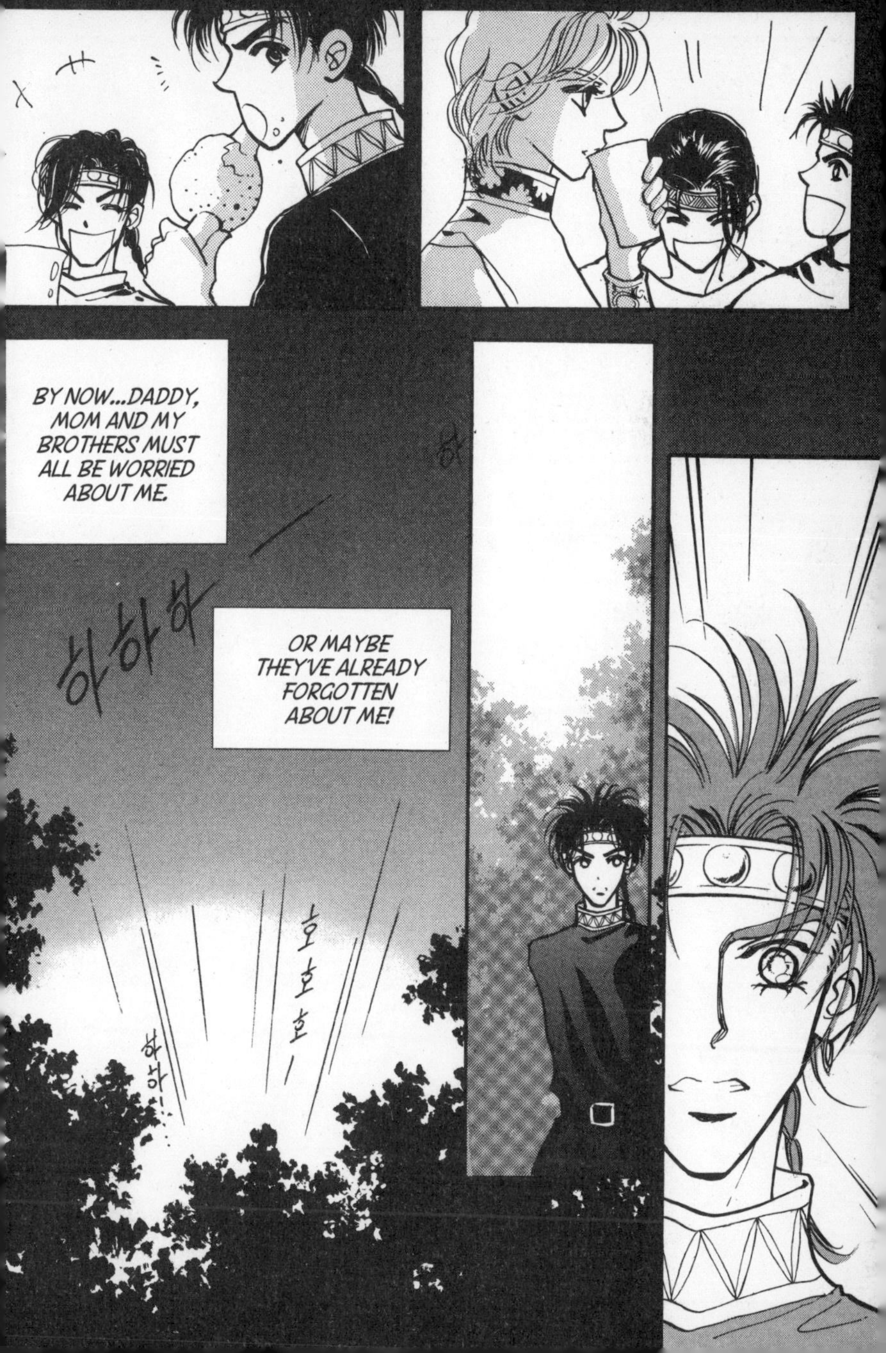
BY NOW...DADDY, MOM AND MY BROTHERS MUST ALL BE WORRIED ABOUT ME.
OR MAYBE THEY'VE ALREADY FORGOTTEN ABOUT ME!
하하하
호호호

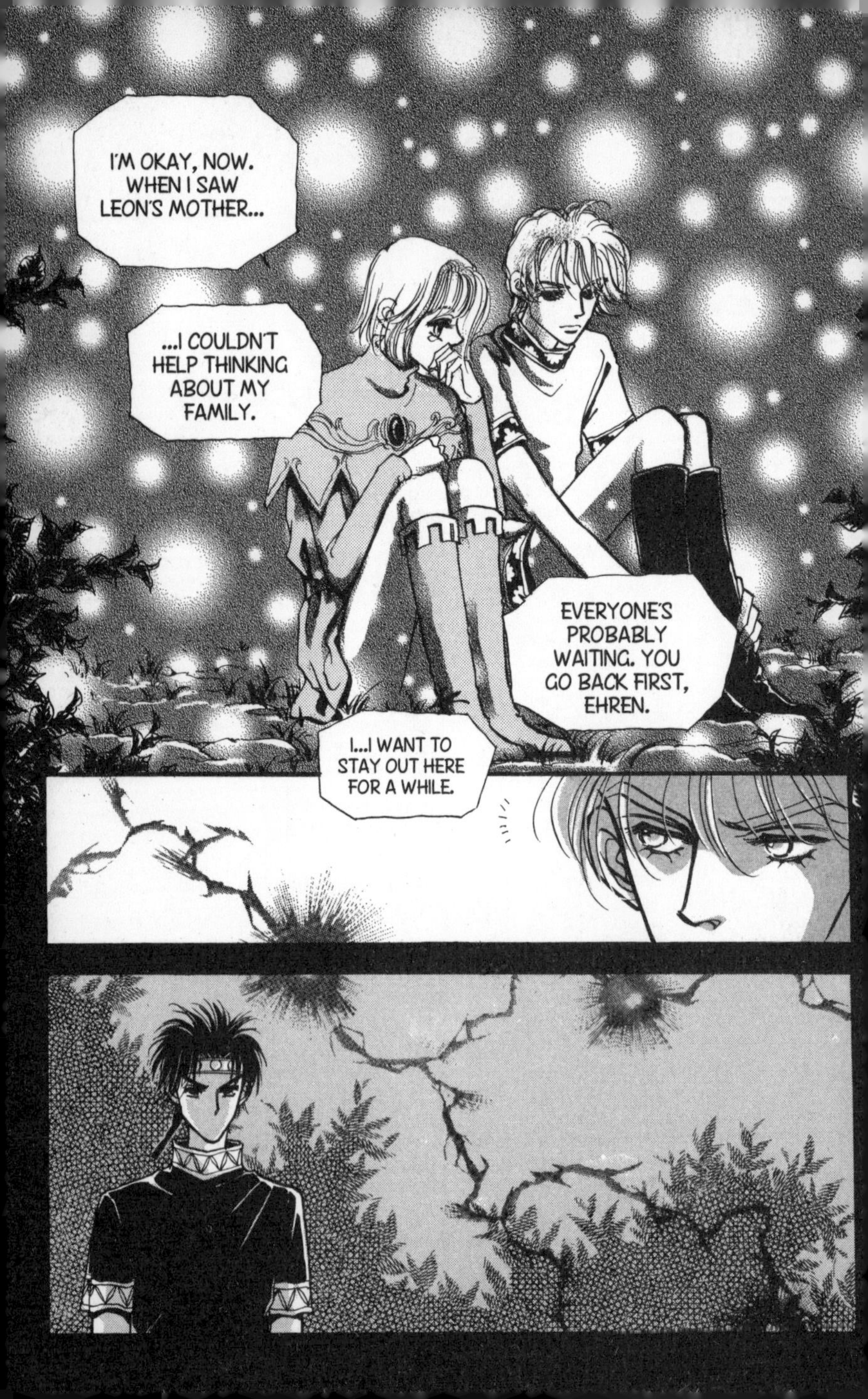
I'M OKAY, NOW. WHEN I SAW LEON'S MOTHER...
...I COULDN'T HELP THINKING ABOUT MY FAMILY.
EVERYONE'S PROBABLY WAITING. YOU GO BACK FIRST, EHREN.
I...I WANT TO STAY OUT HERE FOR A WHILE.

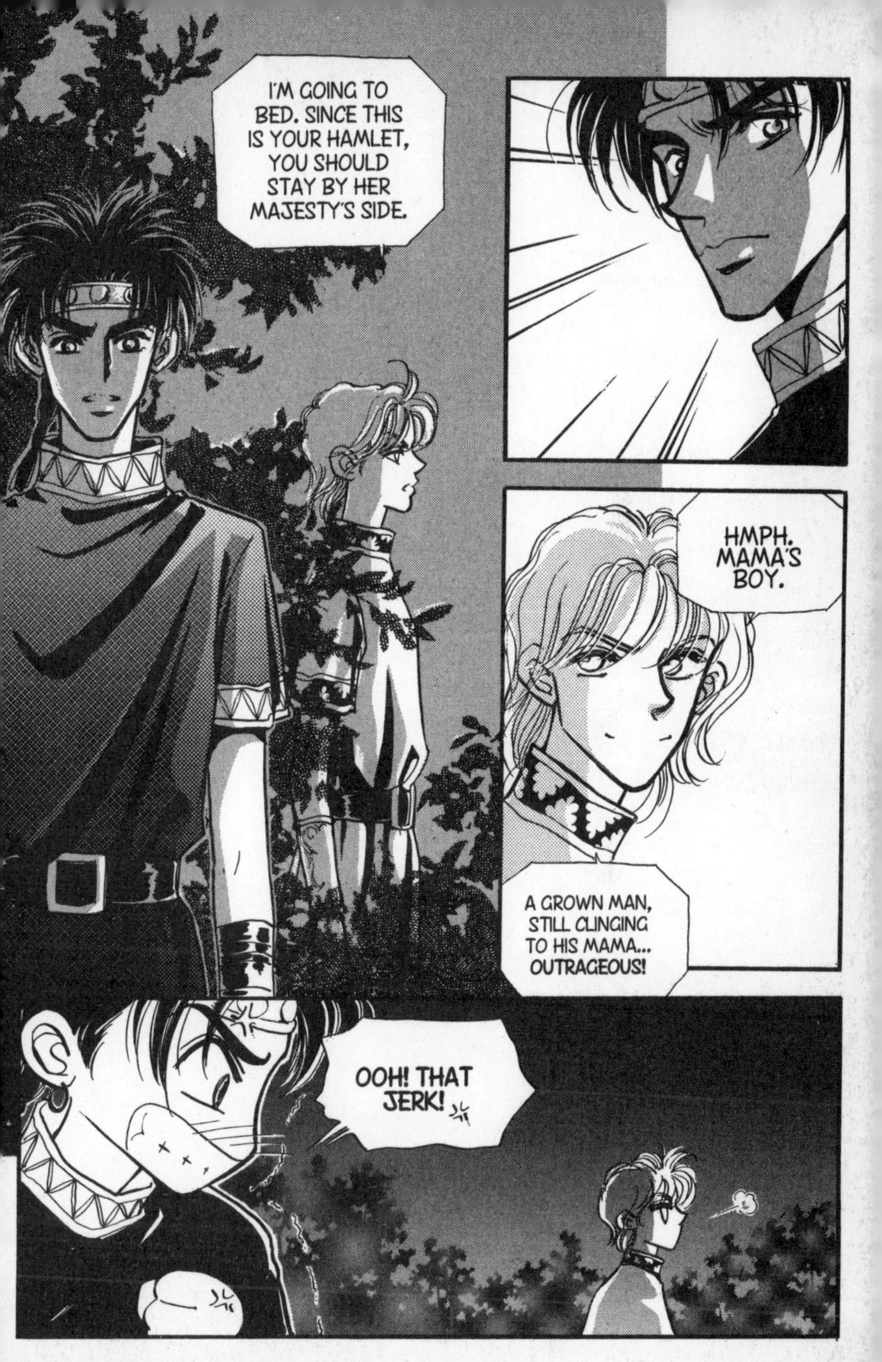
I'M GOING TO BED. SINCE THIS IS YOUR HAMLET, YOU SHOULD STAY BY HER MAJESTY'S SIDE.
HMPH. MAMA'S BOY.
A GROWN MAN, STILL CLINGING TO HIS MAMA... OUTRAGEOUS!
OOH! THAT JERK!

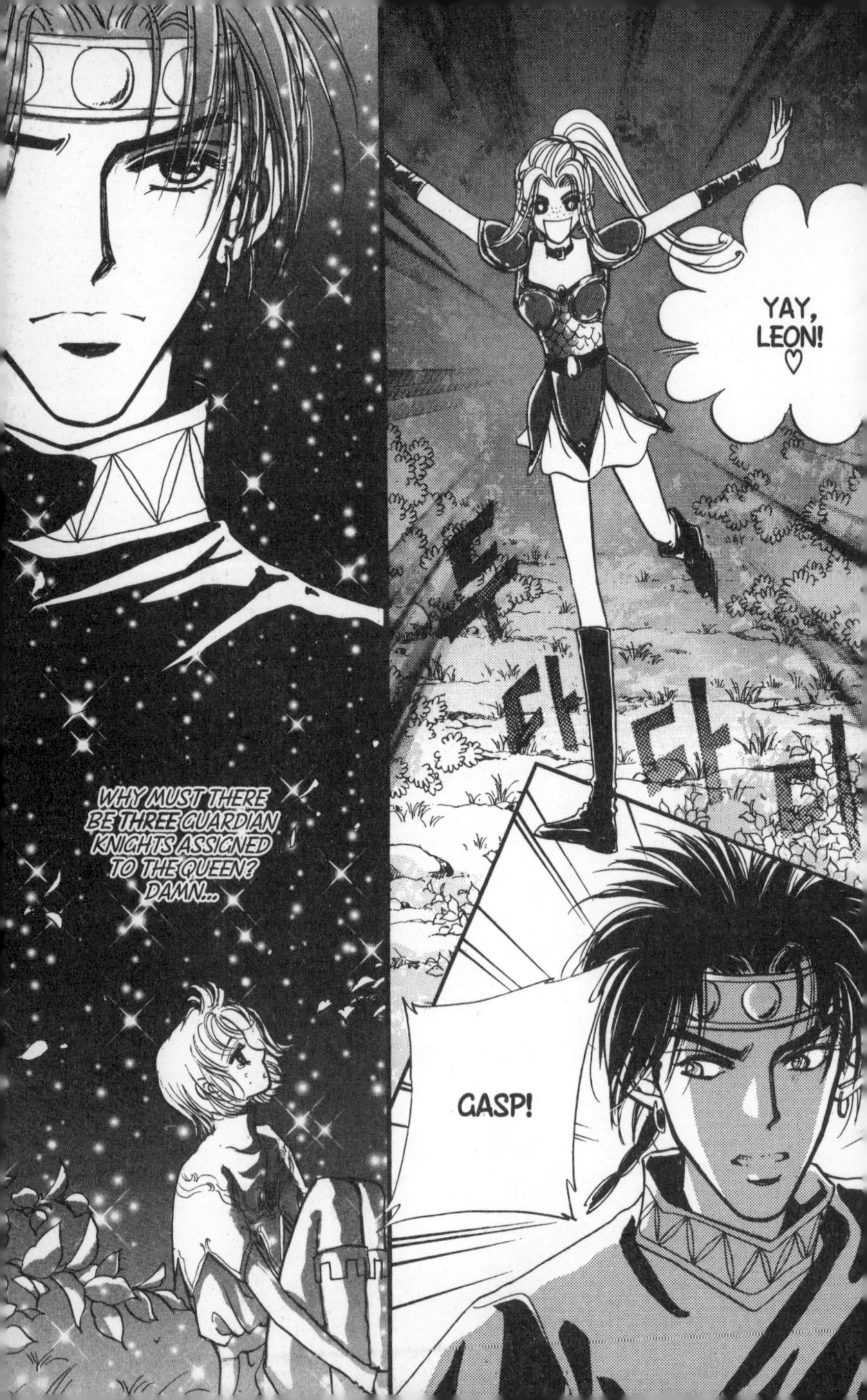
WHY MUST THERE BE THREE GUARDIAN KNIGHTS ASSIGNED TO THE QUEEN? DAMN...
YAY, LEON! ♡
GASP!

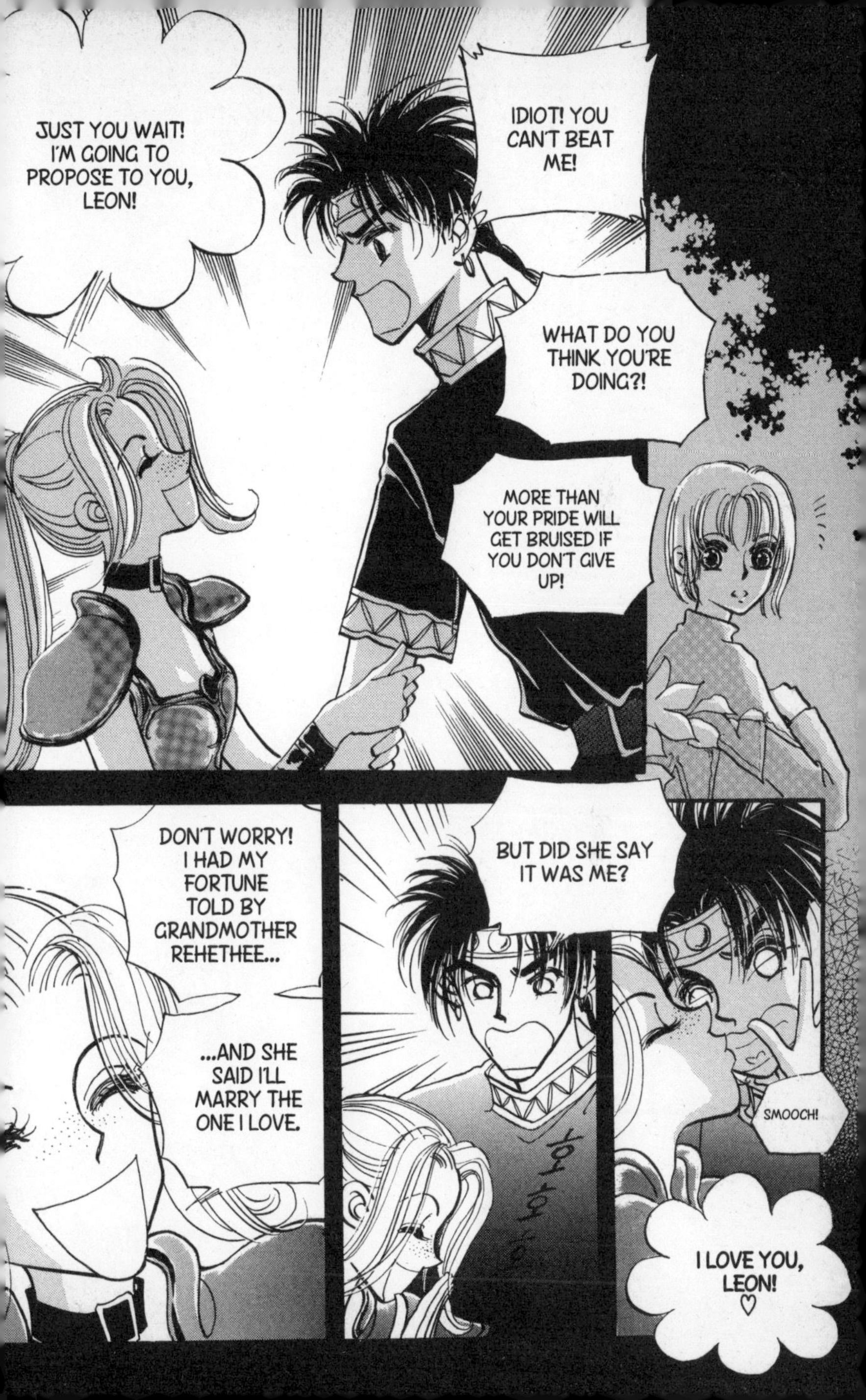
JUST YOU WAIT! I'M GOING TO PROPOSE TO YOU, LEON!
IDIOT! YOU CAN'T BEAT ME!
WHAT DO YOU THINK YOU'RE DOING?!
MORE THAN YOUR PRIDE WILL GET BRUISED IF YOU DON'T GIVE UP!
DON'T WORRY! I HAD MY FORTUNE TOLD BY GRANDMOTHER REHETHEE...
...AND SHE SAID I'LL MARRY THE ONE I LOVE.
BUT DID SHE SAY IT WAS ME?
SMOOCH!
I LOVE YOU, LEON! ♡

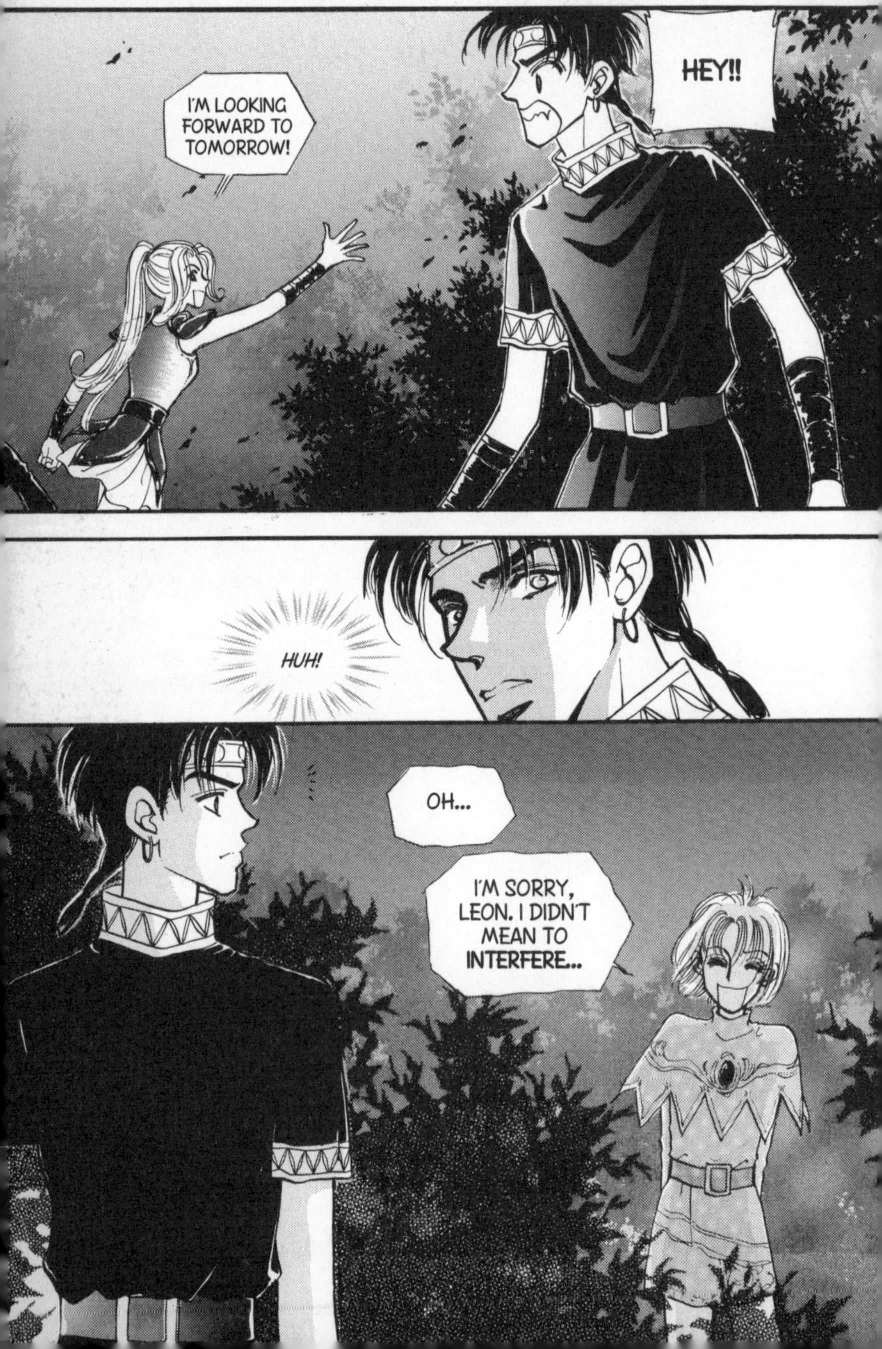
I'M LOOKING FORWARD TO TOMORROW!
HEY!!
HUH!
OH...
I'M SORRY, LEON. I DIDN'T MEAN TO INTERFERE...

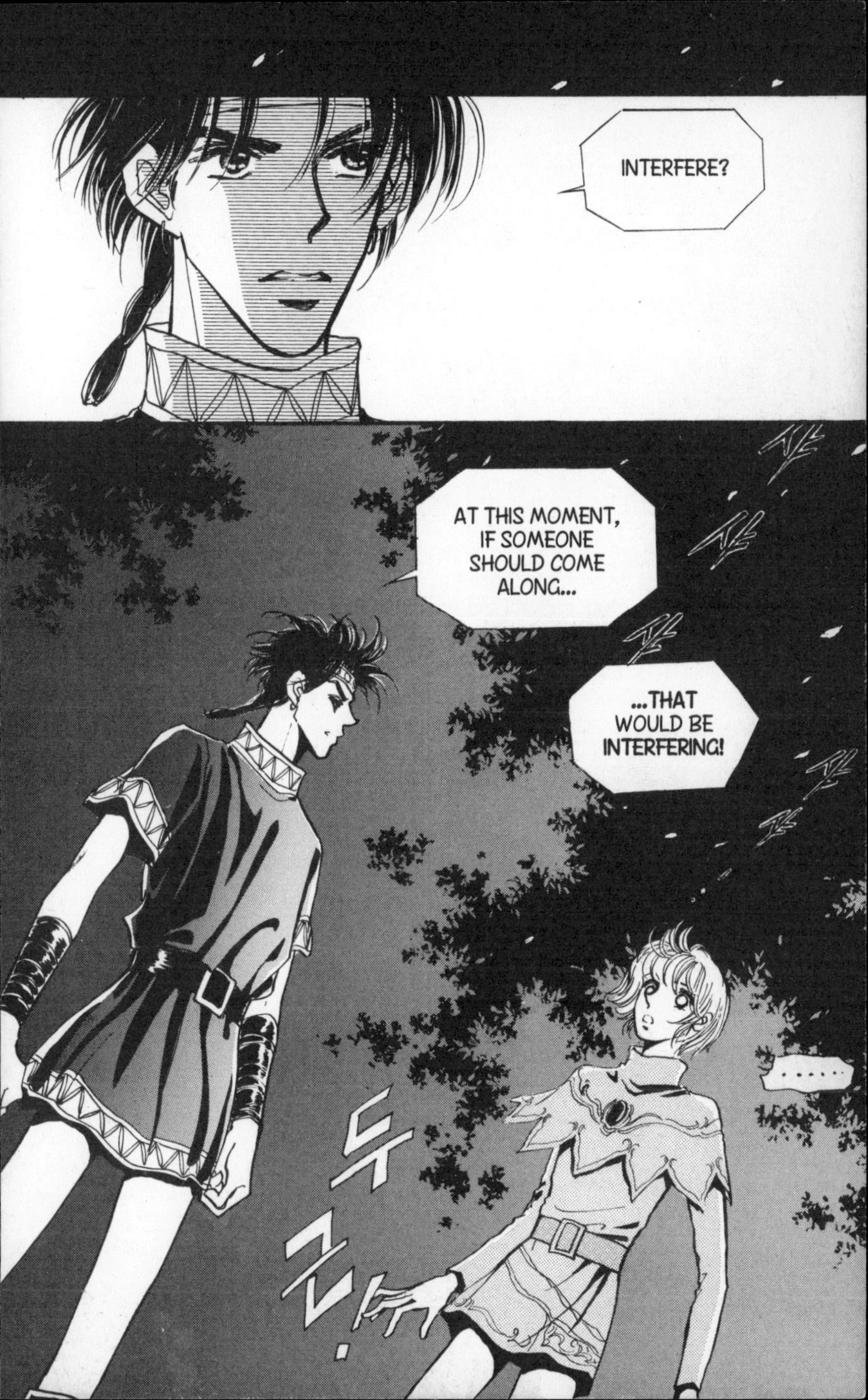
INTERFERE?
AT THIS MOMENT, IF SOMEONE SHOULD COME ALONG...
...THAT WOULD BE INTERFERING!
......

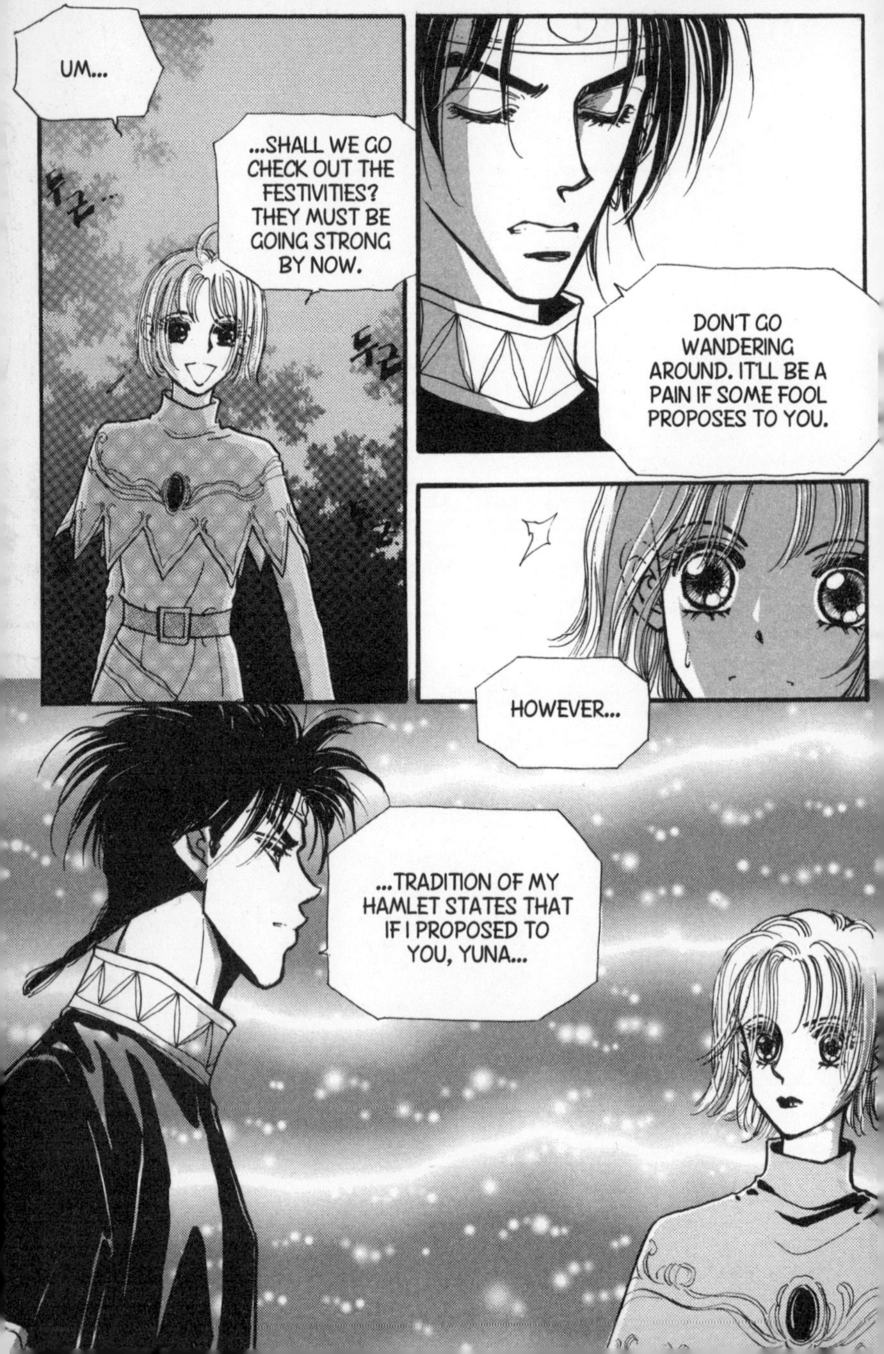
UM...
...SHALL WE GO CHECK OUT THE FESTIVITIES? THEY MUST BE GOING STRONG BY NOW.
DON'T GO WANDERING AROUND. IT'LL BE A PAIN IF SOME FOOL PROPOSES TO YOU.
HOWEVER...
...TRADITION OF MY HAMLET STATES THAT IF I PROPOSED TO YOU, YUNA...

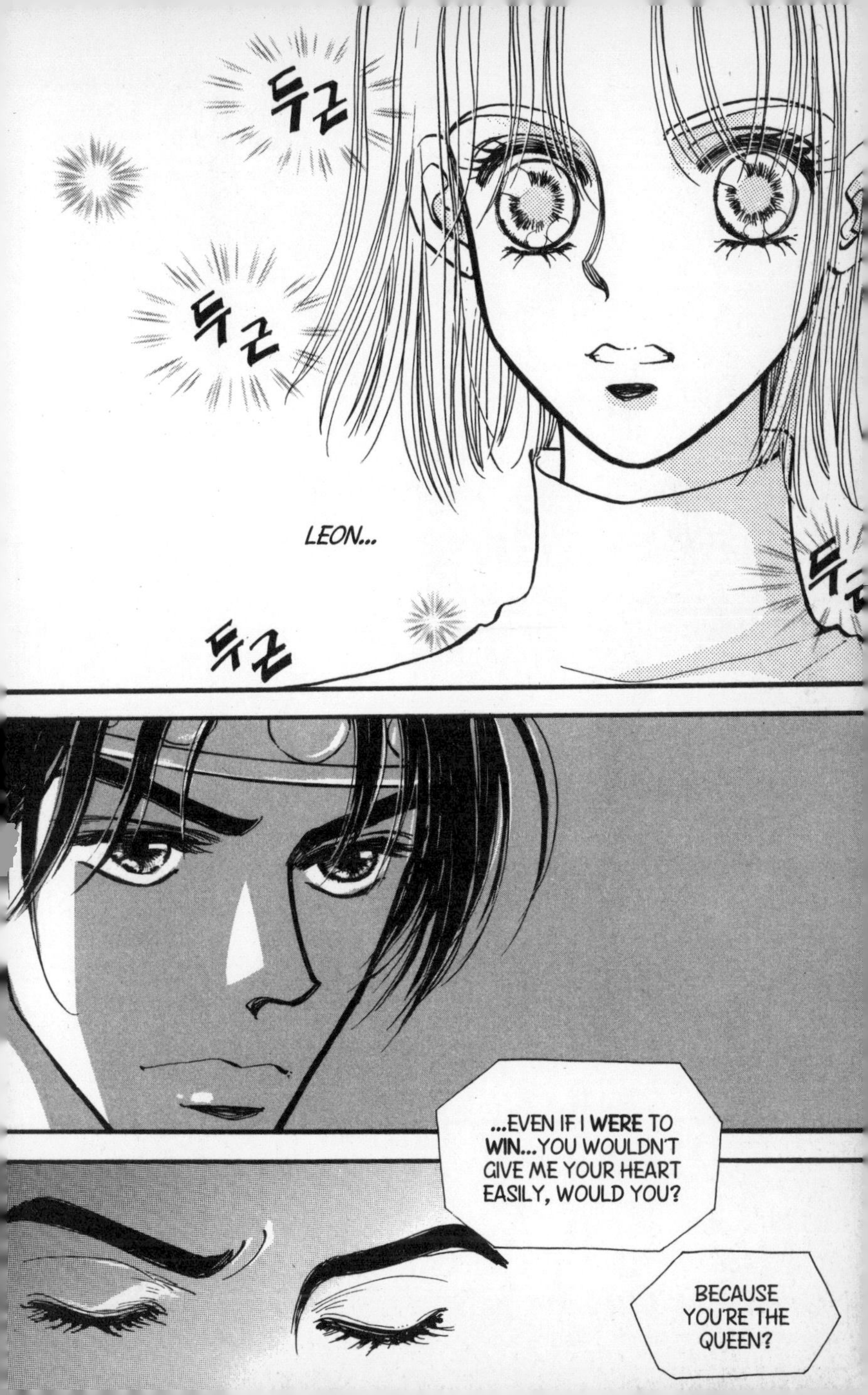
두근
두근
LEON...
두근
두근
...EVEN IF I WERE TO WIN...YOU WOULDN'T GIVE ME YOUR HEART EASILY, WOULD YOU?
BECAUSE YOU'RE THE QUEEN?

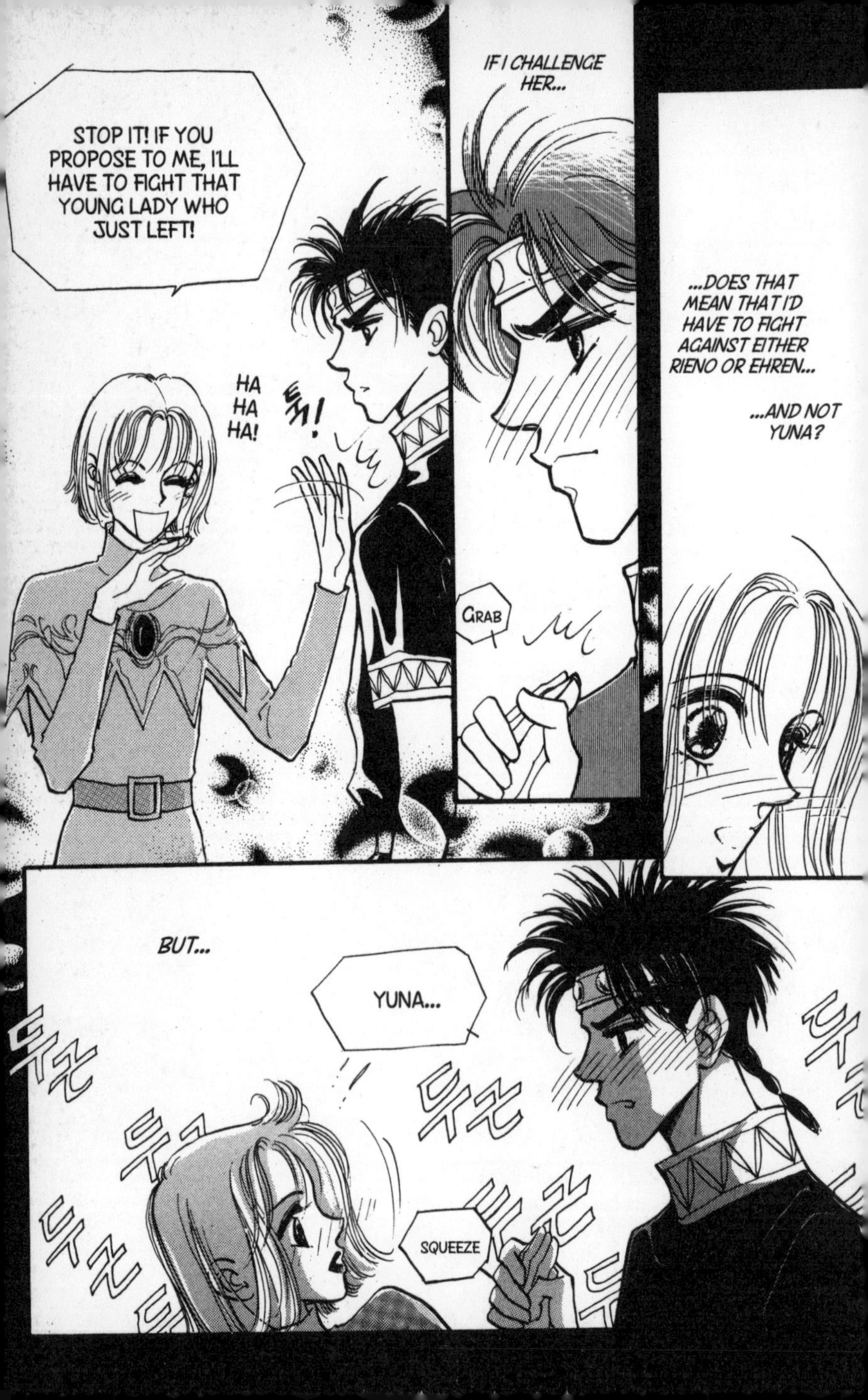
STOP IT! IF YOU PROPOSE TO ME, I'LL HAVE TO FIGHT THAT YOUNG LADY WHO JUST LEFT!
HA HA HA!
IF I CHALLENGE HER...
GRAB
...DOES THAT MEAN THAT I'D HAVE TO FIGHT AGAINST EITHER RIENO OR EHREN...
...AND NOT YUNA?
BUT...
YUNA...
SQUEEZE

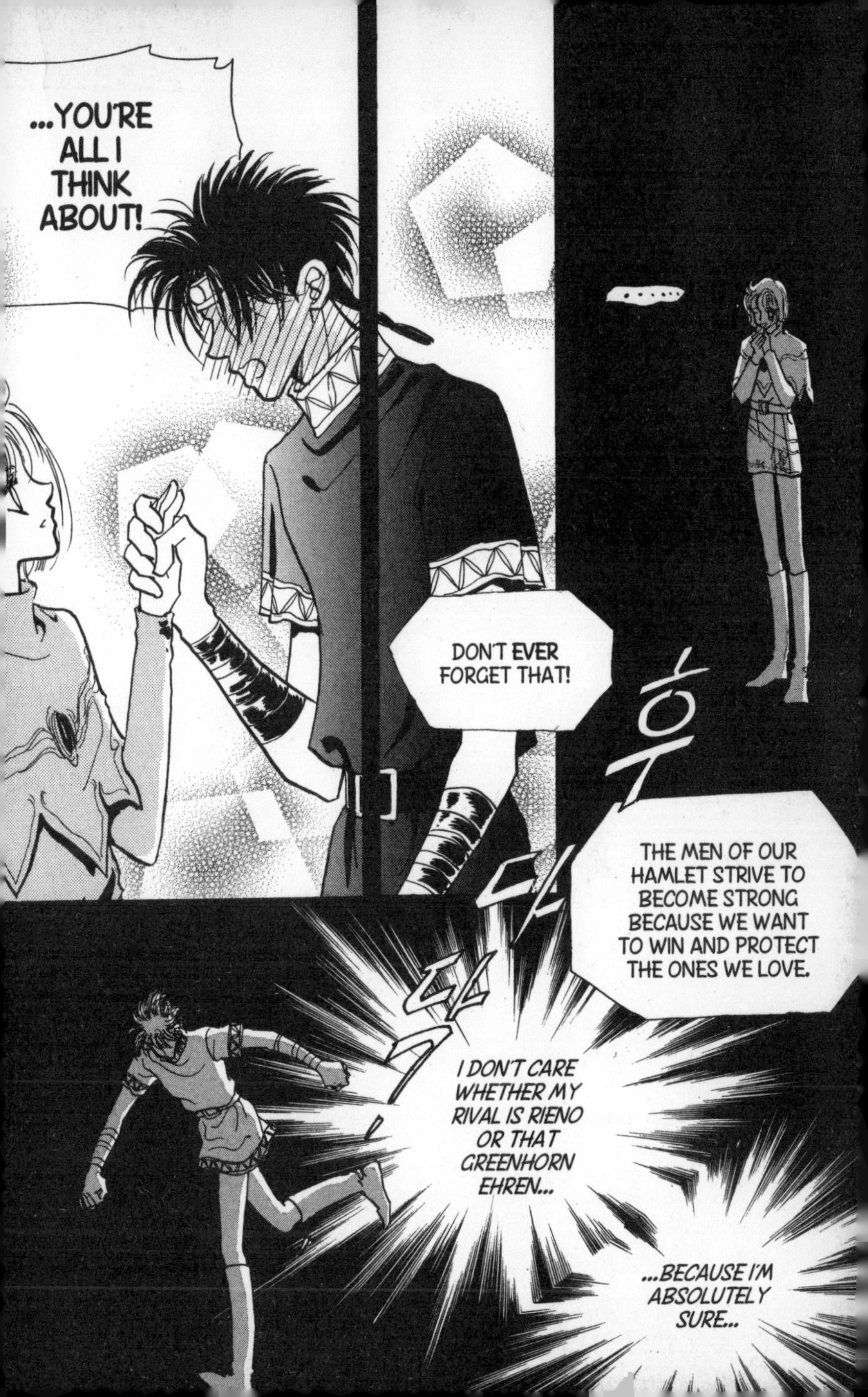
...YOU'RE ALL I THINK ABOUT!
DON'T EVER FORGET THAT!
......
THE MEN OF OUR HAMLET STRIVE TO BECOME STRONG BECAUSE WE WANT TO WIN AND PROTECT THE ONES WE LOVE.
I DON'T CARE WHETHER MY RIVAL IS RIENO OR THAT GREENHORN EHREN...
...BECAUSE I'M ABSOLUTELY SURE...

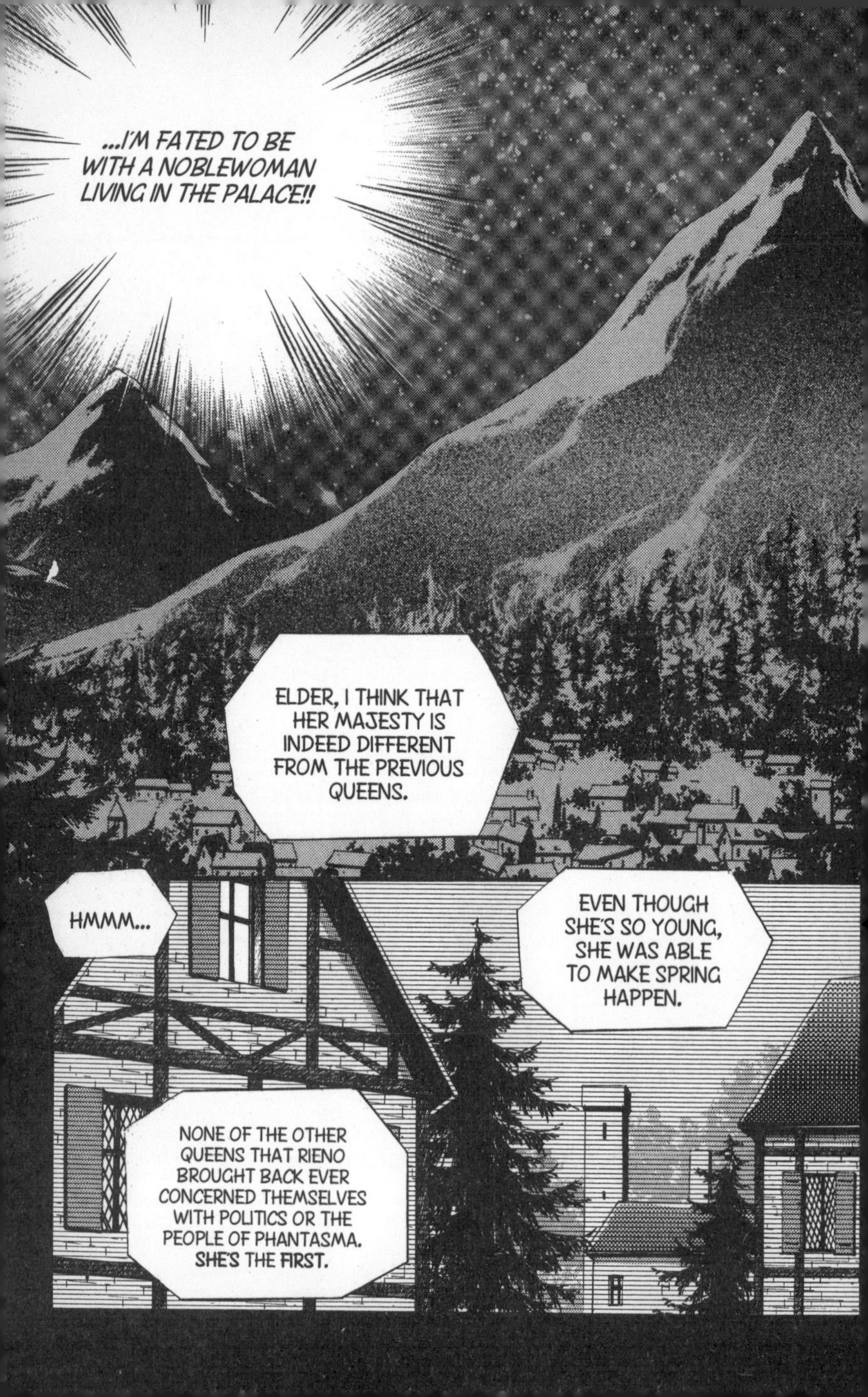

...I'M FATED TO BE WITH A NOBLEWOMAN LIVING IN THE PALACE!!
ELDER, I THINK THAT HER MAJESTY IS INDEED DIFFERENT FROM THE PREVIOUS QUEENS.
HMMM...
EVEN THOUGH SHE'S SO YOUNG, SHE WAS ABLE TO MAKE SPRING HAPPEN.
NONE OF THE OTHER QUEENS THAT RIENO BROUGHT BACK EVER CONCERNED THEMSELVES WITH POLITICS OR THE PEOPLE OF PHANTASMA. SHE'S THE FIRST.

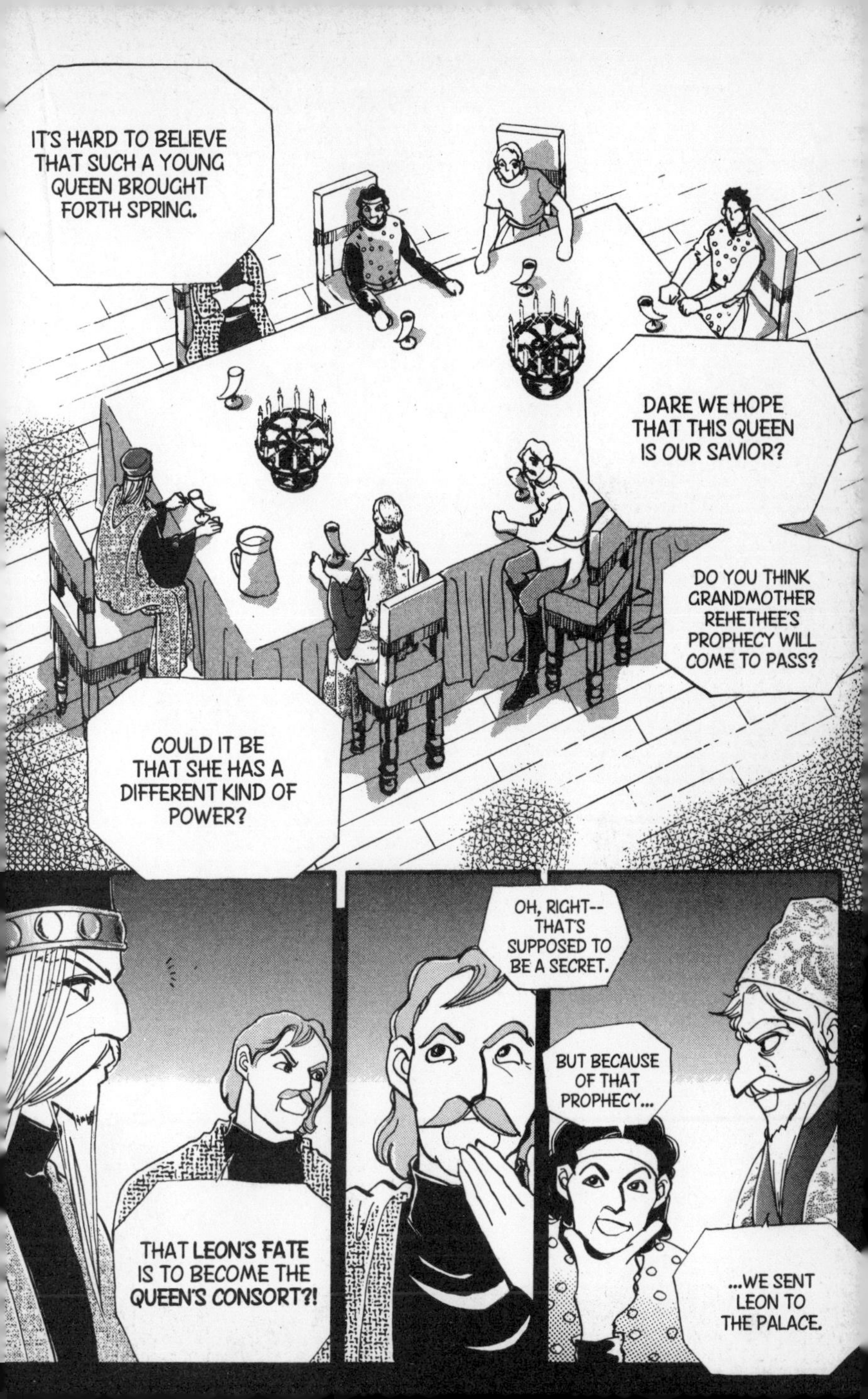
IT'S HARD TO BELIEVE THAT SUCH A YOUNG QUEEN BROUGHT FORTH SPRING.
DARE WE HOPE THAT THIS QUEEN IS OUR SAVIOR?
DO YOU THINK GRANDMOTHER REHETHEE'S PROPHECY WILL COME TO PASS?
COULD IT BE THAT SHE HAS A DIFFERENT KIND OF POWER?
THAT LEON'S FATE IS TO BECOME THE QUEEN'S CONSORT?!
OH, RIGHT-- THAT'S SUPPOSED TO BE A SECRET.
BUT BECAUSE OF THAT PROPHECY...
...WE SENT LEON TO THE PALACE.

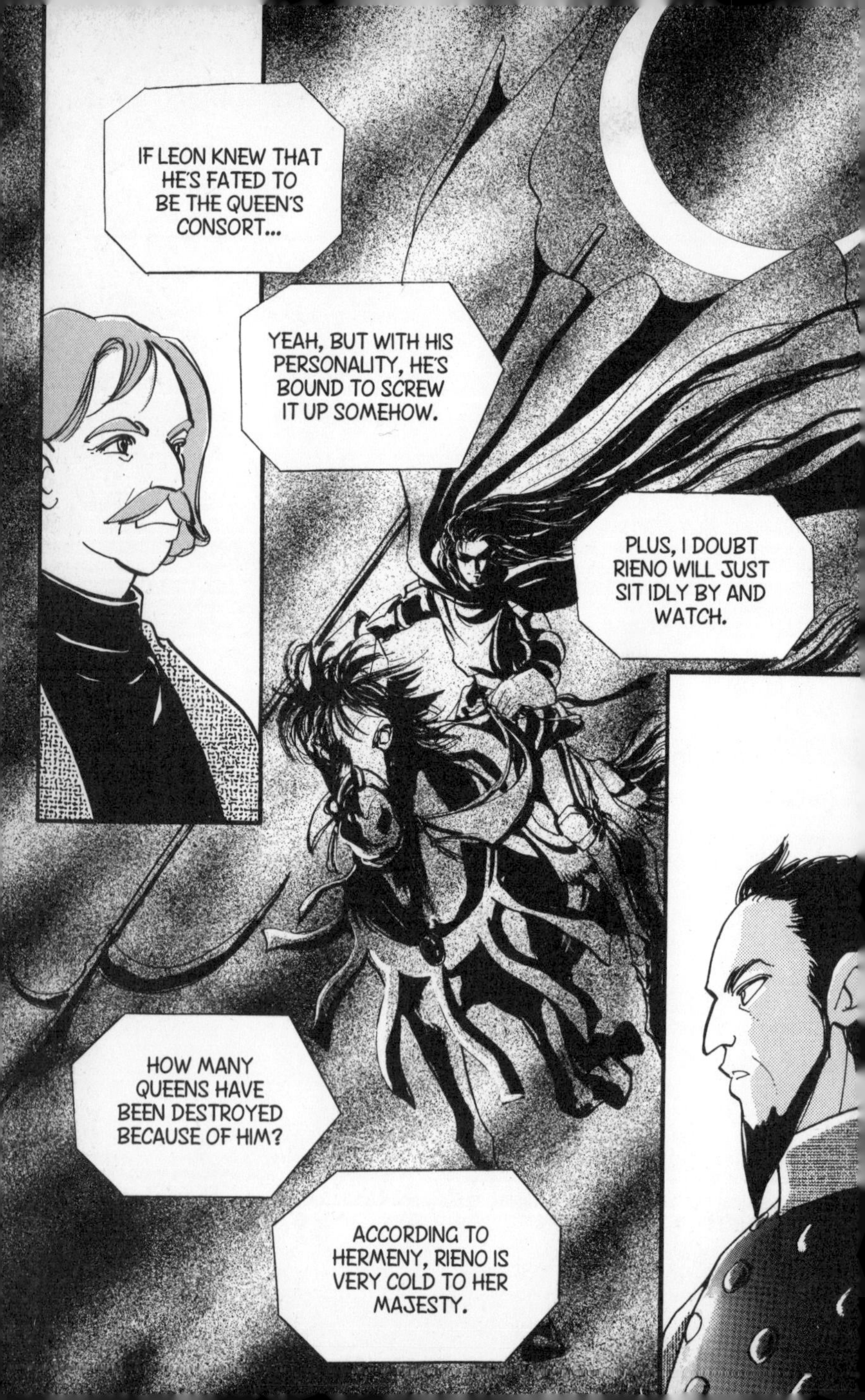
IF LEON KNEW THAT HE'S FATED TO BE THE QUEEN'S CONSORT...
YEAH, BUT WITH HIS PERSONALITY, HE'S BOUND TO SCREW IT UP SOMEHOW.
PLUS, I DOUBT RIENO WILL JUST SIT IDLY BY AND WATCH.
HOW MANY QUEENS HAVE BEEN DESTROYED BECAUSE OF HIM?
ACCORDING TO HERMENY, RIENO IS VERY COLD TO HER MAJESTY.

IF THERE'S ANYTHING WE CAN DO TO HELP LEON, LET'S DO IT.

LET'S DO ALL WE CAN TO HELP BRING HIM AND HER MAJESTY TOGETHER!

HUH?

THAT'S A GREAT IDEA.

IF THE QUEEN WERE TO LOVE ANOTHER MAN BESIDES RIENO, THEN WE'D HAVE HOPE, WOULDN'T WE?

SINCE WE HAVE THE TWO OF THEM RIGHT HERE DURING OUR COUPLE FESTIVAL, LET'S DO WHAT WE CAN TO MAKE THEM A COUPLE!

WE'LL USE WHATEVER MEANS NECESSARY...

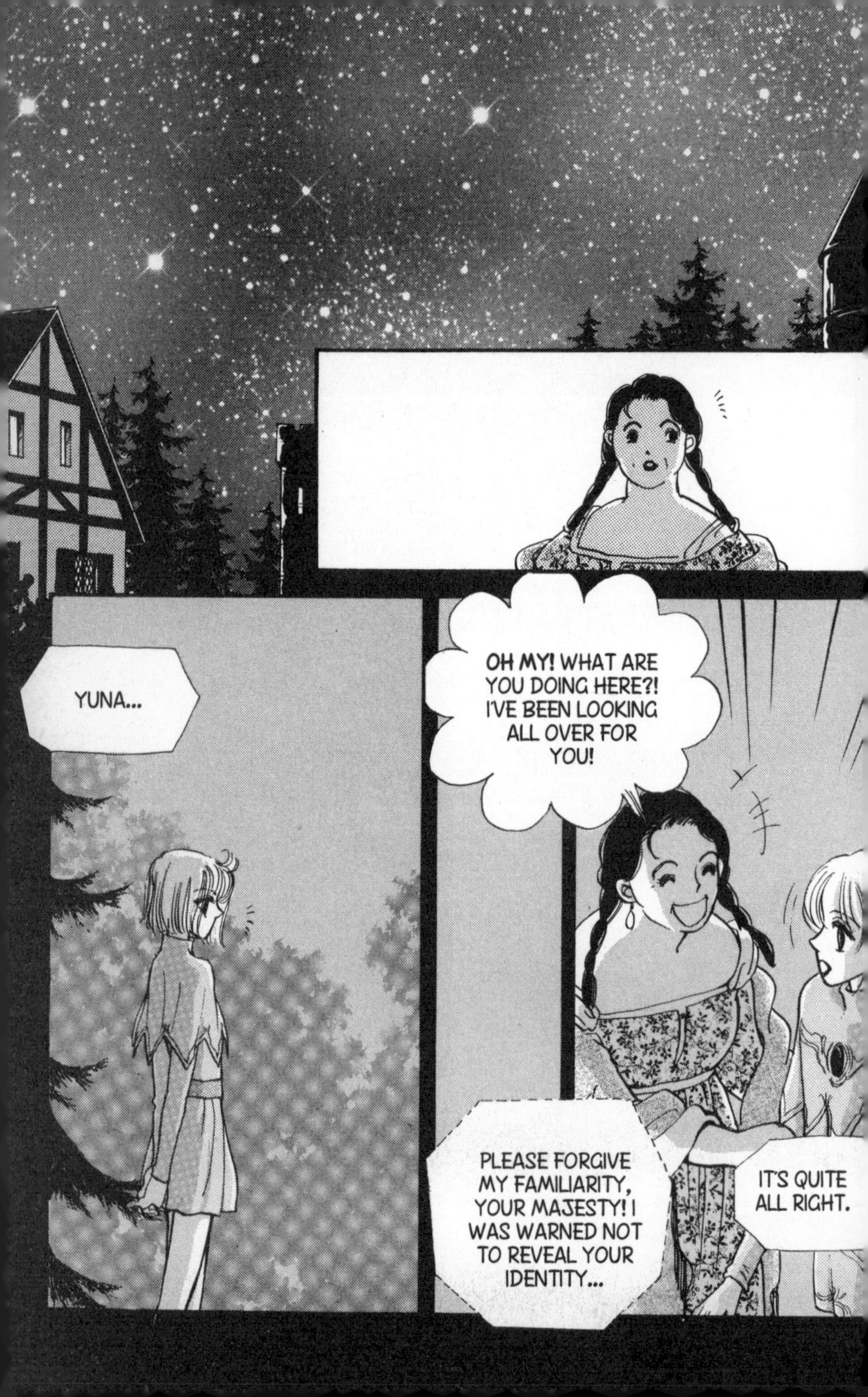
YUNA...
OH MY! WHAT ARE YOU DOING HERE?! I'VE BEEN LOOKING ALL OVER FOR YOU!
PLEASE FORGIVE MY FAMILIARITY, YOUR MAJESTY! I WAS WARNED NOT TO REVEAL YOUR IDENTITY...
IT'S QUITE ALL RIGHT.

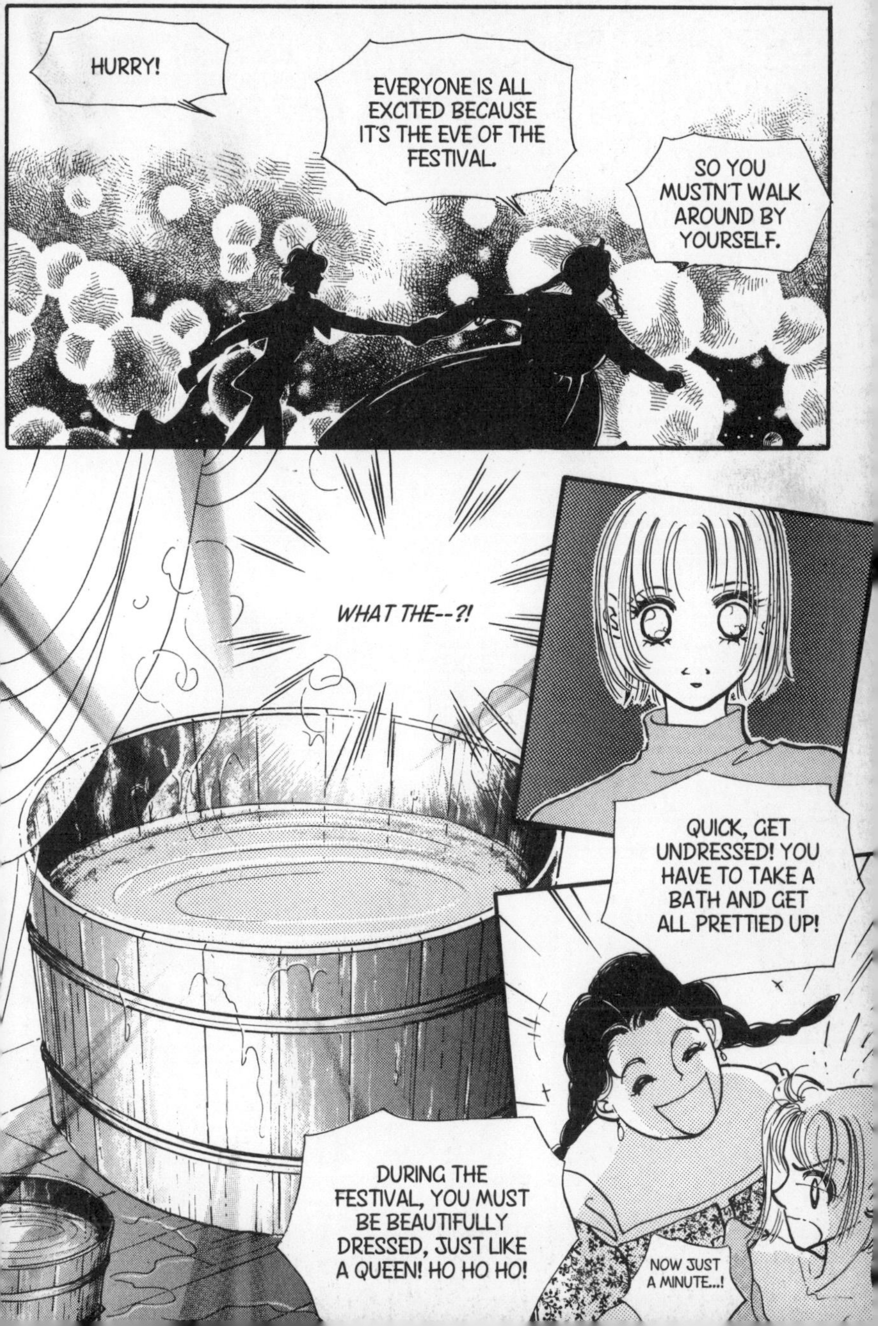
HURRY!
EVERYONE IS ALL EXCITED BECAUSE IT'S THE EVE OF THE FESTIVAL.
SO YOU MUSTN'T WALK AROUND BY YOURSELF.
WHAT THE--?!
QUICK, GET UNDRESSED! YOU HAVE TO TAKE A BATH AND GET ALL PRETTIED UP!
DURING THE FESTIVAL, YOU MUST BE BEAUTIFULLY DRESSED, JUST LIKE A QUEEN! HO HO HO!
NOW JUST A MINUTE...!

TSK TSK...WHAT HAPPENED TO YOUR HAIR?

AND HOW ON EARTH DID YOU DEVELOP MUSCLES LIKE THESE?

A WOMAN'S HAIR IS SO **IMPORTANT**...IT SHOULDN'T BE ALL BUTCHERED LIKE **THIS**!

YET YOUR SKIN IS SO DELICATE...

THANK YOU.

OH, MY...

I'M SORRY...

I WAS THINKING ABOUT MY MOTHER.

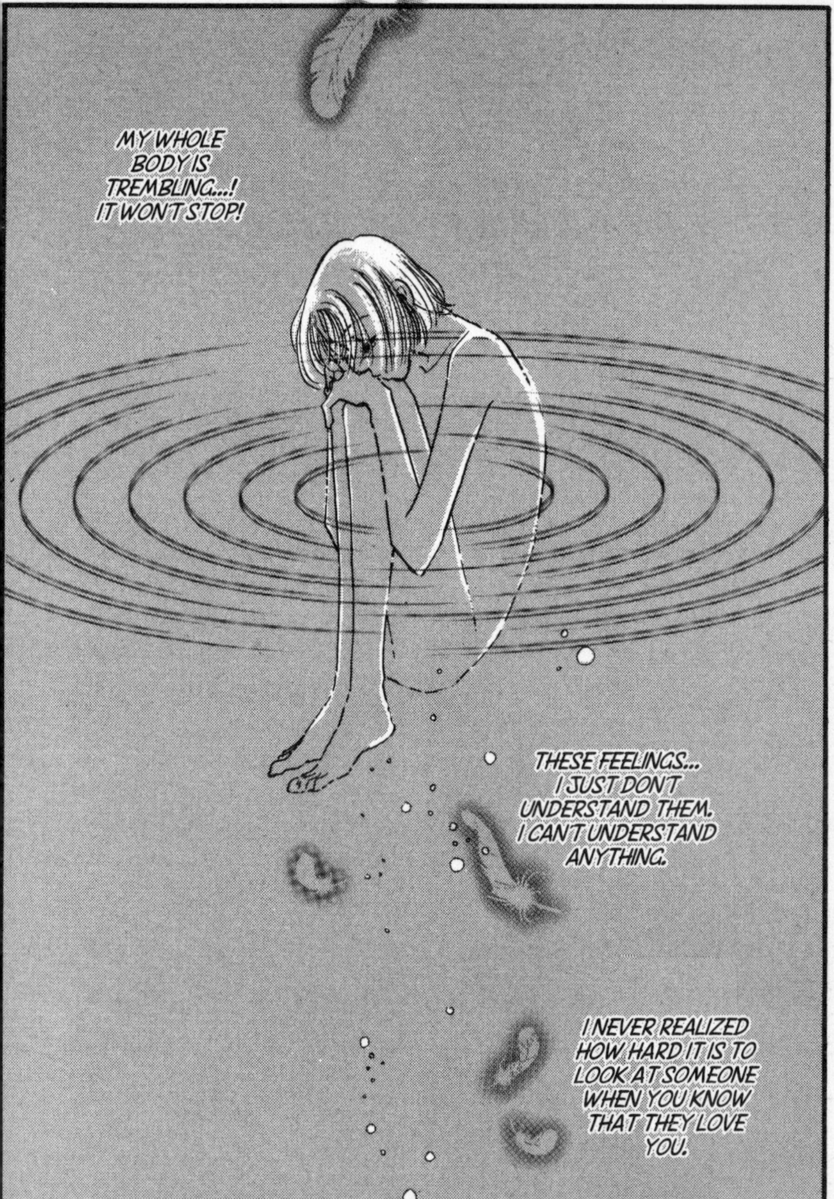
MY WHOLE BODY IS TREMBLING...! IT WON'T STOP!
THESE FEELINGS... I JUST DON'T UNDERSTAND THEM. I CAN'T UNDERSTAND ANYTHING.
I NEVER REALIZED HOW HARD IT IS TO LOOK AT SOMEONE WHEN YOU KNOW THAT THEY LOVE YOU.

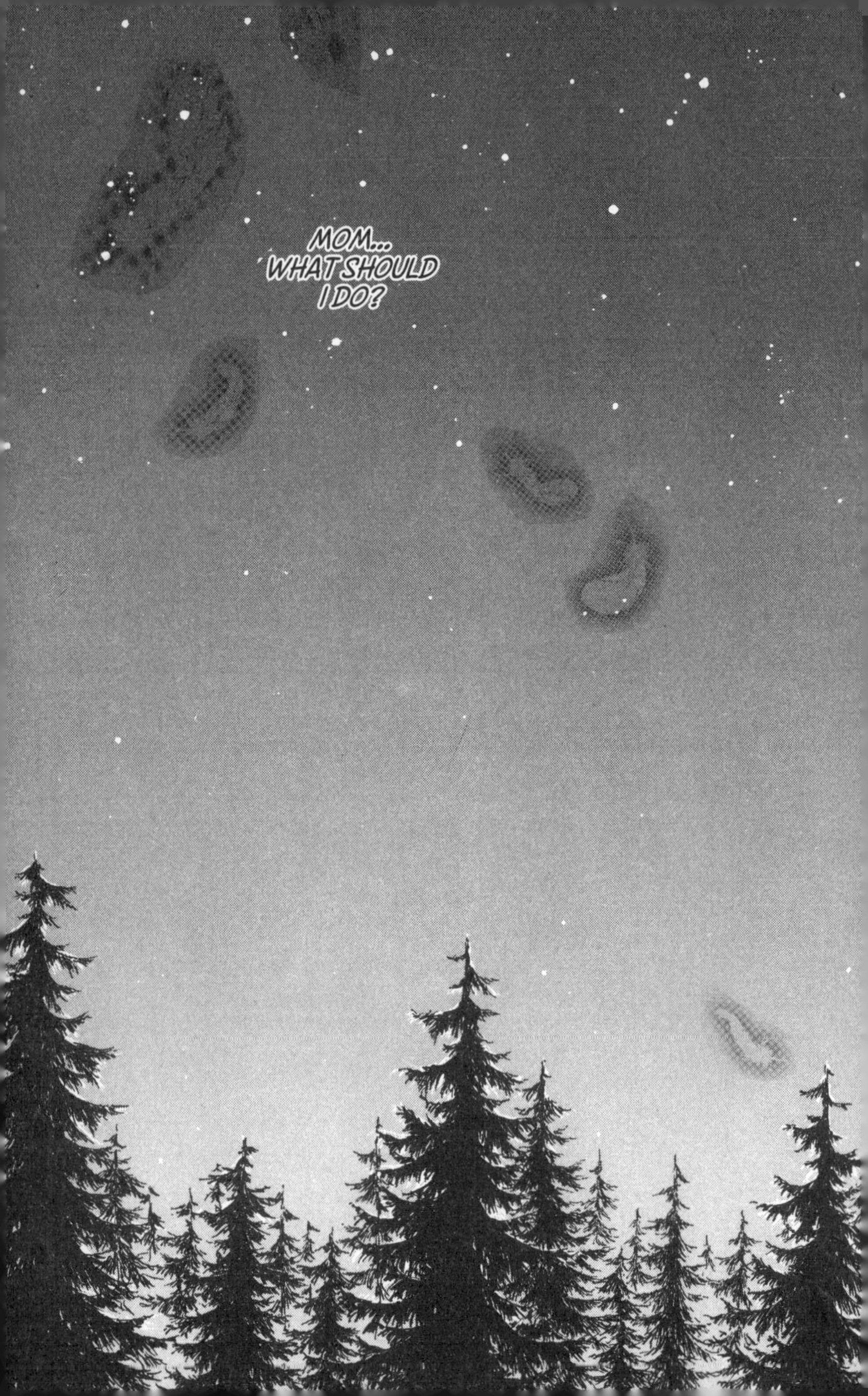
MOM... WHAT SHOULD I DO?

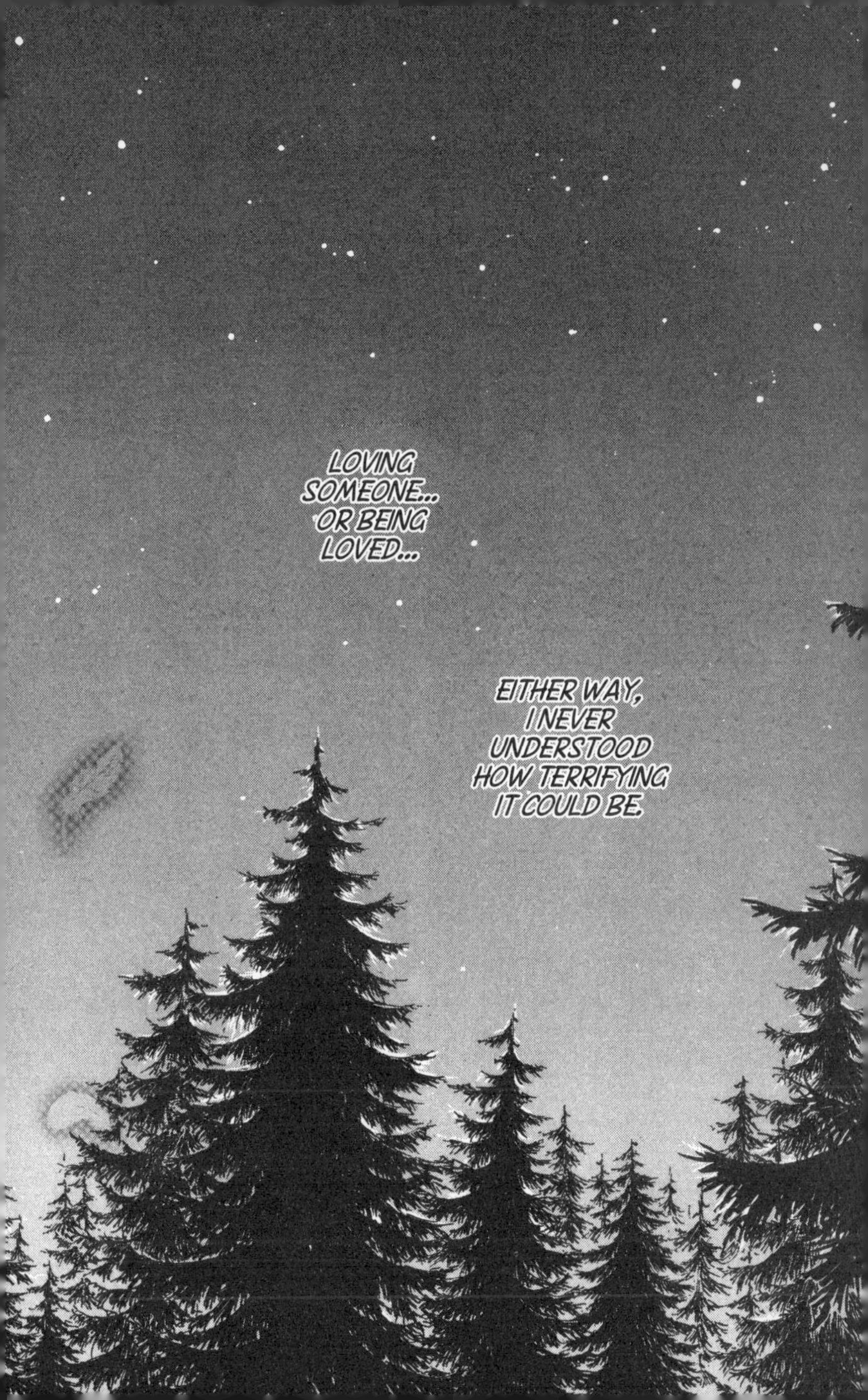
LOVING SOMEONE... OR BEING LOVED...
EITHER WAY, I NEVER UNDERSTOOD HOW TERRIFYING IT COULD BE.

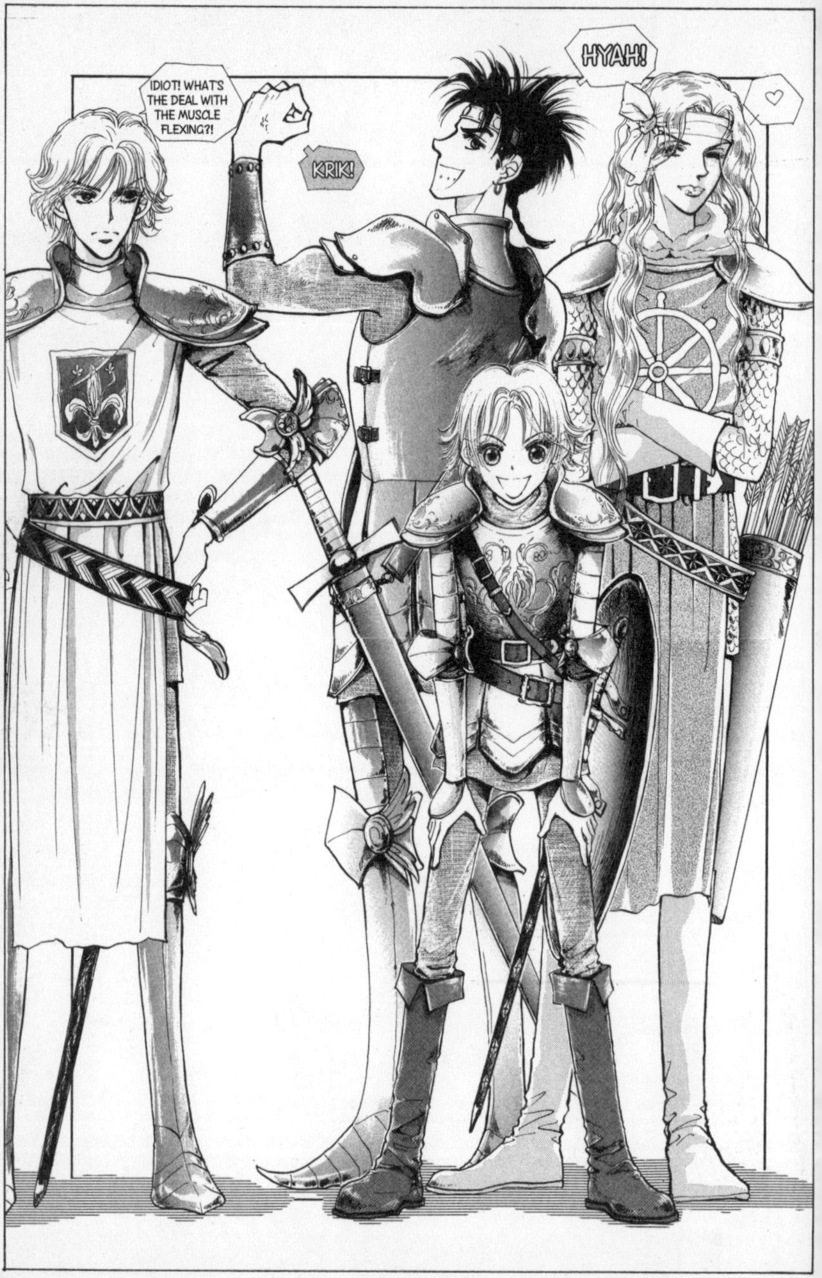
IDIOT! WHAT'S THE DEAL WITH THE MUSCLE FLEXING?!
KRIK!
HYAH!
♡

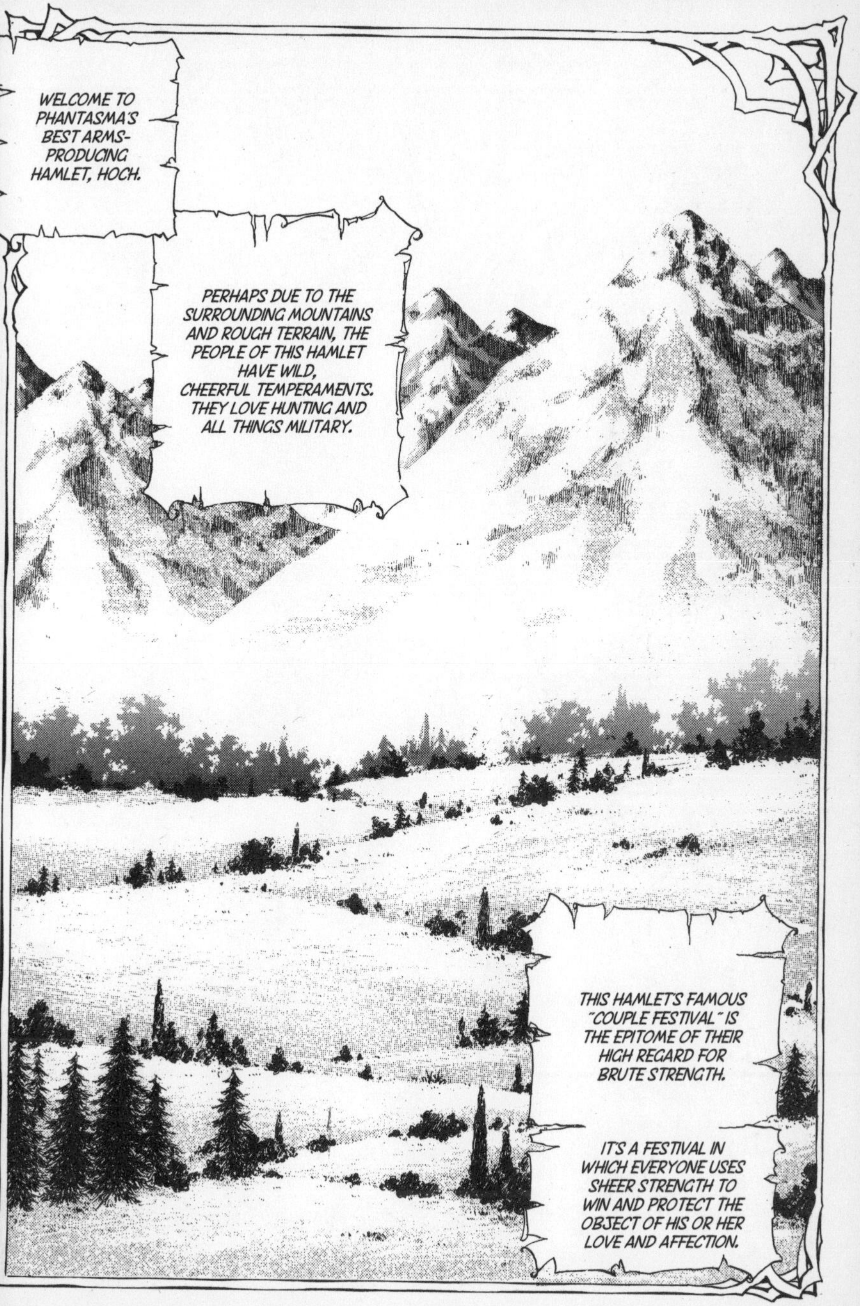
WELCOME TO PHANTASMA'S BEST ARMS-PRODUCING HAMLET, HOCH.
PERHAPS DUE TO THE SURROUNDING MOUNTAINS AND ROUGH TERRAIN, THE PEOPLE OF THIS HAMLET HAVE WILD, CHEERFUL TEMPERAMENTS. THEY LOVE HUNTING AND ALL THINGS MILITARY.
THIS HAMLET'S FAMOUS "COUPLE FESTIVAL" IS THE EPITOME OF THEIR HIGH REGARD FOR BRUTE STRENGTH.
IT'S A FESTIVAL IN WHICH EVERYONE USES SHEER STRENGTH TO WIN AND PROTECT THE OBJECT OF HIS OR HER LOVE AND AFFECTION.

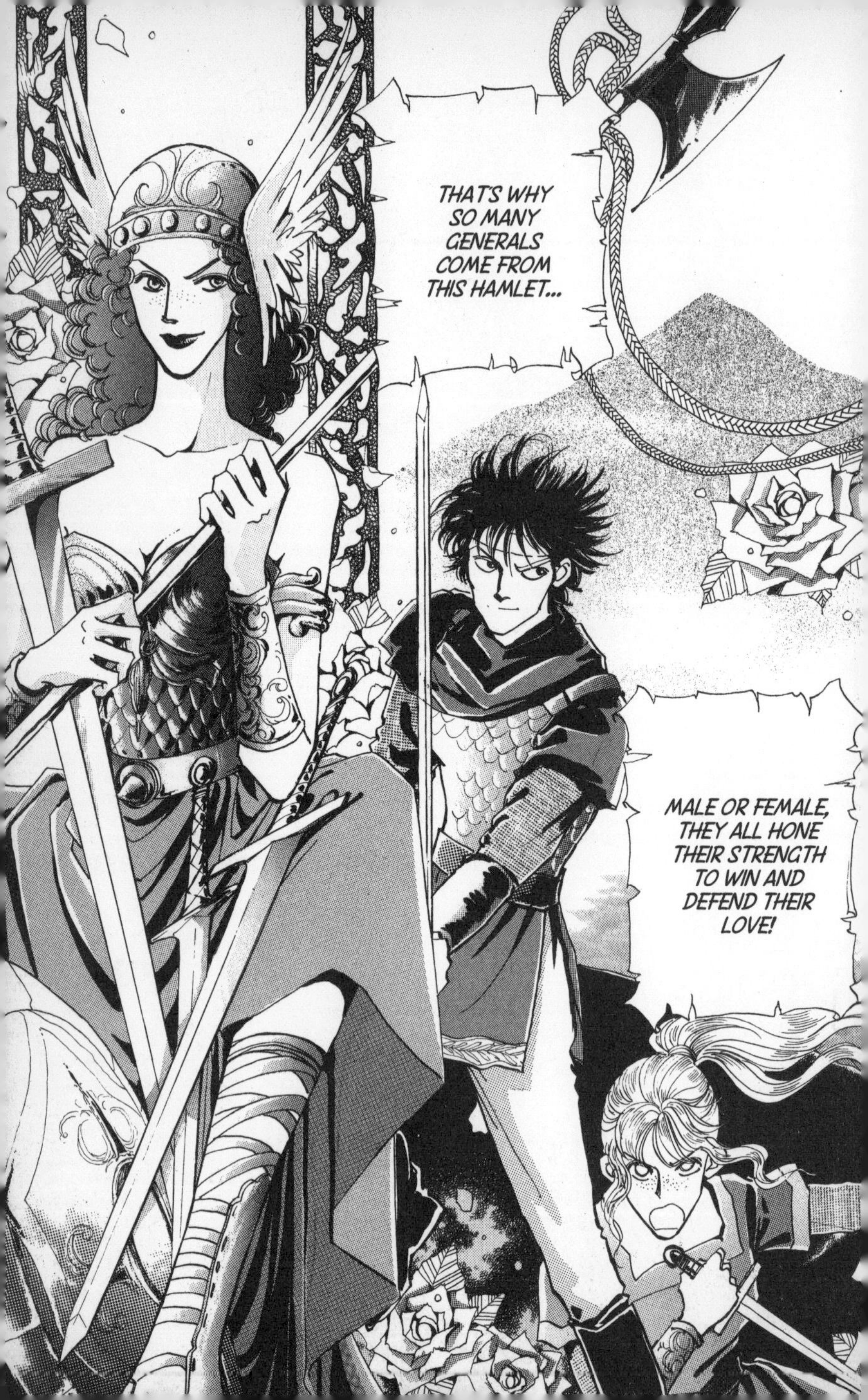
THAT'S WHY SO MANY GENERALS COME FROM THIS HAMLET...
MALE OR FEMALE, THEY ALL HONE THEIR STRENGTH TO WIN AND DEFEND THEIR LOVE!

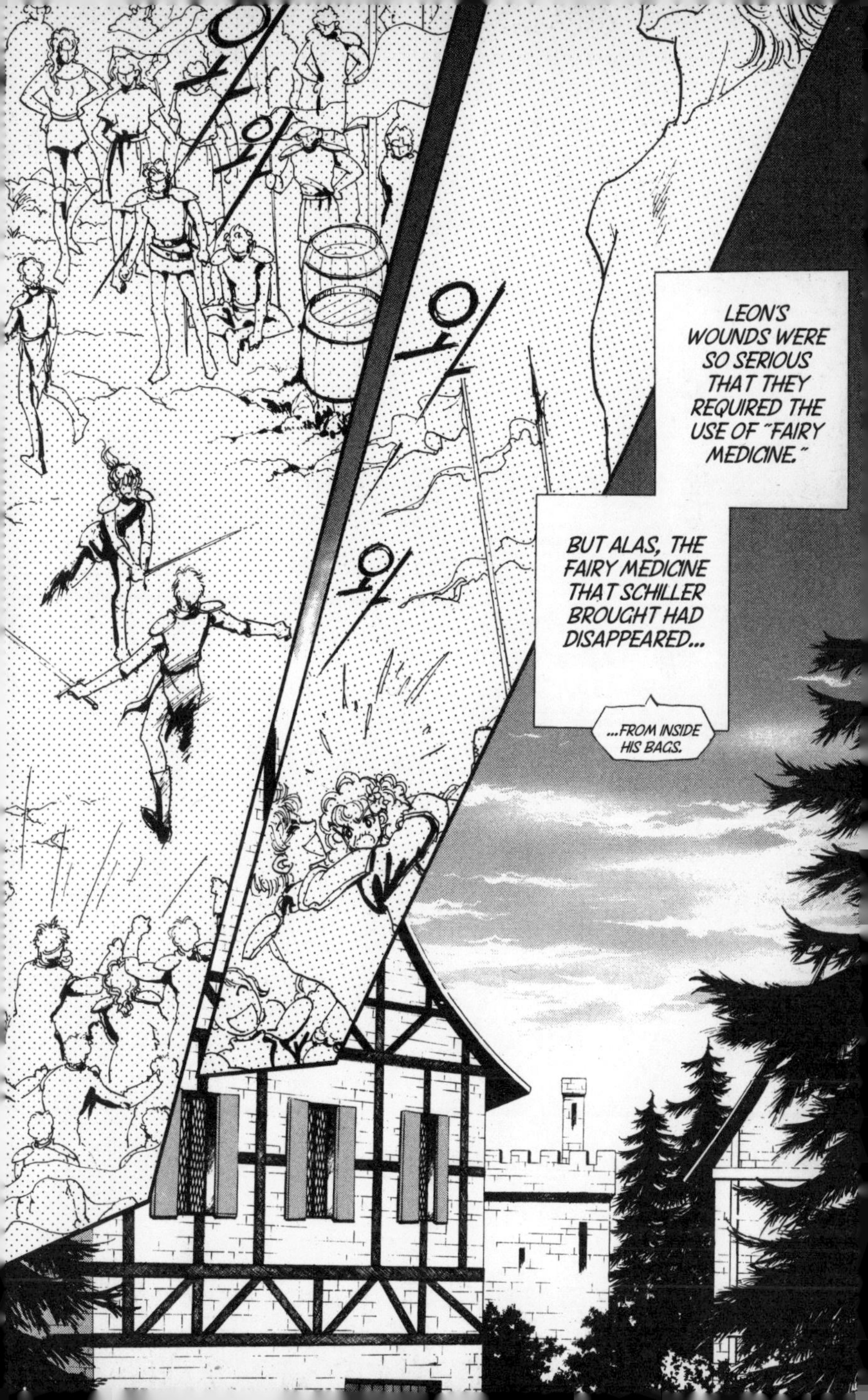
LEON'S WOUNDS WERE SO SERIOUS THAT THEY REQUIRED THE USE OF "FAIRY MEDICINE."
BUT ALAS, THE FAIRY MEDICINE THAT SCHILLER BROUGHT HAD DISAPPEARED...
...FROM INSIDE HIS BAGS.

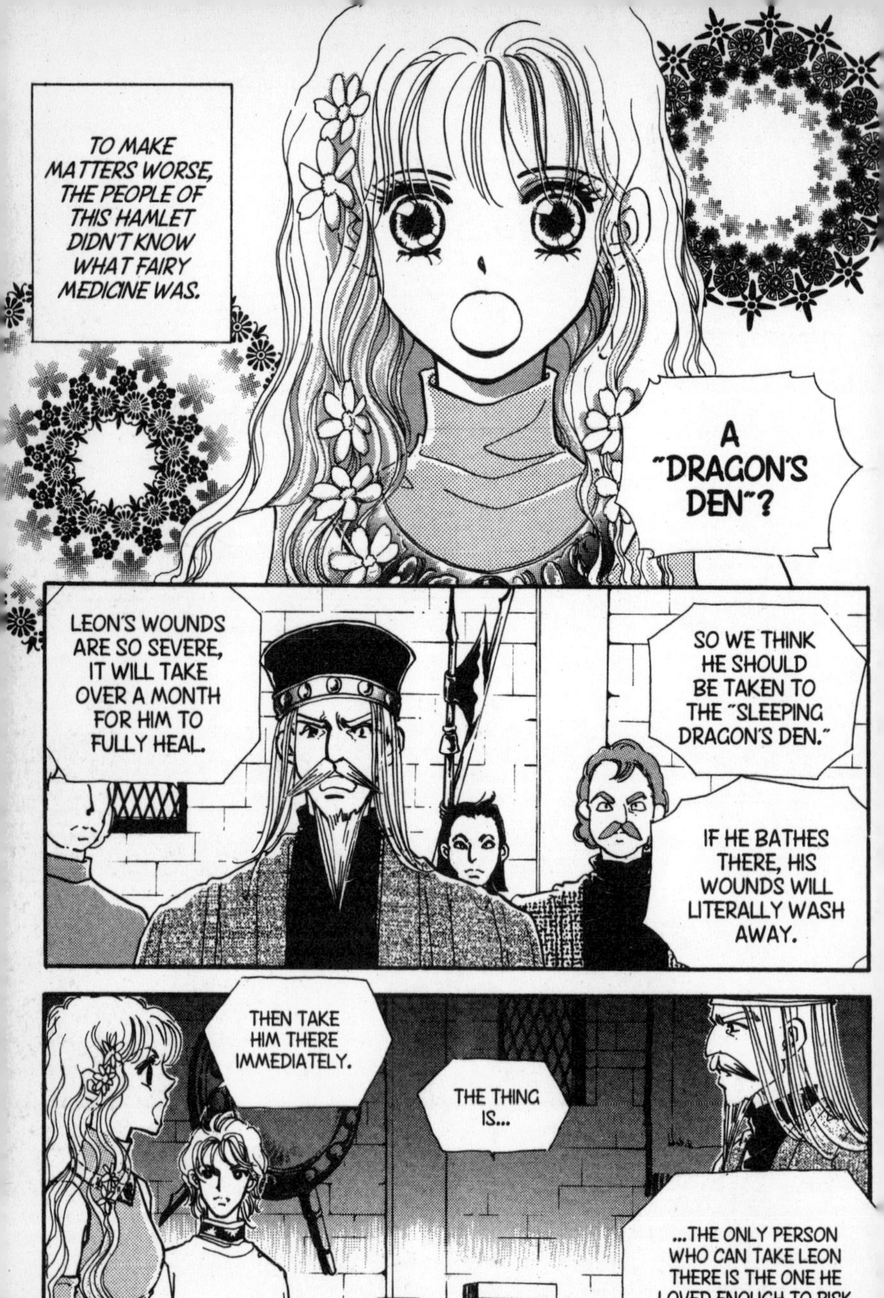
TO MAKE MATTERS WORSE, THE PEOPLE OF THIS HAMLET DIDN'T KNOW WHAT FAIRY MEDICINE WAS.
A "DRAGON'S DEN"?
LEON'S WOUNDS ARE SO SEVERE, IT WILL TAKE OVER A MONTH FOR HIM TO FULLY HEAL.
SO WE THINK HE SHOULD BE TAKEN TO THE "SLEEPING DRAGON'S DEN."
IF HE BATHES THERE, HIS WOUNDS WILL LITERALLY WASH AWAY.
THEN TAKE HIM THERE IMMEDIATELY.
THE THING IS...
...THE ONLY PERSON WHO CAN TAKE LEON THERE IS THE ONE HE LOVED ENOUGH TO RISK HIS LIFE FOR.

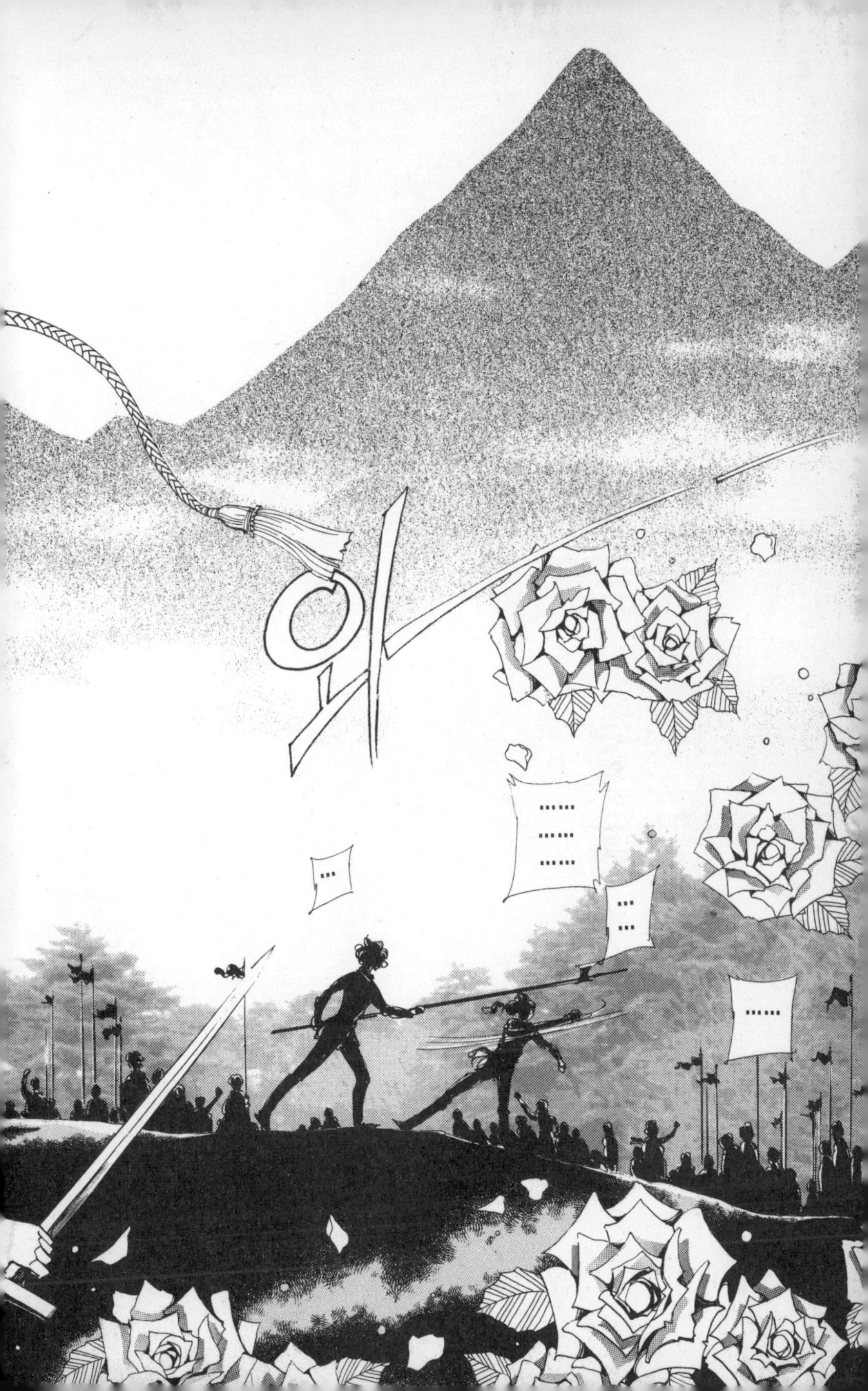
와
……
……
……
……
…
…
……

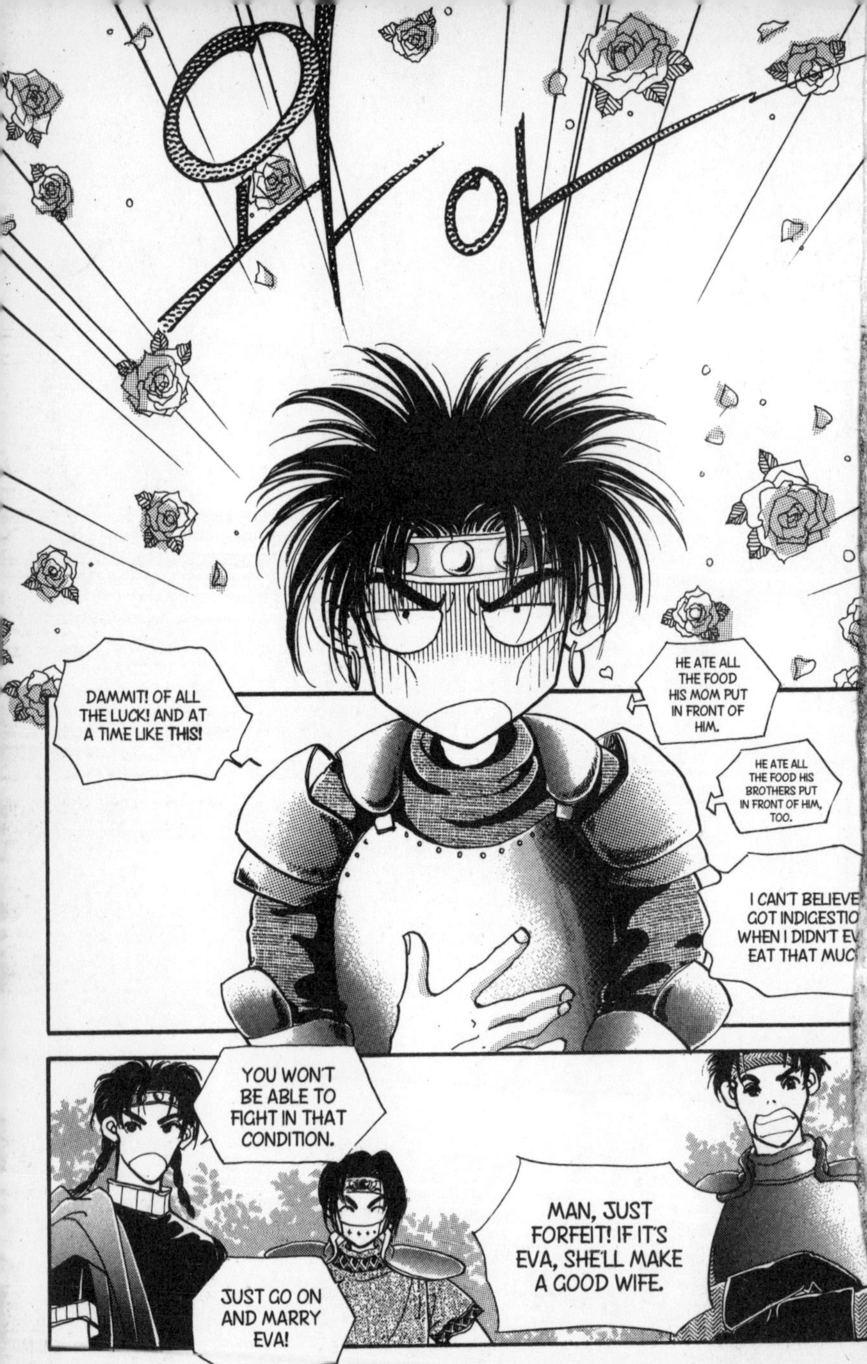
DAMMIT! OF ALL THE LUCK! AND AT A TIME LIKE THIS!
HE ATE ALL THE FOOD HIS MOM PUT IN FRONT OF HIM.
HE ATE ALL THE FOOD HIS BROTHERS PUT IN FRONT OF HIM, TOO.
I CAN'T BELIEVE GOT INDIGESTIO WHEN I DIDN'T EV EAT THAT MUC
YOU WON'T BE ABLE TO FIGHT IN THAT CONDITION.
JUST GO ON AND MARRY EVA!
MAN, JUST FORFEIT! IF IT'S EVA, SHE'LL MAKE A GOOD WIFE.

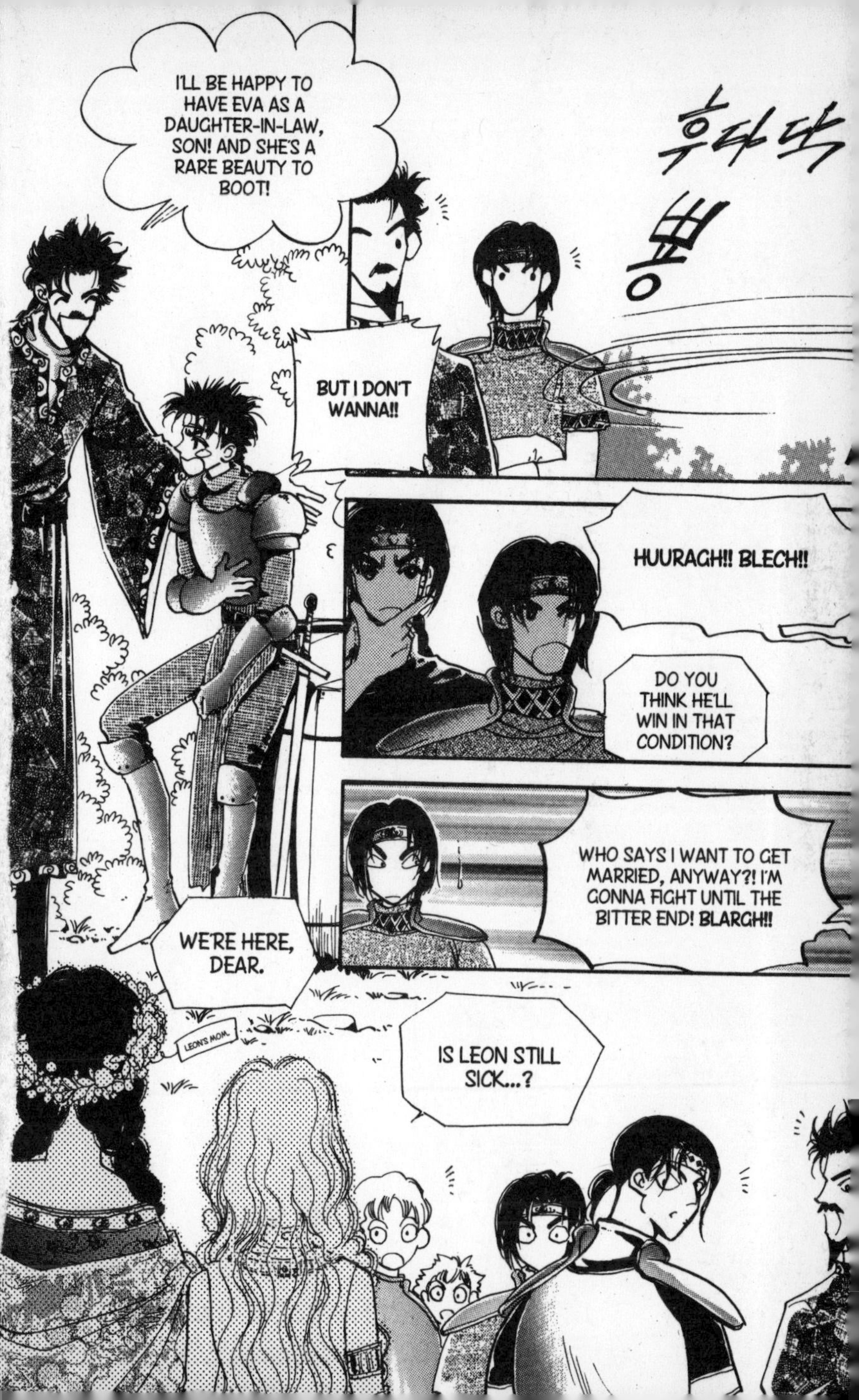

I'LL BE HAPPY TO HAVE EVA AS A DAUGHTER-IN-LAW, SON! AND SHE'S A RARE BEAUTY TO BOOT!
BUT I DON'T WANNA!!
후다닥
뿅
HUURAGH!! BLECH!!
DO YOU THINK HE'LL WIN IN THAT CONDITION?
WHO SAYS I WANT TO GET MARRIED, ANYWAY?! I'M GONNA FIGHT UNTIL THE BITTER END! BLARGH!!
WE'RE HERE, DEAR.
LEON'S MOM.
IS LEON STILL SICK...?

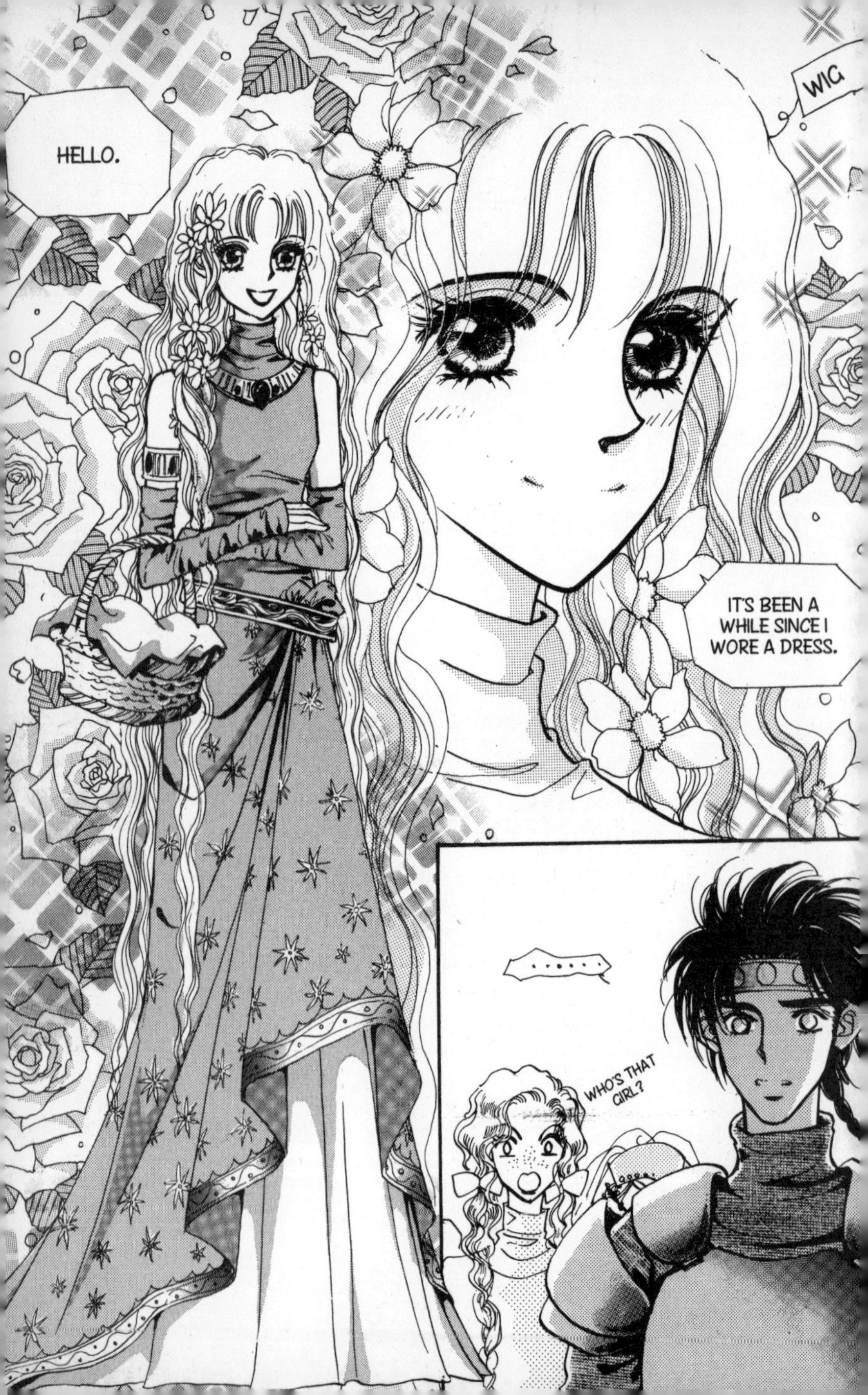
HELLO.
WIG
IT'S BEEN A WHILE SINCE I WORE A DRESS.
......
WHO'S THAT GIRL?

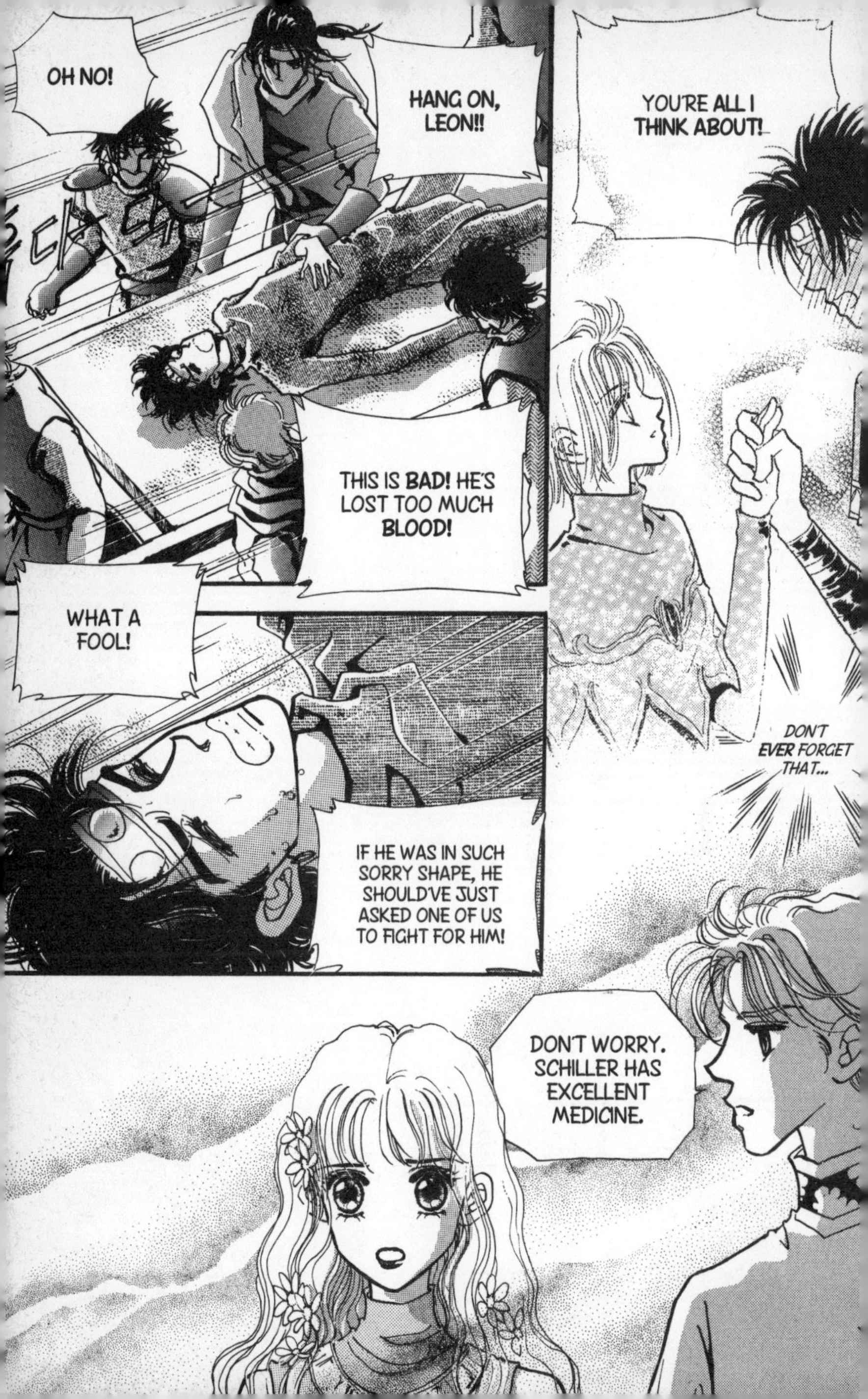
OH NO!
HANG ON, LEON!!
THIS IS BAD! HE'S LOST TOO MUCH BLOOD!
WHAT A FOOL!
IF HE WAS IN SUCH SORRY SHAPE, HE SHOULD'VE JUST ASKED ONE OF US TO FIGHT FOR HIM!
YOU'RE ALL I THINK ABOUT!
DON'T EVER FORGET THAT...
DON'T WORRY. SCHILLER HAS EXCELLENT MEDICINE.

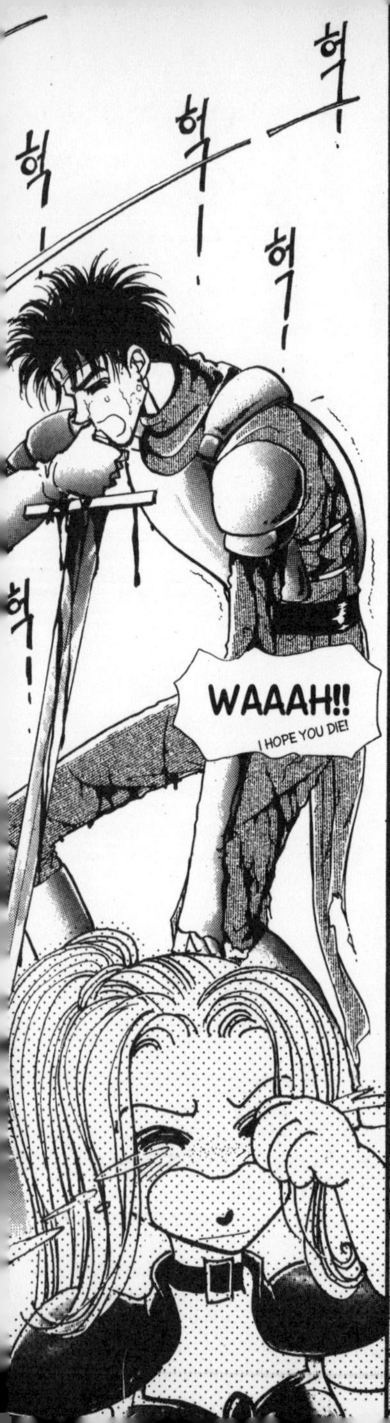
헉
헉
헉
헉
헉
WAAAH!!
I HOPE YOU DIE!
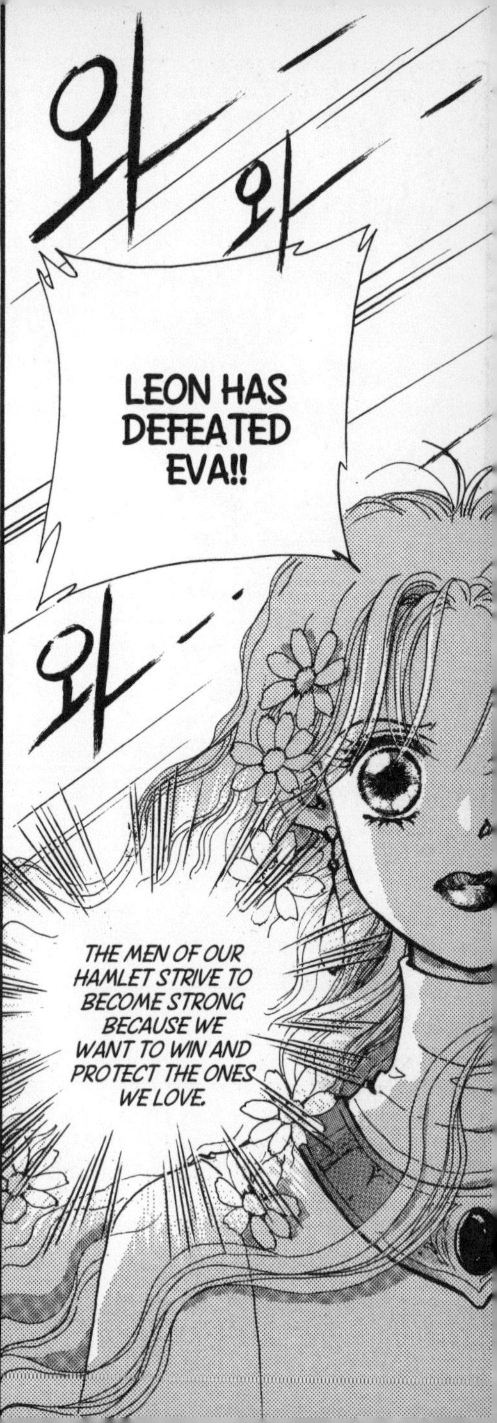
와
와
LEON HAS DEFEATED EVA!!
와
THE MEN OF OUR HAMLET STRIVE TO BECOME STRONG BECAUSE WE WANT TO WIN AND PROTECT THE ONES WE LOVE.

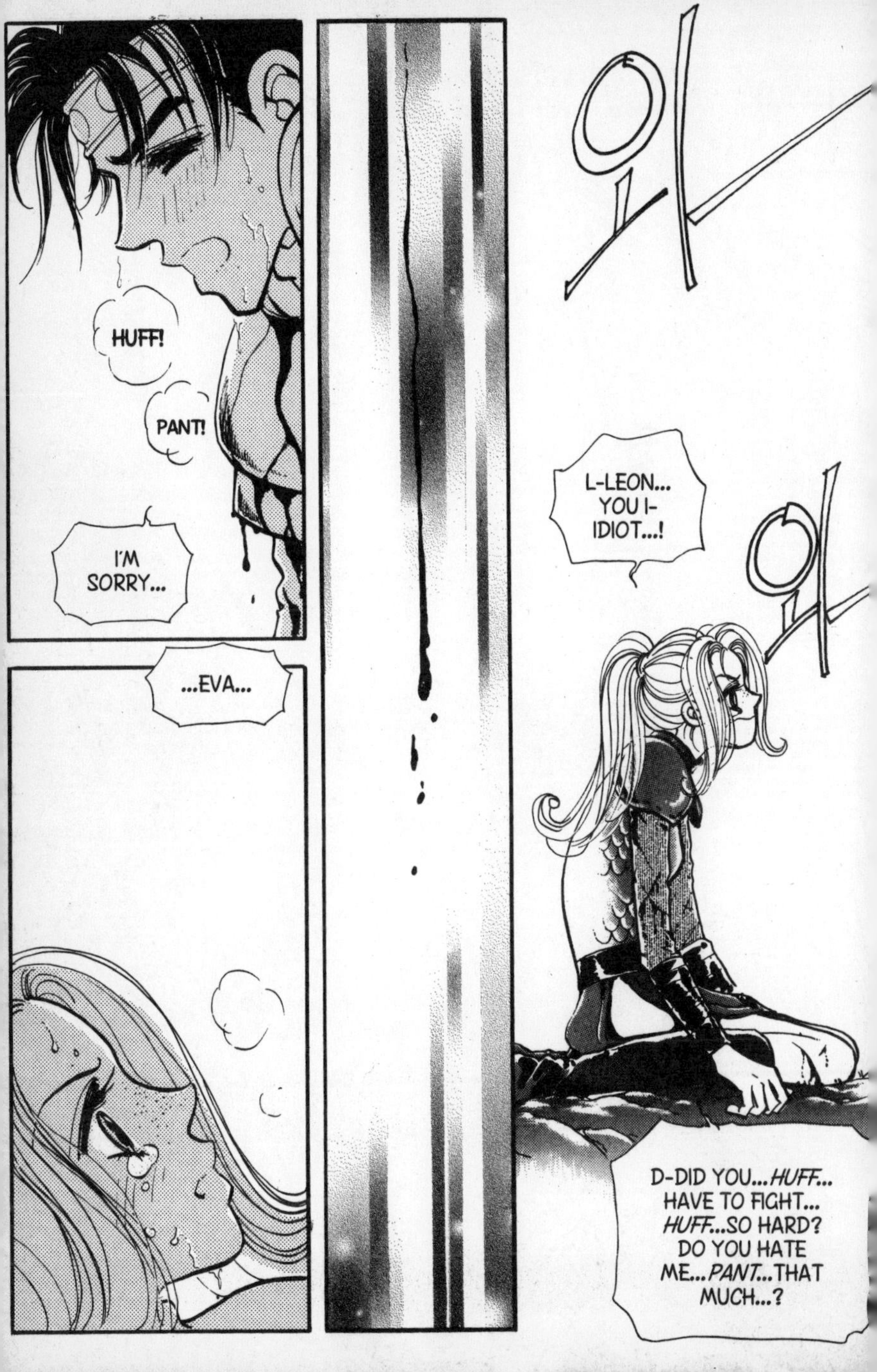
HUFF!
PANT!
I'M SORRY...
...EVA...
L-LEON... YOU I-IDIOT...!
D-DID YOU...*HUFF*... HAVE TO FIGHT... *HUFF*...SO HARD? DO YOU HATE ME...*PANT*...THAT MUCH...?

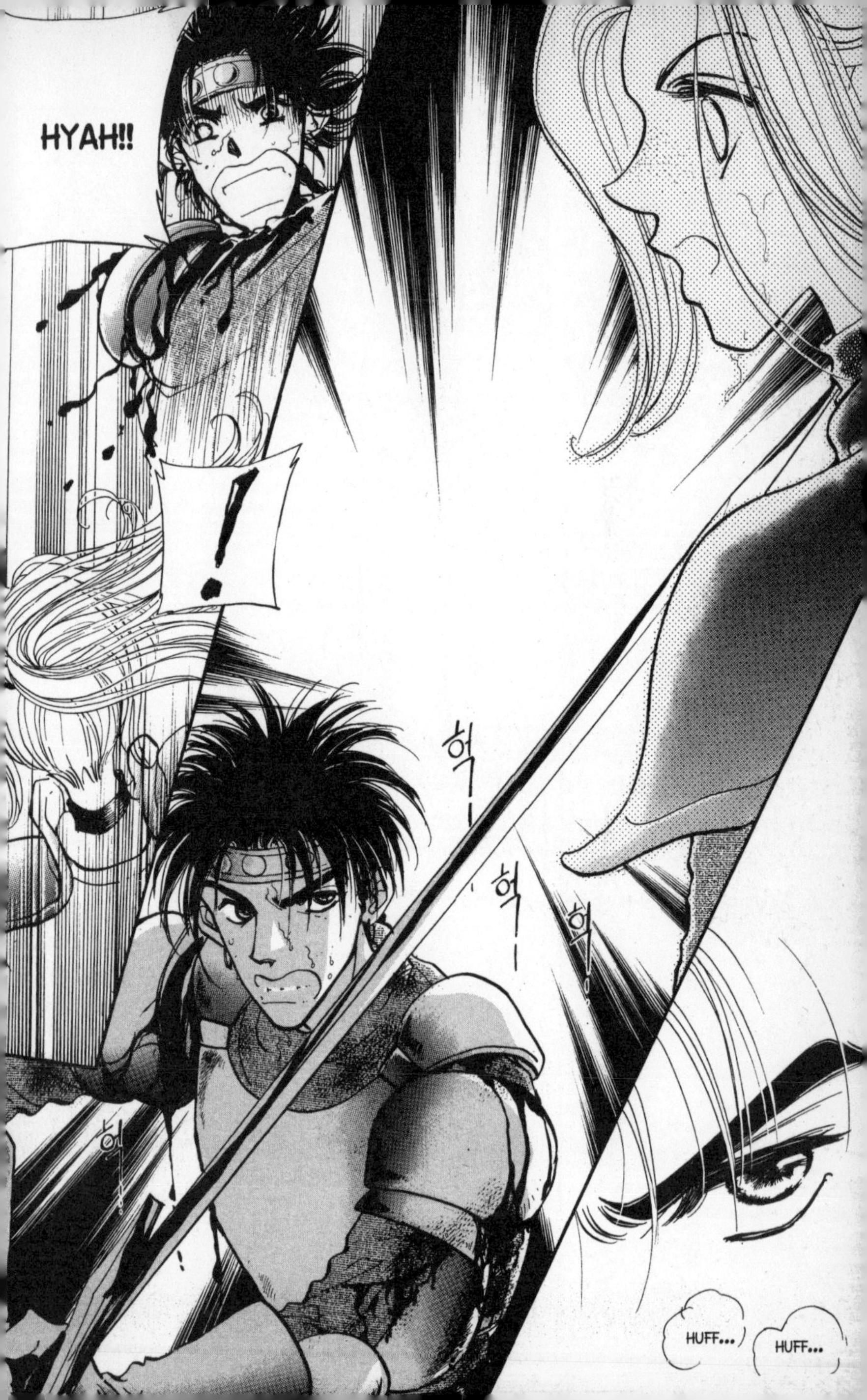
HYAH!!
!
헉
헉
헉
헉
HUFF...
HUFF...

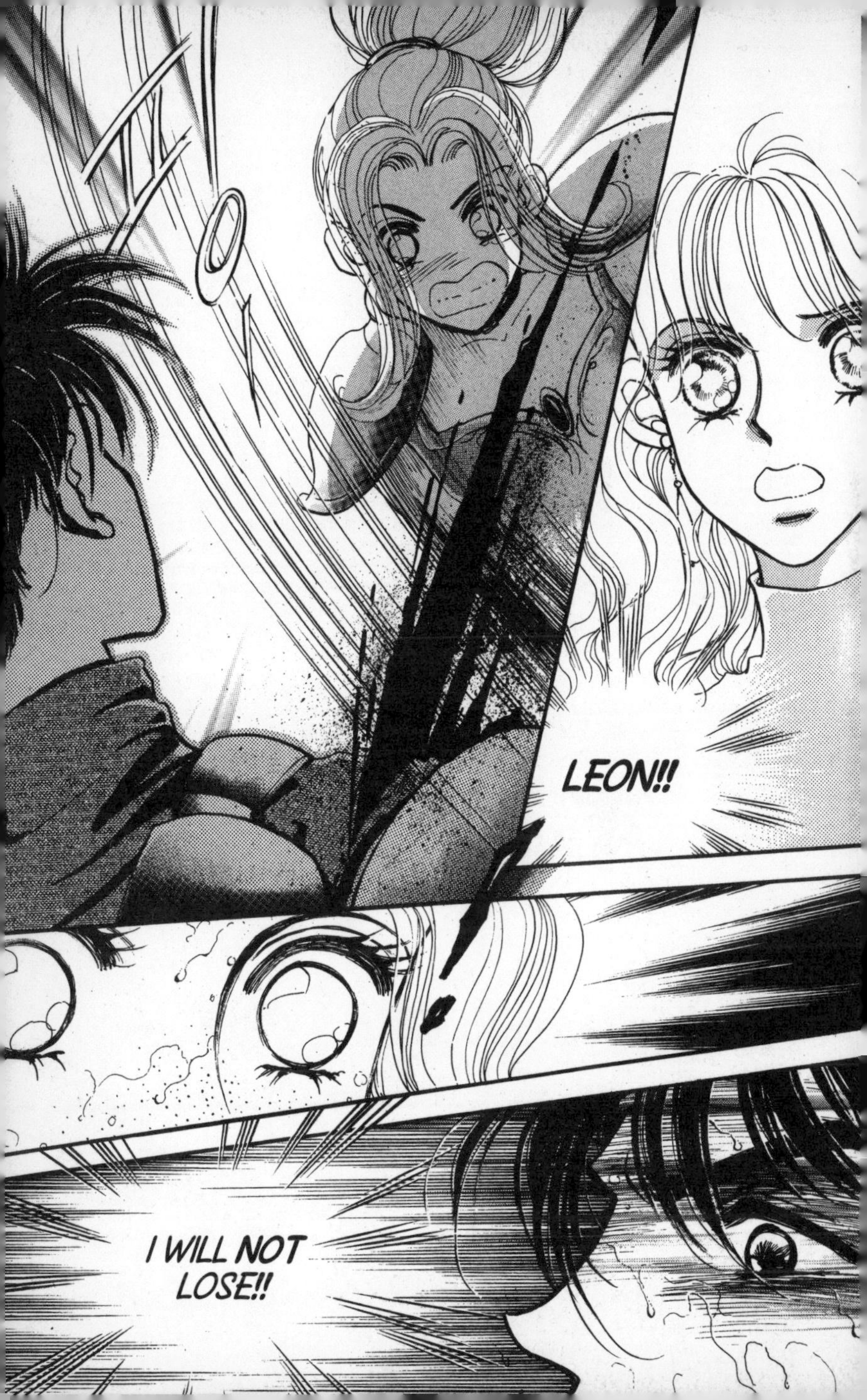
LEON!!
I WILL NOT LOSE!!

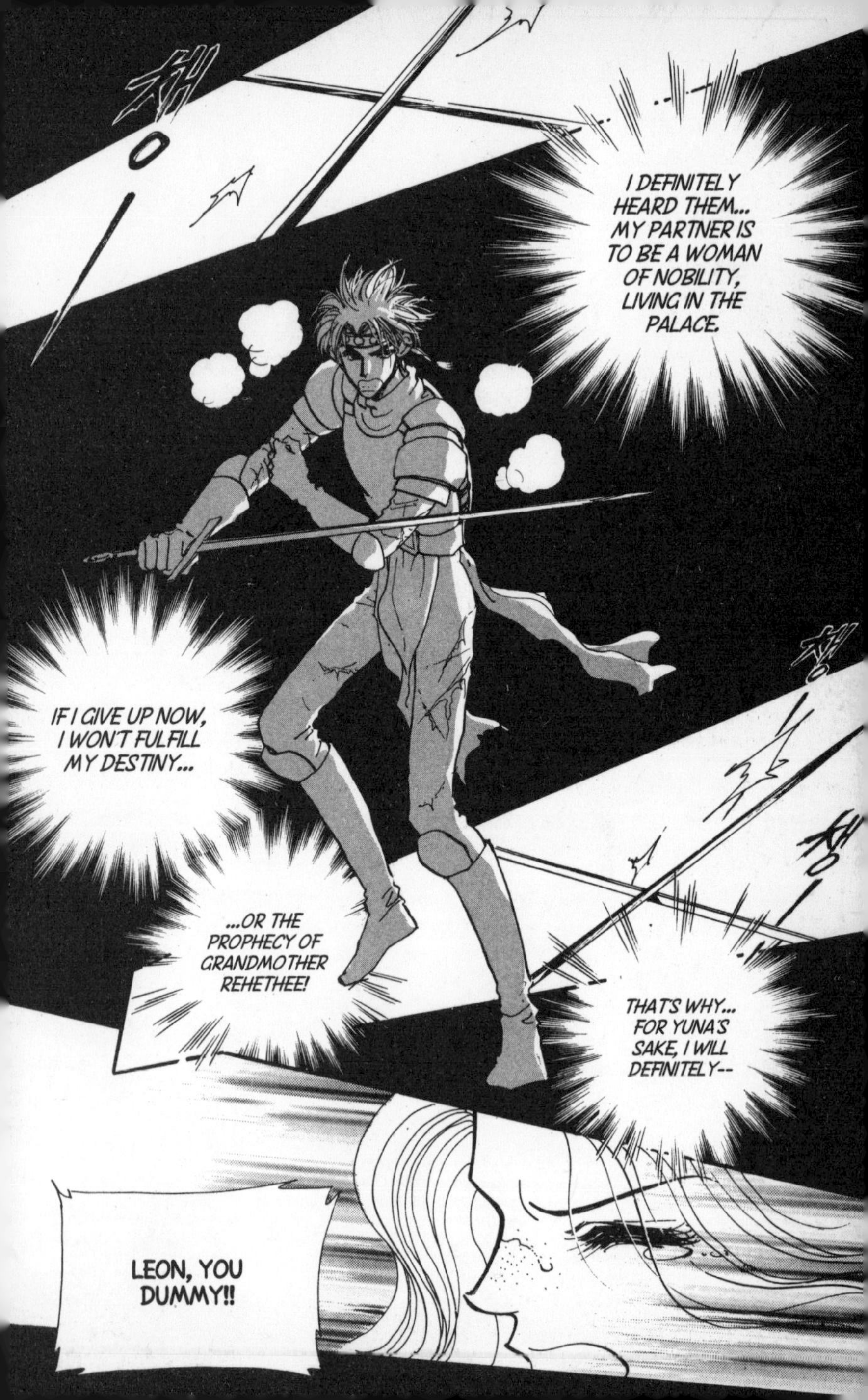

I DEFINITELY HEARD THEM... MY PARTNER IS TO BE A WOMAN OF NOBILITY, LIVING IN THE PALACE.
IF I GIVE UP NOW, I WON'T FULFILL MY DESTINY...
...OR THE PROPHECY OF GRANDMOTHER REHETHEE!
THAT'S WHY... FOR YUNA'S SAKE, I WILL DEFINITELY--
LEON, YOU DUMMY!!

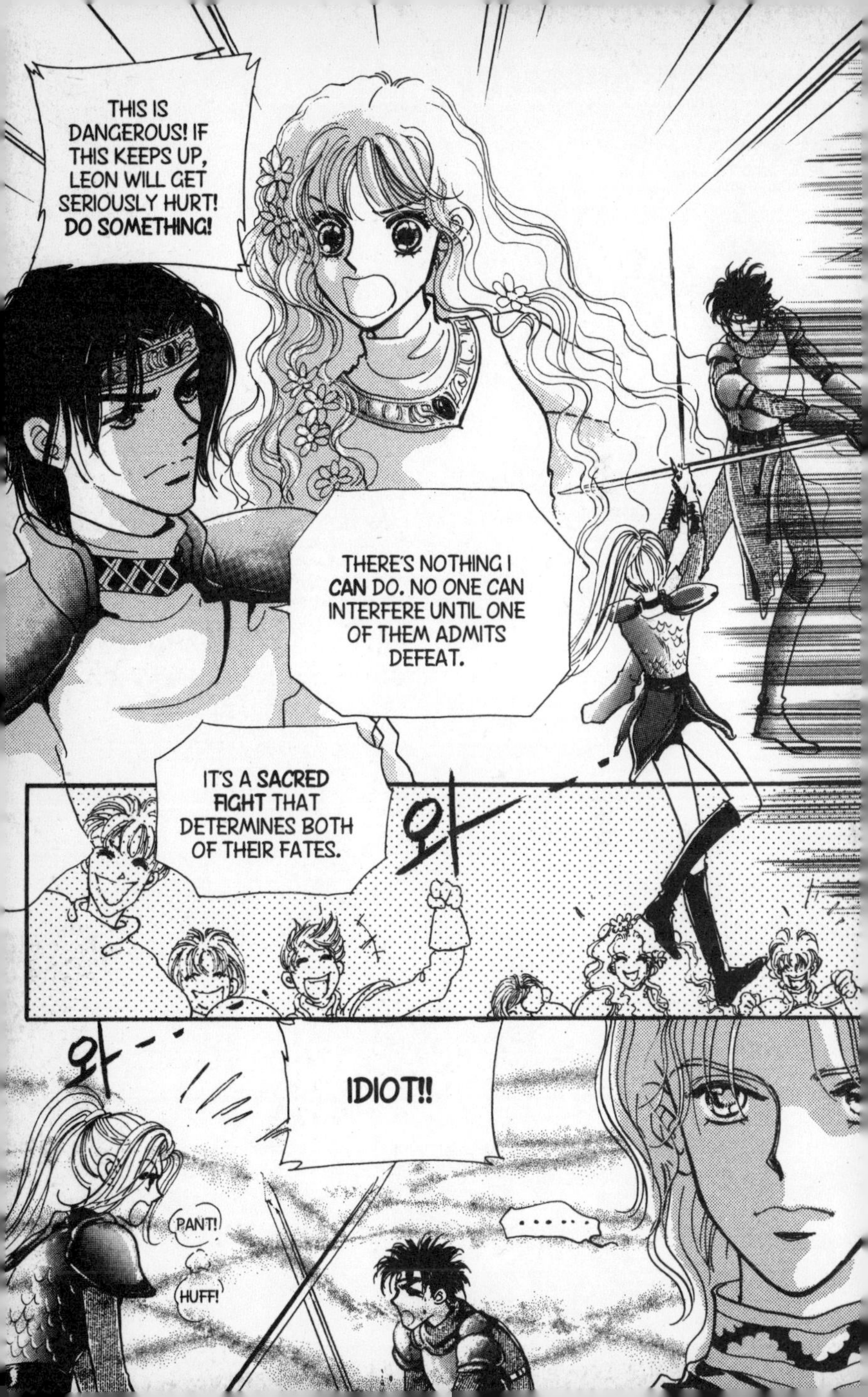
THIS IS DANGEROUS! IF THIS KEEPS UP, LEON WILL GET SERIOUSLY HURT! DO SOMETHING!
THERE'S NOTHING I CAN DO. NO ONE CAN INTERFERE UNTIL ONE OF THEM ADMITS DEFEAT.
IT'S A SACRED FIGHT THAT DETERMINES BOTH OF THEIR FATES.
와
와--
IDIOT!!
PANT!
HUFF!
.....

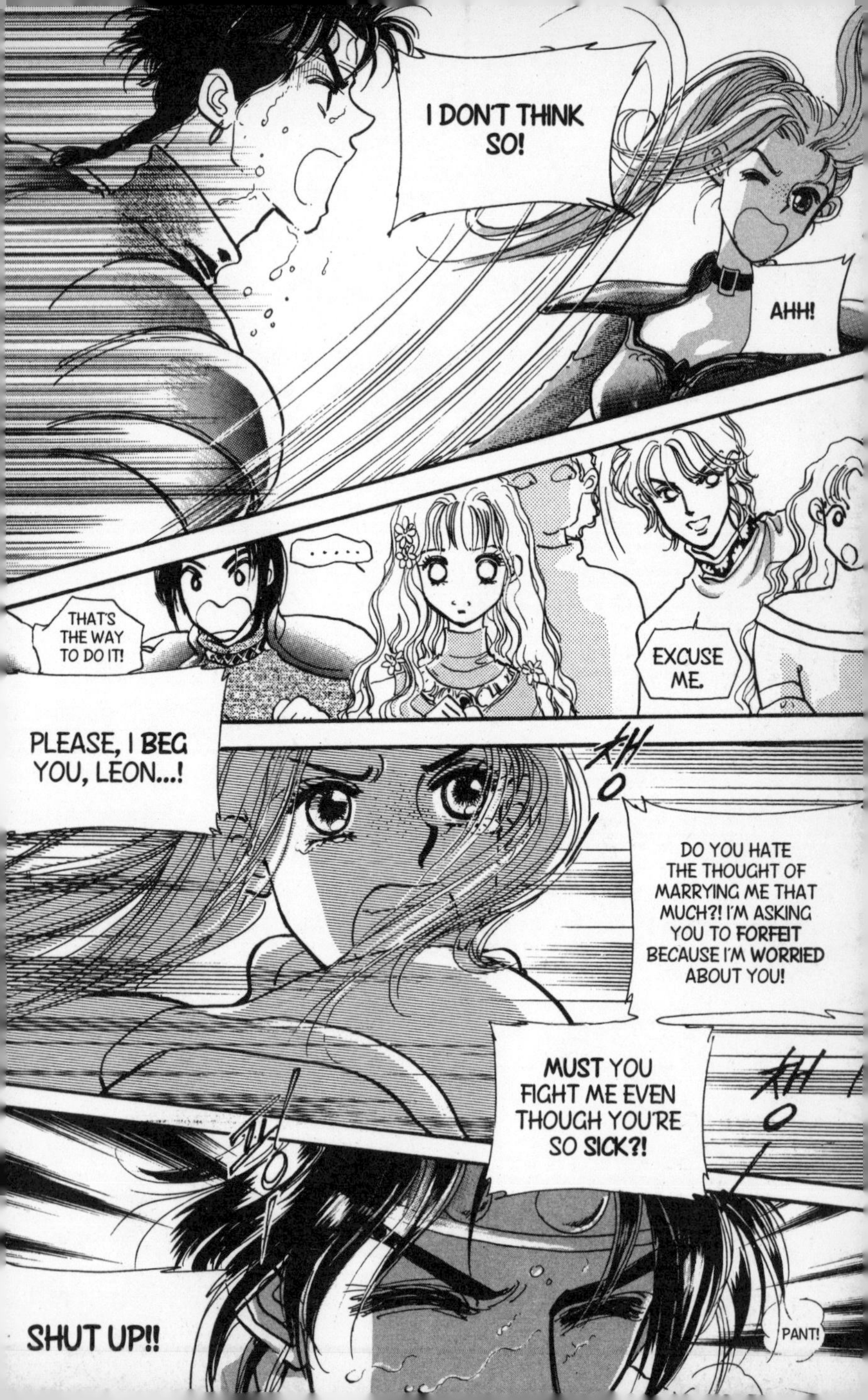
I DON'T THINK SO!
AHH!
THAT'S THE WAY TO DO IT!
.....
EXCUSE ME.
PLEASE, I BEG YOU, LEON...!
DO YOU HATE THE THOUGHT OF MARRYING ME THAT MUCH?! I'M ASKING YOU TO FORFEIT BECAUSE I'M WORRIED ABOUT YOU!
MUST YOU FIGHT ME EVEN THOUGH YOU'RE SO SICK?!
SHUT UP!!
PANT!

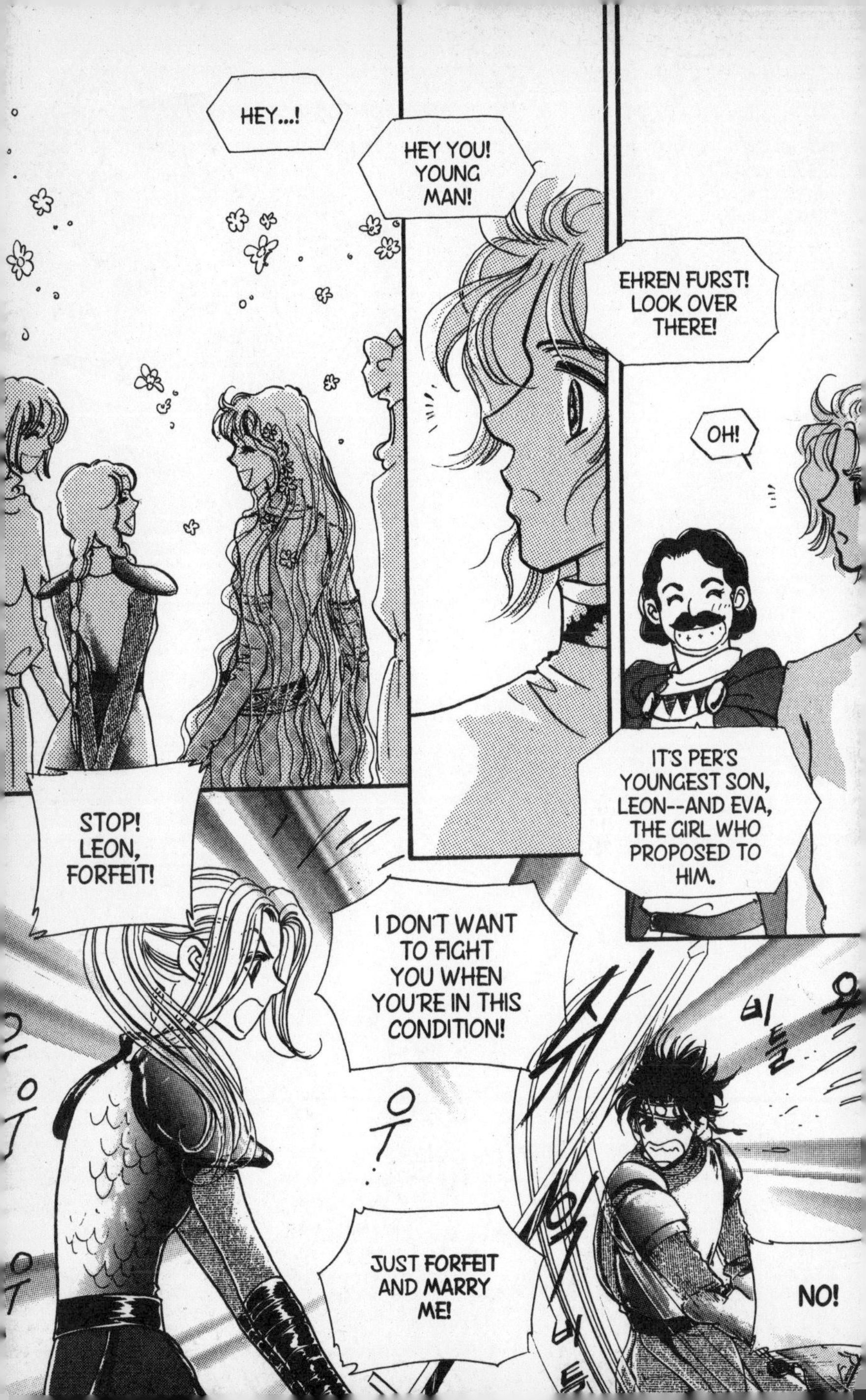
HEY...!
HEY YOU! YOUNG MAN!
EHREN FURST! LOOK OVER THERE!
OH!
IT'S PER'S YOUNGEST SON, LEON--AND EVA, THE GIRL WHO PROPOSED TO HIM.
STOP! LEON, FORFEIT!
I DON'T WANT TO FIGHT YOU WHEN YOU'RE IN THIS CONDITION!
JUST FORFEIT AND MARRY ME!
비틀
NO!

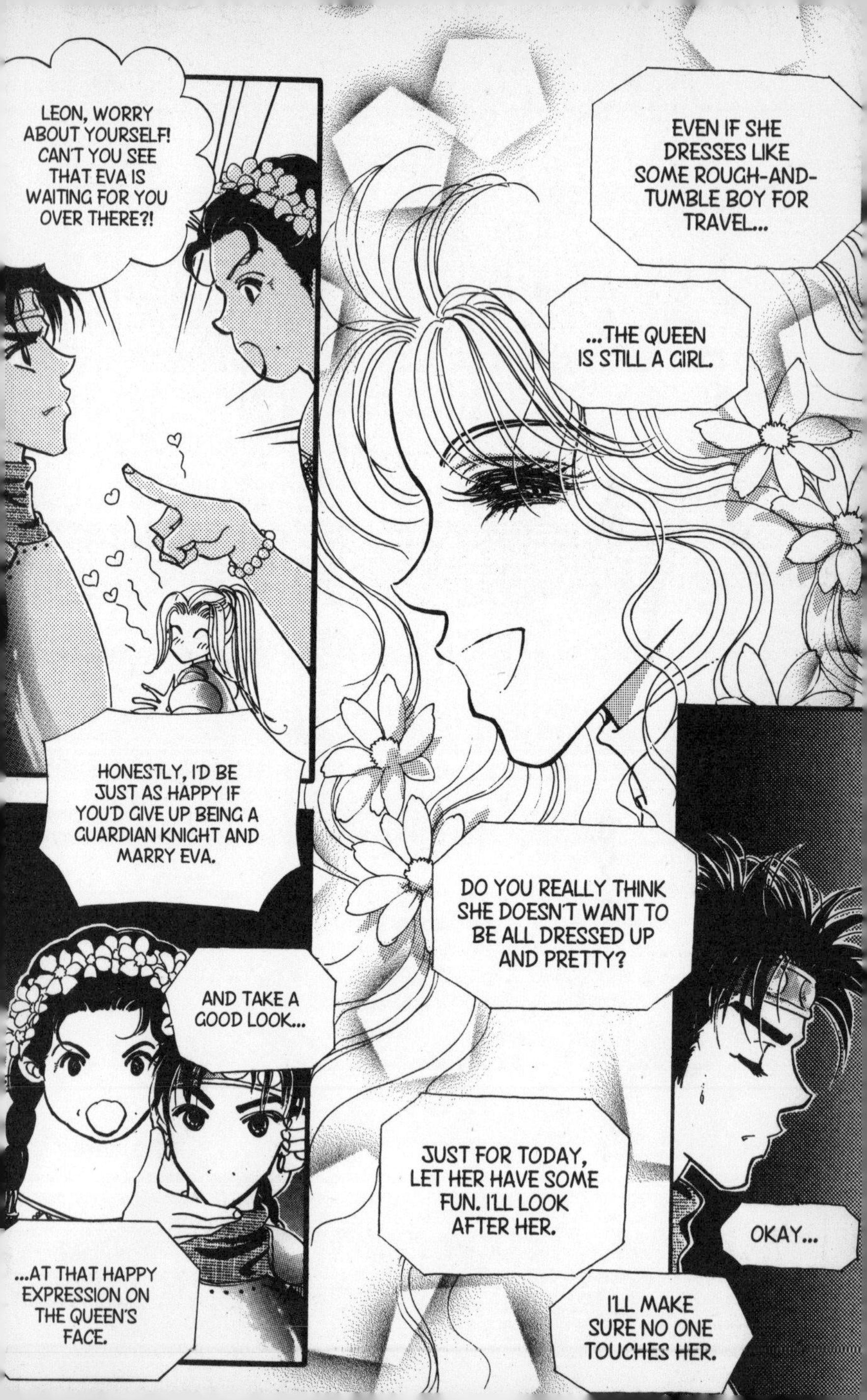
LEON, WORRY ABOUT YOURSELF! CAN'T YOU SEE THAT EVA IS WAITING FOR YOU OVER THERE?!
HONESTLY, I'D BE JUST AS HAPPY IF YOU'D GIVE UP BEING A GUARDIAN KNIGHT AND MARRY EVA.
AND TAKE A GOOD LOOK...
...AT THAT HAPPY EXPRESSION ON THE QUEEN'S FACE.
EVEN IF SHE DRESSES LIKE SOME ROUGH-AND-TUMBLE BOY FOR TRAVEL...
...THE QUEEN IS STILL A GIRL.
DO YOU REALLY THINK SHE DOESN'T WANT TO BE ALL DRESSED UP AND PRETTY?
JUST FOR TODAY, LET HER HAVE SOME FUN. I'LL LOOK AFTER HER.
OKAY...
I'LL MAKE SURE NO ONE TOUCHES HER.

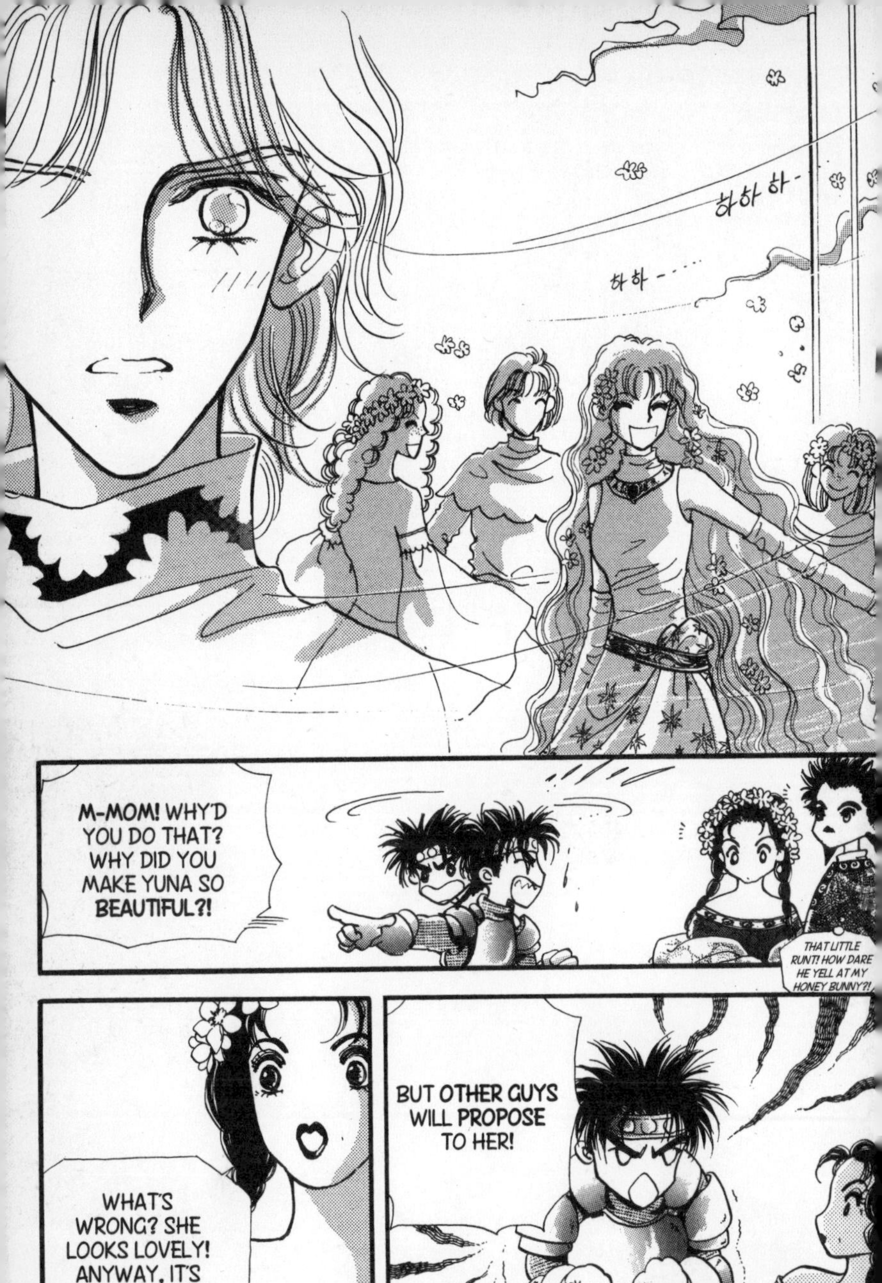

하하 하-
하하-
M-MOM! WHY'D YOU DO THAT? WHY DID YOU MAKE YUNA SO BEAUTIFUL?!
THAT LITTLE RUNT! HOW DARE HE YELL AT MY HONEY BUNNY?!
WHAT'S WRONG? SHE LOOKS LOVELY! ANYWAY, IT'S FESTIVAL TIME!
BUT OTHER GUYS WILL PROPOSE TO HER!

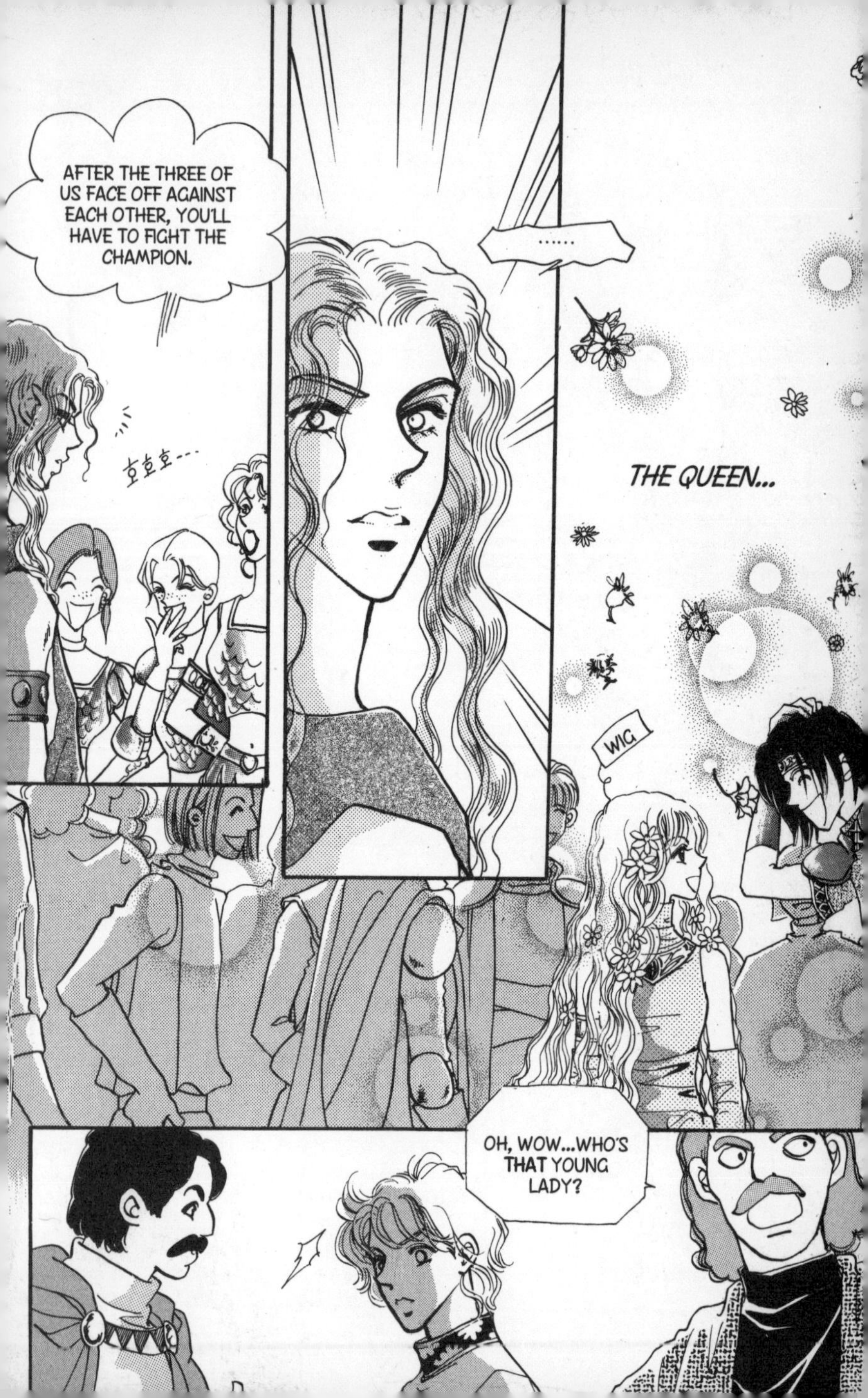
AFTER THE THREE OF US FACE OFF AGAINST EACH OTHER, YOU'LL HAVE TO FIGHT THE CHAMPION.
......
THE QUEEN...
WIG
OH, WOW...WHO'S THAT YOUNG LADY?

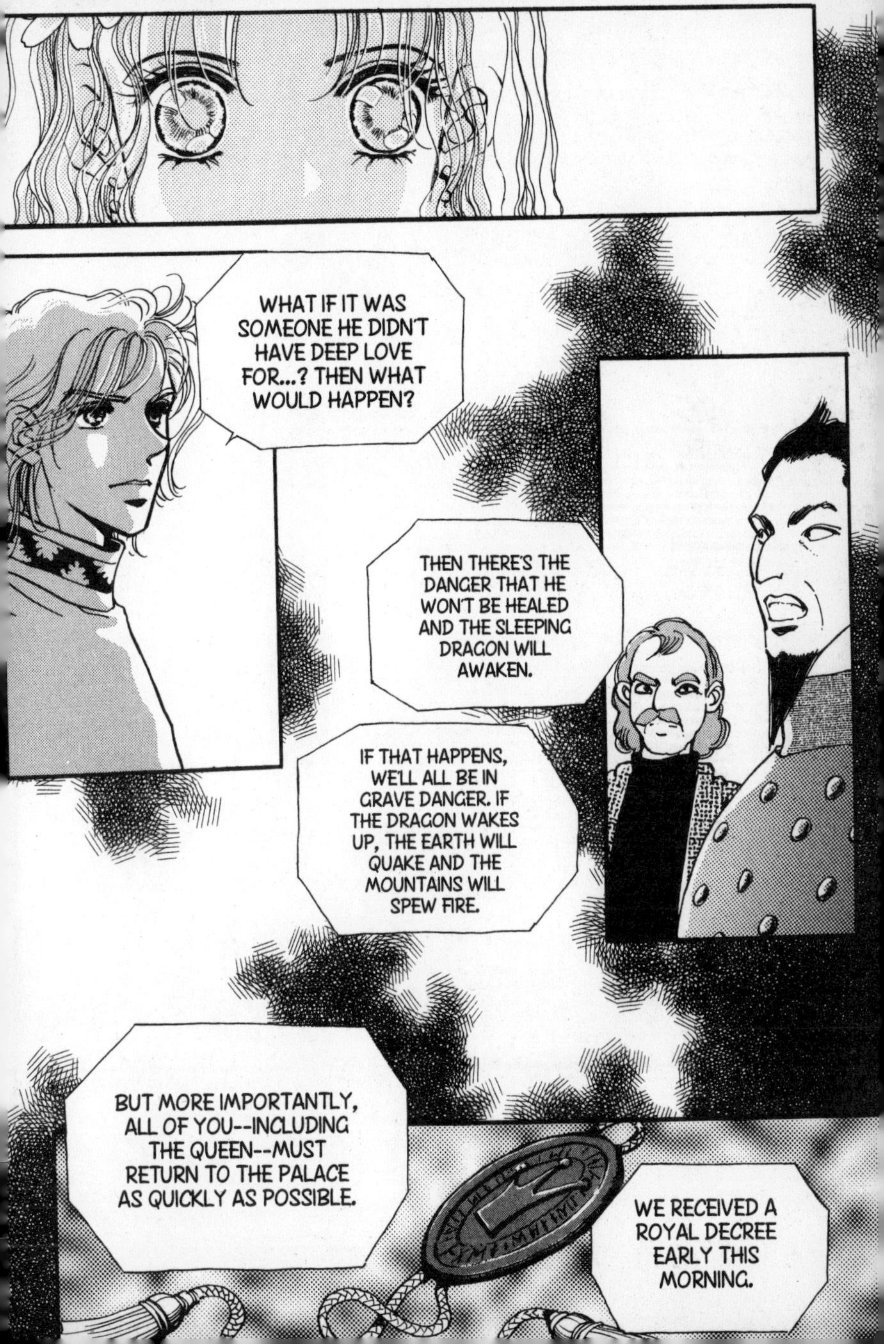
WHAT IF IT WAS SOMEONE HE DIDN'T HAVE DEEP LOVE FOR...? THEN WHAT WOULD HAPPEN?
THEN THERE'S THE DANGER THAT HE WON'T BE HEALED AND THE SLEEPING DRAGON WILL AWAKEN.
IF THAT HAPPENS, WE'LL ALL BE IN GRAVE DANGER. IF THE DRAGON WAKES UP, THE EARTH WILL QUAKE AND THE MOUNTAINS WILL SPEW FIRE.
BUT MORE IMPORTANTLY, ALL OF YOU--INCLUDING THE QUEEN--MUST RETURN TO THE PALACE AS QUICKLY AS POSSIBLE.
WE RECEIVED A ROYAL DECREE EARLY THIS MORNING.

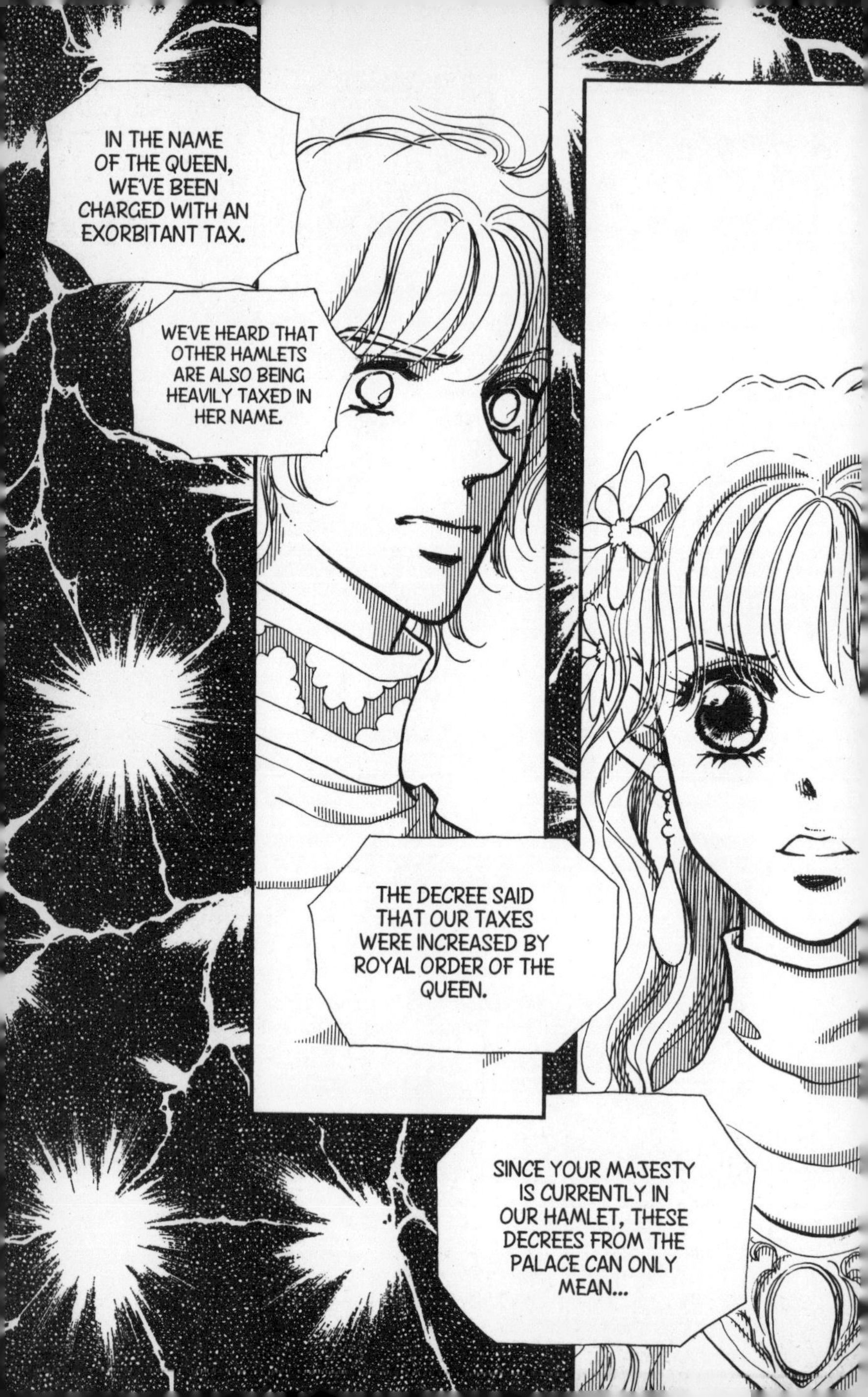
IN THE NAME OF THE QUEEN, WE'VE BEEN CHARGED WITH AN EXORBITANT TAX.
WE'VE HEARD THAT OTHER HAMLETS ARE ALSO BEING HEAVILY TAXED IN HER NAME.
THE DECREE SAID THAT OUR TAXES WERE INCREASED BY ROYAL ORDER OF THE QUEEN.
SINCE YOUR MAJESTY IS CURRENTLY IN OUR HAMLET, THESE DECREES FROM THE PALACE CAN ONLY MEAN...

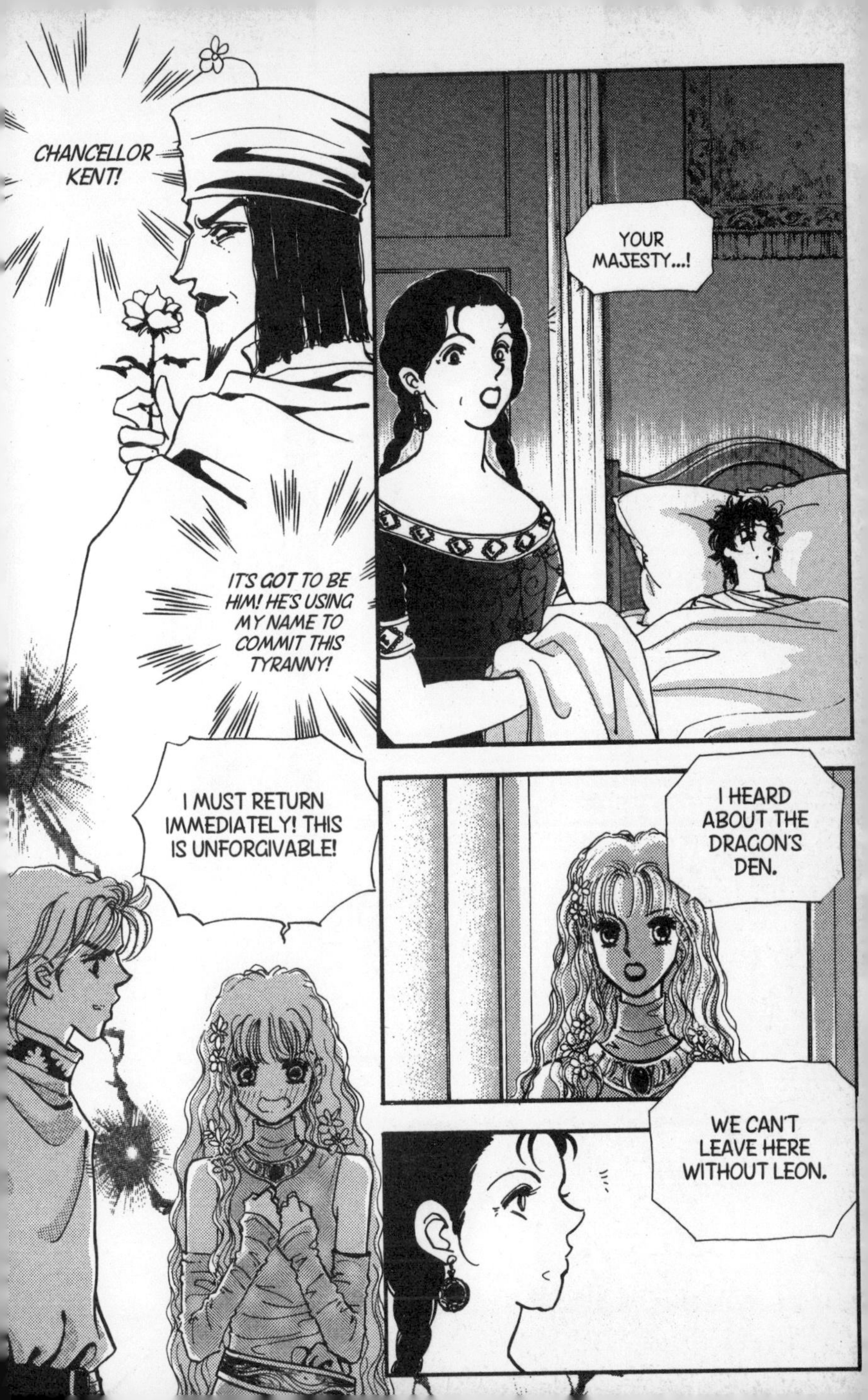

CHANCELLOR KENT!
IT'S GOT TO BE HIM! HE'S USING MY NAME TO COMMIT THIS TYRANNY!
I MUST RETURN IMMEDIATELY! THIS IS UNFORGIVABLE!
YOUR MAJESTY...!
I HEARD ABOUT THE DRAGON'S DEN.
WE CAN'T LEAVE HERE WITHOUT LEON.

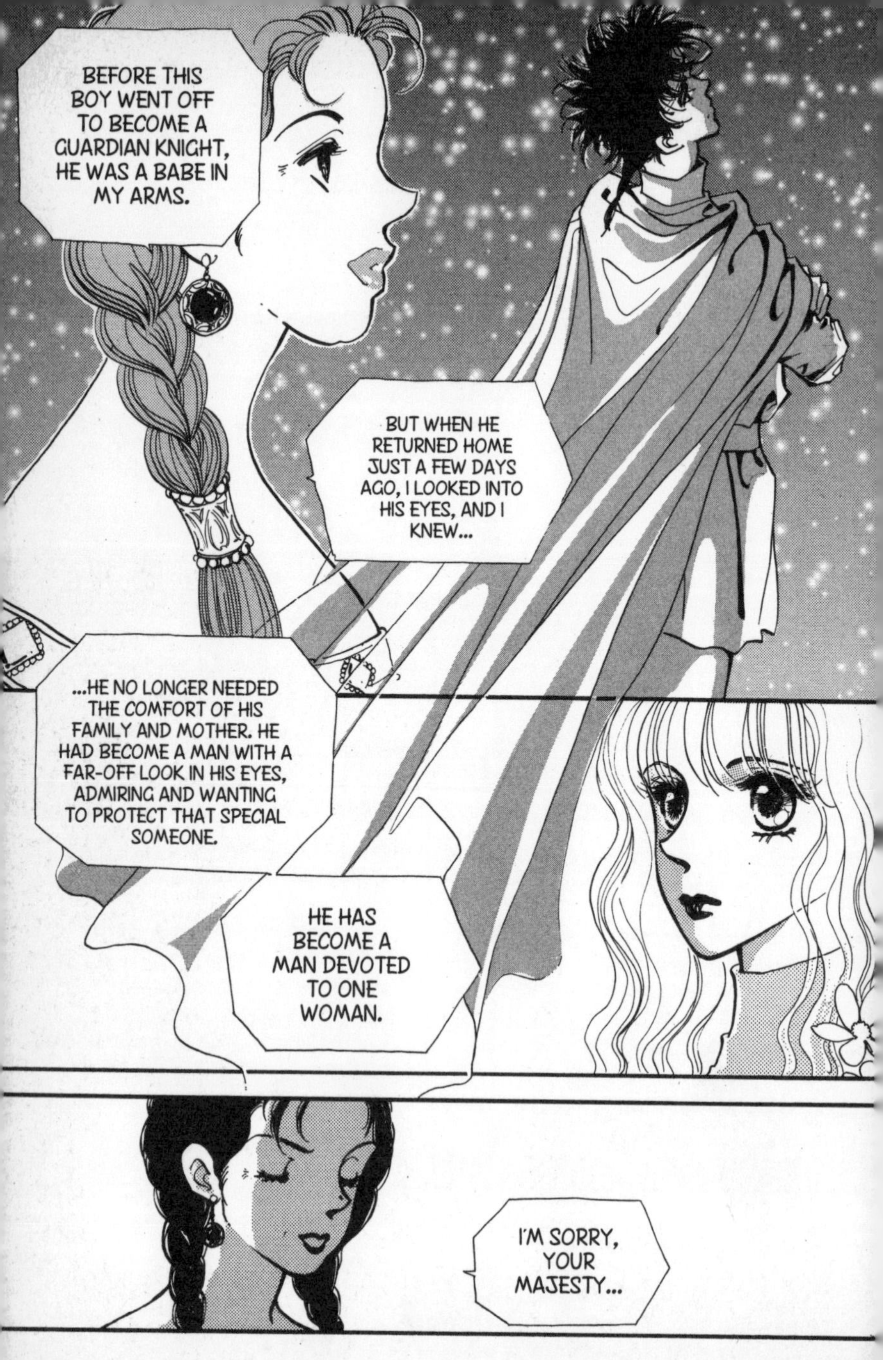
BEFORE THIS BOY WENT OFF TO BECOME A GUARDIAN KNIGHT, HE WAS A BABE IN MY ARMS.
BUT WHEN HE RETURNED HOME JUST A FEW DAYS AGO, I LOOKED INTO HIS EYES, AND I KNEW...
...HE NO LONGER NEEDED THE COMFORT OF HIS FAMILY AND MOTHER. HE HAD BECOME A MAN WITH A FAR-OFF LOOK IN HIS EYES, ADMIRING AND WANTING TO PROTECT THAT SPECIAL SOMEONE.
HE HAS BECOME A MAN DEVOTED TO ONE WOMAN.
I'M SORRY, YOUR MAJESTY...

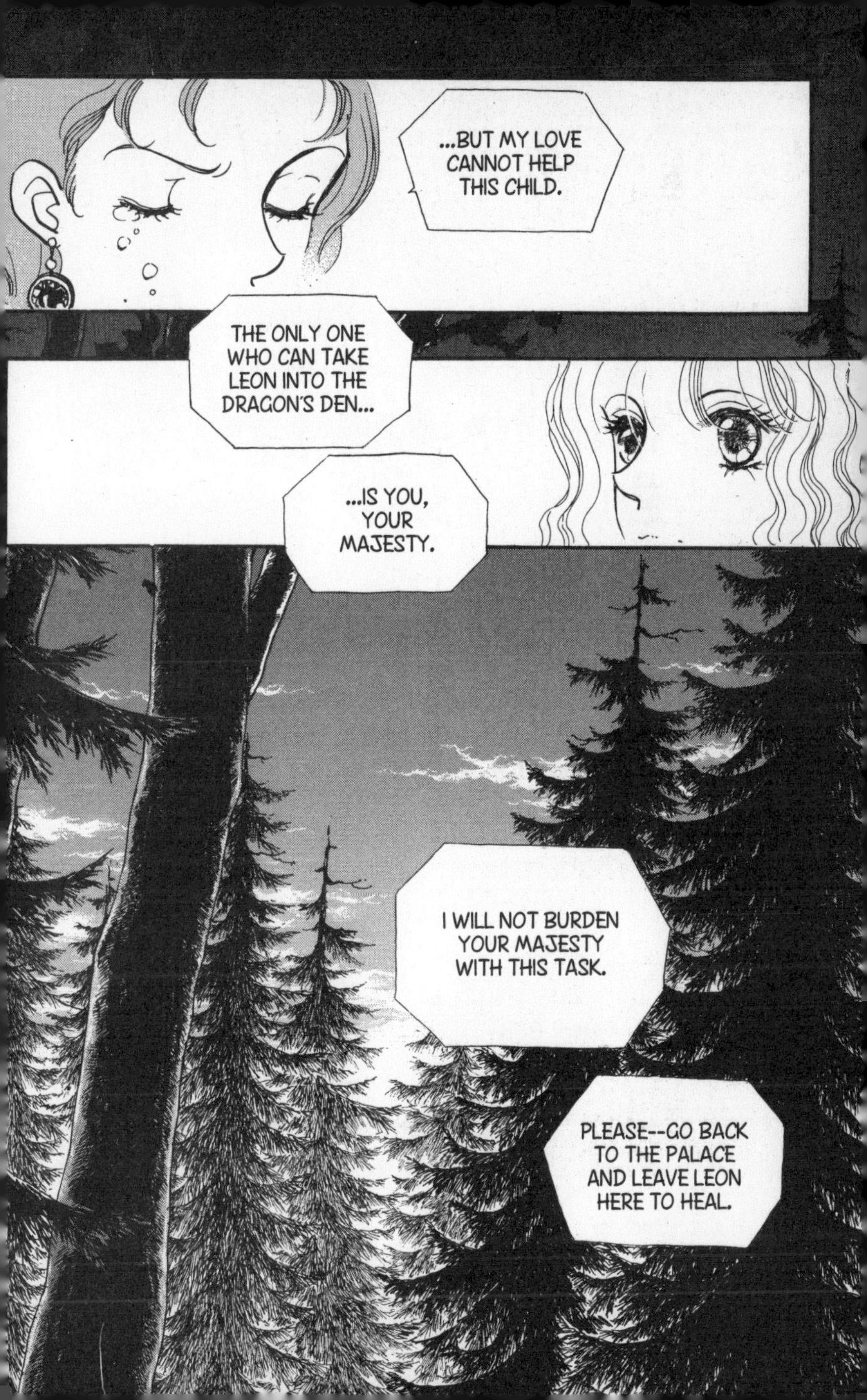
...BUT MY LOVE CANNOT HELP THIS CHILD.
THE ONLY ONE WHO CAN TAKE LEON INTO THE DRAGON'S DEN...
...IS YOU, YOUR MAJESTY.
I WILL NOT BURDEN YOUR MAJESTY WITH THIS TASK.
PLEASE--GO BACK TO THE PALACE AND LEAVE LEON HERE TO HEAL.

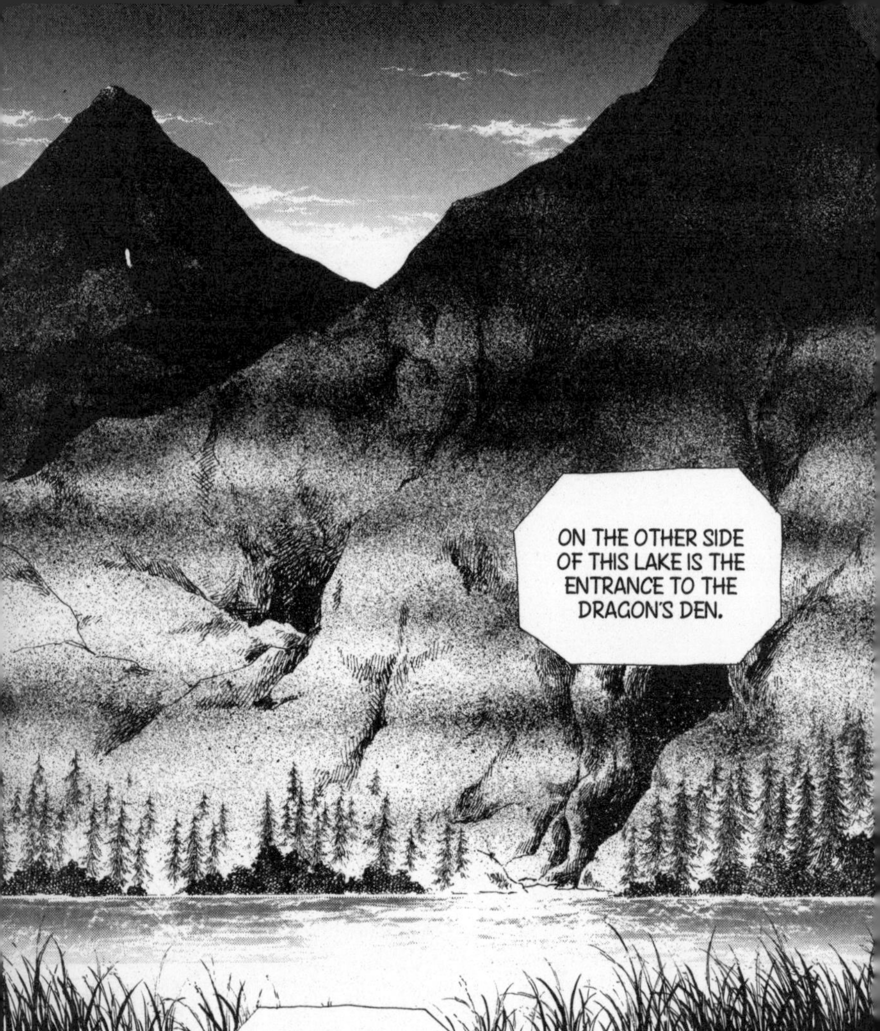
ON THE OTHER SIDE OF THIS LAKE IS THE ENTRANCE TO THE DRAGON'S DEN.
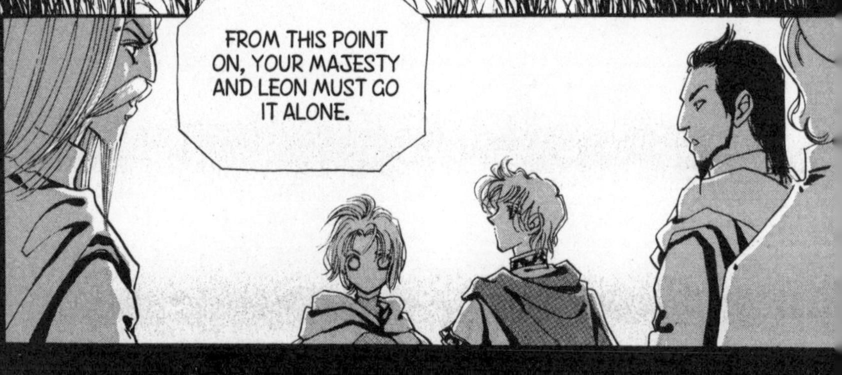
FROM THIS POINT ON, YOUR MAJESTY AND LEON MUST GO IT ALONE.

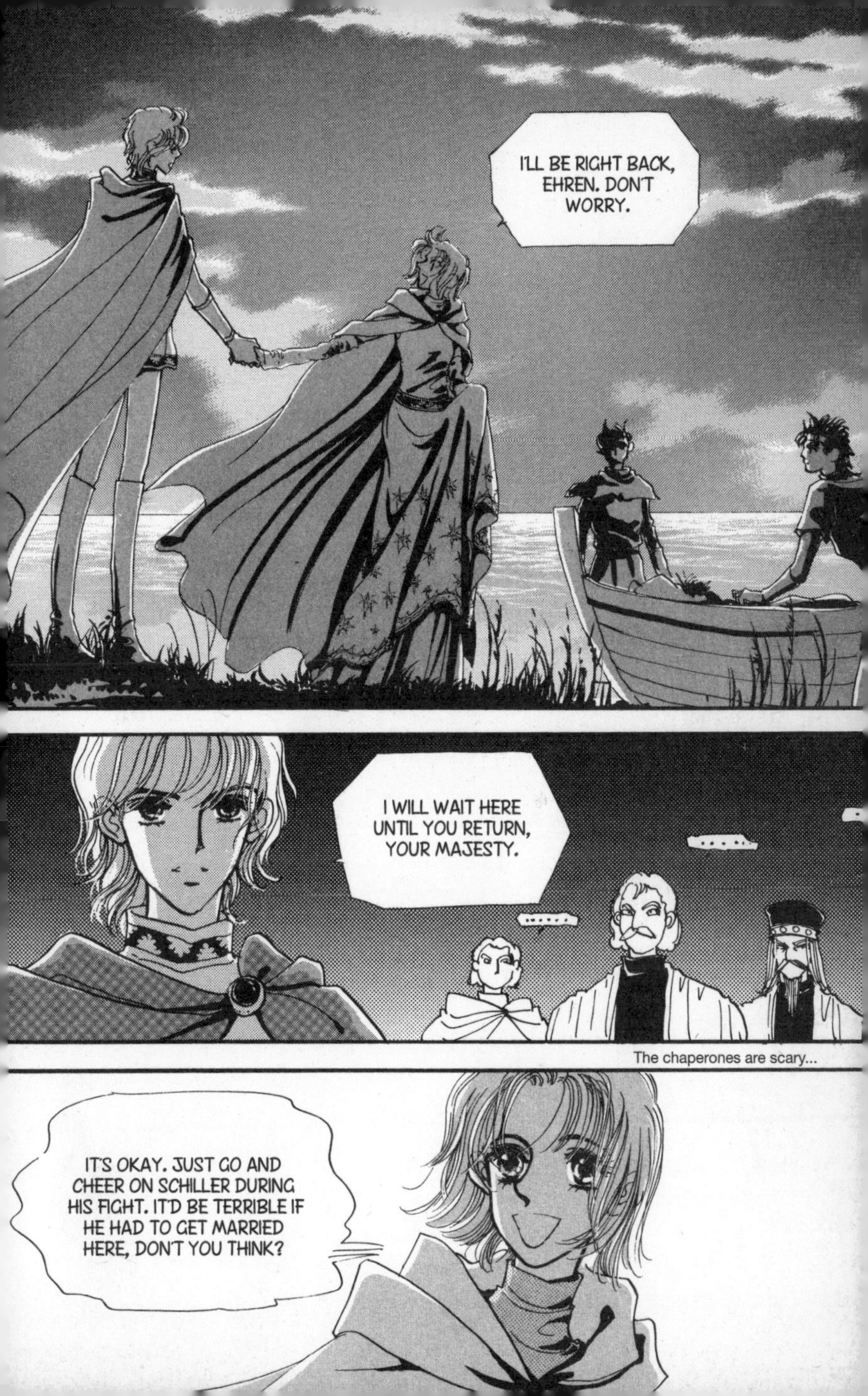
I'LL BE RIGHT BACK, EHREN. DON'T WORRY.
I WILL WAIT HERE UNTIL YOU RETURN, YOUR MAJESTY.
.....
.....
The chaperones are scary...
IT'S OKAY. JUST GO AND CHEER ON SCHILLER DURING HIS FIGHT. IT'D BE TERRIBLE IF HE HAD TO GET MARRIED HERE, DON'T YOU THINK?

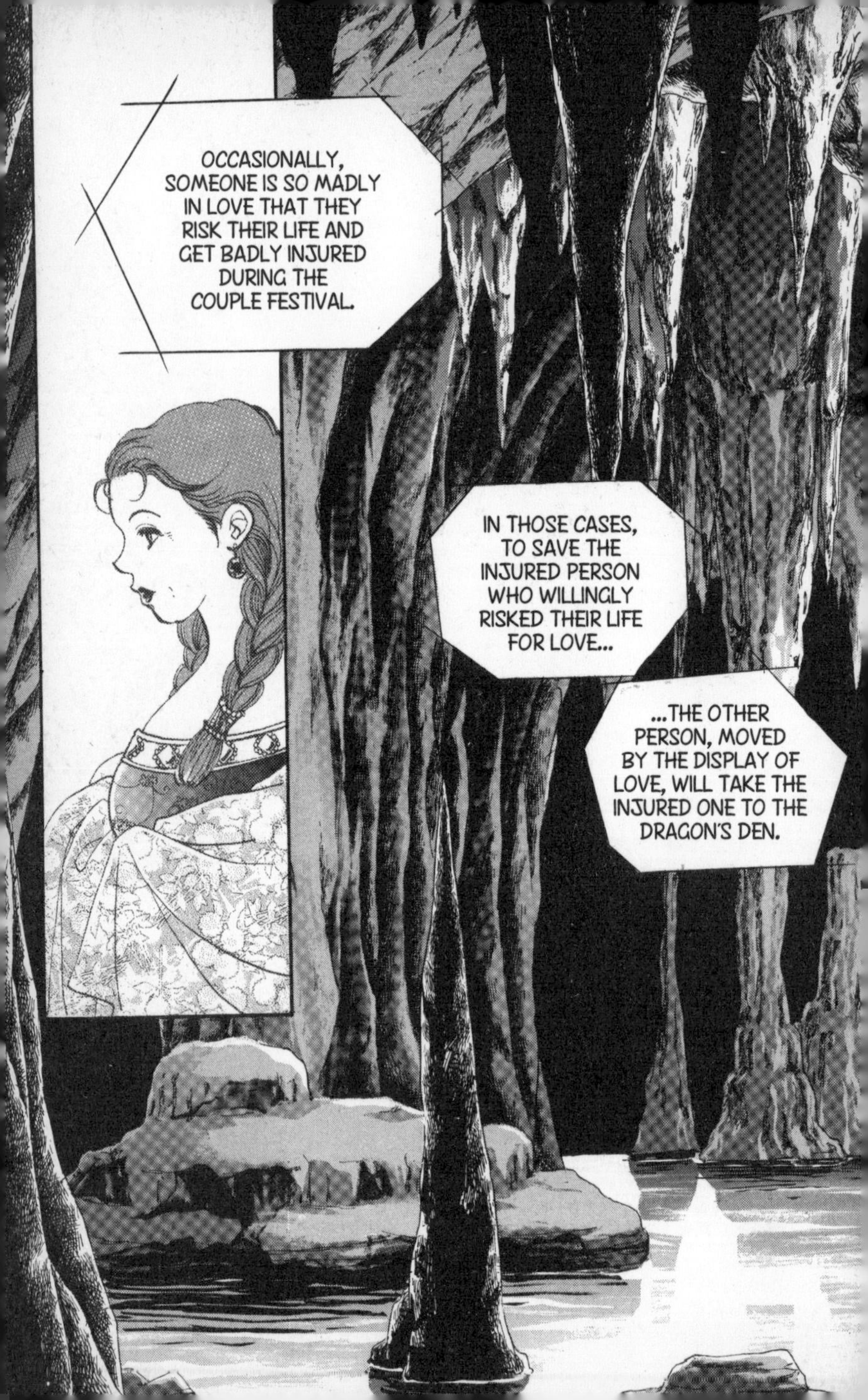
OCCASIONALLY, SOMEONE IS SO MADLY IN LOVE THAT THEY RISK THEIR LIFE AND GET BADLY INJURED DURING THE COUPLE FESTIVAL.
IN THOSE CASES, TO SAVE THE INJURED PERSON WHO WILLINGLY RISKED THEIR LIFE FOR LOVE...
...THE OTHER PERSON, MOVED BY THE DISPLAY OF LOVE, WILL TAKE THE INJURED ONE TO THE DRAGON'S DEN.

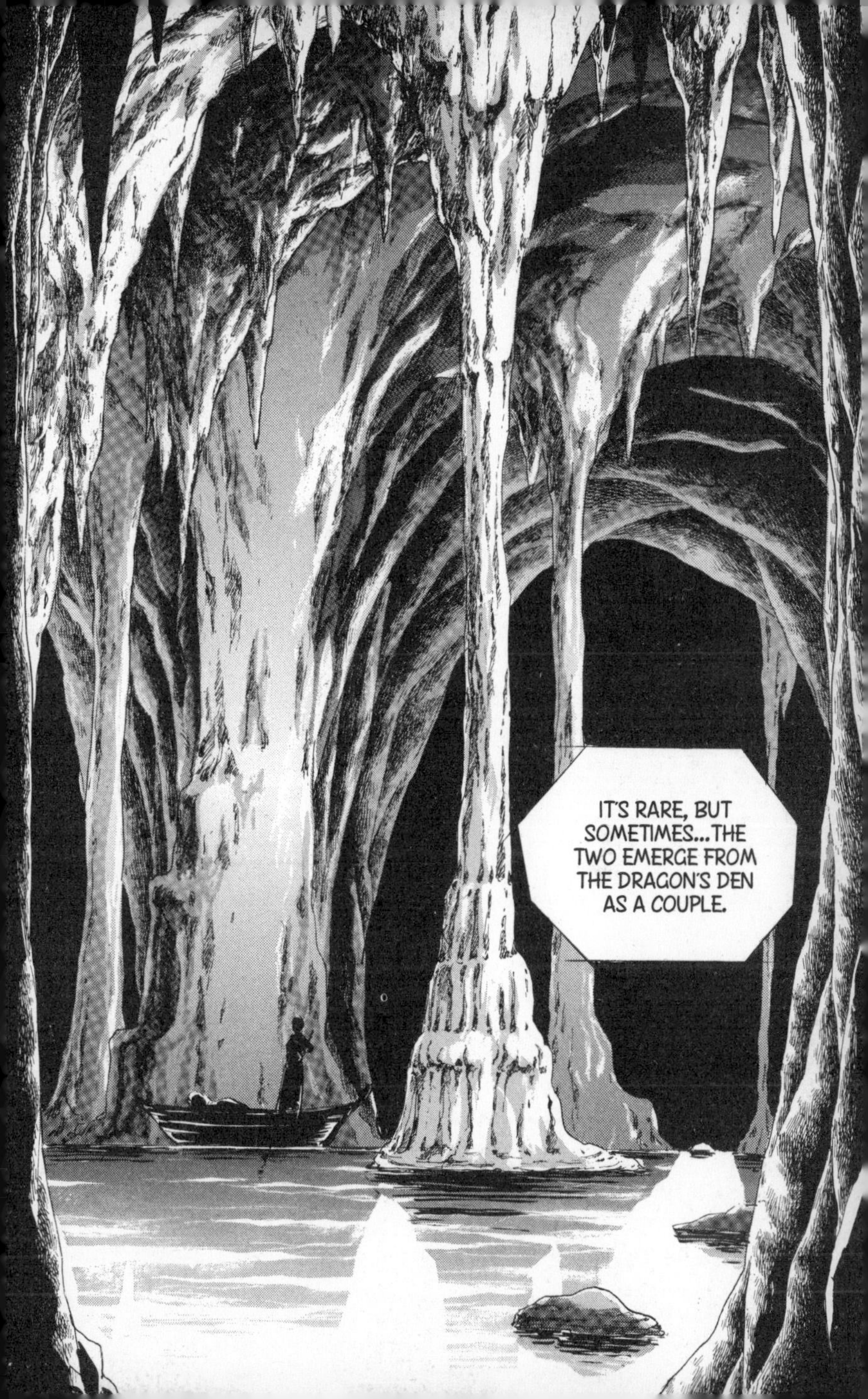
IT'S RARE, BUT SOMETIMES...THE TWO EMERGE FROM THE DRAGON'S DEN AS A COUPLE.

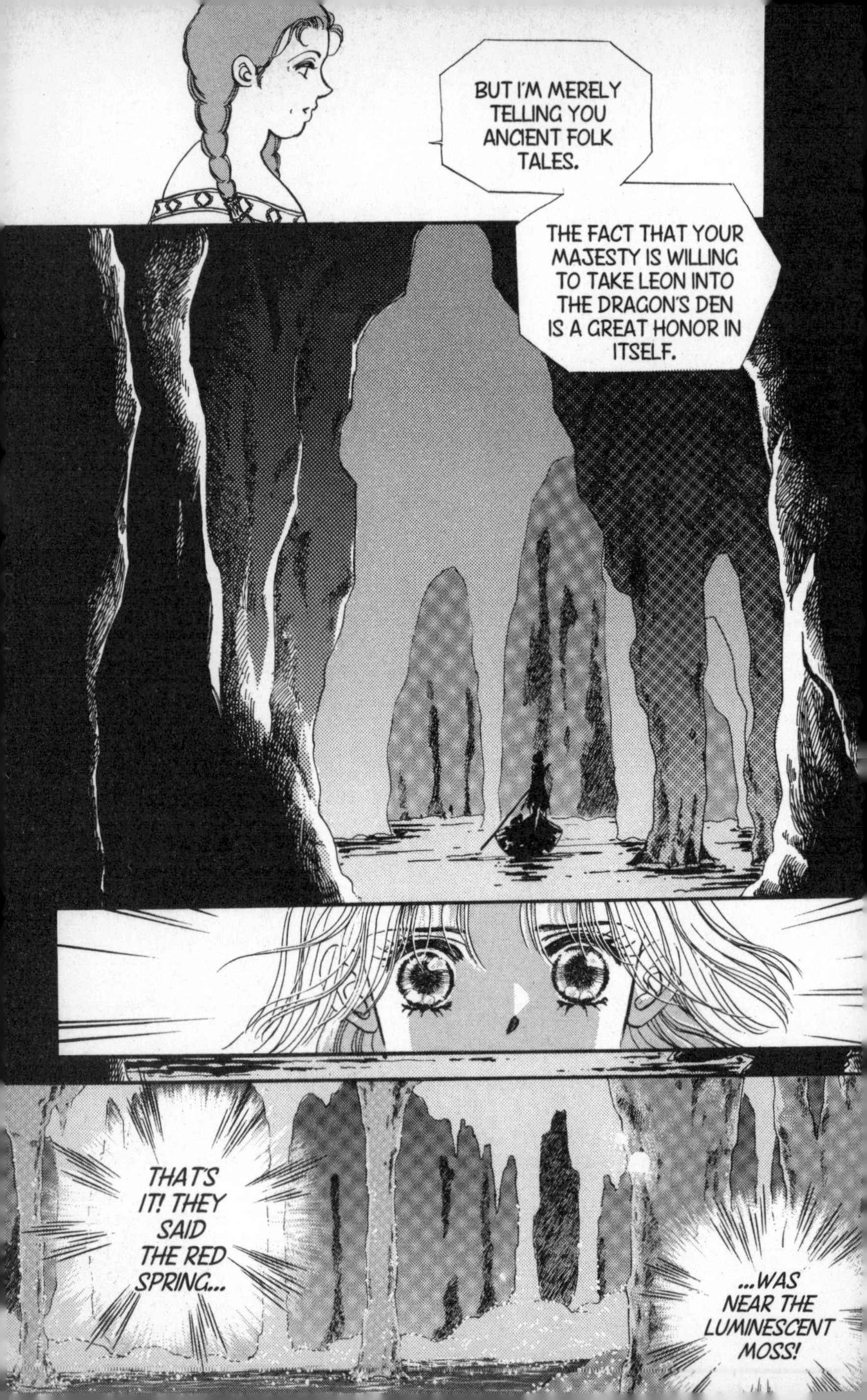
BUT I'M MERELY TELLING YOU ANCIENT FOLK TALES.
THE FACT THAT YOUR MAJESTY IS WILLING TO TAKE LEON INTO THE DRAGON'S DEN IS A GREAT HONOR IN ITSELF.
THAT'S IT! THEY SAID THE RED SPRING...
...WAS NEAR THE LUMINESCENT MOSS!

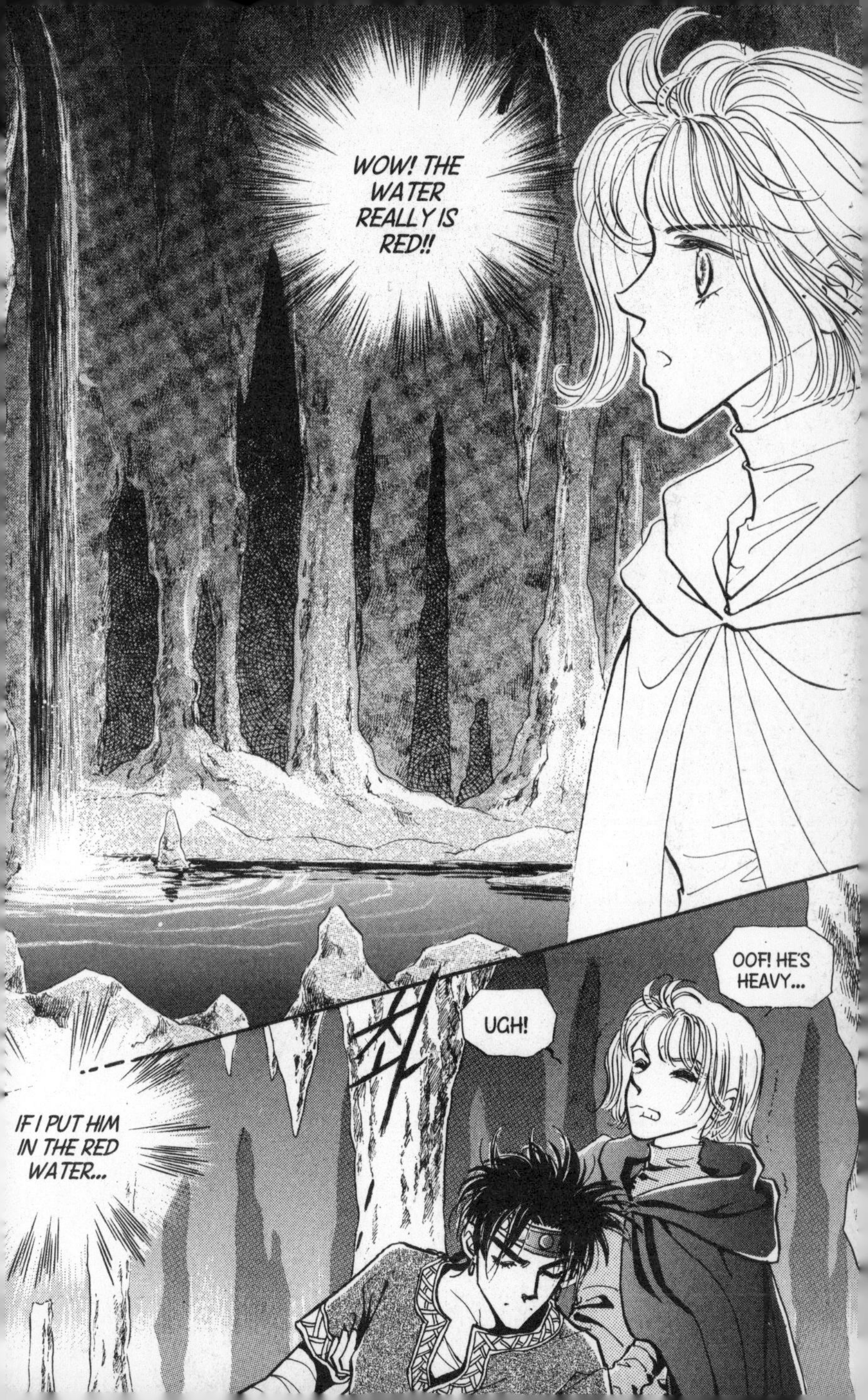
WOW! THE WATER REALLY IS RED!!
IF I PUT HIM IN THE RED WATER...
UGH!
OOF! HE'S HEAVY...

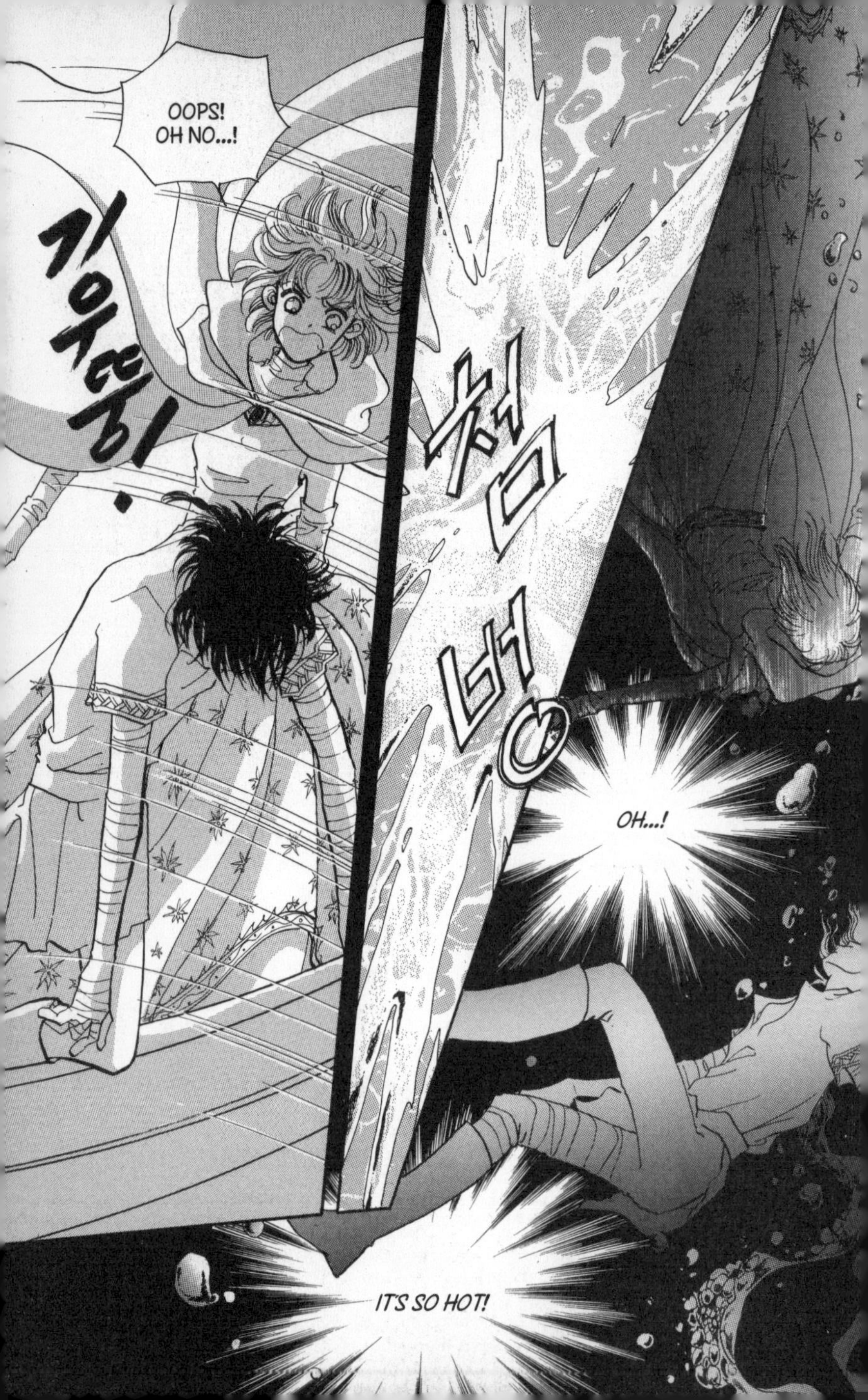
OOPS!
OH NO...!
첨벙
OH...!
ITS SO HOT!

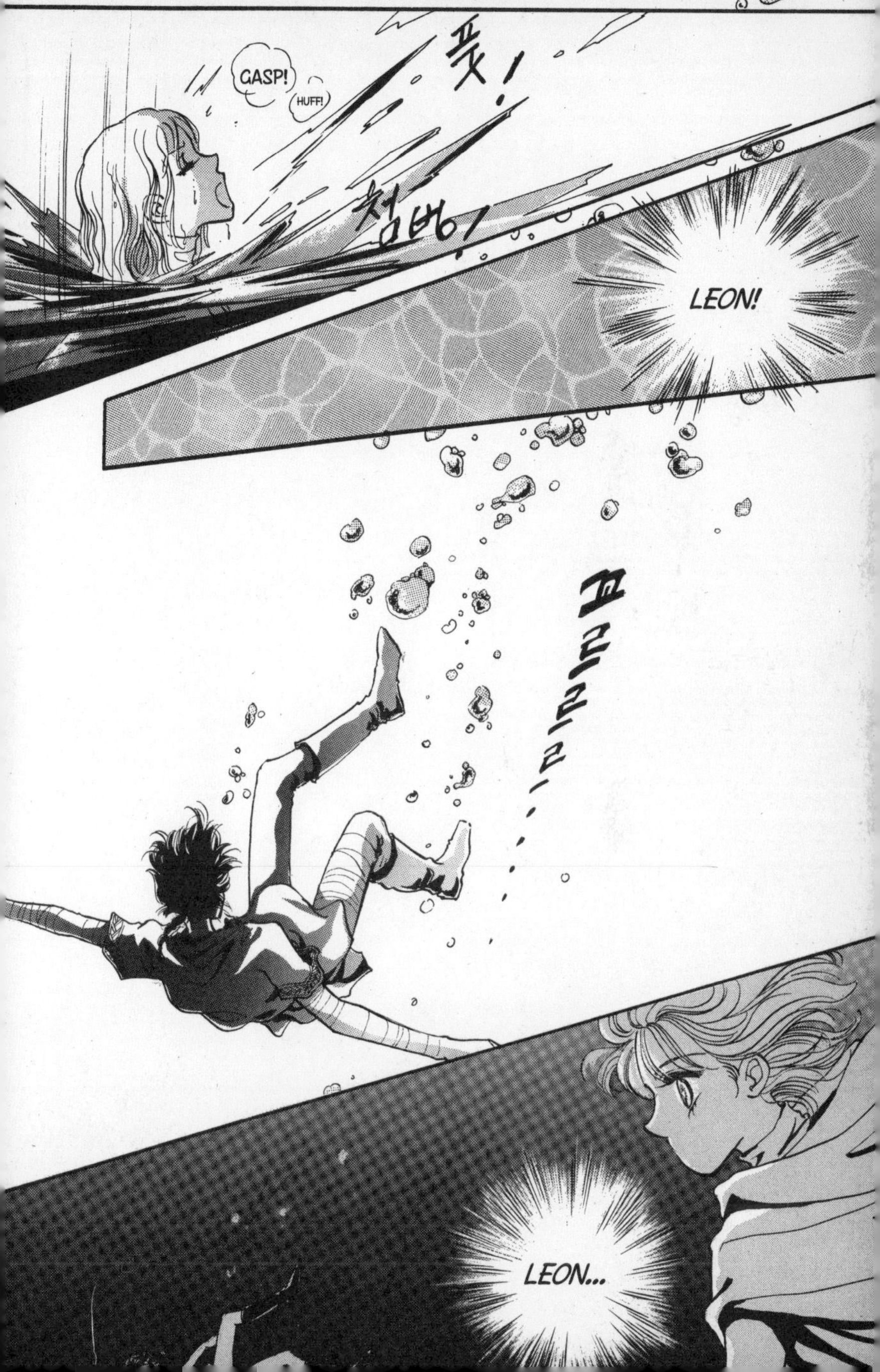
GASP!
HUFF!
풋!
첨벙!
LEON!
프르르르...
LEON...

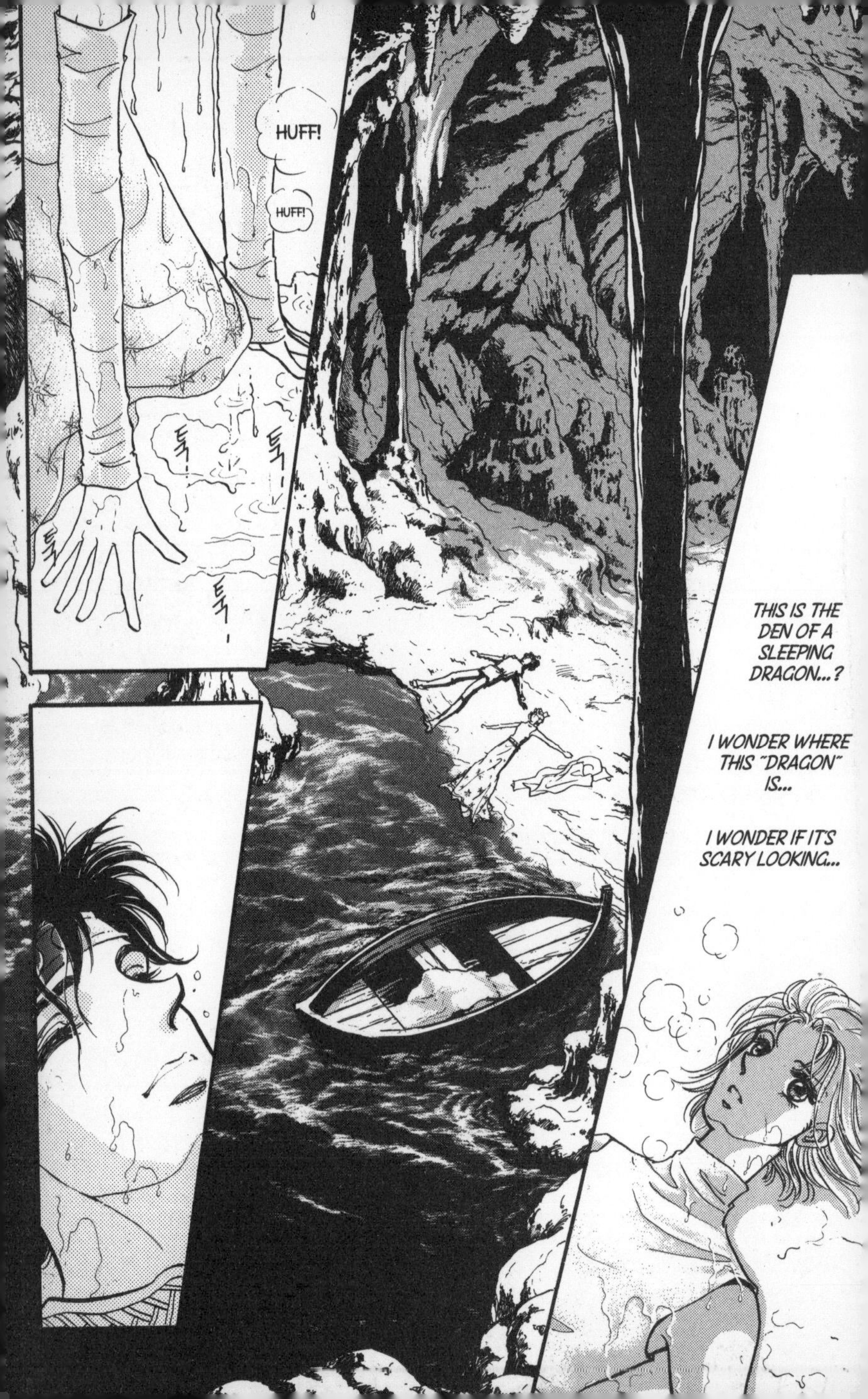
HUFF!
HUFF!
툭
툭
툭
툭
THIS IS THE DEN OF A SLEEPING DRAGON...?
I WONDER WHERE THIS "DRAGON" IS...
I WONDER IF IT'S SCARY LOOKING...

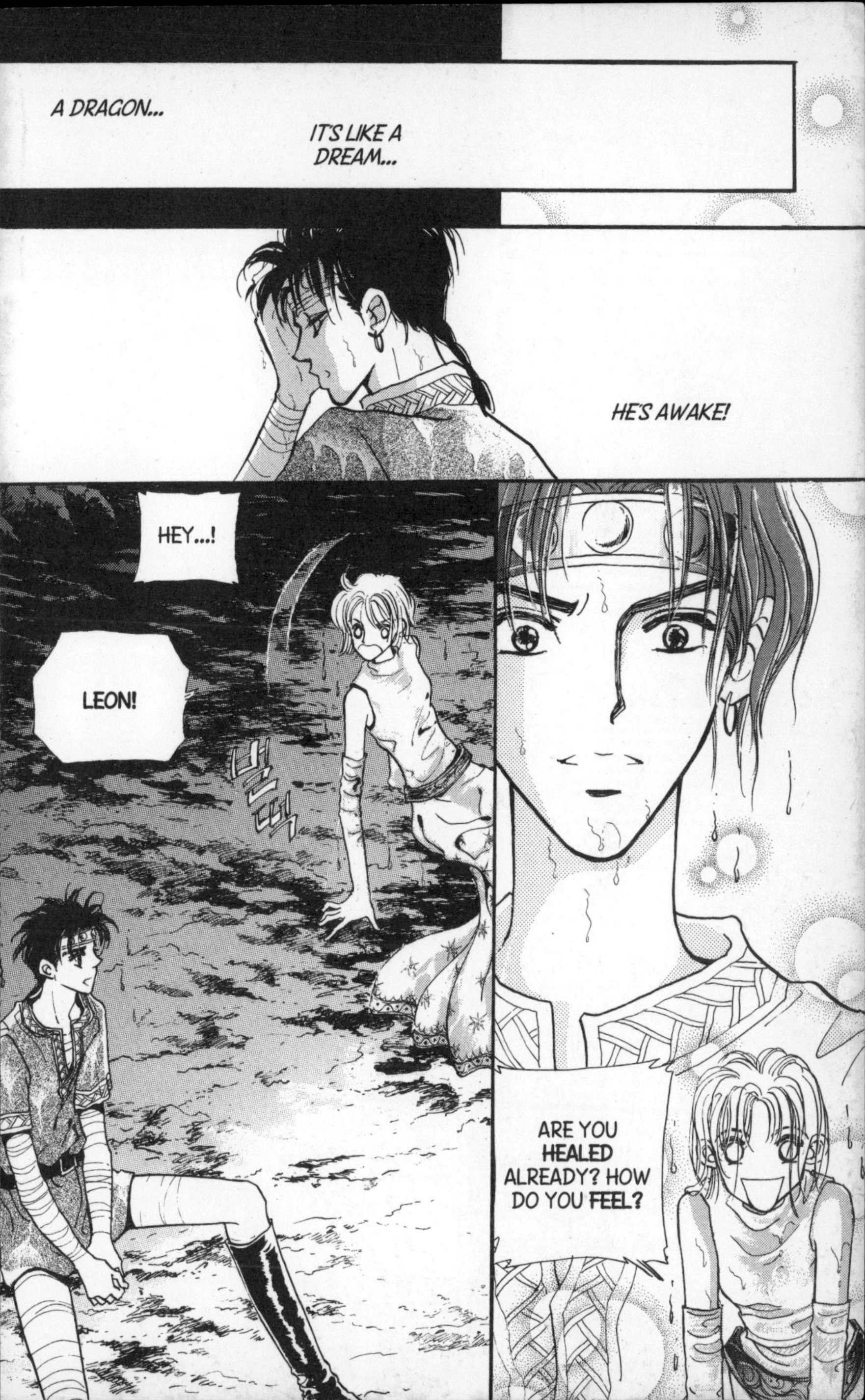
A DRAGON...
IT'S LIKE A DREAM...
HE'S AWAKE!
HEY...!
LEON!
벌떡
ARE YOU HEALED ALREADY? HOW DO YOU FEEL?

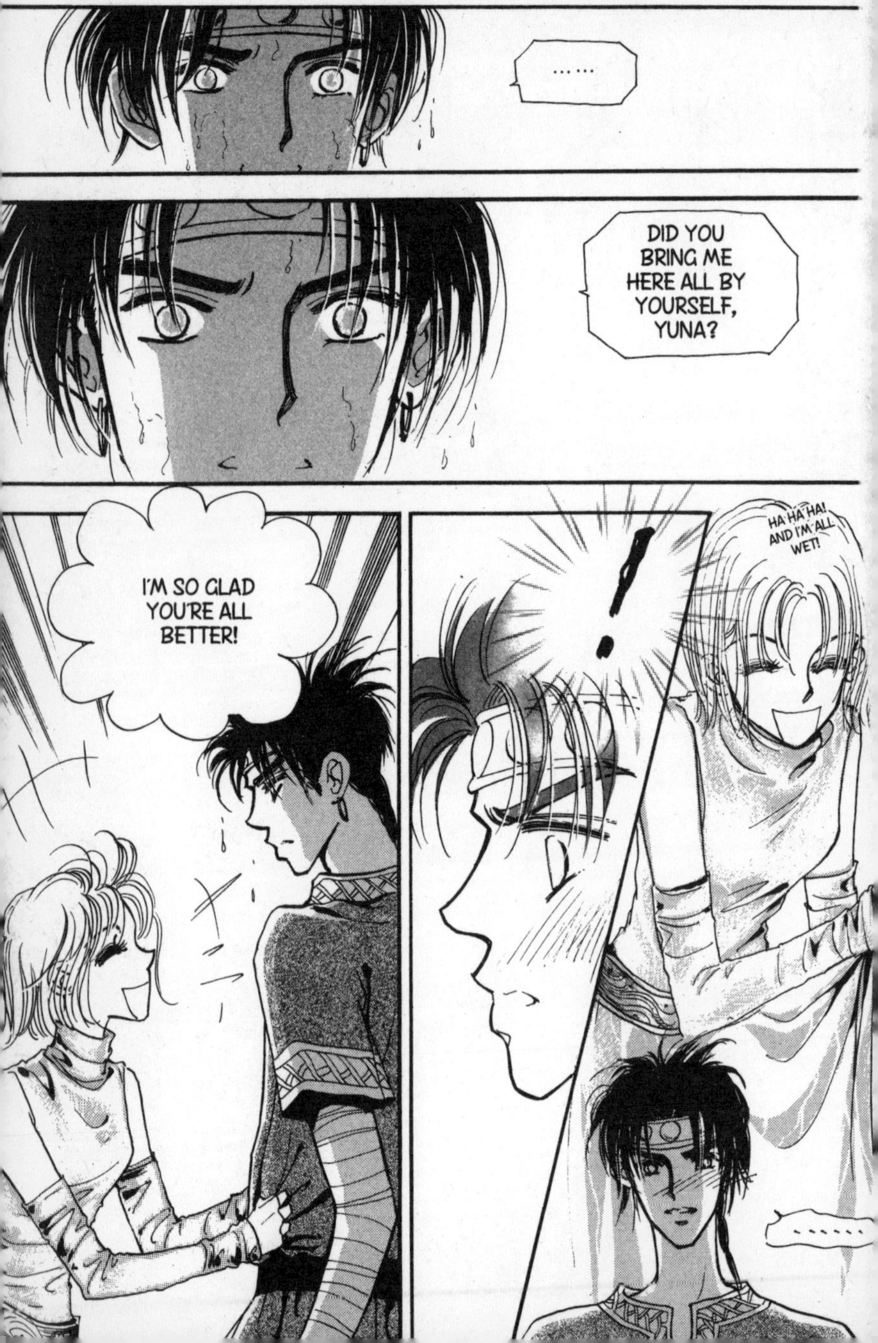
......
DID YOU BRING ME HERE ALL BY YOURSELF, YUNA?
I'M SO GLAD YOU'RE ALL BETTER!
!
HA HA HA! AND I'M ALL WET!
......

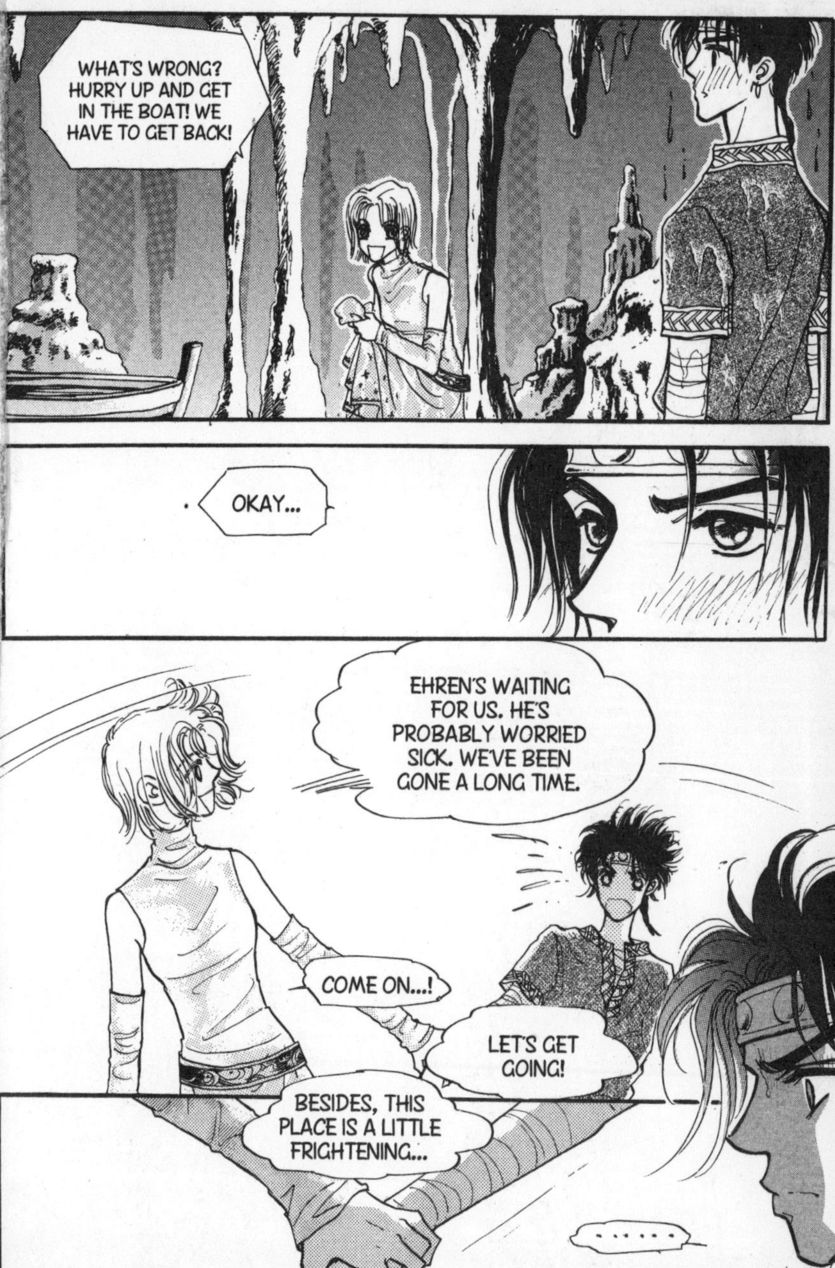
WHAT'S WRONG? HURRY UP AND GET IN THE BOAT! WE HAVE TO GET BACK!
OKAY...
EHREN'S WAITING FOR US. HE'S PROBABLY WORRIED SICK. WE'VE BEEN GONE A LONG TIME.
COME ON...!
LET'S GET GOING!
BESIDES, THIS PLACE IS A LITTLE FRIGHTENING...
......

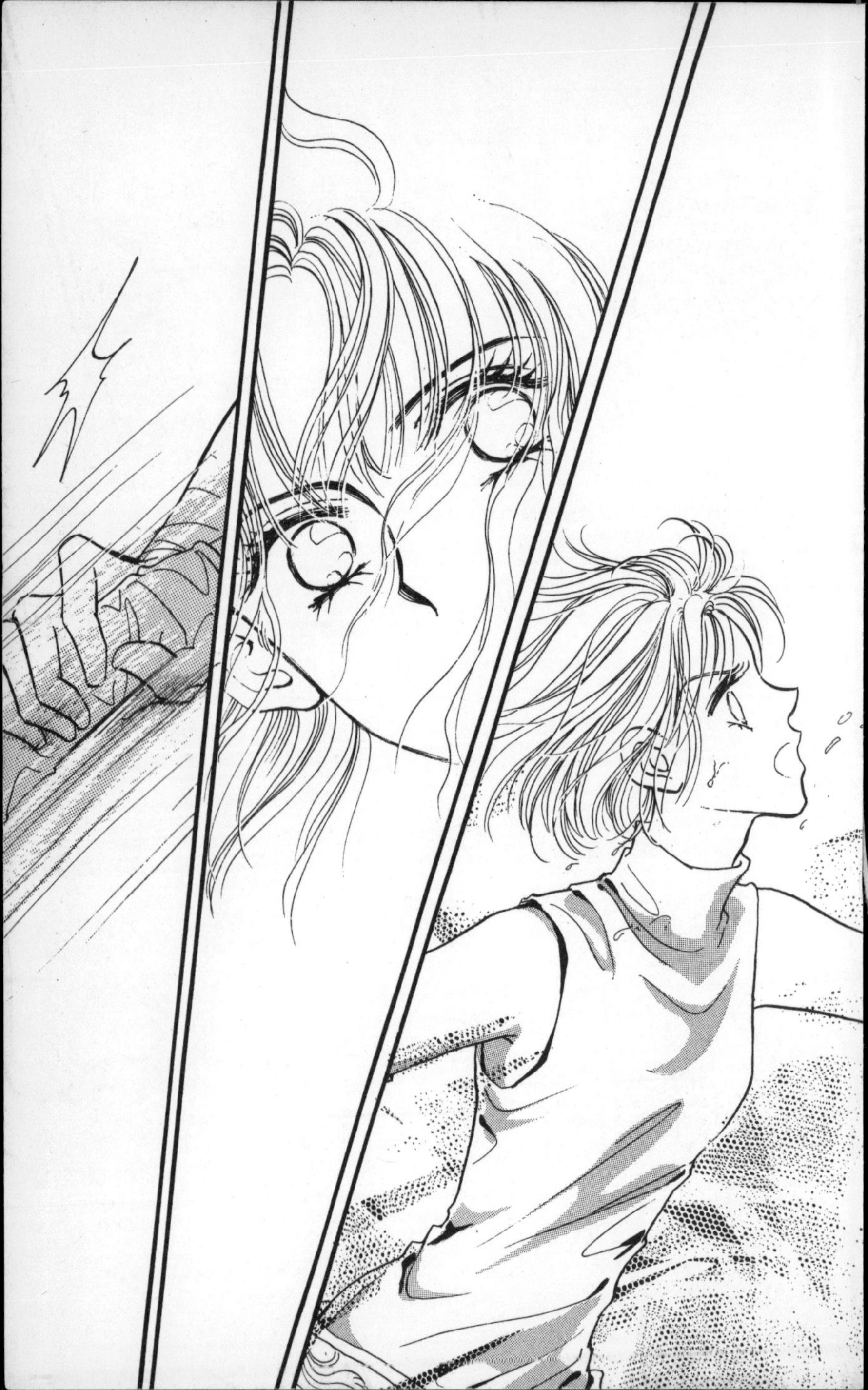

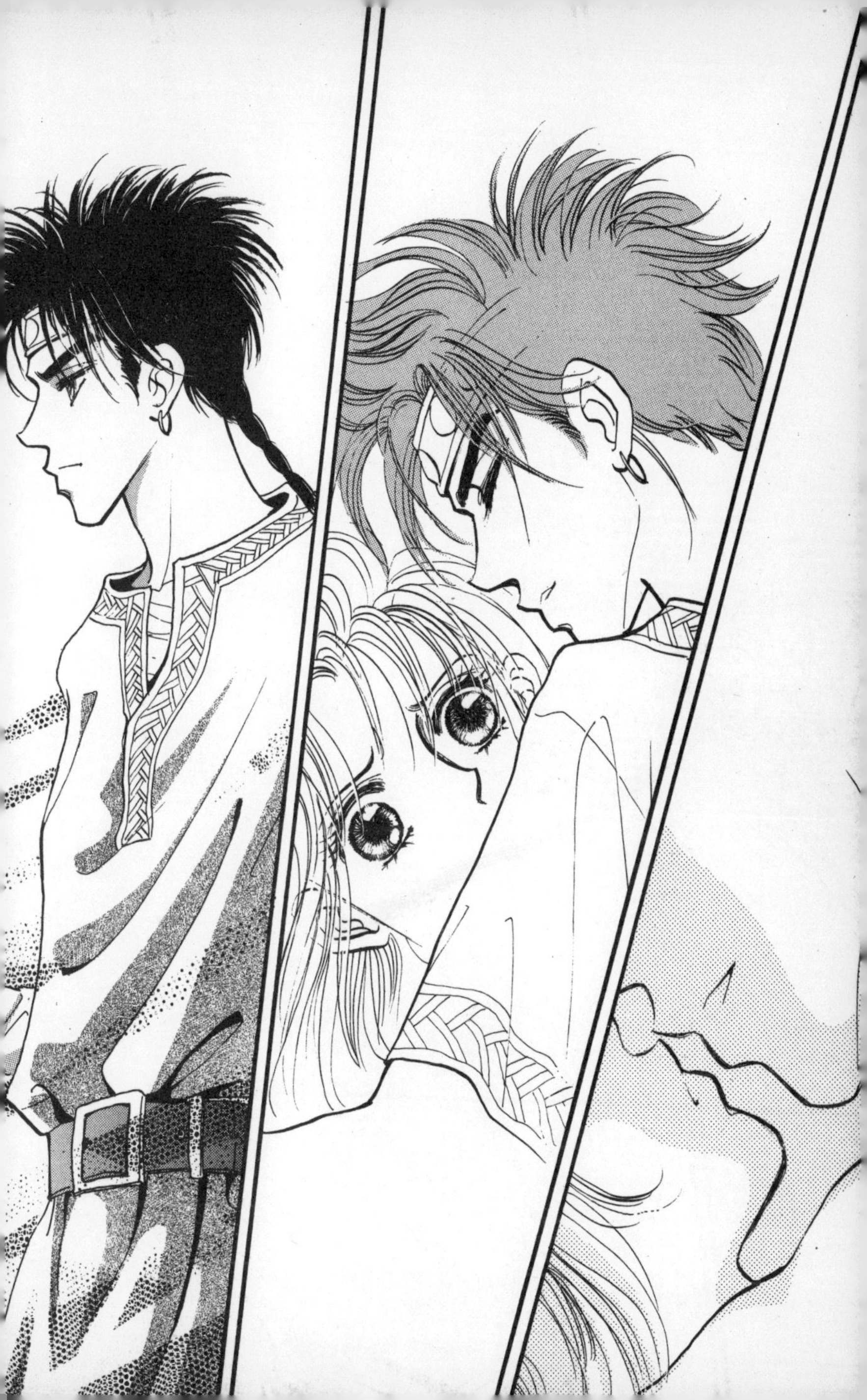

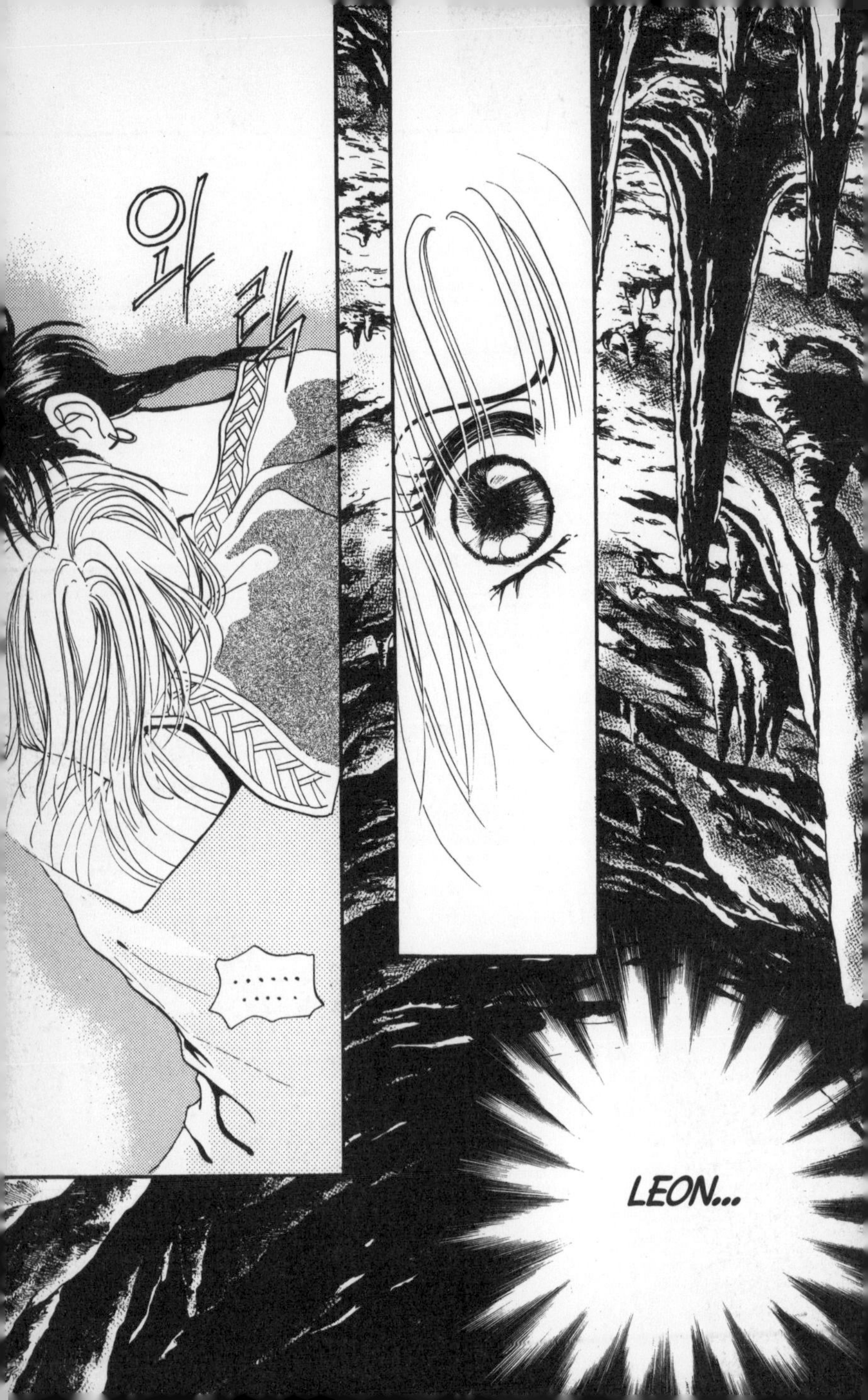
와락
......
LEON...

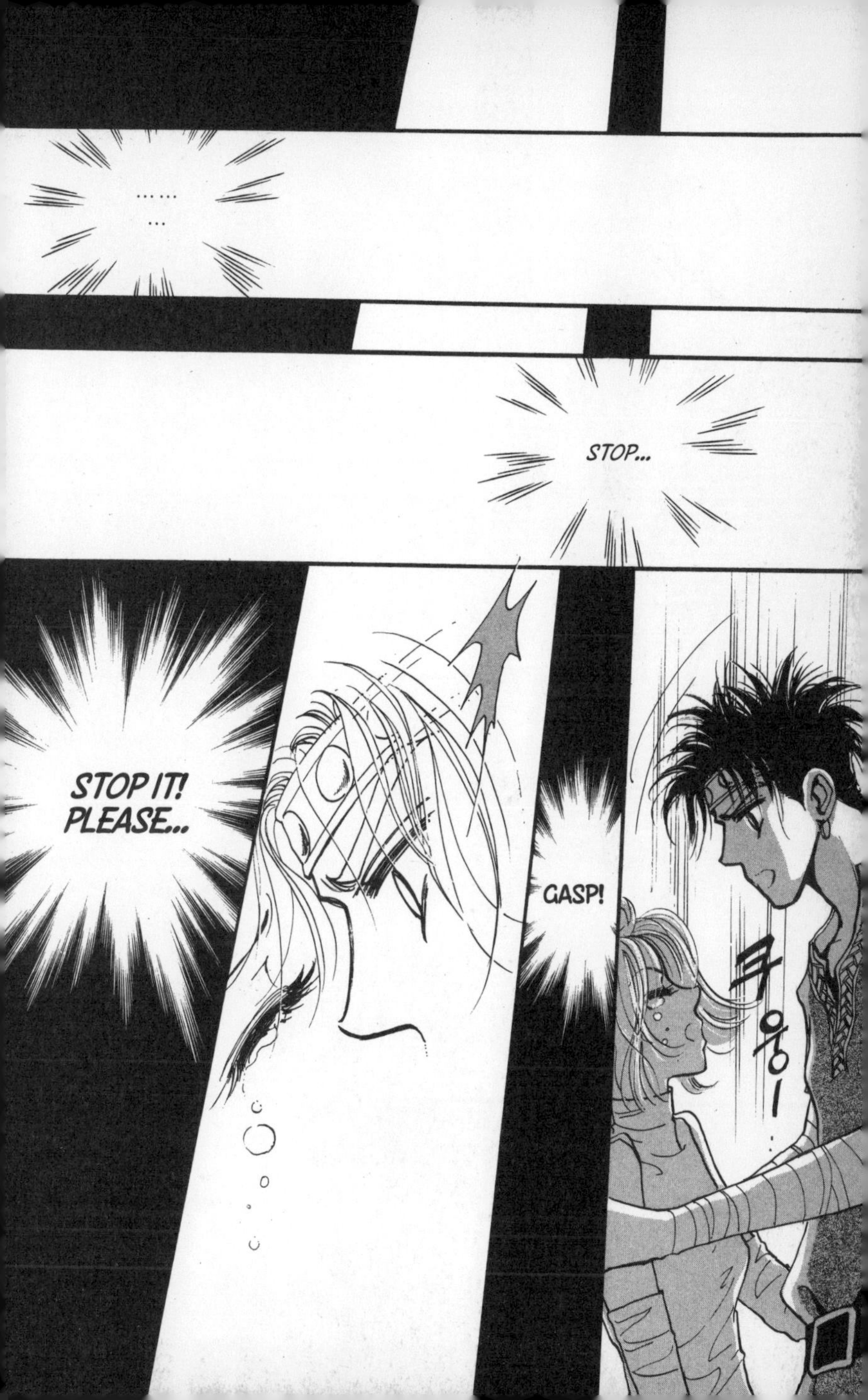
......
...
STOP...
STOP IT! PLEASE...
GASP!
쿠웅!

I'M SORRY...

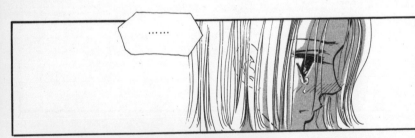

. . . . . .

I'LL DO WHATEVER IT TAKES FOR YOU TO FORGIVE ME.

BUT KNOW THAT I TRULY LOVE YOU.
NOT AS THE QUEEN...
...BUT AS A WOMAN. I LOVE YOU SO VERY MUCH!
YUNA...
I'M...
...SORRY.

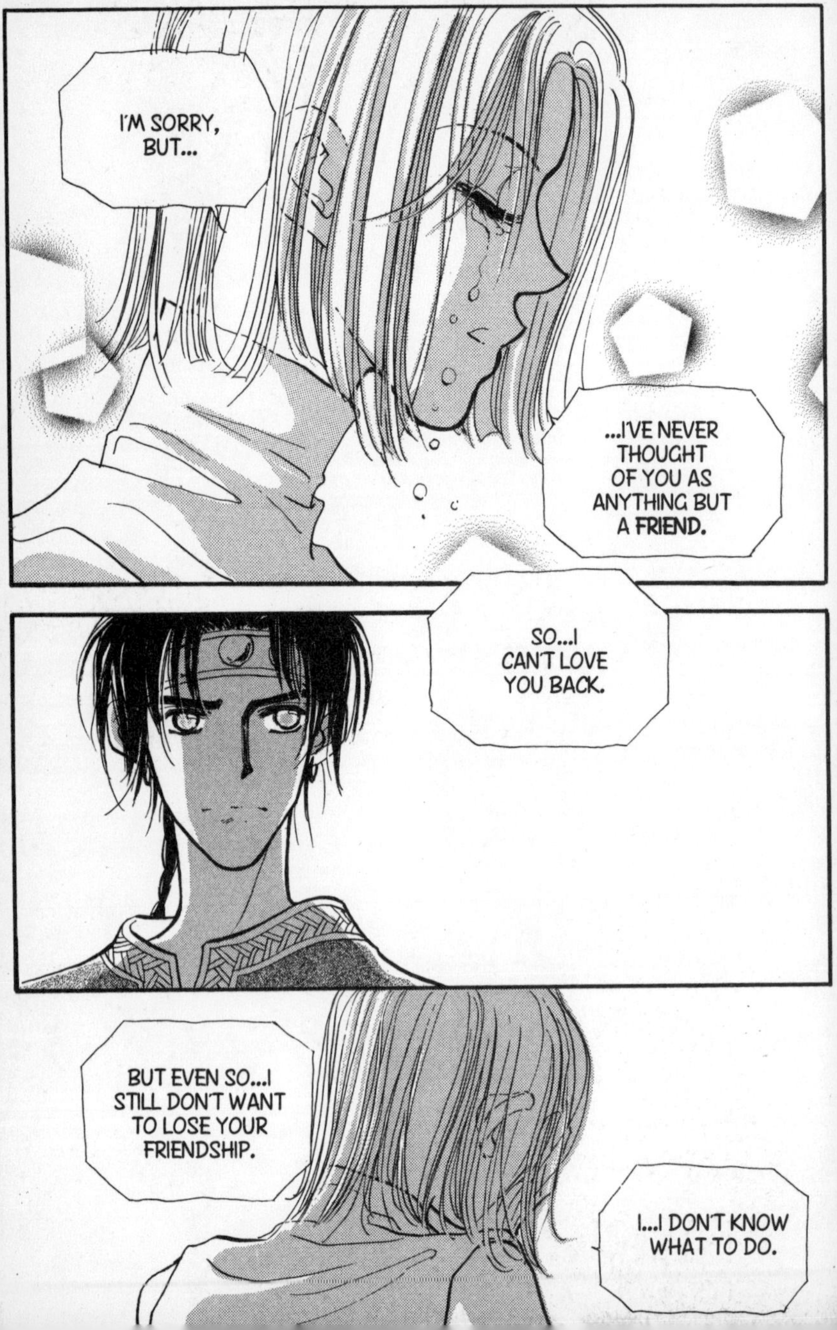
I'M SORRY, BUT...
...I'VE NEVER THOUGHT OF YOU AS ANYTHING BUT A FRIEND.
SO...I CAN'T LOVE YOU BACK.
BUT EVEN SO...I STILL DON'T WANT TO LOSE YOUR FRIENDSHIP.
I...I DON'T KNOW WHAT TO DO.

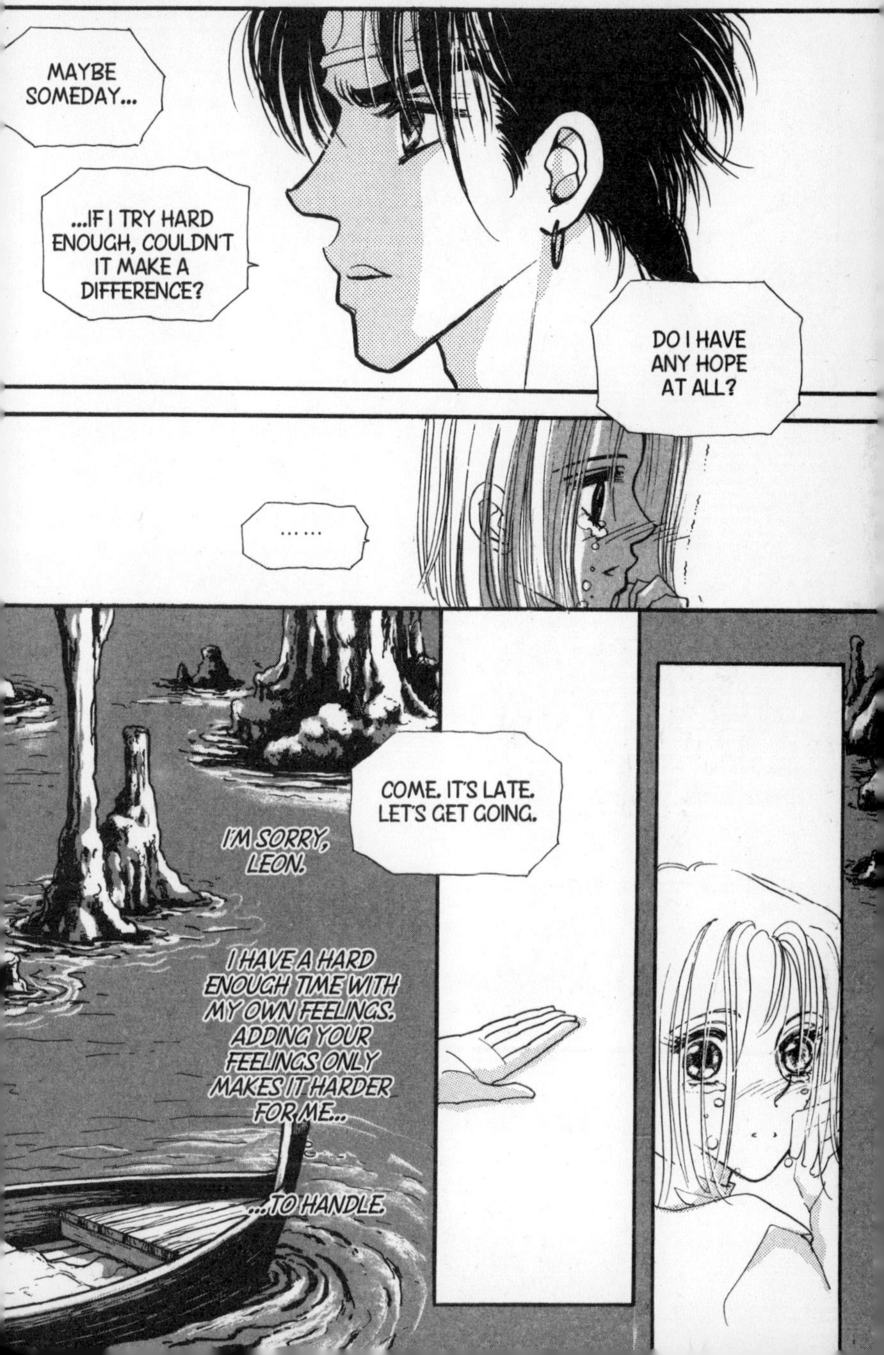
MAYBE SOMEDAY...
...IF I TRY HARD ENOUGH, COULDN'T IT MAKE A DIFFERENCE?
DO I HAVE ANY HOPE AT ALL?
......
I'M SORRY, LEON.
I HAVE A HARD ENOUGH TIME WITH MY OWN FEELINGS. ADDING YOUR FEELINGS ONLY MAKES IT HARDER FOR ME...
...TO HANDLE.
COME. IT'S LATE. LET'S GET GOING.

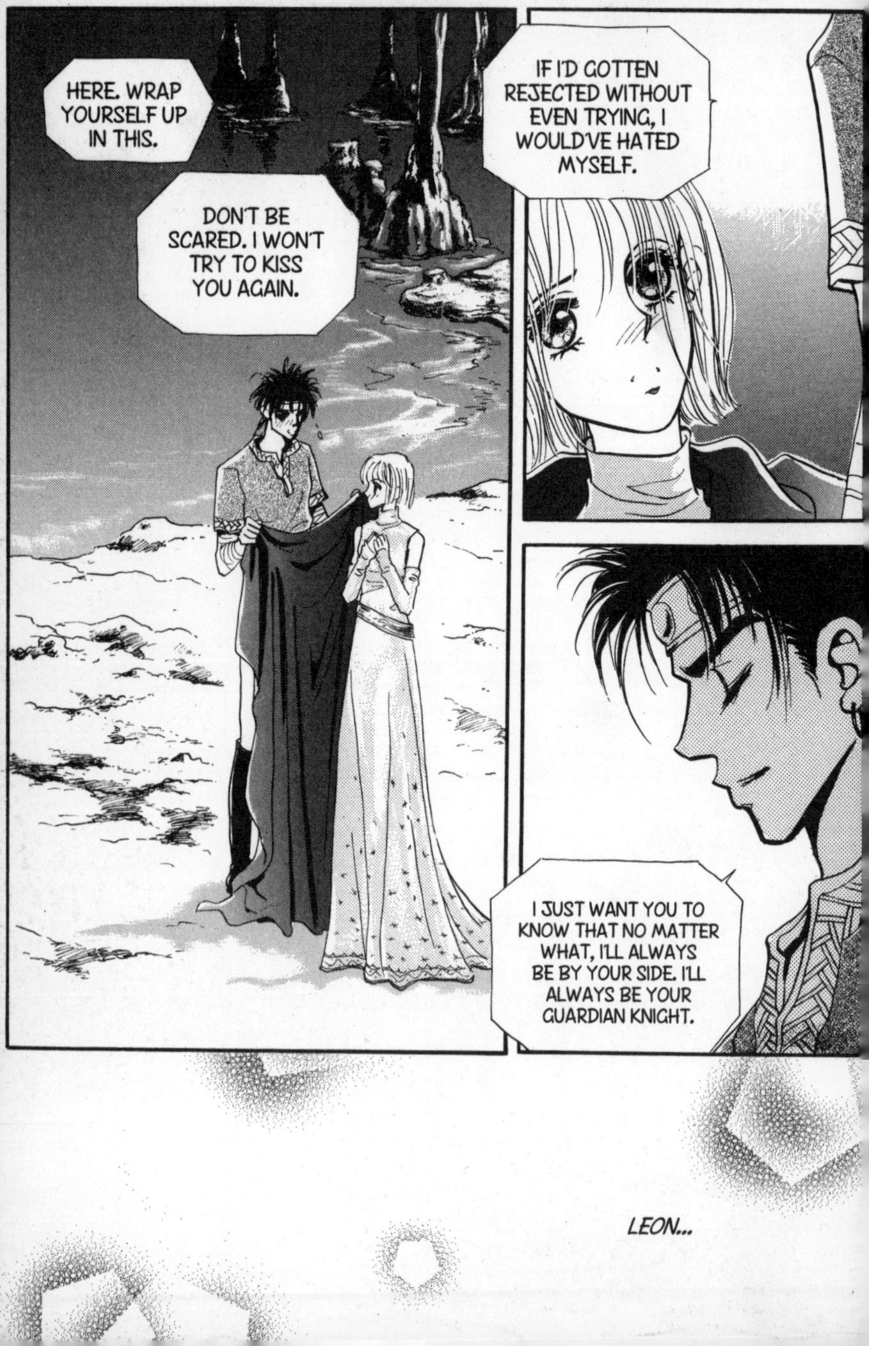
HERE. WRAP YOURSELF UP IN THIS.
DON'T BE SCARED. I WON'T TRY TO KISS YOU AGAIN.
IF I'D GOTTEN REJECTED WITHOUT EVEN TRYING, I WOULD'VE HATED MYSELF.
I JUST WANT YOU TO KNOW THAT NO MATTER WHAT, I'LL ALWAYS BE BY YOUR SIDE. I'LL ALWAYS BE YOUR GUARDIAN KNIGHT.
LEON...

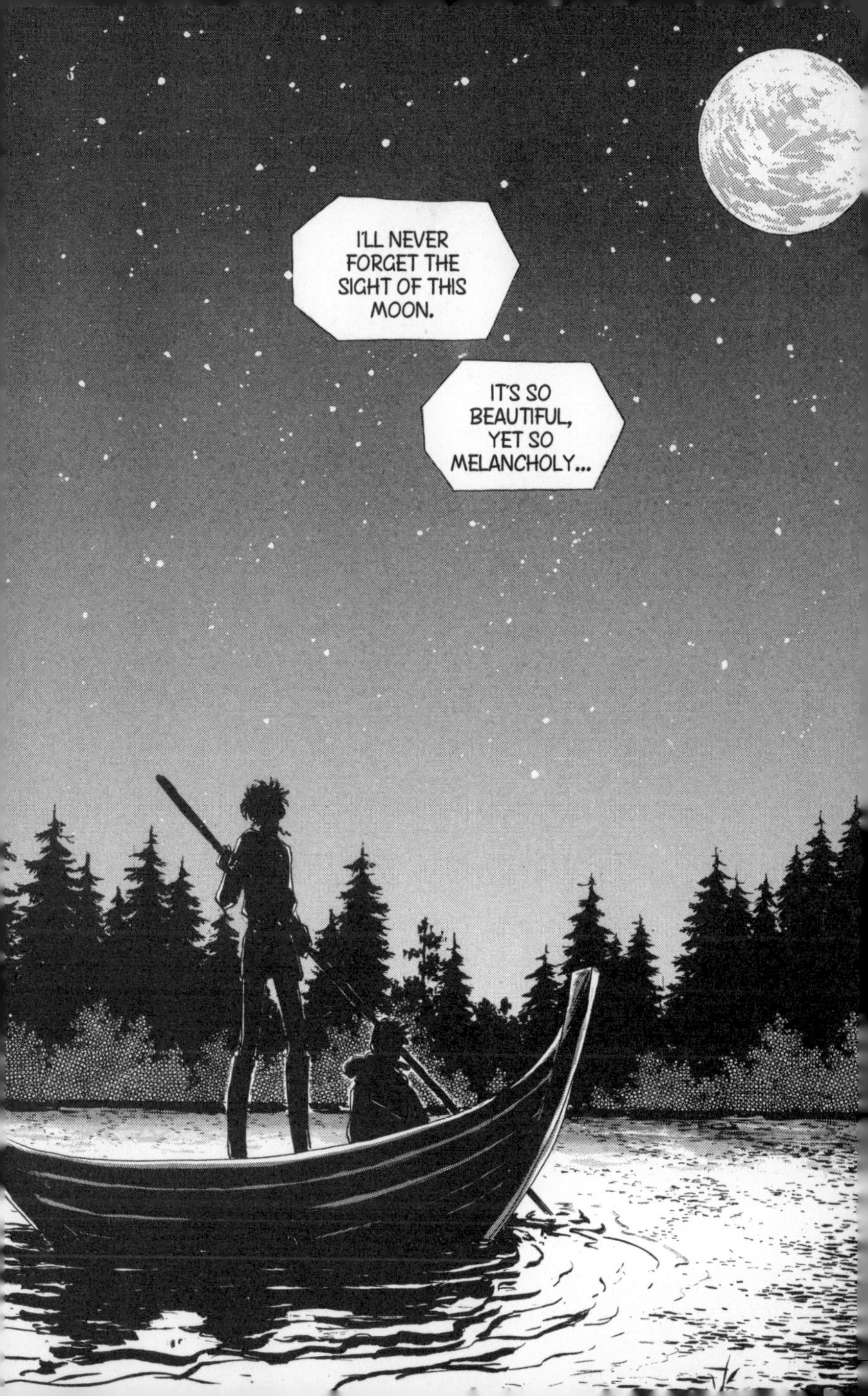
I'LL NEVER FORGET THE SIGHT OF THIS MOON.
IT'S SO BEAUTIFUL, YET SO MELANCHOLY...

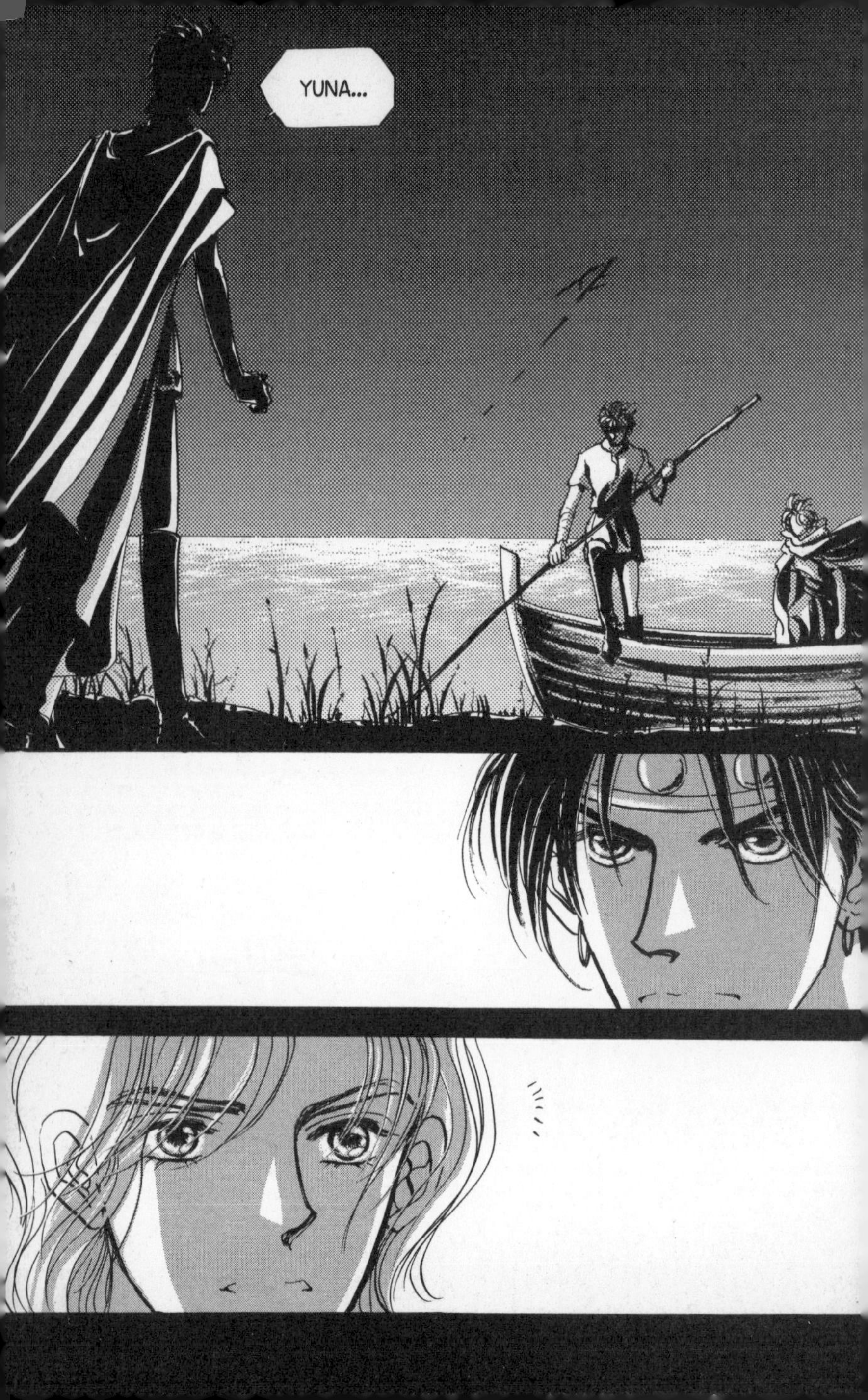
YUNA...

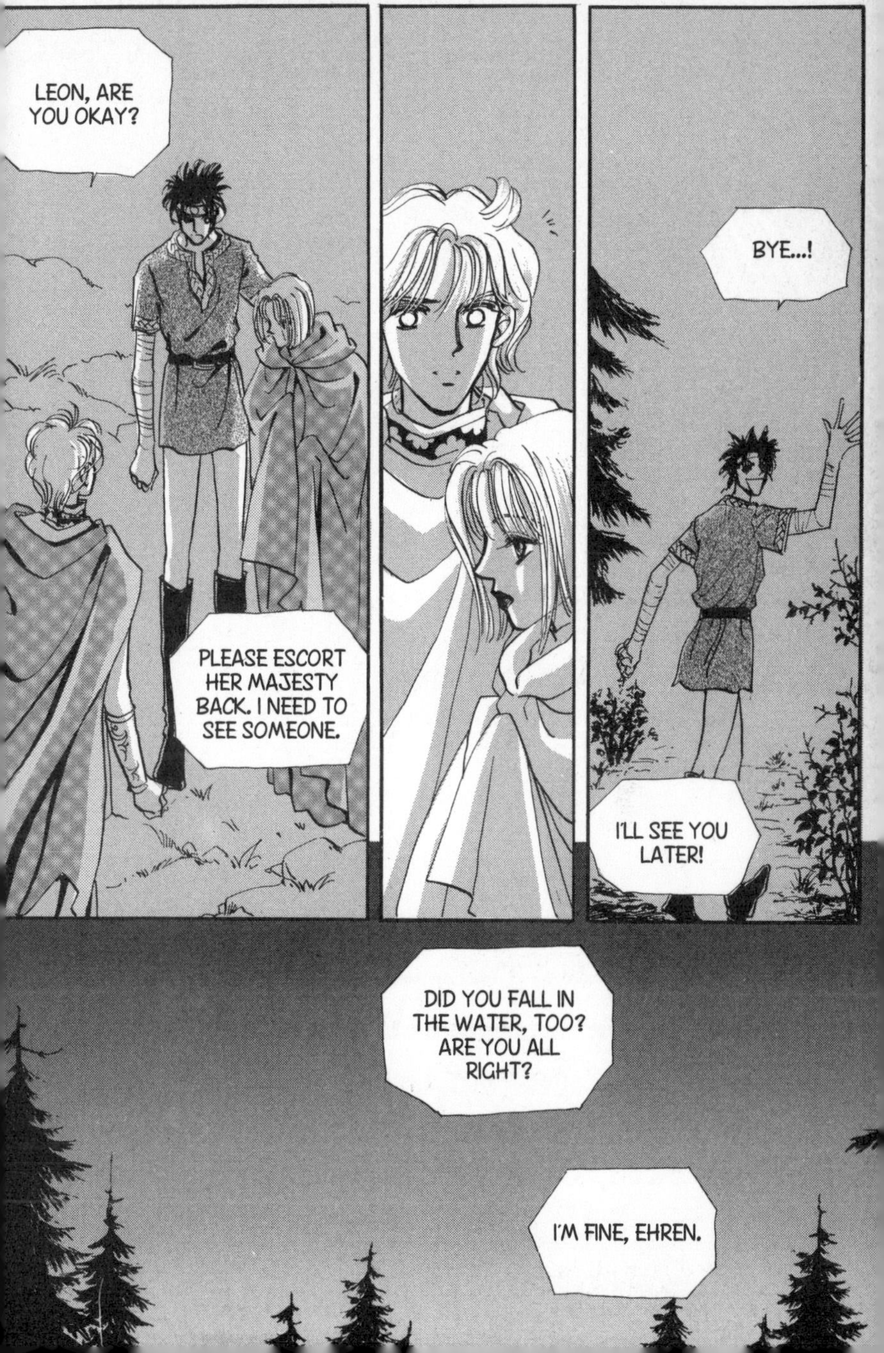
LEON, ARE YOU OKAY?
PLEASE ESCORT HER MAJESTY BACK. I NEED TO SEE SOMEONE.
BYE...!
I'LL SEE YOU LATER!
DID YOU FALL IN THE WATER, TOO? ARE YOU ALL RIGHT?
I'M FINE, EHREN.

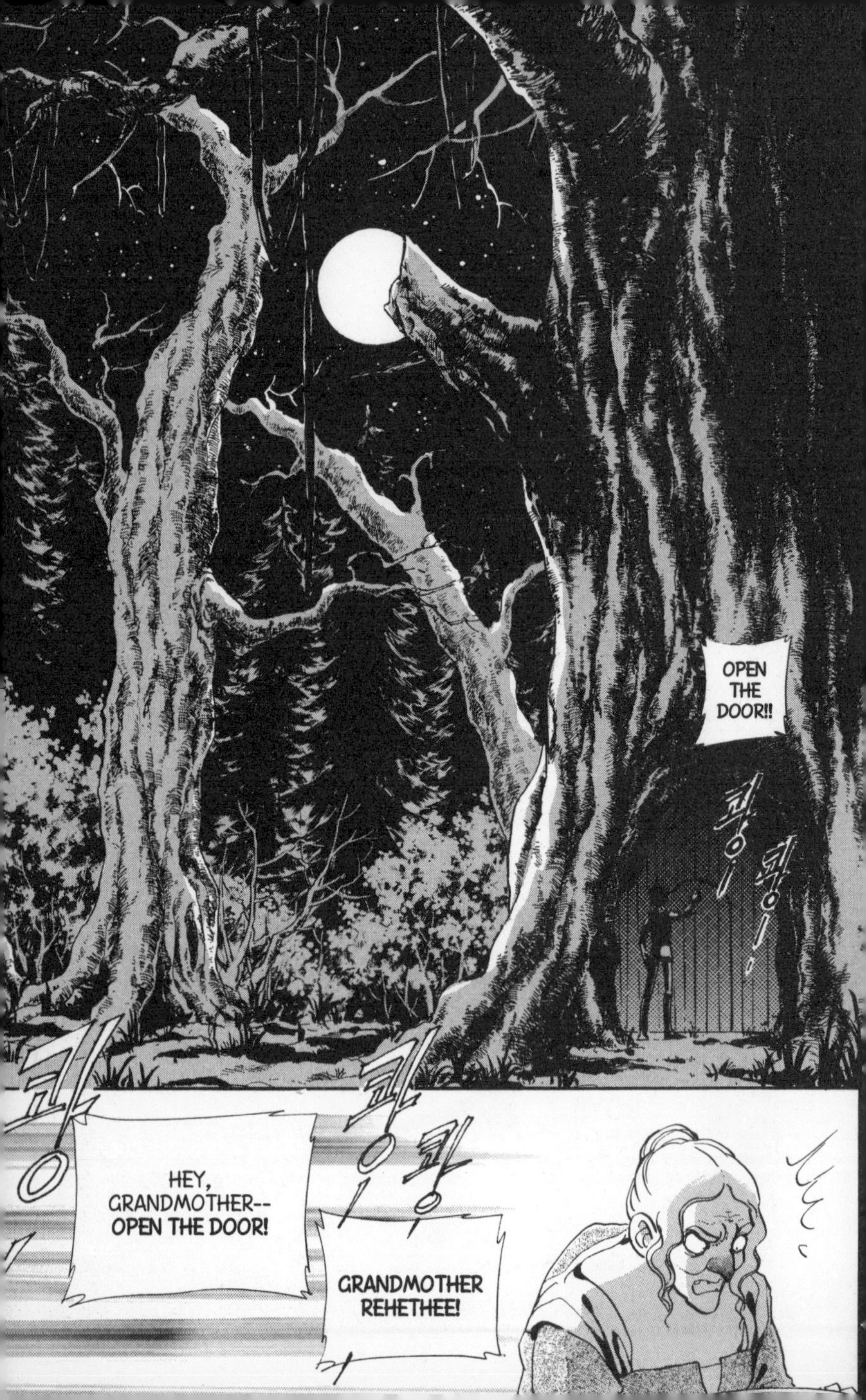
OPEN THE DOOR!!
HEY, GRANDMOTHER-- OPEN THE DOOR!
GRANDMOTHER REHETHEE!

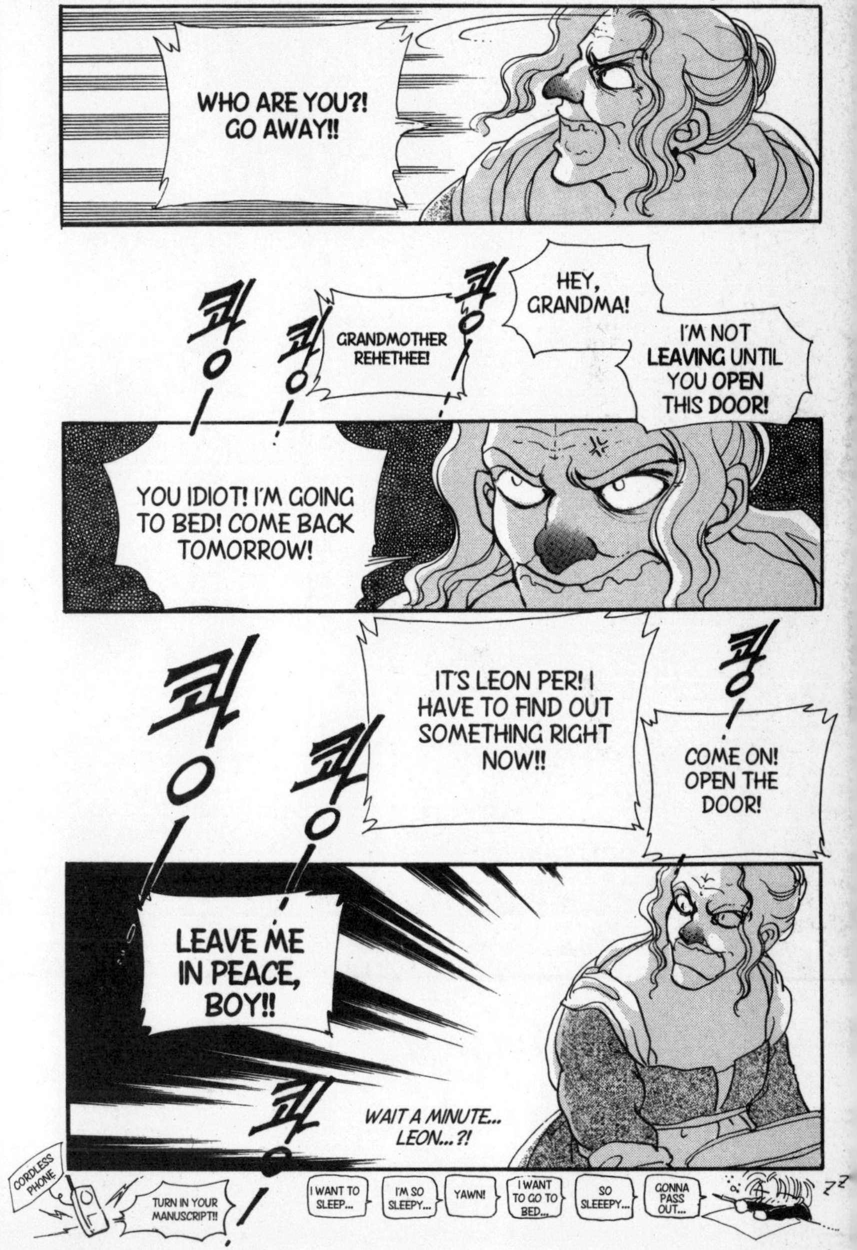
WHO ARE YOU?! GO AWAY!!
쾅!
쾅!
GRANDMOTHER REHETHEE!
쾅!
HEY, GRANDMA!
I'M NOT LEAVING UNTIL YOU OPEN THIS DOOR!
YOU IDIOT! I'M GOING TO BED! COME BACK TOMORROW!
쾅!
쾅!
IT'S LEON PER! I HAVE TO FIND OUT SOMETHING RIGHT NOW!!
쾅!
COME ON! OPEN THE DOOR!
LEAVE ME IN PEACE, BOY!!
쾅!
WAIT A MINUTE... LEON...?!
CORDLESS PHONE
TURN IN YOUR MANUSCRIPT!!
I WANT TO SLEEP...
I'M SO SLEEPY...
YAWN!
I WANT TO GO TO BED...
SO SLEEEPY...
GONNA PASS OUT...
ZZ

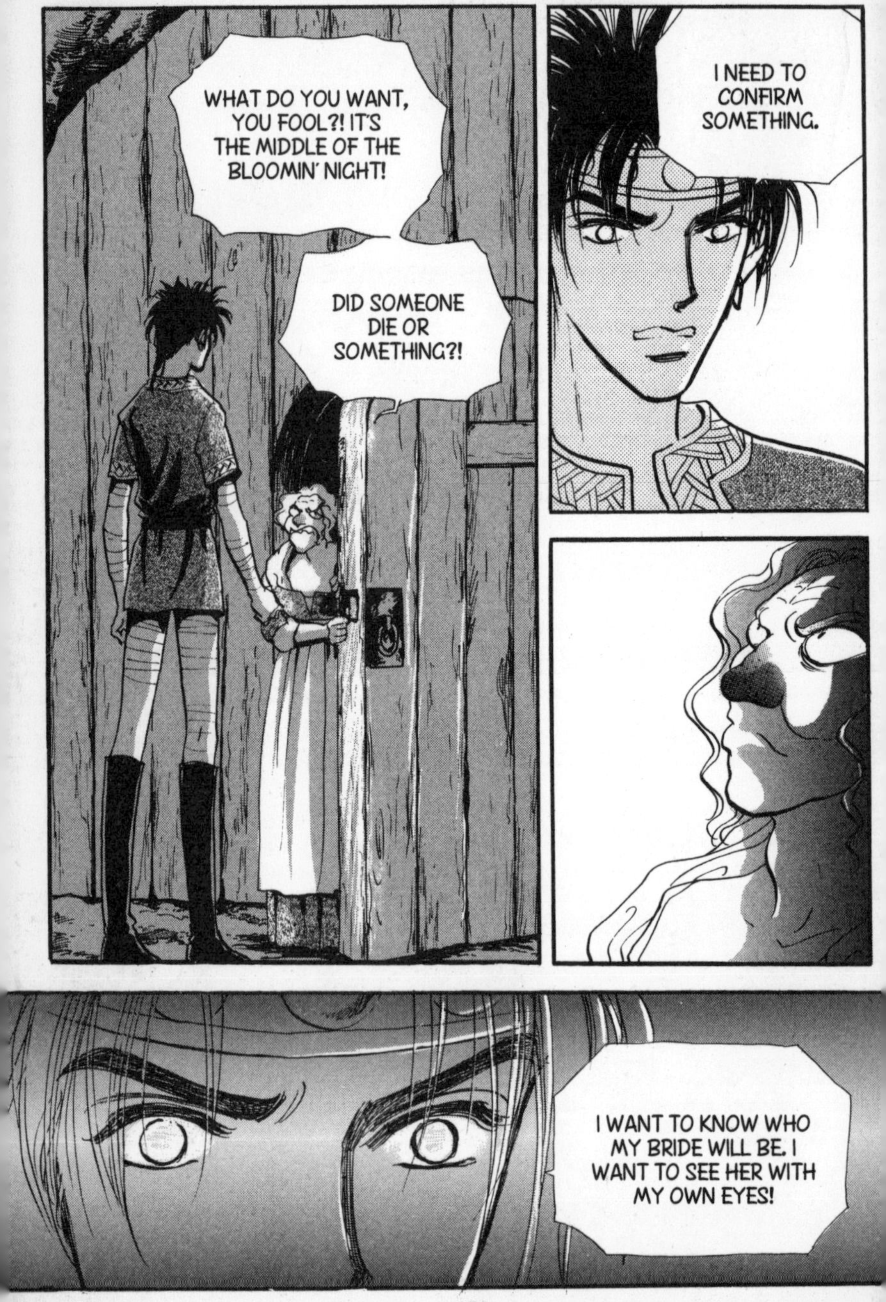
WHAT DO YOU WANT, YOU FOOL?! IT'S THE MIDDLE OF THE BLOOMIN' NIGHT!
DID SOMEONE DIE OR SOMETHING?!
I NEED TO CONFIRM SOMETHING.
I WANT TO KNOW WHO MY BRIDE WILL BE. I WANT TO SEE HER WITH MY OWN EYES!

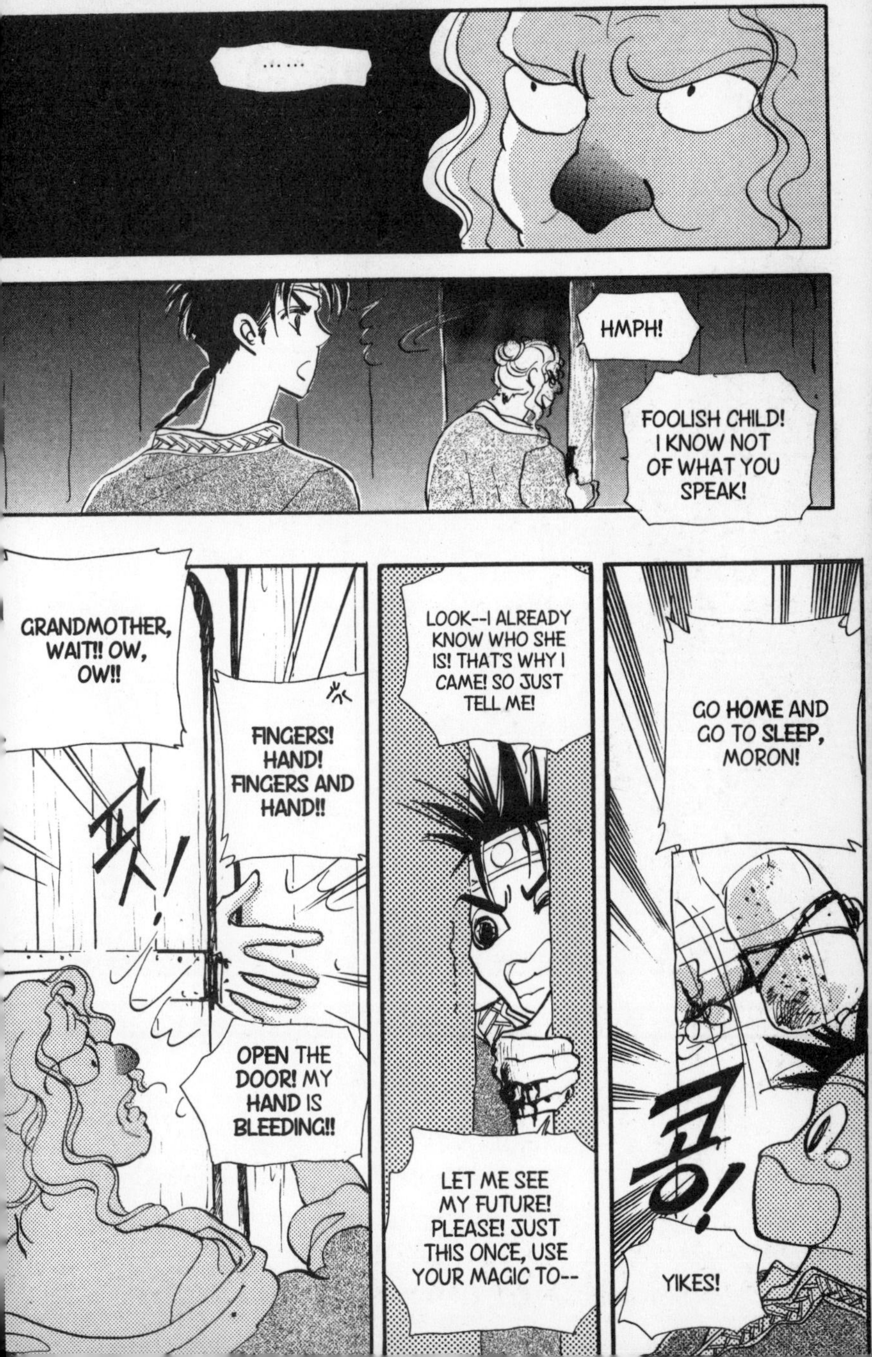
……
HMPH!
FOOLISH CHILD! I KNOW NOT OF WHAT YOU SPEAK!
GRANDMOTHER, WAIT!! OW, OW!!
FINGERS! HAND! FINGERS AND HAND!!
OPEN THE DOOR! MY HAND IS BLEEDING!!
LOOK--I ALREADY KNOW WHO SHE IS! THAT'S WHY I CAME! SO JUST TELL ME!
LET ME SEE MY FUTURE! PLEASE! JUST THIS ONCE, USE YOUR MAGIC TO--
GO HOME AND GO TO SLEEP, MORON!
YIKES!

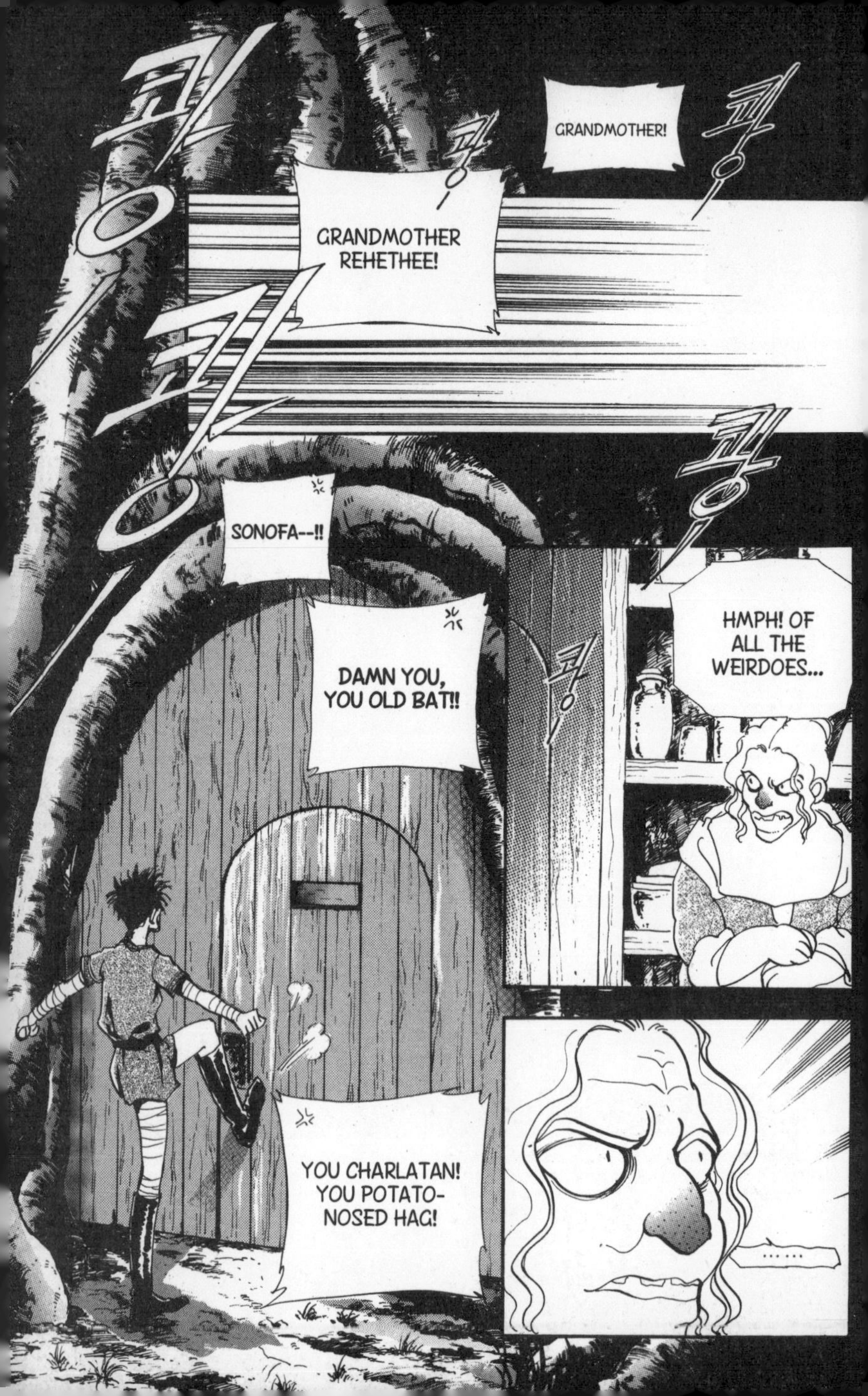
GRANDMOTHER!
GRANDMOTHER REHETHEE!
SONOFA--!!
DAMN YOU, YOU OLD BAT!!
YOU CHARLATAN! YOU POTATO-NOSED HAG!
HMPH! OF ALL THE WEIRDOES...
......

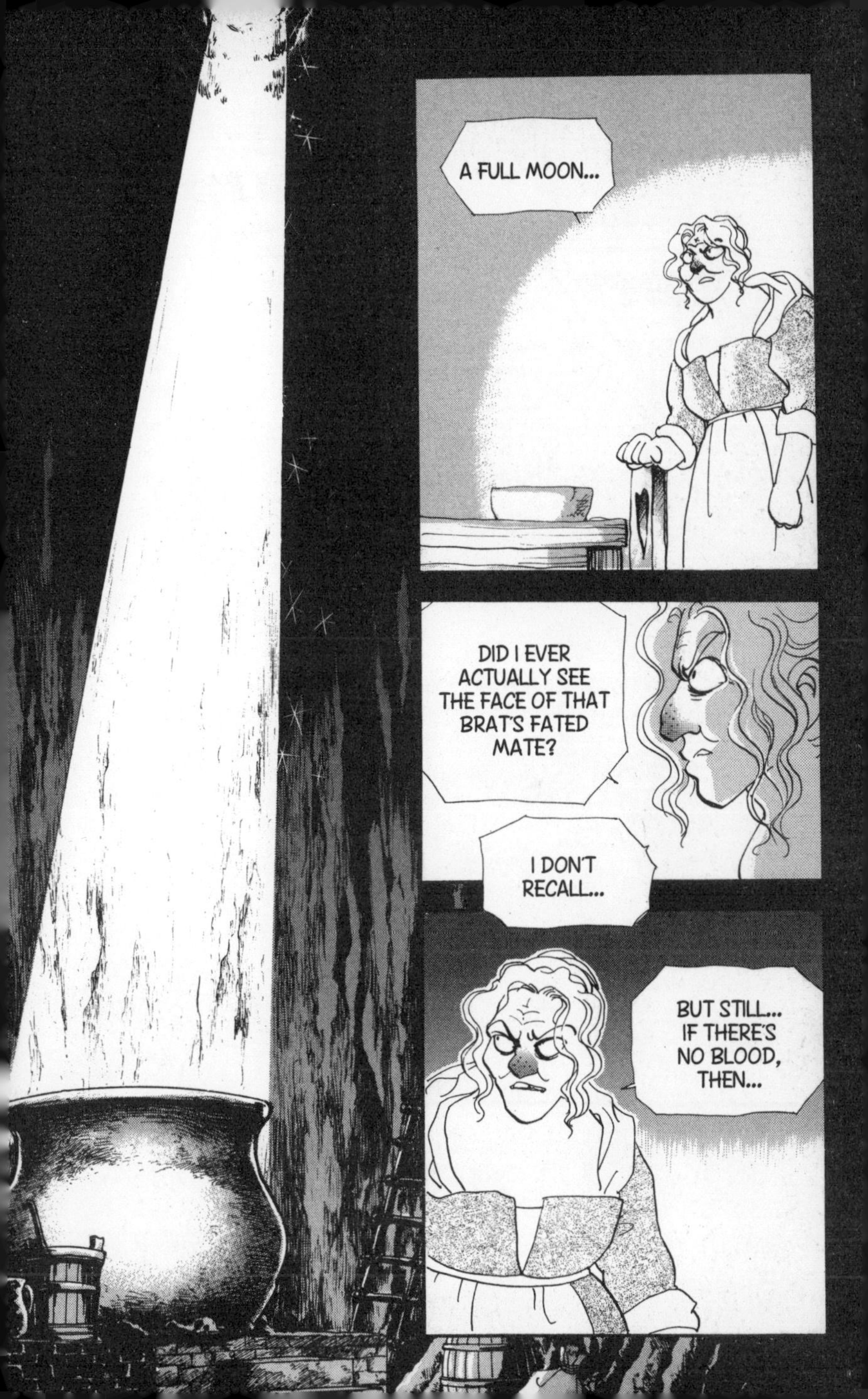
A FULL MOON...
DID I EVER ACTUALLY SEE THE FACE OF THAT BRAT'S FATED MATE?
I DON'T RECALL...
BUT STILL... IF THERE'S NO BLOOD, THEN...

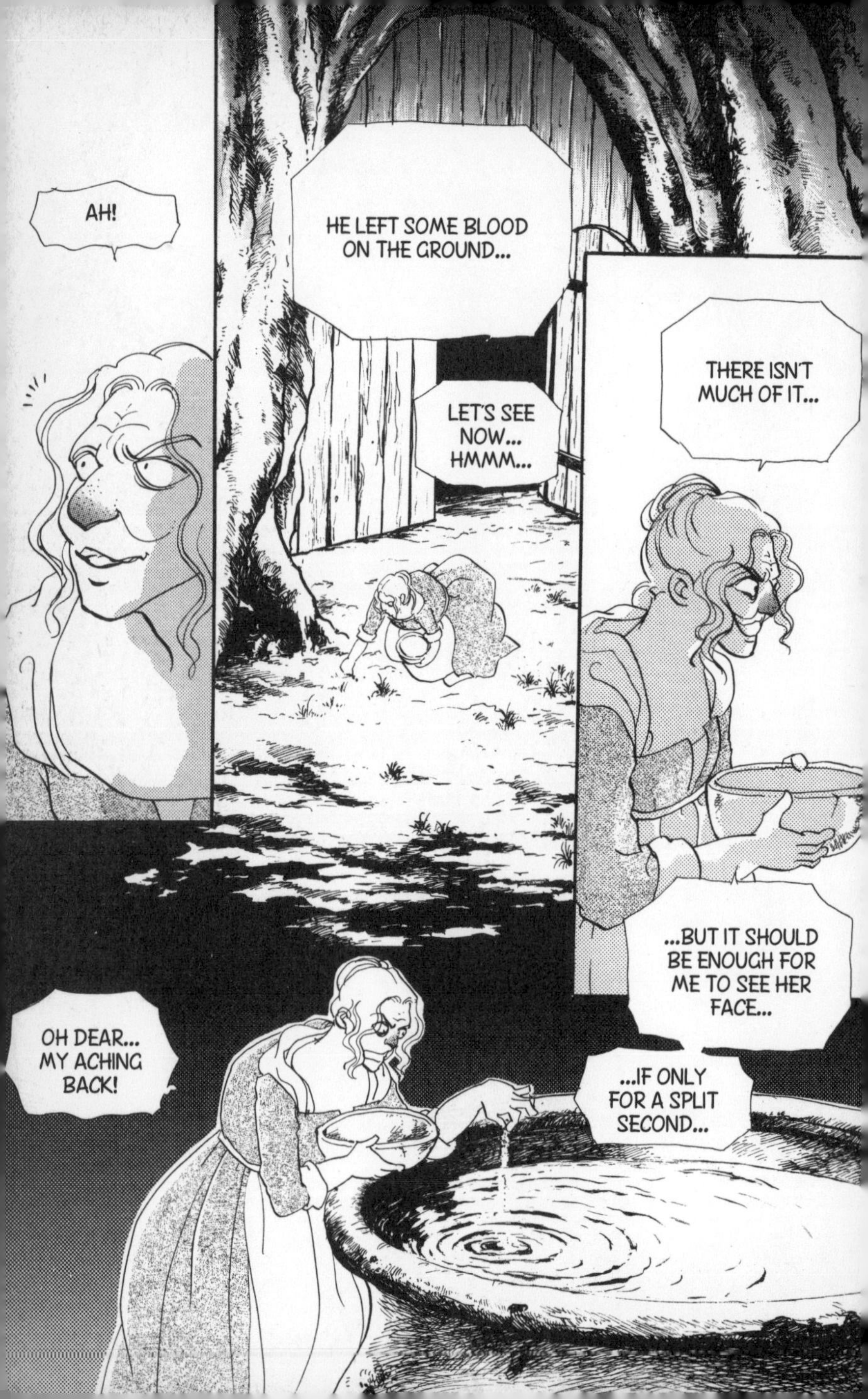
AH!
HE LEFT SOME BLOOD ON THE GROUND...
LET'S SEE NOW... HMMM...
THERE ISN'T MUCH OF IT...
...BUT IT SHOULD BE ENOUGH FOR ME TO SEE HER FACE...
OH DEAR... MY ACHING BACK!
...IF ONLY FOR A SPLIT SECOND...

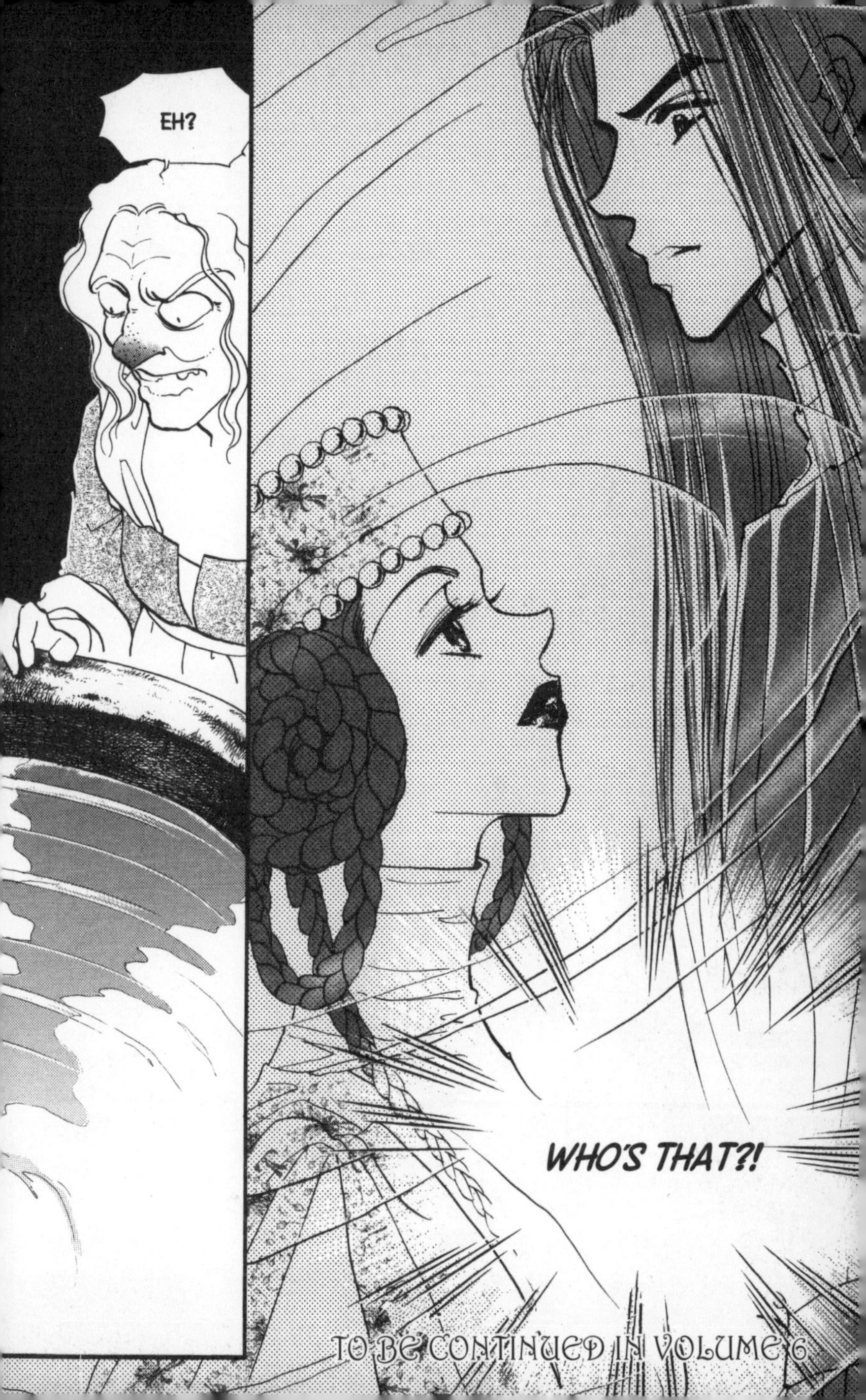
EH?
WHO'S THAT?!
TO BE CONTINUED IN VOLUME 6

The Queen's Knight: A Short Story
SD version...!!

The Queen and the Knights ♡

Journey

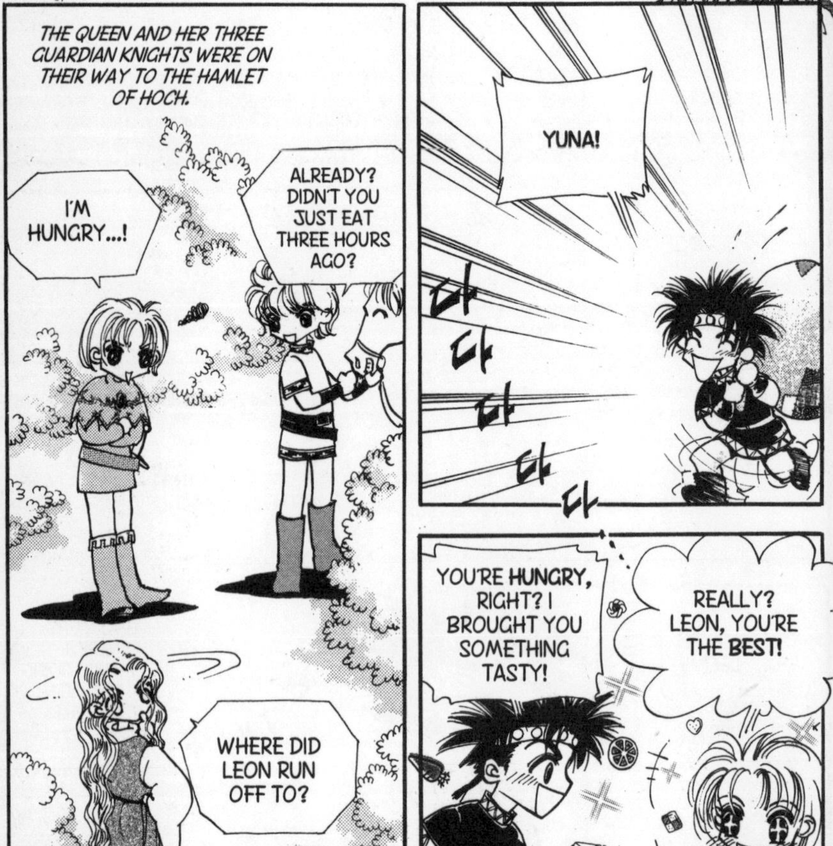

THE QUEEN AND HER THREE GUARDIAN KNIGHTS WERE ON THEIR WAY TO THE HAMLET OF HOCH.
I'M HUNGRY...!
ALREADY? DIDN'T YOU JUST EAT THREE HOURS AGO?
WHERE DID LEON RUN OFF TO?
YUNA!
다 다 다 다 다
YOU'RE HUNGRY, RIGHT? I BROUGHT YOU SOMETHING TASTY!
REALLY? LEON, YOU'RE THE BEST!

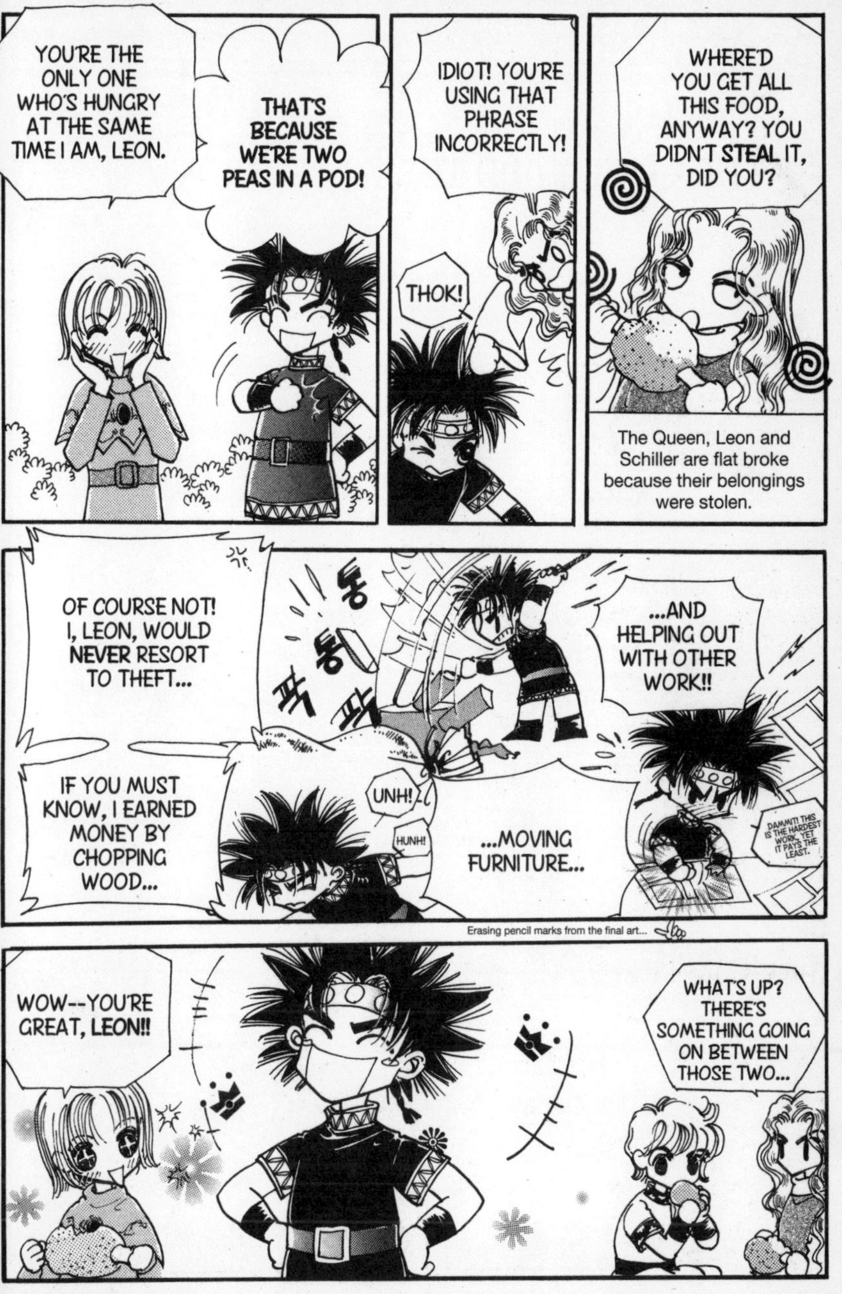
YOU'RE THE ONLY ONE WHO'S HUNGRY AT THE SAME TIME I AM, LEON.
THAT'S BECAUSE WE'RE TWO PEAS IN A POD!
IDIOT! YOU'RE USING THAT PHRASE INCORRECTLY!
THOK!
WHERE'D YOU GET ALL THIS FOOD, ANYWAY? YOU DIDN'T STEAL IT, DID YOU?
The Queen, Leon and Schiller are flat broke because their belongings were stolen.
OF COURSE NOT! I, LEON, WOULD NEVER RESORT TO THEFT...
통
통
딱
딱
...AND HELPING OUT WITH OTHER WORK!!
IF YOU MUST KNOW, I EARNED MONEY BY CHOPPING WOOD...
UNH!
HUNH!
...MOVING FURNITURE...
DAMMIT! THIS IS THE HARDEST WORK, YET IT PAYS THE LEAST.
Erasing pencil marks from the final art...
WOW--YOU'RE GREAT, LEON!!
WHAT'S UP? THERE'S SOMETHING GOING ON BETWEEN THOSE TWO...

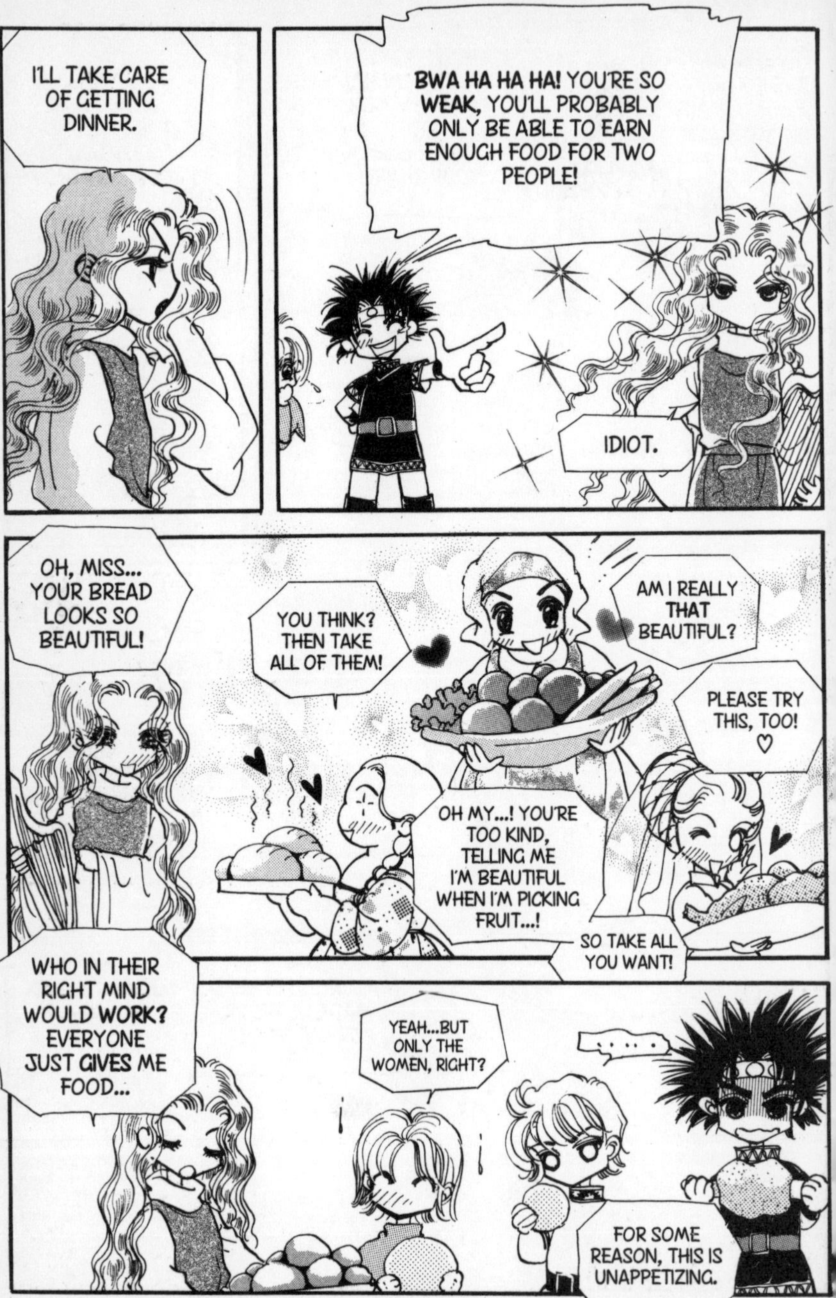
I'LL TAKE CARE OF GETTING DINNER.
BWA HA HA HA! YOU'RE SO WEAK, YOU'LL PROBABLY ONLY BE ABLE TO EARN ENOUGH FOOD FOR TWO PEOPLE!
IDIOT.
OH, MISS... YOUR BREAD LOOKS SO BEAUTIFUL!
YOU THINK? THEN TAKE ALL OF THEM!
AM I REALLY THAT BEAUTIFUL?
PLEASE TRY THIS, TOO! ♡
OH MY...! YOU'RE TOO KIND, TELLING ME I'M BEAUTIFUL WHEN I'M PICKING FRUIT...!
SO TAKE ALL YOU WANT!
WHO IN THEIR RIGHT MIND WOULD WORK? EVERYONE JUST GIVES ME FOOD...
YEAH...BUT ONLY THE WOMEN, RIGHT?
.....
FOR SOME REASON, THIS IS UNAPPETIZING.

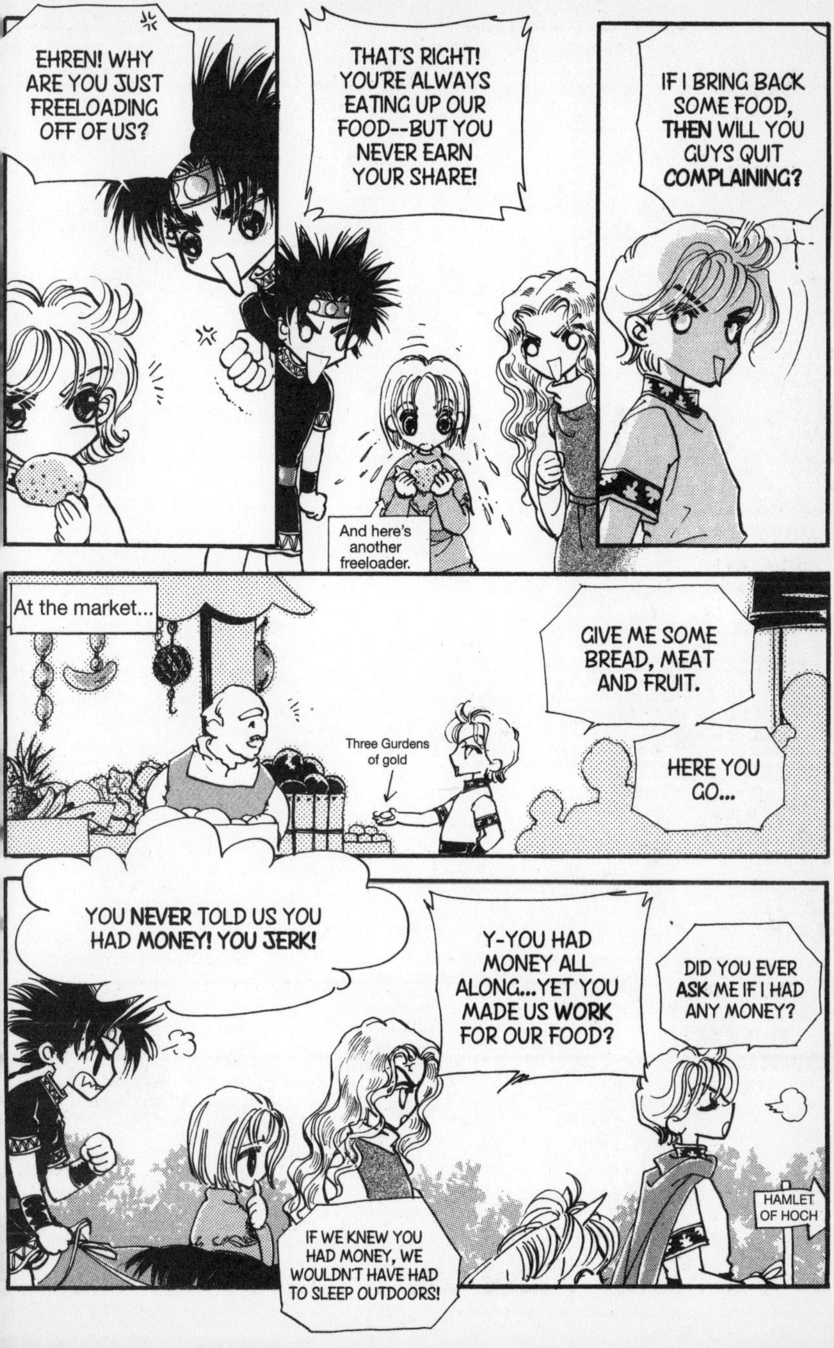
EHREN! WHY ARE YOU JUST FREELOADING OFF OF US?
THAT'S RIGHT! YOU'RE ALWAYS EATING UP OUR FOOD--BUT YOU NEVER EARN YOUR SHARE!
And here's another freeloader.
IF I BRING BACK SOME FOOD, THEN WILL YOU GUYS QUIT COMPLAINING?
At the market...
Three Gurdens of gold
GIVE ME SOME BREAD, MEAT AND FRUIT.
HERE YOU GO...
YOU NEVER TOLD US YOU HAD MONEY! YOU JERK!
Y-YOU HAD MONEY ALL ALONG...YET YOU MADE US WORK FOR OUR FOOD?
DID YOU EVER ASK ME IF I HAD ANY MONEY?
IF WE KNEW YOU HAD MONEY, WE WOULDN'T HAVE HAD TO SLEEP OUTDOORS!
HAMLET OF HOCH

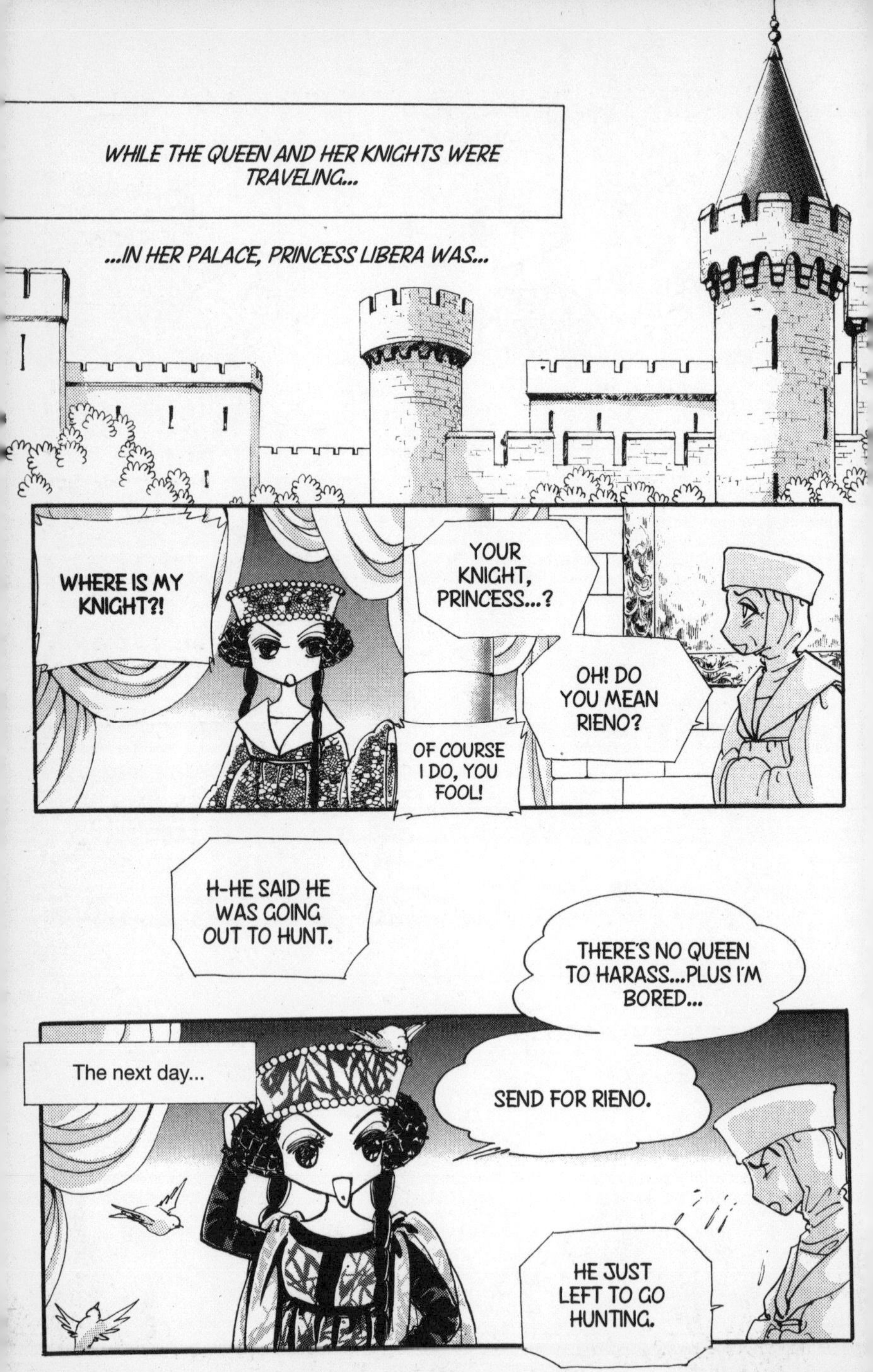
WHILE THE QUEEN AND HER KNIGHTS WERE TRAVELING...
...IN HER PALACE, PRINCESS LIBERA WAS...
WHERE IS MY KNIGHT?!
YOUR KNIGHT, PRINCESS...?
OH! DO YOU MEAN RIENO?
OF COURSE I DO, YOU FOOL!
H-HE SAID HE WAS GOING OUT TO HUNT.
THERE'S NO QUEEN TO HARASS...PLUS I'M BORED...
The next day...
SEND FOR RIENO.
HE JUST LEFT TO GO HUNTING.

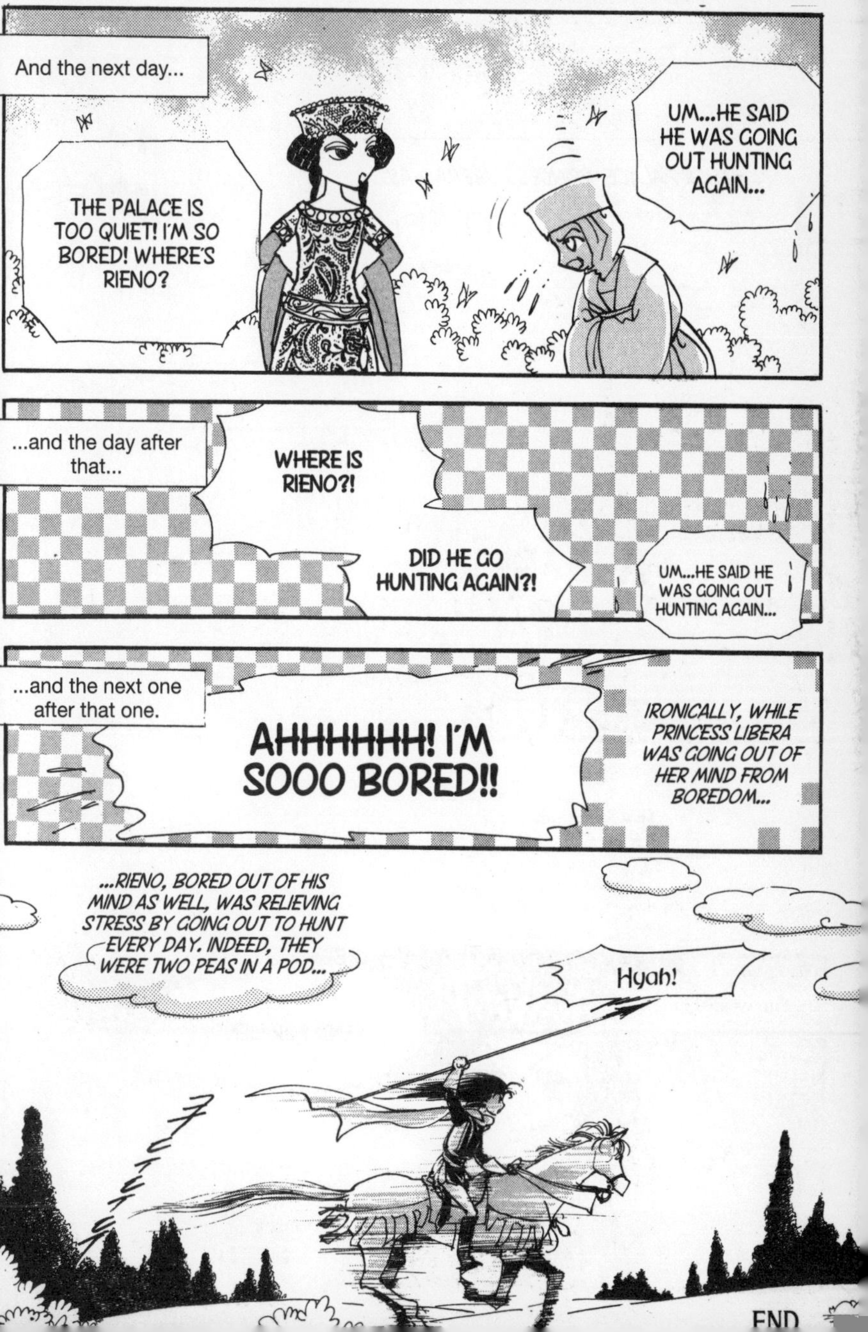

And the next day...
THE PALACE IS TOO QUIET! I'M SO BORED! WHERE'S RIENO?
UM...HE SAID HE WAS GOING OUT HUNTING AGAIN...
...and the day after that...
WHERE IS RIENO?!
DID HE GO HUNTING AGAIN?!
UM...HE SAID HE WAS GOING OUT HUNTING AGAIN...
...and the next one after that one.
AHHHHHH! I'M SOOO BORED!!
IRONICALLY, WHILE PRINCESS LIBERA WAS GOING OUT OF HER MIND FROM BOREDOM...
...RIENO, BORED OUT OF HIS MIND AS WELL, WAS RELIEVING STRESS BY GOING OUT TO HUNT EVERY DAY. INDEED, THEY WERE TWO PEAS IN A POD...
Hyah!
END

IN THE NEXT VOLUME OF...

THE QUEEN'S KNIGHT

YUNA RETURNS TO ELYSIAN AND CONFRONTS
KENT ABOUT THE POLICY "CHANGES" HE MADE
IN HER ABSENCE...BUT THE SLIMY CHANCELLOR
WON'T GO DOWN WITHOUT MANAGING TO
SLING SOME MUD OF HIS OWN.
LATER, YUNA PARTICIPATES IN A HUNT IN THE
FOREST OF DARKNESS TO BRING SPRING BACK TO
PHANTASMA...BUT LITTLE DOES SHE KNOW THAT
KENT HAS SENT SOME OF HIS WARRIORS INTO
THE FOREST ON A MISSION OF REVENGE, WHERE
THE HUNTER BECOMES THE HUNTED!

COMING SOON!

TOKYOPOP SHOP

WWW.TOKYOPOP.COM/SHOP

HOT NEWS!
Check out the TOKYOPOP SHOP! The world's best collection of manga in English is now available online in one place!

Check out all the sizzling hot merchandise and your favorite manga at the shop!

I Luv Halloween Glow-in-the-Dark STICKERS!

BIZENGHAST POSTER

PRINCESS AI POSTCARDS

WWW.TOKYOPOP.COM/SHOP

I LUV HALLOWEEN

I LUV HALLOWEEN BUTTONS & STICKERS

- LOOK FOR SPECIAL OFFERS
- PRE-ORDER UPCOMING RELEASES
- COMPLETE YOUR COLLECTIONS

I LUV HALLOWEEN © Keith Giffen and Benjamin Roman. Princess Ai © & ™ TOKYOPOP Inc. Bizenghast © M. Alice LeGrow and TOKYOPOP Inc.

LIFE
BY KEIKO SUENOBU

Ordinary high school teenagers...
Except that they're not.

OT
OLDER TEEN
AGE 16+

© Keiko Suenobu

READ THE ENTIRE FIRST CHAPTER ONLINE FOR FREE:

Ayumu struggles with her studies, and the all-important high school entrance exams are approaching. Fortunately, she has help from her best bud Shii-chan, who is at the top of the class. But when the test results come back, the friends are surprised: Ayumu surpasses Shii-chan's scores and gets into the school of her choice—without Shii-chan! Losing her friend is so painful for Ayumu that she starts cutting herself to ease her sorrow. Finally, Ayumu seeks comfort in a new friend, Manami. But will Manami prove to be the friend that Ayumu truly needs? Or will Ayumu continue down a dark path?

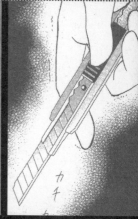

LIFE
Volume 1
Keiko Suenobu

It's about real teenagers...

It's about real high school...

It's about real life.

SPOTLIGHT — TOKYOPOP MANGA SUPPLEMENT

FRUITS BASKET
BY NATSUKI TAKAYA

Fruits Basket™

Tohru Honda was an orphan with no place to go…until the mysterious Sohma family offers her a place to call home. Tohru's ordinary high school life is turned upside down when she's introduced to the Sohmas' world of magical curses and family intrigue. Discover for yourself the Secret of the Zodiac, and find out why *Fruits Basket* has won the hearts of readers the world over!

THE BESTSELLING MANGA IN THE U.S.!

© Natsuki Takaya

TEEN AGE 13+

FOR MORE INFORMATION VISIT WWW.TOKYOPOP.COM